The New Technology of Financial Crime

Financial crime is a trillion-dollar industry that is likely to continue to grow exponentially unless new strategies of prevention and control can be developed. This book covers a wide range of topics related to financial crime commission, victimization, prevention, and control. The chapters included in this book closely examine cyber-victimization in their investigation of online fraud schemes that have resulted in new categories of crime victims as the result of identity theft, romance fraud schemes, phishing, ransomware, and other technology-enabled online fraud strategies. This book also offers new strategies for both financial crime prevention and financial crime control designed to reduce both offending and victimization. It will be a great resource for researchers and students of Criminology, Sociology, Law, and Information Technology.

The chapters in this book were originally published in the journal *Victims & Offenders.*

Donald Rebovich, Ph.D., Distinguished Professor of Criminal Justice at Utica College, USA, is the Executive Director of the Center for Identity Management & Information Protection (CIMIP). Prior to coming to Utica College, Dr Rebovich served as the Research Director for the National White-Collar Crime Center (NW3C) and the American Prosecutors Research Institute of the National District Attorneys Association (NDAA).

James M. Byrne, Ph.D., is a professor in the School of Criminology and Justice Studies at the University of Massachusetts Lowell, USA. He is the Director of the Global Community Corrections Initiative (www.globcci.org) and Editor-in-Chief of the journal *Victims & Offenders.* Dr Byrne is the co-editor of *The Global Impact of the COVID-19 Pandemic on Institutional and Community Corrections* (Routledge, 2021), and is currently completing a new book *The Technology Revolution in Criminal Justice: A Global Review* (Routledge, forthcoming).

The New Technology of Financial Crime

New Crime Commission Technology, New Victims, New Offenders, and New Strategies for Prevention and Control

Edited by
Donald Rebovich and James M. Byrne

Routledge
Taylor & Francis Group
LONDON AND NEW YORK

First published 2023
by Routledge
4 Park Square, Milton Park, Abingdon, Oxon, OX14 4RN

and by Routledge
605 Third Avenue, New York, NY 10158

Routledge is an imprint of the Taylor & Francis Group, an informa business

British Library Cataloguing-in-Publication Data
A catalogue record for this book is available from the British Library

ISBN13: 978-1-032-19202-4 (hbk)
ISBN13: 978-1-032-19203-1 (pbk)
ISBN13: 978-1-003-25810-0 (ebk)

DOI: 10.4324/9781003258100

Typeset in Minion Pro
bycodeMantra

Publisher's Note
The publisher accepts responsibility for any inconsistencies that may have arisen during the conversion of this book from journal articles to book chapters, namely the inclusion of journal terminology.

Contents

Citation Information

The following chapters were originally published in *Victims & Offenders*, volume 16, issue 3 (2021). When citing this material, please use the original page numbering for each article, as follows:

Chapter 1

The Dynamics of Business, Cybersecurity and Cyber-Victimization: Foregrounding the Internal Guardian in Prevention
David Buil-Gil, Nicholas Lord, and Emma Barrett
Victims & Offenders, volume 16, issue 3 (2021) pp. 286–315

Chapter 2

Phishing Evolves: Analyzing the Enduring Cybercrime
Adam Kavon Ghazi-Tehrani and Henry N. Pontell
Victims & Offenders, volume 16, issue 3 (2021) pp. 316–342

Chapter 3

Online Fraud Victimization in China: A Case Study of Baidu Tieba
Claire Seungeun Lee
Victims & Offenders, volume 16, issue 3 (2021) pp. 343–362

Chapter 4

Interrelationship between Bitcoin, Ransomware, and Terrorist Activities: Criminal Opportunity Assessment via Cyber-Routine Activities Theoretical Framework
Hannarae Lee and Kyung-Shick Choi
Victims & Offenders, volume 16, issue 3 (2021) pp. 363–384

Chapter 5

The Use of Military Profiles in Romance Fraud Schemes
Cassandra Cross and Thomas J. Holt
Victims & Offenders, volume 16, issue 3 (2021) pp. 385–406

Chapter 6

The Distillation of National Crime Data into A Plan for Elderly Fraud Prevention: A Quantitative and Qualitative Analysis of U.S. Postal Inspection Service Cases of Fraud against the Elderly
Donald Rebovich and Leslie Corbo
Victims & Offenders, volume 16, issue 3 (2021) pp. 407–430

Chapter 7

Organized Crime as Financial Crime: The Nature of Organized Crime as *Reflected in Prosecutions and Research*
Jay S. Albanese
Victims & Offenders, volume 16, issue 3 (2021) pp. 431–443

Chapter 8

Preventing Identity Theft: Perspectives on Technological Solutions from Industry Insiders
Nicole Leeper Piquero, Alex R. Piquero, Stephen Gies, Brandn Green, Amanda Bobnis, and Eva Velasquez
Victims & Offenders, volume 16, issue 3 (2021) pp. 444–463

Chapter 9

Forecasting Identity Theft Victims: Analyzing Characteristics and Preventive Actions through Machine Learning Approaches
Xiaochen Hu, Xudong Zhang, and Nicholas P. Lovrich
Victims & Offenders, volume 16, issue 4 (2021) pp. 465–494

Chapter 10

The Identification of a Model Victim for Social Engineering: A Qualitative Analysis
Kevin F. Steinmetz
Victims & Offenders, volume 16, issue 4 (2021) pp. 540–564

Notes on Contributors

Jay S. Albanese, Wilder School of Government & Public Affairs, Virginia Commonwealth University, Richmond, USA.

Emma Barrett, Department of Criminology, University of Manchester, UK.

Amanda Bobnis, Development Services Group, Inc., Bethesda, USA.

David Buil-Gil, Department of Criminology, University of Manchester, UK.

James M. Byrne, School of Criminology and Justice Studies, University of Massachusetts Lowell, USA.

Kyung-Shick Choi, Department of Applied Social Sciences, Boston University, USA.

Leslie Corbo, Justice Studies, Utica College, USA.

Cassandra Cross, Cybersecurity Cooperative Research Centre, Brisbane, Australia; School of Justice, Queensland University of Technology, Brisbane, Australia.

Adam Kavon Ghazi-Tehrani, Department of Criminology and Criminal Justice, University of Alabama, Tuscaloosa, USA.

Stephen Gies, Development Services Group, Inc., Bethesda, USA.

Brandn Green, Development Services Group, Inc., Bethesda, USA.

Thomas J. Holt, School of Justice, Queensland University of Technology, Brisbane, Australia; School of Criminal Justice, Michigan State University, Lansing, USA.

Xiaochen Hu, Department of Criminal Justice, Fayetteville State University, USA.

Claire Seungeun Lee, School of Criminology and Justice Studies, University of Massachusetts Lowell, USA.

Hannarae Lee, Department of Criminal Justice, Bridgewater State University, USA.

Nicholas Lord, Department of Criminology, University of Manchester, UK.

Nicholas P. Lovrich, School of Politics, Philosophy and Public Affairs, Washington State University, Pullman, USA.

Alex R. Piquero, Department of Sociology, University of Miami, USA; Monash University, Melbourne, Australia.

Nicole Leeper Piquero, Department of Sociology, University of Miami, USA.

Henry N. Pontell, Department of Sociology, John Jay College of Criminal Justice, New York City, USA.

Donald Rebovich, School of Business and Justice, and Executive Director, The Center for Identity Management and Information Protection (CIMIP), Utica College, USA.

Kevin F. Steinmetz, Department of Sociology, Anthropology, and Social Work, Kansas State University, Manhattan, USA.

Eva Velasquez, Identity Theft Resource Center, San Diego, USA.

Xudong Zhang, Department of Computer Science, Graduate Center of the City University of New York, USA.

Introduction

Donald Rebovich and James M. Byrne

Financial crime is a growing crime problem throughout the world, in large part due to recent advances in information technology and communication. It has been described by financial crime experts as a trillion-dollar global industry that takes an enormous social and economic toll on the lives it touches. The primary goal of this edited collection is to explore the many dimensions of financial crime from the perspectives of victims (both individual and organizational) and offenders. We were particularly interested in aspects of financial crime that focused on the evolution of methods of financial crime facilitated through technological advances, vulnerable groups being exploited by offenders, and the consequences of financial crime victimization. Finally, we were interested in prevention and enforcement strategies utilizing new technology to address the problem of financial crime. The following collection examines the problem of financial crime in its global context, with authors from academia who specialize in the study of financial crime, and with authors from private and public sector entities involved in the prevention and control of financial crime.

The focus of our special issue is on the impact of new technology on financial crime. The chapters included in this collection examine a wide range of topics related to financial crime commission, victimization, prevention, and control. Authors address timely issues and the following questions: How has technology hastened the growth of financial crime both nationally (i.e., in the United States) and internationally? In what environments are financial crime most likely to flourish? What part does organized crime play in financial crime activities? What are the groups most susceptible to being victimized by enterprising perpetrators of financial crimes, and why? And finally, what role can society play in enhancing efforts to prevent financial crime victimization in the future?

Organization of the Book

One of the primary themes of this book is to demonstrate how advances in technology have become a central force in bolstering the ability of fraudsters to exploit the weaknesses of potential victims, enabling offenders to capitalize on a lack of preventive knowledge by certain groups, and thus opening these groups to criminal exploitation.

The lead chapter focuses on the effects of such exploitation on the business community. David Buil-Gil, Nicholas Lord, and Emma Barrett analyze the dynamics of online business activities, cybersecurity measures, and cyber-victimization. They spotlight how digital space and digital systems are a core operating context for most businesses and associated activities, whether entering into economic relations with customers purchasing goods and services, storing and sharing information, or undertaking commercially sensitive activities that involve confidential data. Consequently, cybersecurity becomes a primary concern for businesses operating within digital (and often) global economies. The authors explain how digital space offers new opportunities for varied financial crimes, including frauds, that may be enabled by, or dependent on, internet-connected systems. The most common crime types identified include business e-mail compromise and e-mail account compromise, non-payment and non-delivery fraud, and investment scams.

In the next chapter, Adam Ghazi-Tehrani and Henry Pontell zero in on electronic "phishing," the fraudulent attempt to obtain sensitive information by disguising oneself as a trustworthy entity via electronic communication. Their research is based on interviews with approximately 60 information technology security professionals, "hackers," and academic researchers. Based on a thematic review of these interviews, the authors describe how this form of victim exploitation has quickly evolved beyond original low-skill schemes that relied on casting "a wide net." They find that the frequency of all types of phishing has risen dramatically in recent years. Their study provides an overview of the current state of phishing, the expected technological advances and developments in the near future, and the best prevention and enforcement strategies that can effectively be implemented.

The next technology-oriented chapter, by Claire S. Lee, spotlights victimization in one of the most densely populated nations in the world with a rapidly growing financial crime problem: China. When it comes to online populations and markets, China has some of the largest in the world. As a result, Chinese cybercriminals have more opportunities to target and access victims. While researchers in Western countries have examined internet fraud victimization and offenses in virtual communities in their own global regions, a relatively small body of research on these phenomena has been conducted in non-Western societies. Lee's research attempts to address this research shortfall by analyzing internet fraud victimization in Chinese online communities.

The fourth chapter of our book examines how bitcoin and ransomware can serve as new financing sources for terrorists. Authors Hannarae Lee and Kyung-Shick Choi argue that conveniences afforded to all from technological development have been reached at an astonishing level with the invention of cryptocurrencies like bitcoin being at the forefront. They hypothesize that the same unique characteristics of bitcoin that attract the general public may also attract criminals (e.g. cybercriminals and terrorists) looking for a fast and convenient way of transferring money. Since cybercriminals usually demand their ransom using bitcoin, the unlawful use of bitcoin can be tied to the increase in ransomware attacks in recent years. Due to this apparent connection, there is a continuous speculation about the relationship between terrorist activities and the use of bitcoin. They analyze the dynamic properties of bitcoin prices, ransomware attacks, and terrorist activities, using three different data sources. First, to measure the changes in bitcoin price, the authors analyzed daily bitcoin trading data from the Yahoo Financial website for a seven-year period. Second, they examined search queries from Google and Wikipedia. And third, they examined trend data from the Global Terrorism Database (GTD).

New victims of financial crime are the focus in our next two chapters. Those in the military are examined as ripe targets for fraud via the use of dating sites as a lure for the commission of "romance fraud." Casandra Cross and Thomas Holt note that in 2019, romance fraud was one of the highest categories of financial loss associated with fraud in many countries. The authors examine romance fraud reports made by individuals to Scamwatch (an Australian fraud reporting portal). During a thirteen-month review period, in I in 8 reports, offenders were identified as having employed the military narrative to target victims. Their chapter examines the ways that the military narrative is used by romance fraud offenders and provides a profile of both those who were initially targeted and those who were successfully defrauded.

The elderly population was the targeted financial crime victimization group examined in the next chapter included in our book. Criminal cases from the U.S. Postal Inspection Service (USPIS) were analyzed by authors Donald Rebovich and Leslie Corbo and researchers from the Identity Management and Information Protection Center (CIMIP) of Utica College. This study centered on frauds committed against victims aged 55 years and older with the primary objective being to uncover key empirical information on characteristics of victims of elderly fraud, those who commit these crimes, and the methods they employ to commit these fraudulent acts in order to develop characteristic profiles for each category to serve as the foundation for fraud awareness programs. One of the key findings they report is that elderly fraud cases in which the technological naivete of victims was manipulated by group offenders using multiple methods of attack were the most successful in defrauding senior citizens.

The next two chapters describe new strategies and initiatives designed to either prevent or control this new generation of financial crimes. First, Jay Albanese examines the role of organized groups in the commission of financial crimes, focusing on financial crime cases actually investigated and prosecuted that involved organized crime groups. Dr. Albanese contends that what has been sorely lacking thus far is a comparison of actual cases of organized financial crime (i.e., investigated and prosecuted) to determine the extent to which organized financial crime prosecutions parallel the nature of larger policy debate and typologies about the various types of organized crime that pose the greatest public threat. Data are presented to examine the extent to which the policy and research discussions about organized financial crime match the organized crimes found in practice. This article attempts to answer the question – Does the nature of organized financial crime reflected in the research literature match the nature of organized financial crime investigated and prosecuted by authorities?

The next two chapters focus on the prevention and control of identity theft and provide compelling support for the inclusion of professionals from the field in the development of identity theft and identity fraud prevention strategies. First, authors, Nicole Piquero, Alex Piquero, Stephen Gies, Brandn Green, Amanda Bobnis, and Eva Velasquez, emphasize that identity crime is one the fastest growing economic crimes in the United States with an estimated 26 million American citizens per year falling victim to various forms of identity-based crimes. The authors' study contributes to the scholarship on financial crimes facilitated through identity-based criminal activity. The authors examine the views on technological approaches to the prevention of identity theft among 50 professionals working in identity-based crime victim services, including those from the public sector and private industry. Interviews of these industry "insiders" are the source of valuable insights into the most effective paths to take in the quest to prevent future identity crimes. Next, authors, Xiaochen Hu, Xudong Zhang, and Nicholas Lovrich, apply the latest developments in machine learning approaches to the problem of identity theft. To study identity theft, the authors examined survey data on over 220,000 respondents drawn from three separate waves (2012, 2014, and 2016) of the National Crime Victimization Survey Identity Theft Supplement (NCVS-ITS). Their analyses demonstrate the potential advantages of applying machine learning to the study of identity theft victimization in order to more accurately identify the characteristics of identity theft victims. The authors offer effective strategies for the prevention of identity theft, while also highlighting the limitations of commercial identity theft companies in preventing identity theft.

The final chapter of our collection, Kevin Steinmetz offers a unique analysis of the characteristics of model victims of internet-facilitated frauds based on interviews with 37 security auditors who use "social engineering techniques to test information security systems" (Steinmetz, this volume). The results of his analyses provide a portrait of the model victim of internet-facilitated financial frauds. Steinmetz concludes his chapter with a discussion of the implications of his research for both policy and practice.

The Dynamics of Business, Cybersecurity and Cyber-Victimization: Foregrounding the Internal Guardian in Prevention

David Buil-Gil, Nicholas Lord, and Emma Barrett

ABSTRACT

Private organizations suffer great losses due to cybersecurity incidents, and they invest increasing resources to prevent attacks, but little is known about the effectiveness of cybersecurity measures for prevention. Based on the framework of Routine Activity Theory, this paper analyzes the impact of companies' online activities and cybersecurity measures on victimization. Our analysis of the UK Cybersecurity Breaches Survey shows that the most promising ways to minimize cyber-attacks and their impacts is to invest in in-house cybersecurity human resources and enhance the employees' online self-protection by providing cybersecurity training, rather than just basic software protection and guidance about strong passwords.

Introduction

The digital space and digital systems are core operating contexts for most businesses and their associated activities, whether entering into economic relations with customers purchasing goods and services, storing and sharing data, or undertaking commercially sensitive activities that involve confidential information (Office for National Statistics, 2019). As a result, one-eighth of the UK National Gross Domestic Product depends directly on the digital economy (National Audit Office, 2019). The digital space, however, offers many new opportunities for crimes, including frauds, that may be enabled by, or dependent on, Internet-connected systems. In 2017, the UK Annual Fraud Indicator estimated that frauds were responsible for £140 billion losses for the private sector, £40 billion losses for the public sector and £6.8 billion losses for individuals (Crowe, 2017), and a report published by the National Audit Office (2017) identified that more than half of all frauds were committed online. Other cybersecurity risks, such as malware and denial of service attacks targeting businesses, have also increased in recent years (National Cyber Security Centre, 2017). Given that the private sector is a primary target of cybersecurity attacks and suffers from the greatest economic losses, private companies are investing more resources every day to prevent cybersecurity threats (EY, 2019; Levi et al., 2015), but little is known about the effectiveness of these measures to prevent cyber-attacks (e.g., Bilodeau et al., 2019; Rantala, 2008; Richards, 2009; Williams et al., 2019).

Despite the considerable financial losses suffered by businesses as a result of cybersecurity attacks, criminological research has typically focused on studying cyber-victimization among individual citizens (e.g., Holt & Bossler, 2016; Leukfeldt & Yar, 2016; Marcum et al., 2010). This is likely to be due to the lack of available and reliable sources of data to examine cybersecurity attacks on businesses. To fill this gap in literature, this article analyzes the dynamics of online business activities, cybersecurity measures, and cyber-victimization. This article aims to illuminate which cybersecurity measures are effective in preventing cybersecurity breaches and attacks, and which measures are inefficient or ineffective. Based on the theoretical framework of Routine Activity Theory (RAT; Cohen & Felson, 1979) and considering the suitability of crime targets by their value, inertia, visibility, and accessibility ("VIVA"), this paper analyzes how certain online activities and protective measures implemented by organizations affect their likelihood of falling victims to cyber-attacks. Thus, the original contribution of this paper is to show the utility of RAT for understanding businesses' victimization by cybersecurity attacks and breaches, and more specifically to foreground the internal guardian and personal self-protection as effective ways to minimize cybersecurity attacks and their impacts. This research is concerned mainly with businesses' victimization by cyber-dependent crimes such as computer viruses, spam, hacking, and denial of service attacks (Wall, 2007).

The remainder of this paper is organized as follows. Section 2 examines the role of businesses' online activities and cybersecurity measures for cybercrime prevention. Section 3 applies the notions of guardianship and the VIVA to business victimization by cybersecurity attacks. Section 4 introduces the data and methods used. Section 5 presents the results of our models. Finally, section 6 discusses the results and presents conclusions and implications.

Businesses online activities, cybersecurity and cyber-victimization

Few empirical studies have analyzed cybercrimes suffered by organizations. In this section we summarize the results of the main research analyzing the impact of organizations' cybersecurity measures and online activities on cybercrime victimization.

Rantala (2008) analyzed data from the 2005 US National Computer Security Survey and found that 67% of the 7,818 participant companies had suffered at least one cybersecurity incident in the previous year. The most common cybercrimes suffered by organizations were spyware, adware, phishing, and spoofing. Richards (2009) conducted a survey of 4,000 businesses in Australia and found that the most common types of cybercrime suffered by organizations were virus and malware infections, and the most prevalent impact of cybercrime on businesses was the corruption of hardware or software. Moreover, Richards (2009) showed that only 8% of victims reported cybersecurity incidents to the police, which highlights the value of survey data and the limitations of relying on police-recorded incidents for cybercrime research (Kemp et al., 2020). HISCOX (2018) surveyed 4,103 professionals responsible for the cybersecurity of UK small businesses and found that 30% had suffered cybersecurity breaches in the previous year. Incidents had an average direct cost of £25,700 (e.g., ransom paid, hardware replaced). Bilodeau et al. (2019) analyzed a survey of 10,794 businesses in Canada and found that 21% of organizations were impacted by cybersecurity incidents at least once in the last 12 months (mainly scam, online fraud, phishing and computer viruses). Williams et al. (2019) surveyed 751 businesses in the UK in order to analyze insider cybercrime victimization and found that less than 10% of organizations reported experiencing insider cyber-victimization.

The prevalence of cybercrimes, however, varies across business sectors and sizes, and certain cybersecurity measures appear to have better results for cybercrime prevention than others. For example, Rantala (2008) found that telecommunication businesses, computer system design companies and manufacturers of durable goods have a higher prevalence of cyber-victimization, whereas administrative support, finance, and food service businesses suffer from greatest economic losses. Forestry, fishing, hunting, and agriculture businesses had the lowest victimization rates. Bilodeau et al. (2019) show that banking institutions, universities, and pipeline transportation companies suffer more cyber-attacks than other business sectors. Large companies tend to report the largest expenditures on cybersecurity, but these are also more likely to be targeted by cybercriminals and suffer the greatest financial losses (Bilodeau et al., 2019; Levi et al., 2015; Rantala, 2008; Richards, 2009).

Regarding the use of cybersecurity measures for prevention, Rantala (2008) observed that companies that outsource all or part of their cybersecurity to external providers have, on average, a higher prevalence of cybersecurity incidents, while companies with in-house cybersecurity services suffer fewer attacks. There are, however, different types of outsourced security practices. For instance, companies that outsource their physical security are much more likely to report cybercrimes than companies with in-house physical security, but organizations with outsourced network watch centers have a smaller prevalence of incidents than those with in-house network watch centers (Rantala, 2008). This shows the need to distinguish between outsourced and in-house forms of guardianship when analyzing cybercrime victimization among businesses. Similarly, others argue that the best measures to prevent future cyber-attacks are to encourage employees and managers to become self-protected by increasing cyber threat awareness at all levels of an organization, having a dedicated cybersecurity budget, and instituting ongoing cybersecurity training (HISCOX, 2018; Williams et al., 2019). Williams et al. (2019) also show that companies with a cybersecurity manager appear to suffer more risk of cyber-victimization than companies without cybersecurity managers, but they argue that this may be because previous criminal victimization motivates businesses to adopt new security measures.

Rantala (2008) noted that most companies report that the use of antivirus software, internal controls, e-mail filters and firewalls are all inadequate to prevent cybersecurity incidents, whereas companies tend to report that biometrics, digital certificates, password generators and encryption are more adequate cybersecurity measures. Moreover, organizations where employees are provided with business-owned laptops reduce their risk of cybercrime victimization (Rantala, 2008), and companies that store confidential data are more likely to suffer cyber-attacks than companies that do not store confidential customer information (Williams et al., 2019). Finally, Williams et al. (2019) did not find statistically significant associations between use of social media, e-commerce systems, WIFI networks and personal devices and insider cybercrime victimization.

Williams et al. (2019) argue that organizations' chances of suffering cyber-attacks may be reduced by applying cybersecurity measures aimed at preventing offenders from getting in contact with suitable targets under the absence of guardians (either by increasing the awareness and self-protection of employees or using measures to hinder the access to targets and making targets less visible online). They suggest applying RAT to understand how companies' characteristics and online protective measures can reduce the risk of online victimization.

Routine activities, the VIVA and cyber-attacks

Individual citizens' cyber-victimization has been primarily analyzed through a RAT lens (e.g., Bossler et al., 2012; Buil-Gil et al., 2020; Leukfeldt & Yar, 2016). RAT explains crime opportunities by the convergence in space and time of a potential offender, a suitable target and the absence of a guardian capable of protecting such target (Cohen & Felson, 1979). As Miró Llinares and Johnson (2017, p. 889) argue, "cybercrime can only happen when, through IT, an offender – or the outcome of his or her actions (e.g., when malware is opened) – converges at a certain place in cyberspace at a given moment with a suitable target in the absence of a guardian capable of preventing the event". In digital contexts, criminals can target many victims simultaneously, thus increasing opportunities for the triple convergence described by RAT (Miró Llinares & Johnson, 2017; Miró-Llinares & Moneva, 2020; Yar, 2005).

Others argue that the elements of VIVA (originally described by Cohen & Felson, 1979 to explain the suitability of crime targets under the RAT) are key to assessing the attractiveness of online targets of crime (Yar, 2005). In the context of cybercrimes in e-commerce systems, Newman and Clarke (2003) argued that the Internet allows for an increased "visibility" and "accessibility" to crime targets, due to the absence of capable online guardians and the frequency and variety of everyday activities that individual users conduct online. Leukfeldt and Yar (2016) studied the effect of the elements of VIVA on six types of online crimes suffered by individual victims and concluded that the digital "visibility" of users (i.e., the extent of online routine activities) increases the risk of cybercrime victimization. Leukfeldt and Yar (2016) also showed that the use of antivirus software (a form of technical guardianship) does not prevent most types of cybercrimes, using certain operating systems and browsers ("accessibility" to targets) may increase malware infections, and the users' knowledge and awareness of online risks (i.e., personal guardianship or self-protection) reduce the risk of victimization by hacking and stalking. Similarly, many have shown that improving users' education about information security and promoting safe online behaviors is key to preventing various cybercrimes (Bossler & Holt, 2009; Bossler et al., 2012). Some argue that actions taken by individual persons to protect themselves should not be studied as forms of guardianship, but as self-protection strategies, since the guardian was originally conceptualized as a third party external to the victim and the offender (Miró Llinares, 2015).

This paper uses the theoretical framework of RAT and the VIVA to analyze the impact of organizations' online activities and cybersecurity measures on victimization by cybersecurity attacks. More specifically, we analyze which forms of online personal, social, and technical guardianship are effective in preventing cybercrime victimization, and which elements of VIVA can be used to explain cybercrime suffered by organizations.

Capable guardianship and self-protection

Capable guardians serve to protect the targets and potential victims from crime victimization. Some cybercrime researchers argue that, in cyberspace, the guardian can take the form of personal and technical self-protection as well as formal and informal forms of social control (e.g., Holt & Bossler, 2008, 2016; Marcum et al., 2010); while others argue that the concept of "capable guardian" only refers external parties (e.g., parents, neighbors, friends, line managers, colleagues, police), who reduce the likelihood of cybercrime victimization (Miró Llinares, 2015; Miró Llinares & Johnson, 2017). We distinguish among the following forms of guardianship and self-protection in our research:

Technical self-protection

This mainly refers to the use of software security applications to protect digital systems from malicious content. Technical self-protection may refer to the use of access control software, anti-malware, anti-spyware, firewalls, antivirus software, and other software aimed at defending computer systems against intrusions and unauthorized use of resources. Research has shown that software protection is usually not enough to prevent cybercrime victimization (e.g., Leukfeldt & Yar, 2016; Rantala, 2008).

Personal self-protection

This describes those behaviors and actions taken by employees to protect themselves and the company from internal and external cybersecurity attacks (Miró Llinares, 2015). Thus, it refers to behavioral changes that those working in an organization can take to become better informed about digital risks and mitigate potential cybersecurity threats (Bossler et al., 2012). Personal self-protection can involve, for example, the use of strong passwords, general awareness about digital risks, avoiding doing business with suppliers that fail to adhere to cybersecurity standards, or attending cybersecurity seminars and training (Klein, 1990; Williams et al., 2019).

In-house guardianship

In the context of individual cybercrime prevention, the concept of "social guardianship" is used to refer to family or peers who protect the victim from an attack (Holt & Bossler, 2016). "Social guardianship" measures actions taken by someone other than the potential victim to protect the latter from becoming a victim of crime. Here we distinguish between in-house and outsourced forms of social guardianship, given that previous research has found that these have different effects on businesses' cybercrime victimization (Rantala, 2008). "In-house guardianship" refers to whether companies implement internal cybersecurity controls and have members of the staff dedicated to cybersecurity (e.g., employees whose role includes information security, board members with responsibility for cybersecurity). In other words, by "in-house guardianship" we refer to actions taken by personnel with cybersecurity responsibility within the company to protect the organizations' systems.

Outsourced guardianship

Many businesses outsource their cybersecurity to third-party expert companies. Outsourced cybersecurity services appear to have different effects on cybercrime victimization than in-house cybersecurity teams. For instance, Rantala (2008) observed that those organizations who outsource their physical security, equipment decommissioning, periodic audits, risk assessments, disaster recovery plans, or the regular review of systems are more likely to report cyber-attacks than those businesses that have in-house teams to conduct these activities. Thus, by "outsourced guardianship" we measure actions taken by third-party companies to protect the cybersecurity of the organization.

Value

Those individuals and objects which cybercriminals perceive to be more valuable are those that are more frequently targeted (Holt et al., 2020). While offline "value" is frequently associated with monetary worth, in cyberspace it tends to be an expression of information (as a route to financial gain): "the focus of cybercrime, therefore, is to acquire information in order to extract its value" (Wall, 2007, p. 36). This is why Yar (2005) argues that most cybercrime targets are "informational" in nature. Information held by businesses can be exploited for financial gain, including by holding data to ransom, using confidential information to facilitate fraud, or selling customer details to other criminals to be used in identity fraud. Those businesses with confidential customer information, for instance, may be perceived as more valuable by cybercriminals (Williams et al., 2019).

Inertia

Cohen and Felson (1979) original concept of "inertia" refers to an object's physical properties (size, weight, shape) that define the ease with which it can be removed. Since objects in cyberspace are not defined by physical properties, the notion of "inertia" takes on a different meaning in cybercrime. Some argue that the volume of data of electronic files and their technological specifications retain inertia properties, since these offer resistance for the target to be taken or copied (Yar, 2005). Other cybersecurity measures, such as the use of encryption, may also be seen as forms of inertia, since they impede or make it difficult for offenders to remove valuable information from compromised files and infected systems (Rantala, 2008).

Visibility

Objects and individuals that are more visible to offenders are more likely to become crime targets. Online, targets become visible to cybercriminals through users' communication and interaction with others: "when goods are introduced, voluntarily or not, and if they are not protected, they are exposed to risk, but they will only be suitable targets when they become visible to the offender" (Miró Llinares, 2015, p. 51). The more interaction an object or user has with others online, the higher its visibility and the more likely it is of becoming a target of a cybercrime. Newman and Clarke (2003) argued that the variety of activities that Internet users conduct increase their online visibility, and Leukfeldt and Yar (2016) showed that users' online visibility is one of the main predictors of most forms of cyber-victimization (see also Marcum et al., 2010).

Accessibility

The concept of "accessibility" refers to the ease with which offenders can come into direct contact with a target. As argued by Leukfeldt and Yar (2016), while in the physical world "accessibility" refers to the characteristics of micro places that allow offenders to approach targets, in cyberspace the accessibility is party determined by the operating systems and web browsers used by users, since offenders *access* the target by abusing the holes in such systems. Restricting the access to confidential files or information to certified users also reduces the accessibility to data (Miró Llinares & Johnson, 2017). For instance, Rantala (2008) probed businesses' perceptions of adequacy of cybersecurity measures and found that the use of biometrics and digital certificates were considered adequate cybersecurity measures.

Data and methods

This section introduces the data and modeling approaches used to analyze cybersecurity attacks to UK businesses and charities. After describing the UK Cybersecurity Breaches Survey (CSBS) and its sampling strategy, we present our dependent variables, predictors, and control variables. Finally, we introduce the modeling approaches used in this paper.

Cybersecurity breaches survey

The CSBS is a survey of UK businesses and charities that records information about digital threats faced by organizations and preventive measures to deter cybersecurity attacks and breaches. It has been conducted annually since 2016, and this paper examines data recorded in its 2018 edition. The survey included a quantitative random probability sample of 1,519 businesses and 569 charities, and qualitative interviews with 50 organizations. We have been granted access to the quantitative dataset, but not the interviews, to conduct this research.

The CSBS sample is designed to be representative of all UK businesses across different sizes and sectors and all charities across all income bands (Department for Digital, Culture, Media & Sport, 2018). The sampling frame is all private companies and nonprofit organizations (whole organizations, not local establishments) with more than one employee, including universities, schools and colleges. Public sector organizations are not included in the sample, since these are typically subject to high cybersecurity standards. Businesses in the agriculture, forestry and fishing sectors are also excluded from the sample given their relative lack of e-commerce. Organizations without computers, websites, or online presence and sole traders are also excluded.

The sample of businesses is proportionately stratified by UK regions and disproportionately stratified by the organizations' size and sector. This is done to effectively include medium and large businesses in the sample, which represent only a small proportion of all UK companies. Post-survey weighting is then used to correct for disproportionate stratification. Similarly, the sample of charities is proportionately stratified by country and disproportionately stratified by income bands to allow for a sample of high-income charities (Department for Digital, Culture, Media & Sport, 2018). Interviews were conducted using Computer-Assisted Telephone Interviewing (CATI) between October and December 2017.

Non-interlocking Random Iterative Method (RIM) was used by the original survey administrators to compute survey weights that allow adjusting for non-response bias and disproportionate sampling. Thus, the weighted sample is representative of the UK population of businesses and charities. RIM weighting by size and sector is used for businesses and RIM by income band and country for charities (Department for Digital, Culture, Media & Sport, 2018). Table 1 summarizes the characteristics of the sampled businesses and charities before and after applying the survey weights.

Table 1. Characteristics of businesses and charities sampled (frequency and percentage).

	Unweighted	Weighted
Business or charity (n = 2088)		
Business (including social enterprise)	1502 (71.9%)	1509 (72.3%)
Charity or voluntary sector organization	569 (27.3%)	569 (27.2%)
Don't know	17 (0.8%)	10 (0.5%)
Sector of business (n = 1519)		
Retail and wholesale	217 (14.3%)	280 (18.4%)
Administration or real estate	150 (9.9%)	190 (12.5%)
Construction	145 (9.5%)	189 (12.4%)
Food or hospitality	119 (7.8%)	151 (9.9%)
Finance or insurance	105 (6.9%)	25 (1.6%)
Health, care or social work	101 (6.6%)	73 (4.8%)
Information or communication	99 (6.5%)	93 (6.1%)
Other	583 (38.4%)	517 (34.0%)
Income, turnover or sales (n = 2088)		
Less than £100,000	344 (16.5%)	636 (30.4%)
£100,000 to less than £500,000	455 (21.8%)	524 (25.1%)
£500,000 to less than £5 million	488 (23.4%)	449 (21.5%)
£5 million or more	418 (20.0%)	127 (6.1%)
Don't know	383 (18.3%)	352 (16.8%)
Companies' size (employees, volunteers or trustees) (n = 2088)		
1 to 9	789 (37.8%)	1203 (57.6%)
10 to 49	600 (28.7%)	750 (35.9%)
50 to 249	384 (18.4%)	110 (5.3%)
More than 250	315 (15.1%)	25 (1.2%)
Digital characteristics (n = 2088; categories are not exclusive)		
E-Mail addresses for your organization	1945 (93.2%)	1881 (90.1%)
A website or blog	1808 (86.6%)	1663 (79.7%)
Accounts on social media sites	1396 (66.9%)	1205 (57.2%)
The ability for users to make transactions online	727 (34.8%)	544 (26.1%)
Personal information about customers, users or donors held electronically	1347 (64.5%)	1102 (52.8%)

Cybersecurity Breaches Survey 2018

Dependent variables

We apply various regression modeling approaches to explain three dependent variables: (a) the likelihood of suffering at least one cybersecurity breach or attack in the last 12 months, (b) the likelihood of suffering at least one negative impact or outcome due to cyber-attacks in the last 12 months, and (c) the number of cybersecurity attacks in the last 12 months. The first measure distinguishes organizations that have suffered at least one form of cyber-victimization from those that have not suffered any cyber-attack, which is the most common measure of cyber-victimization used in previous research (e.g., Bossler et al., 2012; Leukfeldt & Yar, 2016; Williams et al., 2019). The second measure discriminates those UK businesses and charities that have suffered negative outcomes or impacts due to cybersecurity attacks from those that have not, in order to analyze the overall harm of cyber-victimization (see Paoli et al., 2018). And the third measures the number of attacks reported by each organization, which allows us to analyze whether variables that explain the binary outcome of cyber-victimization also explain the number of crimes (Hope, 2015).

Table 2 shows the frequency and percentage of organizations reporting various types of cybersecurity incidents. The most prevalent type of victimization is the receipt of fraudulent e-mails by members of the staff (reported by 27.5% of the weighted sample), followed by the impersonation of the organization by third parties (10.3% of weighted organizations) and the infection of computers by viruses (8.9%). The least common forms of cyber-victimization were hacking of bank accounts (2.7%), unauthorized use of hardware or

Table 2. Proportion of businesses and charities that reported being victims of different forms of cybersecurity breaches or attacks during the last 12 months (weighted).

	Frequency and percentage
Staff receiving fraudulent e-mails or being directed to fraudulent websites	575 (27.5%)
People impersonating your organization in e-mails or online	215 (10.3%)
Computers infected with other viruses, spyware or malware	186 (8.9%)
Unauthorized use or hacking of PCs or networks by people outside your company	108 (5.2%)
Computers infected with ransomware	106 (5.1%)
Attacks that try to take down your website or online services	92 (4.4%)
Hacking or attempted hacking of online bank account	56 (2.7%)
Unauthorized use of computers, networks or servers by staff (even if accidental)	50 (2.4%)
Any other type of cybersecurity breaches or attacks	38 (1.8%)
Victims of at least one cybersecurity breach	764 (36.6%)

Cybersecurity Breaches Survey 2018

software by staff members (2.4%) and other cybersecurity attacks (1.8%). In total, 36.6% of companies were victims of at least one form of cybersecurity attack in the last year.

With regards to the effect of cybersecurity attacks on organizations, 21.2% of companies reported suffering at least one negative impact or outcome due to cyber-attacks in the last year. As shown in Table 3, the most common impacts were the implementation of new measures to prevent future attacks (reported by 13.4% of the weighted sample), the use of additional staff time to deal with a breach (11.8%) and staff being stopped from carrying their daily work due to an attack (9.6%). Only 0.6% of organizations lost assets, trade secrets or intellectual property, 0.5% had to offer compensations or discounts to customers, and the 0.4% were fined by regulators or authorities or had to cover other legal costs.

More specifically, concerning the economic impact of cyber-victimization, 84.3% of the weighted sample of organizations reported no economic impact and 6.3% reported an economic impact of less than £500 (see Table 4). Only 1.4% of companies report financial losses greater than £10,000.

Table 3. Proportion of companies that have experienced negative impacts or outcomes due to cybersecurity breaches or attacks during the last 12 months (weighted).

	Frequency and percentage
New measures needed to prevent future breaches	280 (13.4%)
Additional staff time to deal with the breach or attack	246 (11.8%)
Stopped staff from carrying out day-to-day work	201 (9.6%)
Temporary loss of access to files or networks	170 (8.1%)
Any other repair or recovery costs	145 (6.9%)
Software or systems corrupted or damaged	112 (5.4%)
Website or online services taken down or made slower	80 (3.8%)
Lost access to third-party services you rely on	55 (2.6%)
Prevented provision of goods or services to customers	45 (2.2%)
Money was stolen	41 (2.0%)
Complaints from customers	38 (1.8%)
Permanent loss of files (other than personal data)	38 (1.8%)
Loss of revenue or share value	30 (1.4%)
Reputational damage	27 (1.3%)
Discouraged from carrying out a future business activity	24 (1.1%)
Personal data altered, destroyed or taken	15 (0.7%)
Lost or stolen assets, trade secrets or intellectual property	13 (0.6%)
Goodwill compensation or discounts given to customers	10 (0.5%)
Fines from regulators or authorities, or associated legal costs	9 (0.4%)
Victims of at least one cybersecurity breach with at least one negative impact	442 (21.2%)

Cybersecurity Breaches Survey 2018

Table 4. Economic impact of cybersecurity attacks on businesses and charities (weighted).

Economic impact	Frequency and percentage
None	1347 (84.3%)
Less than £500	100 (6.3%)
£500 to less than £1,000	33 (2.1%)
£1,000 to less than £5,000	71 (4.4%)
£5,000 to less than £10,000	24 (1.5%)
£10,000 to less than £20,000	12 (0.8%)
£20,000 to less than £50,000	8 (0.5%)
£50,000 to less than £100,000	0 (0.0%)
£100,000 to less than £500,000	1 (0.1%)
£500,000 or more	0 (0.0%)
NAs	491

Cybersecurity Breaches Survey 2018

Table 5. Summary statistics about cybersecurity attacks on businesses and charities (weighted).

	Min.	1st q.	Mean	Median	3rd q.	Max.
At least one cybersecurity attack (0/1)	0	0	0.37	0	1	1
At least one cybersecurity attack – excluding fraudulent e-mails (0/1)	0	0	0.23	0	0	1
At least one negative impact due to cybersecurity attack (0/1)	0	0	0.21	0	0	1
Number of cybersecurity attacks – original	0	0	283.30	0	1	397,795
Number of cybersecurity attacks – transformed by single square root	0	0	2.56	0	1	630
Number of cybersecurity attacks – transformed by double square root	0	0	0.59	0	1	25

Cybersecurity Breaches Survey 2018

Table 5 shows the summary statistics of our dependent variables. The binary measures of suffering at least one cybersecurity attack (including and excluding fraudulent e-mails) and suffering at least one negative impact or outcome do not show extreme distributions and can be analyzed by using logistic regressions for binary outcomes. However, the number of cybersecurity breaches is affected by a zero-inflated distribution and extreme values, which have a large impact on the sample's average and variance. A few organizations reporting a large number of cyber-attacks affect the assumptions underlying statistical modeling and the robustness of our analyses. We apply a simple, but efficient, double square root transformation (or fourth root transformation) to stabilize the effect of large values and allow analyzing the number of cybersecurity attacks. The double square root transformation is applied because the single square root transformation did not effectively reduce the influence of extreme values. The double square root transformation is a well-known solution for skewed positive count variables used to diminish the impact of large numbers of crime victimization on the sample (see Xie et al., 2002, 2000). This data-transformation approach is preferred over other approaches since it can be easily performed also in the presence of zeros. Moreover, this transformation allows analyzing the full sample without the need to delete outliers.

After transforming the dependent variable of number of cyber-attacks, the transformed average number of cybersecurity incidents faced by businesses is 0.59 and the maximum is 25. Nevertheless, the distribution of the number of cybersecurity attacks faced by companies still shows a zero-inflated distribution (see Figure 1), given that 64.5% of companies did not report any cybersecurity attacks in the previous year. In other words, most businesses and charities suffered zero breaches and attacks. Thus, the assumption of normal distribution is

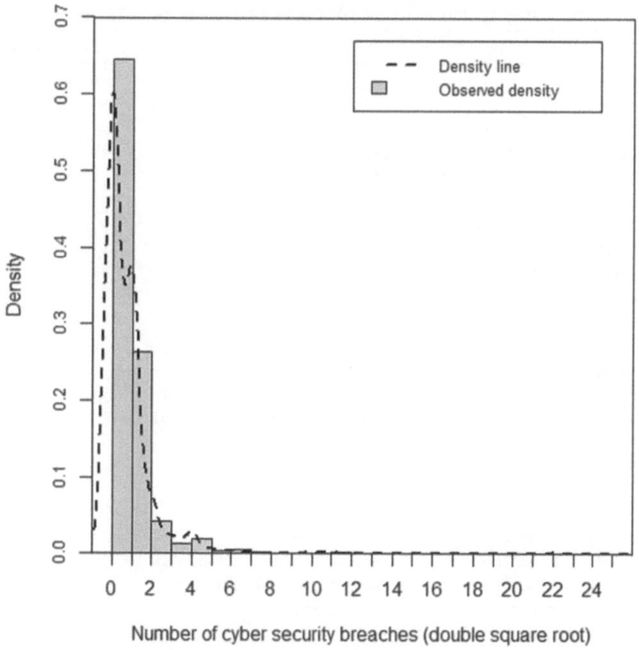

Figure 1. Distribution of number of cybersecurity breaches and attacks reported by businesses and charities (transformed by double square root).

not met, and traditional linear models cannot be used. Instead, we use a Hurdle Negative Binomial model for zero-inflated data to analyze the number of cybersecurity breaches faced by organizations (see Section 4.5).

Predictors

We will examine which cybersecurity measures effectively reduce the likelihood of falling victim to cybersecurity attacks, and which measures are inefficient or counter effective. Aside from the income and the digital characteristics of each company (e.g., use of social media, website or blog, personal information held electronically), which are summarized above in Table 1, we will also analyze those cybersecurity measures and online activities that may have an effect on the businesses' victimization by cybersecurity attacks. We use the companies' income and the measure of storing personal data electronically as proxy measures of "value" (see Leukfeldt & Yar, 2016; Wall, 2007; Williams et al., 2019). Various measures of online presence (use of social media, websites, and institutional e-mail addresses, amongst others) are used as indicators of the companies' "visibility" to the general public (Miró Llinares, 2015; Newman & Clarke, 2003).

Amongst all cybersecurity measures reported by UK businesses and charities, the most commonly used are the application of software updates (applied by 87.1% of the weighted sample), updated malware protection (85.2%) and use of firewalls with appropriate configuration (83.4%). These three represent forms of technical self-protection (Holt & Bossler, 2016; Leukfeldt & Yar, 2016). Restricting IT access rights to specific users, which is

Table 6. Cybersecurity measures to prevent or manage breaches or attacks (weighted).

	Frequency and percentage
Applying software updates	1818 (87.1%)
Update malware protection	1779 (85.2%)
Firewalls with appropriate configuration	1741 (83.4%)
Restricting IT admin and access rights to specific users	1558 (74.6%)
Backing up data securely via means other than a cloud service	1367 (65.5%)
Guidance on acceptably strong passwords	1277 (61.2%)
Security controls on company-owned devices (e.g., laptops)	1225 (58.7%)
Externally-hosted web services	1211 (58.0%)
Only allowing access via company-owned devices	1182 (56.6%)
Backing up data securely via a cloud service	1105 (52.9%)
Outsourced provider that manages cybersecurity	866 (41.5%)
Monitoring of user activity	751 (36.0%)
Staff members whose role include information security	745 (35.7%)
Encrypting personal data	738 (35.4%)
Business-as-usual health checks to identify cybersecurity risks (last 12 months)	683 (32.7%)
A segregated guest wireless network	620 (29.7%)
Company directors are given updates around cybersecurity at least monthly	596 (28.6%)
Board members with responsibility for cybersecurity	592 (28.4%)
Formal policy covering cybersecurity risks	533 (25.5%)
A risk assessment covering cybersecurity risks (last 12 months)	469 (22.4%)
Someone has attended seminars or training on cybersecurity (last 12 months)	439 (21.0%)
Health checks beyond regular to identify cybersecurity risks (last 12 months)	423 (20.3%)
Internal audit to identify cybersecurity risks (last 12 months)	405 (19.4%)
Cyber risks documented in the Business Continuity Plan	365 (17.5%)
Require suppliers to adhere to cybersecurity standards or good practices	242 (11.6%)
Formal cybersecurity incident management processes	235 (11.3%)
Cyber risks documented in Company-level risk register	219 (10.5%)
Cyber risks documented in an Internal Audit Plan	200 (9.6%)
Cyber risks documented in Departmental risk registers	167 (8.0%)
Specific cybersecurity insurance policy	162 (7.8%)
Invested in threat intelligence (last 12 months)	150 (7.2%)

Cybersecurity Breaches Survey 2018

a measure of "access", was also used by a large proportion of organizations (74.6%). Table 6 presents the frequency and percentage of companies that use each cybersecurity measure.

In our regression models, we will only analyze as independent variables those cybersecurity measures that are related to at least one form of guardianship (or self-protection) or at least one of the elements of VIVA (Cohen & Felson, 1979; Yar, 2005). We will also analyze those measures implemented to facilitate the detection of digital vulnerabilities associated with one or multiple elements of VIVA (e.g., extraordinary checks to identify and document risks) and organizations' perceived preparedness for cybersecurity (i.e., agree that the company has enough people with the right skills and knowledge to effectively manage cybersecurity). Most predictors have been recoded as binary variables to distinguish between companies that apply and do not apply each measure. The companies' income was recoded as five dummy variables.

Moreover, we note that some explanatory variables have been aggregated to reduce the number of predictors in our models, in order to keep the models parsimonious and avoid multicollinearity. In this case, variables were aggregated directly by recoding various categorical questions asked within the surveys to binary measures of software protection, preparedness for cybersecurity, extraordinary cybersecurity checks, online platforms, and cybersecurity training. However, future research may explore the use of Latent Class Analysis to construct data-driven multidimensional constructs. For example, a new variable of "basic software protection" has been constructed from the variables "applying software updates", "update malware protection" and "firewalls with appropriate configuration", giving a score of 1 to those businesses that implement the three of them (74.6% of the weighted sample) and a score of 0 to the others. Similarly, a measure of perceived preparedness for cybersecurity is recoded from the questions "people dealing with cybersecurity in our organization have the right cybersecurity skills and knowledge to do this job effectively" and "we have enough people dealing with cybersecurity in our organization to effectively manage the risks". We assign a score 1 when the organization agrees with both statements (59.9%) and 0 otherwise. Having enough staff dedicated to cybersecurity may not be enough to prevent incidents if such group of people do not have adequate cybersecurity expertise, and having staff with cybersecurity skills may not be enough to reduce attacks if they are very few.

A variable of "extraordinary cybersecurity checks" has been recoded from those measures identifying activities other than business-as-usual to identify digital risks (i.e., internal audit, ad-hoc check beyond regular processes, risk assessment, threat intelligence, external audit), with a score of 1 given to companies that undertook at least one of them in the last year (44.6% of the sample). We have also merged the measures of having a website and social media accounts, since these were highly correlated, to create a new variable that distinguishes those organizations that have both website and social media (54.0%) from the others. And the variable "cybersecurity training" measures those companies in which someone has attended at least one cybersecurity seminar or conference or attended internal or external training on cybersecurity in the last year (21.0% of weighted sample).

Control variables

To minimize the risk of confounding bias, we include two groups of control variables in our models. First, we incorporate nine dummy variables to distinguish between companies' sectors (see Table 1), given that certain sectors are known to be more frequently victimized than others (Bilodeau et al., 2019; Rantala, 2008; Richards, 2009). Second, the models also control for five dummy variables of total economic investment in cybersecurity, which allow examining whether cybersecurity breaches are affected by the cybersecurity measures included in the models or other investments in cybersecurity ignored by our models.

With regards to the organizations' overall economic investment in cybersecurity, most companies do not directly invest financial resources on this. As shown in Table 7, the

Table 7. Economic investment in cybersecurity by companies' turnover (weighted).

		Companies' turnover			
		Less than £100,000	£100,000 to £500,000	£500,000 to £5 M	£5 M or more
Investment in cybersecurity					
	Don't invest	357 (66.0%)	145 (21.3%)	110 (28.3%)	16 (16.7%)
	Less than £1,000	151 (28.0%)	206 (44.3%)	120 (30.9%)	19 (19.4%)
	£1,000 to less than £10,000	31 (5.8%)	98 (21.1%)	121 (31.1%)	33 (33.9%)
	£10,000 to less than £50,000	1 (0.2%)	15 (3.2%)	27 (6.9%)	21 (20.9%)
	£50,000 or more	0 (0.0%)	1 (0.1%)	10 (2.7%)	9 (9.2%)
	n	540	465	388	98
	%	100	100	100	100

Cybersecurity Breaches Survey 2018
Note: n = 1491 (NAs excluded)

proportion of businesses that do not invest in cybersecurity is large even among companies with large turnovers.

Methods: modeling strategy

We will make use of logistic regressions for binary outcomes to analyze the companies' likelihood of suffering at least one cybersecurity breach or attack in the last year (including and excluding fraudulent e-mails) and the companies' likelihood of suffering at least one negative outcome or impact due to cybersecurity attacks in the last year. We will use a Hurdle negative binomial regression for zero-inflated data to analyze the number of breaches suffered by UK businesses and charities.

Binary logistic regression is used to analyze the association between the likelihood of suffering at least one cybersecurity attack or at least one negative outcome and all independent and control variables (see Bonney, 1987). We will examine the Odds Ratio (OR) of each predictor and control variable, which is an indicator of the likelihood that the outcome under study (i.e., cybercrime victimization or negative outcome) occurs in one group (e.g., organizations that use basic software protection) relative to the odds of the reference group (e.g., no basic software protection). The R package "stats" is used to fit the logistic regression models (R Core Team, 2020).

Hurdle negative binomial regression for zero-inflated data is used to model the organizations' number of cybersecurity breaches or attacks in last 12 months. Hurdle regression models are used to analyze discrete dependent variables with an excess of zeros, as is our case (see Figure 1). It is a two-part modeling approach: the first part, the zero Hurdle model, estimates the binary outcome of having suffered zero or non-zero breaches or attacks in the last 12 months, whereas the second part, the so-called truncated Negative Binomial model, estimates the number of crimes suffered by companies with at least one reported victimization (see Cameron & Trivedi, 2005; Zeileis et al., 2008). As with binary logistic regression models, we will examine the predictors' OR relative to the reference group. We use the "pscl" R package to fit the Hurdle negative binomial models (Jackman, 2020). We also considered the use of zero-inflated negative binomial regression models to analyze the number of cyber-attacks reported by organizations, but the Hurdle model showed better indices of goodness-of-fit (see subsection 5.4) and adjusted better to our data. In short, Hurdle models assume that there is one process to explain whether organizations are victimized or not and a second process that determines the number of crimes suffered by organizations with non-zero crime counts, while zero-inflated models assume that the process that explains the number of crimes may also explain suffering zero cyber-attacks. Arguably, the Hurdle model allows for more direct interpretations in a field where regression models for zero-inflated data have rarely been applied before, although future research may also apply zero-inflated models to examine if results are consistent across modeling approaches.

Predicting cybersecurity breaches

This section is divided as follows: subsection 5.1 presents the results of the models estimated to explain the likelihood of falling victim to at least one cybersecurity attack, subsection 5.2 shows the results of the model estimated to explain the likelihood of suffering at least one negative impact due to cybersecurity attacks, subsection 5.3 presents the results of the Hurdle models of number of attacks reported by organizations, and subsection 5.4 presents model diagnostics.

Predicting odds of falling victim to cybersecurity attacks

Table 8 shows the binary logistic regression models used to predict the likelihood that organizations report at least one form of cybersecurity attack and at least one form of negative impact or outcome due to cybersecurity attacks. Model 1 shows the results of the model predicting the odds of falling victim to least one cybersecurity attack, Model 2 presents the results of the model predicting cybersecurity attacks (excluding fraudulent e-mails), and Model 3 shows the results of the model predicting negative impacts or outcomes due to cyber-attacks.

First, in Model 1, Table 8, we can see that all business sectors are more likely to suffer cybersecurity attacks than charities or voluntary sector organizations, except for businesses dedicated to food and hospitality, which show an OR smaller than 1 but not significant. For instance, companies in the construction sector are almost three times more likely to report cyber-attacks than charities, and businesses dedicated to the information or communication sector are 2.5 times more likely to be targeted by cybercriminals than charities. Second, organizations that invest more financial resources in cybersecurity are also those with higher odds of suffering at least one attack. As an example, organizations that invest £10,000 or more in cybersecurity are 2.5 times more likely to report at least one cyber-attack than companies that do not invest financial resources in cybersecurity.

The organization's income is significantly associated with the likelihood of suffering at least one cyber-victimization: companies that earn £5 million or more every year are more than 3 times more likely to suffer at least one cyber-attack than companies with incomes smaller than £100,000. Organizations that are visible online via their website and social media, externally-hosted website, guest wireless network or institutional e-mail addresses are all statistically more likely to report suffering cybersecurity breaches or attacks than organizations without such visibility. For example, companies with externally-hosted websites are 80% more likely to suffer cyber-attacks than companies without websites or with internally-hosted websites, and organizations with institutional e-mail addresses are 88% more likely to report at least one attack than businesses and charities without organizational e-mail addresses.

The encryption of personal data shows a statistically significant positive association with victimization by cybersecurity attacks: organizations that encrypt personal data are 49% more likely to report suffering attacks than organizations that do not encrypt information or do not deal with personal data. Organizations that use basic software protection are 42% more likely to report at least one cyber-attack compared to companies that do not use software protection programs; whereas the monitoring of users' activity seems to reduce the likelihood of cyber-victimization by 20%. Organizations that have one board member with responsibility for cybersecurity and update their directors about cybersecurity monthly are around 30% more likely to report at least one cyber-attack than companies without these measures. And finally, businesses and charities that perceive themselves to have enough staff with cybersecurity skills and knowledge to prevent cyber-attacks are 28% less likely to reporting falling victims to at least one cybercrime than companies that do not agree with

Table 8. Binary logistic regression models to predict odds of suffering at least one cybersecurity attack in last year (1 = experienced victimization) and at least one negative impact or outcome due to cybersecurity breaches (1 = experienced negative outcome).

	Model 1 (at least one cybersecurity attack)			**Model 2** (at least one cybersecurity attack, excluding fraudulent e-mails)			**Model 3** (at least one negative impact/outcome due to cyber-attacks)		
	OR	95% CI		OR	95% CI		OR	95% CI	
(Intercept)	0.03***	0.02	0.06	0.03***	0.01	0.05	0.02***	0.01	0.04
Control variables									
Company sector (ref: charity or voluntary sector organization)									
Administration or real estate	2.04**	1.30	3.21	1.54	0.92	2.58	1.05	0.61	1.78
Construction	2.96***	1.87	4.70	2.34**	1.39	3.95	1.87*	1.09	3.19
Finance or insurance	2.23^{+}	0.91	5.64	1.87	0.70	4.79	1.08	0.38	2.85
Information or communication	2.46**	1.44	4.24	3.02***	1.70	5.37	1.77^{+}	0.97	3.20
Health, care or social work	1.26	0.67	2.34	1.24	0.60	2.49	1.00	0.47	2.04
Food or hospitality	0.86	0.51	1.44	1.04	0.57	1.88	0.64	0.33	1.20
Retail and wholesale	1.64*	1.07	2.50	0.99	0.60	1.63	0.94	0.57	1.58
Others	1.70**	1.18	2.46	1.66*	1.09	2.55	1.29	0.83	1.99
Economic investment in cybersecurity (ref: no investment)									
Less than £1,000	1.77***	1.33	2.35	1.49*	1.06	2.11	2.27***	1.58	3.29
£1,000 to £10,000	1.92***	1.35	2.73	1.95**	1.31	2.91	2.25***	1.47	3.46
£10,000 or more	2.52**	1.45	4.45	2.39**	1.36	4.21	2.49**	1.38	4.48
Don't know	1.21	0.84	1.73	1.32	0.87	1.99	1.61*	1.03	2.52
Independent variables									
Technical self-protection (ref: no)									
Basic software protection	1.42*	1.06	1.90	0.87	1.14	1.94	1.09	0.76	1.57
Personal self-protection (ref: no)									
Training on cybersecurity	0.80	0.61	1.05	0.80	0.74	1.31	0.75^{+}	0.55	1.01
Guidance strong passwords	1.08	0.84	1.39	0.98	0.96	1.88	0.95	0.71	1.29
Require that suppliers adhere to CS standards	1.13	0.82	1.55	1.35^{+}	0.62	1.22	1.40^{+}	1.00	1.97
In-house guardianship (ref: no)									
Monitoring of user activity	0.80^{+}	0.63	1.02	0.71*	0.80	1.41	0.76^{+}	0.58	1.00
Control company devices	0.92	0.72	1.18	1.06	0.97	1.64	0.84	0.63	1.13
Extraordinary CS checks	1.15	0.91	1.46	1.20	0.59	1.07	1.67***	1.26	2.21
Board member on CS	1.30*	1.03	1.65	1.26^{+}	1.04	1.77	1.18	0.90	1.55
CS updates to director at least monthly	1.32*	1.04	1.68	1.36*	1.15	2.33	1.12	0.85	1.49
Enough people with skills/ knowledge dealing with CS	0.72*	0.56	0.92	0.59***	0.44	0.78	0.61**	0.45	0.82
Outsourced guardianship (ref: no)									
Outsourced provider CS	1.18	0.93	1.49	1.48**	0.54	0.92	1.50**	1.14	1.98
Value (ref: Less than £100,000)									
£100,000 to £500,000	1.38^{+}	0.99	1.92	1.50*	1.01	2.25	1.72*	1.13	2.63
£500,000 to £5 million	1.93***	1.35	2.76	2.35***	1.55	3.58	2.16***	1.40	3.39
£5 million or more	3.11***	1.84	5.29	4.89***	2.82	8.56	4.47***	2.53	7.96
Don't know	1.43^{+}	0.97	2.14	1.78*	1.12	2.86	1.84*	1.12	3.04
Personal data electronically (ref: no)	0.98	0.79	1.23	0.88	0.83	1.45	1.08	0.83	1.41
Inertia (ref: no)									
Encrypting personal data	1.49***	1.17	1.88	1.37*	0.92	1.57	1.57**	1.20	2.05
Visibility (ref: no)									
Transactions online	0.96	0.74	1.23	1.09	0.78	2.45	0.90	0.67	1.20
Institution e-mail addresses	1.88*	1.17	3.13	1.35	1.18	2.02	1.73	0.92	3.56
Website and social media	1.57***	1.24	1.99	1.54**	1.16	1.99	1.59**	1.20	2.11
Externally-hosted web	1.80***	1.43	2.27	1.52**	1.03	1.75	1.67***	1.26	2.23
Guest wireless network	1.38**	1.09	1.76	1.34*	0.64	1.03	1.49**	1.13	1.95
Accessibility (ref: no)									
Employees don't use personal devices to work	0.86	0.70	1.07	0.81^{+}	1.15	2.33	0.82	0.64	1.05
Restricting access rights	0.95	0.72	1.27	1.63**	0.79	1.30	1.21	0.85	1.74
Backing up data securely	1.03	0.83	1.29	1.01	1.05	1.78	0.96	0.74	1.24
PseudoR^2	0.20			0.19			0.19		
Log-likelihood	−1116.23			−1036.49			−1022.74		

n = 2088; $^{+}$significant at 10% level, *sig. 5%, **sig. 1%, ***sig. 0.1%

this statement. All the other independent variables show non-significant associations with our dependent variable.

It is important to bear in mind, nevertheless, that the measure of falling victim to cyber-attacks at least once is partly affected by organizations reporting that staff receive fraudulent e-mails or are being directed to fraudulent websites, which was reported by 27.5% of the sample. In order to check whether our results are disproportionately affected by this type of cyber-victimization, we have fitted the same model after recoding the dependent variable to include only those companies that reported at least one cyber-attack other than receiving fraudulent e-mails. This reduces the proportion of organizations suffering cyber-attacks from 37% to 23% of our sample. The results of the model fitted after recoding the dependent variable are presented in Model 2, Table 8.

We highlight five important differences observed in the new model, which has a more restrictive measure of suffering at least one cyber-attack: (a) The variables "restricting access rights" and "require that suppliers adhere to cybersecurity standards" become positive and significant, showing that organizations that fall victims to cybercrimes more severe than receiving fraudulent e-mails may take more drastic measures to protect themselves. (b) Those organizations in which employees do not use personally-owned devices to carry out business activities are statistically less likely to report falling victims to cybercrimes (other than receiving fraudulent e-mails), showing that not allowing employees to use personally-owned devices for work may reduce the likelihood of suffering attacks. (c) Whereas the measures of "basic software protection" and "institutional e-mail addresses" were positive and significant in Model 1, these become negative but not significant after excluding receiving fraudulent e-mails from the list of crimes. (d) The variable "outsourced cybersecurity provider" becomes significant in the model excluding fraudulent e-mail, showing that organizations with outsourced cybersecurity are more likely to suffer cyber-attacks (other than receiving spam) than companies with in-house cybersecurity (or without cybersecurity staff). (e) The association between having enough staff with skills and knowledge to deal with cybersecurity and falling victim to fewer cyber-attacks becomes even stronger: those companies that agree that they have enough staff with the right cybersecurity skills are 41% less likely to report suffering cyber-attacks than organizations that do not have enough staff with cybersecurity skills or knowledge.

Modeling the odds of suffering negative impacts due to cybersecurity attacks

Given that not all cybercrimes produce the same effects on organizations (see Paoli et al., 2018; Rantala, 2008), and some cyber-attacks do not produce direct negative impacts, we replicate the regression models presented above to analyze the likelihood of suffering at least one of the negative impacts or outcomes described in Table 3. The model results are shown in Model 3, Table 8.

In this case, the effect of the organizations' sector is not as significant as it appeared to be in our Models 1 and 2 (used to predict the likelihood of falling victim to a cybersecurity attack). Only two control variables related to the organizations' sector remain statistically significant in our new model: construction companies are 87% more likely than charities, and information and communication businesses are 77% more likely than charities, to report suffering at least one negative impact due to cyber-attacks. Those businesses and charities that invest more financial resources on cybersecurity are also those that are more likely to report suffering the negative impacts of cybersecurity incidents; and the companies' income is a very good indicator of their likelihood of reporting negative cybersecurity impacts (e.g., organizations that earn £5 million or more are 4.5 times more likely to suffer negative impacts than companies whose income is smaller than £100,000).

Online visibility, and more specifically the use of website and social media, externally-hosted websites and guest wireless networks, is associated with an increased likelihood of suffering negative impacts due to cyber-attacks. In this case, the use of institutional e-mail addresses is not a statistically significant predictor. In terms of access to the targets, those organizations in which employees do not use their personal devices to access business information and work are around 20% less likely to suffer negative impacts of cyber-attacks, but this association is not significant. Encrypting personal data is associated with a larger likelihood of reporting negative impacts from cybersecurity attacks, as shown in the previous models. In this case, however, using extraordinary cybersecurity checks becomes significant and positive: those companies that invest in extraordinary checks are 67% more likely to have suffered negative impacts due to cyber-attacks than companies that do not apply these measures.

Organizations in which employees take cybersecurity training or attend cybersecurity seminars are 25% less likely to suffer negative impacts because of cyber-attacks, and UK businesses and charities that monitor the users' activity are 24% less likely to report negative cybersecurity impacts or outcomes. Similarly, companies that perceive that they have enough staff with cybersecurity skills are 39% less likely to suffer negative cybersecurity impacts than organizations that perceive otherwise. On the contrary, organizations that outsource their cybersecurity are 50% more likely to report negative impacts than companies that do not. Having a board member with responsibility for cybersecurity and giving monthly cybersecurity updates to the director do not have statistically significant associations with the negative impacts of cyber-attacks. The rest of the independent variables do not show statistically significant coefficients.

Predicting the number of cybersecurity attacks faced by organizations

In order to analyze the number of victimizations by cybersecurity attacks faced by UK businesses and charities, we make use of a two-part Hurdle negative binomial regression. The first part of the model explains organizations' likelihood of reporting at least one attack (i.e., binary outcome of zero or non-zero cybersecurity incidents), whereas the second part estimates the count of cybercrimes suffered by organizations with at least one reported victimization. Model results are presented in Table 9: Model 1 is estimated from control variables only, Model 2 from independent variables of theoretical interest only, and Model 3 includes all variables.

With regards to the companies' sector, which is used here as a control variable, we can highlight several statistically significant associations. Construction companies are 99% more likely than charities and voluntary sector organizations to report falling victim to cyber-attacks at least once, but the number of attacks faced by those organizations is not significantly larger than the count of attacks reported by charities. Organizations in the administration or real estate sectors are 61% more likely than charities to fall victims to

Table 9. Hurdle negative binomial regression to predict number cybersecurity breaches in last 12 months (transformed by double square root).

	Model 1		Model 2		Model 3	
	Binary	Count	Binary	Count	Binary	Count
	OR	OR	OR	OR	OR (95% CI)	OR (95% CI)
(Intercept)	0.15***	1.11	0.05***	0.10***	0.05 (0.03–0.08)***	0.10 (0.03–0.31)***
Control variables						
Company sector (ref: charity or voluntary sector organization)						
Administration or real estate	2.40***	1.80***			1.61 (1.14–2.28)**	1.89 (1.29–2.72)***
Construction	2.29***	0.76			1.99 (1.40–2.82)***	1.19 (0.75–1.89)
Finance or insurance	2.24**	1.17			1.63 (0.87–3.04)	1.75 (0.82–3.63)
Information or communication	2.55***	2.12***			1.61 (1.09–2.38)*	2.27 (1.55–3.33)***
Health, care or social work	1.28	0.76			1.06 (0.64–1.73)	0.76 (0.36–1.60)
Food or hospitality	1.04	0.66			0.88 (0.57–1.35)	0.64 (0.33–1.26)
Retail and wholesale	1.85***	1.49*			1.41 (1.01–1.97)*	1.85 (1.30–2.70)***
Others	1.85***	1.05			1.53 (1.14–2.05)**	1.13 (0.80–1.60)
Economic investment in cybersecurity (ref: no investment)						
Less than £1,000	2.03***	0.98			1.57 (1.25–1.98)***	0.83 (0.66–1.05)
£1,000 to £10,000	2.84***	0.77*			1.70 (1.29–2.22)***	0.81 (0.60–1.08)
£10,000 or more	3.87***	0.66*			2.06 (1.43–2.97)***	0.75 (0.50–1.13)
Don't know	1.70***	0.47***			1.19 (0.89–1.59)	0.45 (0.31–0.66)***
Independent variables						
Technical self-protection (ref: no)						
Basic software protection			1.57***	1.24	1.36 (1.06–1.74)*	1.23 (0.93–1.66)
Personal self-protection (ref: no)						
Training on cybersecurity			0.87	0.63***	0.84 (0.69–1.02)$^{+}$	0.59 (0.46–0.76)***
Guidance strong passwords			1.07	1.64***	1.03 (0.85–1.25)	1.59 (1.26–2.03)***
Require that suppliers adhere to CS standards			1.10	1.18	1.08 (0.87–1.36)	1.29 (1.02–1.62)*
In-house guardianship (ref: no)						
Monitoring of user activity			0.83*	0.73**	0.85 (0.71–1.01)$^{+}$	0.71 (0.59–0.89)**
Control company devices			0.96	1.02	0.92 (0.76–1.11)	1.03 (0.82–1.26)
Extraordinary CS checks			1.18^{+}	0.79*	1.15 (0.96–1.38)	0.83 (0.67–1.01)$^{+}$
Board member on CS			1.17^{+}	1.19^{+}	1.19 (1.00–1.41)$^{+}$	1.17 (0.96–1.42)
CS updates to director at least monthly			1.30**	1.37***	1.23 (1.03–1.47)*	1.43 (1.17–1.73)***
Enough people with skills/ knowledge dealing with CS			0.78*	1.04	0.76 (0.63–0.93)**	0.87 (0.74–1.02)$^{+}$
Outsourced guardianship (ref: no)						
Outsourced provider CS			1.18^{+}	0.45**	1.11 (0.93–1.33)	0.52 (0.43–0.65)***

(Continued)

Table 9. (Continued).

	Model 1		Model 2		Model 3	
	Binary	Count	Binary	Count	Binary	Count
	OR	OR	OR	OR	OR (95% CI)	OR (95% CI)
Value (ref: Less than £100,000)						
£100,000 to £500,000			1.53***	1.49**	1.14 (0.87–1.51)	1.38 (1.01–1.86)*
£500,000 to £5 million			2.15***	1.57**	1.55 (1.17–2.06)**	1.35 (0.98–1.87)+
£5 million or more			3.21***	0.98	2.18 (1.52–3.13)***	0.79 (0.50–1.23)
Don't know			1.64***	1.11	1.33 (0.97–1.83)+	0.97 (0.66–1.42)
Personal data electronically (ref: no)			1.01	1.69***	0.97 (0.82–1.14)	1.65 (1.34–2.05)***
Inertia (ref: no)						
Encrypting personal data			1.31**	1.29**	1.35 (1.14–1.61)***	1.33 (1.09–1.59)**
Visibility (ref: no)						
Transactions online			0.94	1.08	0.98 (0.81–1.17)	1.09 (0.88–1.34)
Institution e-mail addresses			1.92**	3.89*	1.71 (1.11–2.65)*	3.81 (1.34–10.88)*
Website and social media			1.24*	1.56***	1.35 (1.13–1.61)**	1.67 (1.34–2.10)***
Externally-hosted web			1.79***	0.91	1.70 (1.42–2.04)***	0.81 (0.66–1.01)*
Guest wireless network			1.23*	0.99	1.26 (1.06–1.50)**	1.13 (0.92–1.38)
Accessibility (ref: no)						
Employees don't use personal devices to work			0.94	1.37***	0.95 (0.81–1.11)	1.48 (1.24–1.78)***
Restricting access rights			1.00	0.82	1.02 (0.82–1.28)	0.86 (0.68–1.09)
Backing up data securely			1.12	0.83*	1.10 (0.92–1.29)	0.80 (0.66–0.98)*
Pseudo R^2	0.16		0.27		0.32	
Log-likelihood	−2196.20		−1977.57		−1913.18	

n = 2088; +significant at 10% level, *sig. 5%, **sig. 1%, ***sig. 0.1%

cyber-attacks at least once, and the number of cyber-security attacks faced by administration or real estate companies increases by 89% in contrast to charities. Similarly, retail and wholesale organizations are 41% more likely than charities to fall victim to at least one cyber-attack and the number of attacks increases by 85% when compared to charities. Finally, businesses in the information and communication fields are 61% more likely than charities to suffer cybersecurity attacks at least once, and the number of attacks increases by 2.3 times in comparison to charities.

Economic investment in cybersecurity is a good predictor of both reporting falling victim to at least one cyber-attack and of the number of attacks faced by organizations, but the latter becomes insignificant when incorporating all control and independent variables into the model. In other words, the specific cybersecurity actions included as independent variables in Model 3 explain most of the variation of victimization counts derived from the companies' direct cybersecurity measures, and the overall economic investment in cybersecurity becomes insignificant when the model accounts for those specific measures and actions.

An organization's income/sales is a significant predictor of the binary outcome of non-zero victimization, and companies with incomes/turnover larger than £5 million are 2.2 times more likely to suffer at least one attack than organizations with incomes smaller than £100,000. However, in the count part of the model, this variable is only significant when predicting the number of cyber-attacks faced by businesses with incomes smaller than £5 million. The number of cyber-attacks faced by organizations that hold personal data electronically increases by 65% in comparison to those companies that do not hold personal data electronically.

Organizations with more online visibility (having institutional e-mail addresses, website and social media, externally-hosted website, and guest wireless network) are all more likely to suffer at least one attack than organizations without these characteristics, but only the measures of institutional e-mail addresses and website/social media remain significant in the count part of the model. For instance, organizations with institutional e-mail addresses increase the number of attacks they face by almost four times in comparison to companies without organizational e-mail accounts, and companies with website and social media accounts increase their number of cybersecurity incidents by 67%.

Those organizations whose employees do not use their personal devices to conduct business activity show that the number of cyber-attacks they face increases by 65%, whereas the binary part of the model is not significant. On the contrary, while backing up data securely and conducting extraordinary cybersecurity checks had OR larger than one, but not significant, in the binary part of the model, the OR become smaller than one and significant in the count part: those organizations that back up data securely reduce the number of breaches and attacks by 20%, and those that conduct some form of extraordinary cybersecurity check reduce the number of attacks by 17%. Encrypting personal data is associated with higher odds of suffering at least one cyber-attack and an increased number of cybersecurity incidents. The count part of the model also shows that those organizations that provide guidance on strong passwords and require that suppliers adhere to cybersecurity standards tend to suffer a larger number of cyber-attacks. Businesses and charities with outsourced cybersecurity tend be more likely to suffer at least one cyber-attack, but they also reduce the overall number of incidents they face by 48% in comparison to other organizations.

Three variables are associated with reduced odds of suffering at least one attack and also a decreased number of cyber-victimizations. Organizations that train their staff on cybersecurity have 16% lower odds of suffering at least one attack and reduce the number of cybersecurity incidents by 41%. Companies that monitor users' activity are 15% less likely to suffer at least one cyber-attack and they reduce the number of incidents by 29%. Finally, those companies that perceive they have enough staff with cybersecurity skills and knowledge are 34% less likely to suffer at least one attack and the number of cybersecurity attacks they face is reduced by 13%. However, having basic software protection is associated with 36% increased likelihood of falling victim to at least one cyber-attack, having a board member on cybersecurity is associated with 19% higher odds of suffering at least one cybersecurity incident, and giving monthly cybersecurity updates to the organization's director is associated with 23% higher odds of suffering non-zero attacks and a 43% increased number of cybersecurity incidents.

Model diagnostics

In order to investigate whether the regression models presented above meet the model assumptions and assess whether our results are affected or biased by a small proportion of observations with a large, undue influence, we present some model diagnostics.

In the case of the three binary logistic regression models used to analyze the odds of reporting at least one cybersecurity attack and reporting at least one negative impact due to attacks, and given that we use several predictors and control variables, we assessed the multicollinearity of all variables for each model using variance inflation factors (VIF), as suggested by Miri et al. (2010). Multicollinearity is found when a model is estimated with two or more predictors which are highly linearly related, thus affecting the reliability of the coefficients of individual predictors. As a rule of thumb, a VIF larger than 5 may indicate problematic multicollinearity in our data. In our case we detect no multicollinearity: the largest VIF is 2.62 in the model estimated to predict at least one attack (referred to the predictor "other company sector"), and 2.82 in the model estimated to predict at least one negative impact (referred to the predictor "£500,000 to £5 million invested in cybersecurity"). Moreover, in the three models, the log likelihood values (LLV) are higher (closer to zero) in the model fitted from all control and independent variables, which indicates a better goodness of fit of the full model.

In the case of the Hurdle negative binomial models used to analyze the number of cybersecurity attacks faced by organization, we assess whether the regression fits the data by using a hanging rootogram and the LLV. Figure 2 shows the hanging rootogram of the Hurdle model predicting the number of attacks, which represents the difference between observed and predicted values hanging from the curve. The Hurdle model fits perfectly the number of zeros in the distribution as well as most positive values, but we also observe a slight under-fitting at the counts 3 and 4. In other words, while the model appears to fit the data very well, it may underestimate the number of businesses reporting 3 and 4 cyber-victimizations in the last year. The LLV are also higher in the model fitted from all control and independent variables in comparison to models with fewer variables, which is a good indicator of goodness-of-fit of the full model. Moreover, we compared the goodness-of-it of our Hurdle model with a zero-inflated negative binomial model estimated from the same data, and the Hurdle model shows better results in all indices examined. The Akaike

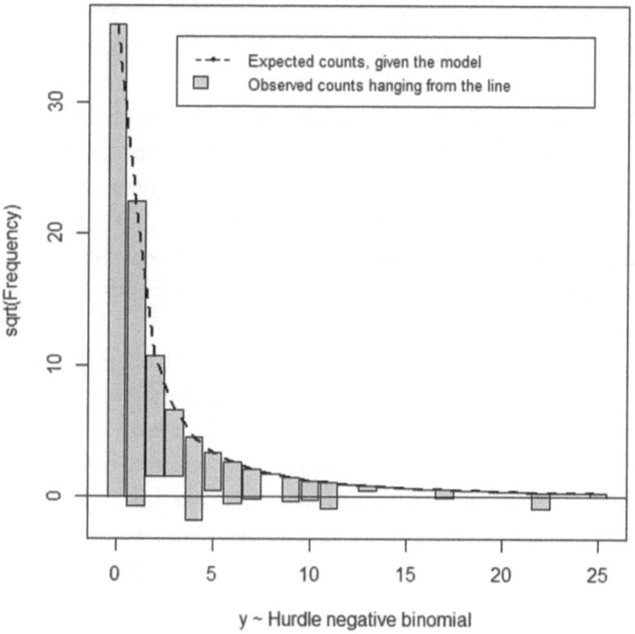

Figure 2. Hanging rootogram of Hurdle negative binomial regression predicting number of cybersecurity attacks (transformed by double square root).

Information Criterion (AIC) and the Bayesian Information Criterion (BIC) are smaller in the Hurdle model (AIC = 3980.2, BIC = 4405.6) than the zero-inflated model (AIC = 4051.6, BIC = 4476.9), and the LLV is higher in the Hurdle model (LLV = −1914.1) than the zero-inflated model (LLV = −1949.7).

Discussion and conclusions

The study of cybercrime victimization suffered by private organizations has been mostly neglected in criminological research due to the lack of available sources of data. Addressing this gap in research is important, given the growing financial impact of cyber-attacks on the private sector (Crowe, 2017; Paoli et al., 2018) and the fact that organizations are investing more resources every year to prevent cybersecurity breaches and attacks (EY, 2019). In this article we have analyzed data recorded by the CSBS 2018 to identify cybersecurity measures which appear more effective at preventing cybersecurity breaches and attacks and which ones do not show significant effects for crime prevention.

We have applied the theoretical framework of RAT and the elements of VIVA to analyze the impact of businesses' online activities and cybersecurity measures, as indicators of various forms of capable guardianship and suitability of crime targets, on cybercrime victimization, as suggested in previous research (e.g., Miró Llinares & Johnson, 2017; Newman & Clarke, 2003; Williams et al., 2019; Yar, 2005). We have combined the use of modeling approaches traditionally used to study cybercrime victimization (i.e., logistic regression models for binary victimization outcomes, see Bossler et al., 2012; Leukfeldt & Yar, 2016; Williams et al., 2019) with novel approaches to analyze the negative impact and harms of cybercrime victimization on organizations (e.g., Paoli et al., 2018) and the number of crimes suffered by businesses and charities. This gives us information not only about the likelihood of organizations reporting falling victim to at least one cybersecurity breach, but also the likelihood of suffering the negative consequences of such criminal activities, and the number of crimes they may face. For instance, the use of Hurdle models for zero-inflated data is an understudied method in criminological research even though it adjusts very well to zero-inflated distributions observed in victimization research (e.g., Hope, 2015; Hope & Trickett, 2008). The use of this triple methodological approach allows us to identify several important findings that advance understanding of the dynamics of business, cybersecurity and cyber-victimization.

Firstly, before applying RAT to interpret the impact of organizations' online activities and cybersecurity measures on cybercrime victimization, we briefly examine the key differences across business sectors. Rantala (2008) had already observed that communication and IT businesses have a higher prevalence of cyber-victimization than other sectors (i.e., a larger proportion of these companies are victimized at least once), but our Hurdle count models show that these companies also suffer from a greater incidence of attacks: the number of cybersecurity incidents faced by communication and IT businesses increases by more than two times compared to charities. This is probably due to the perceived "value" of these companies, since they manage large volumes of personal data (Wall, 2007; Yar, 2005), but also because their online "visibility" and exposure to the general public tends to be large. Surprisingly, finance and insurance companies did not show significant associations with cybercrime victimization in most models. One may argue that even though these organizations plausibly manage highly "valuable" information, they are typically not characterized by a large frequency and variety of visible online activities (in terms of exposure to the general public), which may reduce their "visibility" and overall attractiveness following Cohen and Felson (1979) conceptualization of VIVA. For instance, whereas 54.0% of organizations in our sample have a website and social media, this value is only 37.0% in the case of businesses in the financial and insurance sectors; and while 26.1% of all companies have some sort of functionality to enable online transactions, only 15.0% of financial and insurance businesses have online platforms that allow transactions.

We observe in our models that those organizations that invest more financial resources in cybersecurity are generally more likely to report suffering cyber-attacks and their negative effects. This result appears to be counter-intuitive, as one would expect that allocating more financial resources to cybersecurity would help prevent attacks (Srinidhi et al., 2015), but there are two potential explanations that could account for this. First, we can speculate that decision-making processes in those organizations that, in the first instance, are more likely to suffer attacks will favor major investments in cybersecurity to mitigate risks (Fielder et al., 2016). Thus, results observed in our models may show that organizations that anticipate major cybersecurity threats invest more resources in cybersecurity. There is, however, a second potential interpretation: investing more resources in cybersecurity may enable detecting more crimes, thus enlarging the prevalence of "detected" cybercrime victimization. These interpretations, however, cannot be checked on the basis of cross-sectional methods, and future research should use longitudinal and quasi-experimental methods to illuminate the underlaying causal associations between cybersecurity investment and cyber-attacks victimization.

Our analyses show that organizations' turnover/income is a good predictor of the prevalence and incidence of cyber-attacks reported by companies and the harm these crimes cause. When considering cyber-victimization of individuals, Leukfeldt and Yar (2016) argued that a person's financial characteristics are likely to affect how cyber-attackers view their value. In the case of private organizations, this is even more likely to be the case, given that details of organizations' revenues are often publicly available. Others argue, however, that in cyberspace the "value" is frequently an expression of information as a route to financial gain (Wall, 2007; Yar, 2005), and Williams et al. (2019) found that organizations with confidential customer information were more likely to suffer insider business cybercrime victimization. Our model results show that those organizations that store personal information suffer more cyber-attacks, although this variable does not predict the negative impacts of cybercrime (e.g., loss of access to files, systems corrupted, stopped staff from carrying out their daily work).

Our results also show that those organizations that encrypt personal data as a cybersecurity control are more likely to report suffering cybersecurity incidents and their negative consequences. Although this cybersecurity measure may be interpreted as an indicator of the target's "inertia", since it is intended to create difficulties for criminals to extract meaningful information from compromised files, it may also be an indicator of the target's perceived "value", given that valuable business information will most probably be encrypted when stored digitally (Rantala, 2008). In-depth qualitative studies with cyber-criminals are needed to further understand how they assess the "value" of targets online. As well as signaling that the data being protected by encryption is of value, encrypted systems could be attractive to those criminals who are motivated by the challenge of overcoming digital system defenses rather than simply by the desire to obtain valuable data (Campbell & Kennedy, 2009; Holt et al., 2017). Future research should also analyze whether the use of encryption techniques applied to obstruct illegitimate access to digital systems helps prevent cybersecurity incidents (Noore, 2003).

In terms of visibility, research has shown that those individuals who become visible to offenders by increasing the frequency and variety of activities they conduct online are those who are more frequently targeted (Leukfeldt & Yar, 2016; Marcum et al., 2010; Newman & Clarke, 2003). In the case of businesses' digital victimization, we find evidence that four specific forms of online interaction increase an organization's online visibility and are associated with an increased risk of cyber-attacks: having a website and social media, a externally-hosted website, a guest wireless network, and institutional e-mail addresses. We note, however, that amongst the previous variables, the only ones that are significant to predict the number of cybersecurity incidents are having institutional e-mail addresses and having a website and social media accounts. Those organizations that provide employees with institutional e-mail addresses are particularly affected by receiving fraudulent e-mails, which generally produce less damaging effects than other forms of cybercrime.

Restricting IT administration and access rights to specific users, which may be analyzed as a measure of "access" to targets under the VIVA acronym (Miró Llinares & Johnson, 2017), is associated with a higher likelihood of reporting having suffered at least one cybersecurity attack (excluding fraudulent e-mails). It is, nevertheless, negative but not significant in the models predicting harms of cyber-attacks and the number of cyber-victimizations suffered by organizations. Our interpretation of this finding is that organizations may apply these restrictions to IT administration and access rights after detecting a first attack, and this prevention strategy may help them prevent future attacks and mitigate the negative effects of cybersecurity incidents. As Williams et al. (2019, p. 1127) suggest, "criminal incidents often motivate the adoption of avoidance or security behaviors".

Those organizations that prevent their employees from using their personal devices to conduct business activity tend to report a larger number of cyber-attacks, as shown in the Hurdle count model. This is explained by the frequency of fraudulent e-mails reported by organizations, which would be otherwise received by personal devices instead of company-owned machines. When we exclude receiving fraudulent e-mails from the list of cyber-crimes and estimate logistic regressions of cyber-victimization (other than receiving spam), we observe that this measure may prevent other forms cybercrime but does not prevent receiving fraudulent e-mails.

With regard to the various forms of organizational self-protection analyzed in this paper, we find that when employees are encouraged to become better-informed about cybersecurity (through training and attending seminars) the number of cyber-attacks and their negative impact are reduced (HISCOX, 2018). As argued by Jahankhani (2013, p. 260), perhaps one of the most effective strategies to prevent cybercrimes is "to improve on cognitive development and behavioral skills by developing a set of education, training, and awareness programs specific to Internet exposure risks and cyber behaviors". Moreover, backing up data securely and conducting extraordinary cybersecurity checks also reduce the number of cybercrimes suffered by organizations, but these do not appear to prevent the negative impacts of cybercrime.

Contrary to expectations, providing guidance about strong passwords to employees is associated with a larger number of cybersecurity incidents reported by organizations. This measure does not appear to reduce the number of cybersecurity incidents when applied alone, and it may have a counterproductive effect by allowing organizations to believe they are taking sufficient steps to prevent crime, and that other measures are unnecessary. Previous research had already suggested that guidance on passwords may "lull" organizations into a false sense of security and indirectly lead to increased attacks (e.g., Klein, 1990; Stone et al., 2006). In our sample, 73% of organizations that provide guidance on strong passwords do not encourage employees to take any cybersecurity training, and more than half of those organizations do not monitor users' activity. Thus, encouraging one good cybersecurity practice (in this case, strong passwords) may be dysfunctional more broadly if it deters organizations from instituting other important cybersecurity measures. Moreover, as suggested by the National Cyber Security Centre (2018), those organizations that place unrealistic demands on users in their "strong passwords guidance" (e.g., asking employees to change the password frequently or using long passwords with special characters) may actually lead to a "password overload" which causes that users re-use the same passwords across systems, use predictable passwords or write passwords down in places where they can be easily found.

Requiring suppliers to adhere to cybersecurity standards shows a positive association with the negative harms of cybersecurity attacks, which may indicate that organizations take this decision after suffering the negative impact of a cyber-attack, but this measure does not significantly prevent future cybercrimes. Another explanation may be that organizations that have complex supply chains are more likely to require suppliers to adhere to cybersecurity measures, but they are also more likely to suffer attacks.

The use of basic software protection, as a measure of technical self-protection, does not seem to be an effective measure to prevent cyber-attacks either (Leukfeldt & Yar, 2016; Rantala, 2008). This finding, however, may be explained by the inclusion of fraudulent e-mails as a form of cybercrime in our analyses, since software protection programs do not successfully prevent receiving spam e-mails. After excluding this type of crime from our analyses this variable becomes negative but not significant.

The use of outsourced forms of guardianship, which refers to the hiring of external cybersecurity providers, is associated with a higher likelihood of having suffered at least one cybersecurity attack (Rantala, 2008), but it also reduces the number of cybersecurity incidents suffered by companies. It is plausible that hiring external cybersecurity helps organizations prevent future attacks, but longitudinal studies are needed to further examine the causal associations between hiring outsourced cybersecurity and preventing attacks. (This shows the need for using Hurdle count models in cybercrime research, since this would have remained hidden if we had only used traditional logistic regression models.) Nevertheless, outsourcing cybersecurity does not appear to reduce the likelihood of suffering the negative impacts of cyber-attacks.

On the contrary, enhancing the in-house guardian by developing cybersecurity teams within the organization seems to generate the best results for preventing cyber-attacks and their negative impacts. The monitoring of users' activity is associated with a reduced number of cyber-attacks and it lowers the likelihood to suffer the negative impact of cybercrime. Those organizations that control company devices are less likely to suffer negative impacts or outcomes due to cyber-attacks, although this association is not significant. And finally, while establishing high-level cybersecurity controls (i.e., board members on cybersecurity, monthly cybersecurity updates to the director) is not associated with reduced cyber-attacks (Williams et al., 2019), foregrounding the internal guardian by having enough members of staff with skills and knowledge to manage cybersecurity seems to be the most promising cybersecurity measure to prevent future cyber-attacks and their negative impacts.

In summary, this article shows that the framework established by RAT can be used to further understand cyber-victimization in private organizations. More specifically, our results show that investing in in-house cybersecurity human resources and enhancing employees' online self-protection by providing cybersecurity training, rather than just basic software protection and guidance about strong passwords, are the most promising ways to minimize cyber-attacks and their impacts. These results can be used by researchers to further understand the effect of organizational cybersecurity measures on cybercrime prevention, but our analyses may also serve to guide organizational practices for cybercrime prevention. For instance, these results point toward the need to invest in in-house cybersecurity teams and internal cybersecurity training programs to mitigate cybersecurity risks and prevent future victimization (Jahankhani, 2013; Levi et al., 2015; Williams et al., 2019).

There is, however, a need for new research analyzing cybercrime victimization suffered by businesses and charities in other geographic contexts and using alternative sources of data. National governments from various countries are developing new surveys to record data on cybercrime victimization, which may become key sources of information to further investigate corporate cyber-victimization and to guide businesses' evidence-based cybersecurity practices.

Acknowledgments

The authors would like to thank Jose Pina-Sánchez for comments that greatly improved the manuscript.

Disclosure statement

No potential conflict of interest was reported by the author(s).

ORCID

David Buil-Gil http://orcid.org/0000-0002-7549-6317
Nicholas Lord http://orcid.org/0000-0002-5922-707X
Emma Barrett http://orcid.org/0000-0003-0762-5196

References

Bilodeau, H., Lari, M., & Uhrbach, M. (2019). *Cyber security and cybercrime challenges of Canadian businesses, 2017* (Report No. 85-002-X). The Canadian Centre for Justice Statistics, Statistics Canada.

Bonney, G. E. (1987). Logistic regression for dependent binary observations. *Biometrics*, *43*(4), 951–973. https://doi.org/10.2307/2531548

Bossler, A. M., & Holt, T. J. (2009). On-line activities, guardianship, and malware infection: An examination of routine activities theory. *International Journal of Cyber Criminology*, *3*(1), 400–420. http://www.cybercrimejournal.com/bosslerholtijcc2009.pdf

Bossler, A. M., Holt, T. J., & May, D. C. (2012). Predicting online harassment victimization among a juvenile population. *Youth & Society*, *44*(4), 500–523. https://doi.org/10.1177/0044118X11407525

Buil-Gil, D., Miró-Llinares, F., Moneva, A., Kemp, S., & Díaz-Castaño, N. (2020). Cybercrime and shifts in opportunities during COVID-19: A preliminary analysis in the UK. *European Societies*, 1–13. https://doi.org/10.1080/14616696.2020.1804973

Cameron, A. C., & Trivedi, P. K. (2005). *Microeconomics. Methods and applications*. Cambridge University Press.

Campbell, Q., & Kennedy, D. M. (2009). The psychology of computer criminals. In S. Bosworth, M. E. Kabay, & E. Whyne (Eds.), *Computer security handbook* (*5th* ed.) (pp. 140–160). Wiley.

Cohen, L. E., & Felson, M. (1979). Social change and crime rate trends: A routine activity approach. *American Sociological Review*, *44*(4), 588–608. https://doi.org/10.2307/2094589

Crowe. (2017). *Annual Frau Indicator 2017. Identifying the cost of fraud to the UK economy.*

Department for Digital, Culture, Media & Sport. (2018). *Cyber security breaches survey (Technical annex).*

EY. (2019). *Is cybersecurity about more than protection? EY global information security survey 2018-19.*

Fielder, A., Panaousis, E., Malacaria, P., Hankin, C., & Smeraldi, F. (2016). Decision support approaches for cyber security investment. *Decision Support Systems*, *86*, 13–23. https://doi.org/10.1016/j.dss.2016.02.012

HISCOX. (2018, October 18). *UK small businesses targeted with 65,000 attempted cyber attacks per day*. HISCOX. https://www.hiscoxgroup.com/news/press-releases/2018/18-10–18

Holt, T. J., & Bossler, A. M. (2008). Examining the applicability of lifestyle-routine activities theory for cybercrime victimization. *Deviant Behavior*, *30*(1), 1–25. https://doi.org/10.1080/01639620701876577

Holt, T. J., & Bossler, A. M. (2016). *Cybercrime in progress. Theory and prevention of technology-enabled offenses*. Routledge.

Holt, T. J., Freilich, J. D., & Chermak, S. M. (2017). Exploring the subculture of ideologically motivated cyber-attackers. *Journal of Contemporary Criminal Justice*, *33*(3), 213–233. https://doi.org/10.1177/1043986217699100

Holt, T. J., Leukfeldt, R., & van de Weijer, S. (2020). An examination of motivation and routine activity theory to account for cyberattacks against Dutch web sites. *Criminal Justice and Behavior*, *47*(4), 487–505. https://doi.org/10.1177/0093854819900322

Hope, T. (2015). Understanding the distribution of crime victimization using "British crime survey" data: An exercise in statistical reasoning. In *Oxford handbooks online*. Oxford University Press. https://doi.org/10.1093/oxfordhb/9780199935383.013.41

Hope, T., & Trickett, A. (2008). The distribution of crime victimisation in the population. *International Review of Victimology*, *15*(1), 37–58. https://doi.org/10.1177/026975800801500103

Jackman, S. (2020). *PSCL: Classes and methods for R developed in the political science computational laboratory (R package version 1.5.5) [Computer software]*. United States Studies Centre, University of Sydney.

Jahankhani, H. (2013). Developing a model to reduce and/or prevent cybercrime victimization among the user individuals. In B. Akhgar & S. Yates (Eds.), *Strategic intelligence management: National security imperatives and information and communications technologies* (pp. 258–268). Butterworth-Heinemann.

Kemp, S., Miró-Llinares, F., & Moneva, A. (2020). The dark figure and the cyber fraud rise in Europe: Evidence from Spain. *European Journal on Criminal Policy and Research*. https://doi.org/10.1007/s10610-020-09439-2

Klein, D. V. (1990). "Foiling the cracker": A survey of, and improvements to, password security. *Proceedings of the 2nd USENIX security workshop*, Portland, 5–14.

Leukfeldt, E. R., & Yar, M. (2016). Applying routine activity theory to cybercrime: A theoretical and empirical analysis. *Deviant Behavior*, *37*(3), 263–280. https://doi.org/10.1080/01639625.2015.1012409

Levi, M., Doig, A., Gundur, R., Wall, D., & Williams, M. (2015). *The implications of economic cybercrime for policing* (Research report). City of London Corporation.

Marcum, C. D., Higgins, G. E., & Ricketts, M. L. (2010). Potential factors of online victimization of youth: An examination of adolescent online behaviors utilizing routine activity theory. *Deviant Behavior*, *31*(5), 381–410. https://doi.org/10.1080/01639620903004903

Miri, H., Sarkar, S. K., & Rana, S. (2010). Collinearity diagnostics of binary logistic regression model. *Journal of Interdisciplinary Mathematics*, *13*(3), 253–267. https://doi.org/10.1080/09720502.2010.10700699

Miró Llinares, F. (2015). That cyber routine, that cyber victimization: Profiling victims of cybercrime. In R. G. Smith, R. C. C. Cheung, & L. Y. C. Lau (Eds.), *Cybercrime risks and responses* (pp. 47–63). Palgrave Macmillan.

Miró Llinares, F., & Johnson, S. D. (2017). Cybercrime and place: Applying environmental criminology to crimes in cyberspace. In G. J. N. Bruinsma & S. D. Johnson (Eds.), *The Oxford handbook of environmental criminology* (pp. 883–906). Oxford University Press.

Miró-Llinares, F., & Moneva, A. (2020). Environmental criminology and cybercrime: Shifting focus from the wine to the bottles. In T. Holt & A. Bossler (Eds.), *The Palgrave handbook of international cybercrime and cyberdeviance* (pp. 491–511). Palgrave Macmillan.

National Audit Office. (2017). *Online fraud (report by the comptroller and auditor general)*.

National Audit Office. (2019). *Progress of the 2016-2021 national cyber security programme (report by the comptroller and auditor general)*.

National Cyber Security Centre. (2017). *The cyber threat to UK businesses (2016/2017 Report)*. National Audit Office.

National Cyber Security Centre. (2018, November 19). *Password policy: Updating your approach*. https//www.ncsc.gov.uk/collection/passwords/updating-your-approach.

Newman, G. R., & Clarke, R. V. (2003). *Superhighway robbery: Preventing e-commerce crime*. Willan Publishing.

Noore, A. (2003). A secure conditional access system using digital signature and encryption. *2003 IEEE International Conference on Consumer Electronics*, 220–221. Los Angeles: IEEE. https://doi.org/10.1109/ICCE.2003.1218894

Office for National Statistics. (2019). *E-commerce and ICT activity, UK: 2018 (Statistical bulletin).*

Paoli, L., Visschers, J., & Verstraete, C. (2018). The impact of cybercrime on businesses: A novel conceptual framework and its application to Belgium. *Crime, Law and Social Change, 70*(4), 397–420. https://doi.org/10.1007/s10611-018-9774-y

R Core Team. (2020). *R: A language and environment for statistical computing [Computer software].* R Foundation for Statistical Computing.

Rantala, R. R. (2008). *Cybercrime against businesses, 2005 (Special report).* Bureau of Justice Statistics.

Richards, K. (2009). *The Australian business assessment of computer user security (ABACUS): A national survey (research and public policy series).* Australian Institute of Criminology.

Srinidhi, B., Yan, J., & Tayi, G. K. (2015). Allocation of resources to cyber-security: The effect of misalignment of interest between managers and investors. *Decision Support Systems, 75*, 49–62. https://doi.org/10.1016/j.dss.2015.04.011

Stone, J., & Madigan, E. (2006). A managerial framework for network security. *Proceedings of the 2006 International Conference on telecommunication systems - Modeling and analysis.* Reading: Peen State Berks.

Wall, D. S. (2007). *Cybercrime. The transformation of crime in the information age.* Policy Press.

Williams, M. L., Levi, M., Burnap, P., & Gundur, R. V. (2019). Under the corporate radar: Examining insider business cybercrime victimization through an application of routine activities theory. *Deviant Behavior, 40*(9), 1119–1131. https://doi.org/10.1080/01639625.2018.1461786

Xie, M., Goh, T. N., & Kuralmani, V. (2002). *Statistical models and control charts for high-quality processes.* Springer.

Xie, M., Goh, T. N., & Tang, X. Y. (2000). Data transformation for geometrically distributed quality characteristics. *Quality and Reliability Engineering International, 16*(1), 9–15. https://doi.org/10.1002/(SICI)1099-1638(200001/02)16:1<9::aid-qre278>3.0.CO;2-8

Yar, M. (2005). The novelty of 'cybercrime': An assessment in light of routine activity theory. *European Journal of Criminology, 2*(4), 407–427. https://doi.org/10.1177/147737080556056

Zeileis, A., Kleiber, C., & Jackman, S. (2008). Regression models for count data in R. *Journal of Statistical Software, 27*(8), 1–25. https://doi.org/10.18637/jss.v027.i08

Phishing Evolves: Analyzing the Enduring Cybercrime

Adam Kavon Ghazi-Tehrani and Henry N. Pontell

ABSTRACT

Phishing, the fraudulent attempt to obtain sensitive information by disguising oneself as a trustworthy entity via electronic communication, has quickly evolved beyond low-skill schemes that relied on casting "a wide net." Spear phishing attacks target a particular high-value individual utilizing sophisticated techniques. This study aims to describe the current state of phishing, the expected technological advances and developments of the near future, and the best prevention and enforcement strategies. Data comes from interviews with approximately 60 information technology security professionals, "hackers," and academic researchers. Routine Activity Theory provided an operational framework; while it is an imperfect fit for most crimes, it provides enough explanatory power for cyber-crimes. Interviewees mainly agreed: First, technological advances increase the proliferation of phishing attacks, but also aid in their detection. It has never been easier to conduct a simple attack, but a good attack requires more effort than ever before. Second, phishing is directly responsible financial fraud and, indirectly, as the primary attack vector for ransomware. Third, newer types of attacks utilizing technology, like deepfakes, will make the problem worse in the short-term. Fourth, prevention will come from machine learning and public education akin to WIFI security improvement via the combination of encryption and password awareness.

Introduction

Phishing is an automated form of social engineering whereby criminals use the Internet to fraudulently extract sensitive information from businesses and individuals, often by impersonating legitimate web sites. The high potential for rewards (e.g., through access to bank accounts and credit card numbers), the ease of sending forged e-mail messages impersonating legitimate authorities, and the difficulty law enforcement has in pursuing the criminals responsible have resulted in a surge of phishing attacks in recent years (Egan, 2020). The 2019 "State of the Phish" report found that nearly 90% of organizations experienced targeted phishing attacks in 2019, 84% reported SMS/text phishing (smishing), 83% faced voice phishing (vishing), and the volume of reported e-mail increased 67% year over the previous year (Egan, 2020). Evidence suggests that an increasing number of people shy away from Internet commerce due to the threat of identity fraud, despite the tendency of companies to assume the risk for fraud (Morrison & Firmstone, 2000).

A typical phishing attack begins with an e-mail to the victim, supposedly from a reputable institution, yet actually from the *phisher*. The text of the message commonly warns the user that a problem must be immediately corrected with the user's account. The victim is then led to a *spoofed* website (a fake one designed to resemble the institution's official website) (Alsharnouby et al., 2015). In this passive attack, the web page prompts the victim to enter account information (e.g., username and password) and may also request other personal details, such as the victim's Social Security number, bank account numbers, ATM PINs, etc. All of this information is relayed to the phisher, who can then use it to access the user's accounts (Alsharnouby et al., 2015).

Phishing has remained a costly cybercrime for businesses and individuals. It is directly responsible for financial loss due to fraud, and causes damage indirectly as the primary attack vector for ransomware, where the victim's computer files are locked by intruders until payment is made to them (Gorham, 2020). From 2013–2018 the FBI found that Business E-mail Compromise (BEC) accounted for 12 USD billion in direct losses to US corporations and that ransomware attacks cost corporations 7.5 USD billion in 2019 alone (O'Neill, 2020).

Past studies (Hutchings & Hayes, 2009; Kigerl, 2012; Reyns et al., 2011) have analyzed *phishing* within the Routine Activity theoretical framework. Though various criminological theories have been utilized to explain cyber-crime, including social learning theory, self-control theory, and subcultural theories (Stalans & Donner, 2018), these remain offender-focused methods of explanation. To analyze why *phishing* exists, persists, and what may be done to combat it, situation-focused theory is more appropriate (Wortley & Tilley, 2014). Routine activity (Cohen & Felson, 1979) is a situational theory of crime opportunity that provides a tool for analyzing the efficacy of both technology-focused (*target hardening*) and human-focused (*capable guardians*) efforts to combat *phishing*. This allows policy suggestions that aim to reduce risk of victimization to be tested (Leukfeldt, 2014, 2015; Leukfeldt & Yar, 2016).

This study seeks to define the factors that lead to *phishing* enduring as a crime type and to refine the application of Routine Activity Theory to cyber-crimes. It also aims to describe the current state of phishing, the expected technological advances and developments in the near future, and the current state of prevention and enforcement strategies in order to further improve them.

The paper is presented as follows. First, a literature review summarizes the extent of phishing scholarship and identifies gaps in current research regarding phishing. Second, the methodology for the study is described, including the research plan, data collection and coding issues, research questions and planned analysis. Third, the data are analyzed and findings are presented through a series of "relevant, emergent codes," which allow for the labeling of concepts that become apparent during data collection and analysis. Finally, there is a discussion of the findings regarding phishing in both the present and future, potential control mechanisms, and an assessment of the utility of applying Routine Activity Theory to cyber-crimes in general. Limitations of the study and suggestions for future research are offered, as well as policy implications.

Literature review

Routine Activity Theory

There remains debate within cyber criminology about the similarity of cyber-crimes to terrestrial ones and the viability of using "traditional" criminological theory to analyze digital crimes (Grabosky, 2001). Cohen and Felson's (1979) Routine Activity Theory (RAT), created to explain crime patterns in post-WWII Chicago, is the most frequently applied criminological theory for understanding cyber-crime victimology (Bossler & Holt, 2009; Hutchings & Hayes, 2009; Leukfeldt, 2014, 2015; Leukfeldt et al., 2016; Leukfeldt & Yar, 2016; Ngo & Paternoster, 2011; Pratt et al., 2010; Reyns et al., 2011; Van Wilsem, 2011, 2013). The routine activity approach holds that victimization is influenced by a combination of a *motivated offender*, a *suitable target*, and an *absence of a capable guardian* in a convergence of time and space (Cohen & Felson, 1979). The *motivated offender* is an assumed property, *tuitable targets* are determined by VIVA: Value, Inertia, Visibility, and Access, and *capable guardians* may be people, such as police, or things, such as security cameras (Cohen & Felson, 1979).

Routine Activity Theory has also been advanced since its original conception by Clarke et al. (1999), who extended Cohen and Felson's (1979) work on target suitability to explain the phenomenon of "hot products, " or those that can be stolen easily and that share six key attributes of being CRAVED; they are concealable, removable, available, valuable, enjoyable and disposable (Clarke et al., 1999). Their research suggests that relatively few hot products account for a large proportion of all thefts (Clarke et al., 1999).

The theory is not perfectly adapted for virtual settings, however, and Yar (2005) argues that it is problematic to convert the routine activity approach from real space to cyber space, due to issues of spatiality, temporality, and the tenuous comparison of physical guardians to virtual ones. The critiques presented by Yar (2005) are definitional, rather than practical. For example, Yar (2005) argues that Routine Activity Theory requires both a rhythm, or "regular periodicity with which events occur," and a timing, in which different activities are coordinated "such as the coordination of an offender's rhythms with those of a victim" (Cohen & Felson, 1979, p. 590). *Phishing* is usually an asynchronous act: a compromised e-mail is sent to the intended victim and the victim opens it at some later time. In this case, using a narrow interpretation of Routine Activity Theory, a temporal convergence will not occur. Instead, a wider interpretation allows for the temporal convergence to be between the victim and the *phishing* e-mail, rather than the victim and the offender.

Though every facet of Routine Activity Theory may not map perfectly from real space to virtual space, numerous studies have supported its application for cyber-crimes, generally, and *phishing*, specifically. Hutchings and Hayes (2009) found that users who spend more time online are more likely to be *phished* by increasing their "exposure" as a *suitable target* to possible offenders and that users who do not utilize spam filters (*capable guardians*) are also more likely to fall victim. Bossler and Holt (2009) found similar results when analyzing other types of cyber victimization within a population of colleges students. In their study, Bossler and Holt (2009) discovered that while respondents' general computer use and activities such as playing video games, shopping, or checking e-mail did not have a significant impact on the likelihood of experiencing online victimization, the number of hours respondents spent in chat rooms and using instant message (IM) chat did.

Also, Leukfeldt and Yar (2016) later show that the explanatory power of Routine Activity Theory differs greatly between different types of cyber-crime, but that factors which matter for *phishing*, such as target *value* and *visibility* were significant in predicting victimization. *Phishing* is one type of cyber-crime that seems particularly well-suited to the theory. While the temporal and physical elements are removed via online contact, the combination of a *suitable target* (sensitive information) and the absence of *capable guardian* (an uninformed end-user) would appear to result in a higher likelihood of phishing victimization.

Types of phishing

The vast majority (96%) of phishing attempts are made via e-mail (Verizon, 2019). In the past, these e-mails were poorly-worded, low-effort attempts sent to a large number of people (for example, in batches of hundreds of thousands) with the expectation that even a low response rate (~0.5%) would still yield hundreds of victims (Egan, 2020). Widespread use of "spam" filters, however, has made this brute-force methodology increasingly ineffective and *phishers* have turned to more advanced techniques (Cook et al., 2009). These include: Business E-Mail Compromise (BEC), Smishing, Vishing, Spear phishing, and Whaling (Parmar, 2012).

BEC occurs when a cybercriminal sends an e-mail to a lower-level employee, typically someone who works in the accounting or finance department, while pretending to be the company's CEO or another executive, manager, or supervisor (Mansfield-Devine, 2016b). The goal of these e-mails is often to get their victim to transfer funds to a fake account while preying on the tendency for most employees to not question their workplace superiors (Mansfield-Devine, 2016b).

Smishing is short for "SMS phishing;" SMS is "short message service," the standard the world uses for text messaging (Stembert et al., 2015). Smishing attacks utilize phone text messages as the attack vector, instead of e-mails, partially to bypass SPAM filters and to reach more potential victims. *Vishing*, short for "voice phishing" uses telephone calls to accomplish the same, for similar reasons (Stembert et al., 2015).

Spear phishing has risen in popularity as earlier "simple" mass phishing has declined; a *spear phishing* attack is targeted (Parmar, 2012). Unlike general phishing e-mails, which use spam-like tactics to reach the general population in massive e-mail campaigns, spear phishing e-mails target specific individuals within an organization employing various social engineering tactics to tailor and personalize the e-mails to their intended victims. For example, they may use subject lines that would be topics of interest to the recipients to trick them into opening the message and clicking on links or attachments. *Whaling* is a form of *spear phishing* and can be viewed as the "opposite" of BEC (Stembert et al., 2015): Instead of targeting lower-level individuals within an organization, the cybercriminal aims messaging at high-level executives such as CEOs, CFOs, and COOs in order to trick them into revealing sensitive information and corporate data. These targets are carefully selected because of their access and authority within an organization.

In addition, users with no technological skill at all are able to engage in such activities using *phishing kits* and *phishing-as-a-service. Phishing kits* allow novices to purchase and run pre-built packages and *phishing-as-a-service* allows unskilled offenders to hire someone else to conduct the attack (Thomas et al., 2017).

Studies on phishing

Dhamija et al. (2006) conducted one of the earliest studies investigating why people fall for phishing scams, asking participants to identify various Web sites as legitimate or fake. They found that highly effective phishing sites fooled 90% of their participants and that most browser cues were opaque to these end-users. Victims did not realize that Web pages can be easily copied, and thus incorrectly judged these sites based on their content and their professional appearance. Downs et al. (2006) conducted a complementary study examining phishing e-mail messages that replicated the Dhamija et al. (2006) study, finding that participants used basic and often incorrect heuristics in deciding how to respond to e-mail messages. For example, some participants reasoned that since the business already had their information, it would be safe to give it again. These early studies were largely atheoretical, focusing more on description than explanation.

More recent studies (Leukfeldt, 2015; Leukfeldt et al., 2016) explore the relationships among phishing and cybercriminal networks, social ties, and online forums. For example, research by Leukfeldt et al. (2016) found that social ties play an important role in the origin and growth of the majority of networks that criminals with access to forums are able to use to criminally exploit quickly and easily.

There are studies on *phishing* outside the field of criminology, which focus on education and training. Two studies by Arachchilage and Love (2013, 2014) tested the efficacy of security awareness. These studies showed a significant improvement of participants' *phishing* avoidance behavior after playing a game based on security best practices. Furthermore, the findings suggest that participants' threat perception, safeguard effectiveness, self-efficacy, perceived severity and perceived susceptibility elements positively impact threat avoidance behavior, whereas safeguard cost had a negative impact on it (Arachchilage & Love, 2013, 2014).

Studies on phishing and Routine Activity Theory

As mentioned above in the section on the suitability of Routine Activity Theory for digital crimes, there are few studies on phishing that utilize RAT (Hutchings & Hayes, 2009; Leukfeldt, 2014, 2015). Leukfeldt (2014) and (Leukfeldt, 2015) focus on *suitable targets* and *risk factors*, respectively. Leukfeldt (2014) finds that personal background and financial characteristics play no role in phishing victimization, that having up-to-date antivirus software as a technically capable guardian is an insignificant factor, and that no single, clearly defined group has an increased chance of being a victim. The study concludes that while *target hardening* may help, there are limited opportunities for prevention campaigns aimed at specific target groups or dangerous online activities, making situational crime prevention problematic. There is the suggestion that banks could play the role of capable guardian to potentially mitigate this shortcoming (Leukfeldt, 2014).

Leukfeldt (2015) also compares victimization risk factors for two types of phishing: high-tech phishing (e.g., using malicious software) and low-tech phishing (e.g., using e-mails and telephone calls). The findings show situational crime prevention has to be aimed at groups other than just the users themselves. Criminals are primarily interested in popular online places and the onus is on the owners of these virtual spaces to protect their users from being victimized from both high- and low-tech phishing (Leukfeldt, 2015).

Thus, at present, there remains a clearly-defined gap in our understanding of the utility of RAT to the prevention and control of phishing, which this study seeks to address. At present there are no widely-successful mechanisms, technological or human-focused, to prevent victimization through phishing. The current study seeks to further refine the results of past studies with different data and research questions regarding both the factors behind the evolution of *phishing* and the viability of RAT for guiding policies to combat this ubiquitous form of cybercrime.

Methodology

The study utilizes personal interviews as its data source. This research methodology allows for a deeper understanding of relatively new and undeveloped areas, and for consideration of prominent theoretical issues and policy concerns (Corbin & Strauss, 2008; Creswell & Poth, 2018). Questions were developed which could allow for a better understanding of how phishing may continue to evolve in the future, how it may be better combatted, and to examine both the utility and further development of Routine Activity Theory for cyber-crimes.

A qualitative study is appropriate when the goal of research is to explain a phenomenon by relying on the perception of a person's experience in a given situation (Stake, 2010). As outlined by Creswell (2014), a quantitative approach is also appropriate when a researcher seeks to understand relationships between variables. Because the purpose of this study is to discover relevant factors, both social and technological, to further-develop theory, and suggest control strategies, a qualitative approach is appropriate.

Research questions

In order to define the factors that lead to *phishing* enduring as a crime type and to refine the application of Routine Activity Theory to cyber-crime, and its prevention and control, the following questions were developed:

RQ1: What factors allow *phishing* to exist as a long-term, successful crime type?

RQ2: What *technological* solutions are viable both now and in the future?

RQ3: What *human-focused* prevention strategies are viable now and in the future?

Study participants

The overall sample (N = 62) was drawn through purposive sampling from three distinct, expert, and diverse populations in order to gain the broadest perspective in answers to the research questions: information technology/security professionals, "hackers," and academic researchers. The purposive sampling technique is the deliberate choice of a participant due to the qualities the participant possesses (Etikan, 2016). It is a nonrandom technique that does not need underlying theories or a set number of participants. With purposive sampling, the researcher decides what needs to be known and sets out to find people who can and are willing to provide the information by virtue of knowledge or experience (Barratt et al., 2015). This involves identification and selection of individuals or groups of individuals that are proficient and well-informed with a phenomenon of interest. Unlike random studies, which deliberately include a diverse cross section of ages, backgrounds and cultures, the idea behind purposive sampling is to concentrate on people with particular characteristics who will better be able to assist with the relevant research (Barratt et al., 2015; Etikan, 2016), in this case, those with the most information on *phishing* and cyber-crime victimization.

Though the selected groups varied in age-range, years of experience, and other demographic factors (such as gender balance), the responses to interview questions were overwhelmingly similar. Due to the lack of any significant differences in responses, and the nature of the study (i.e., interviewees are the sources of information, not the object of study themselves), the groups were combined, providing one population for analysis.

The selection of respondents was dictated by the following two guidelines. First, participants must have worked, published, or participated in computer security for at least three years. Second, all participants had to be fluent in the English language, but English did not have to be their native language. Though the majority (N = 38) of interview subjects were based in the United States, there were a number of international participants (N = 24) as well.

Participants were recruited through existing professional networks of the researchers, the American Society of Criminology (ASC), and the Social Science Research Network (SSRN). Many of the participants had been interviewed for a previous project on international cyber-crimes and were willing to participate again. Initial contact for these participants was obtained for the prior project via "cold e-mails" and forum posts on popular cyber security websites such as "Krebs on Security" and "Naked Security."

The interview subjects were asked to respond via e-mail if they were interested in being interviewed on the topic of *phishing* or knew someone who might be. We informed the prospective participant that we hoped to interview approximately 20 people each from industry, enthusiast, and scholarly circles, that the interview would take approximately 30–60 minutes, and would be entirely confidential and anonymous. We initiated contact with 85 individuals and were able to interview 62 of them, for an overall response rate of 72.9%. This is similar to other comparable studies, such as the Leukfeldt research (2014, 2015), which both drew from the same data set at a 47% response rate and the Bossler and Holt research (2009), which had a response rate of 72.3%.

Data collection

A semi-structured, informal interview format was used, consisting of twelve open-ended questions that are in Appendix A. Interviews were conducted primarily by telephone (77.4%, N = 48) or video via FaceTime or Skype (12.9%, N = 8). A number of participants from the hacker group preferred to respond via text, either through e-mail or IRC (9.6%, N = 6). Written or verbal informed consent was provided by each participant before the interview. Each interview was conducted in a single session, and transcribed and coded for each specific question by the primary researcher.

Saturation (Glaser & Strauss, 2009) occurs when the researcher realizes that for a given subject, no new categories emerge from coding responses and therefore, nothing more can be added to the data. It was possible that saturation could occur in this research. Once saturation is reached, the theory or phenomenon is said to be grounded in the data (Charmaz, 2006; Urquhart, 2013). Saturation was realized in this study after the 45th interview, and at that point one group (academics) was underrepresented in the sample. Interviews were continued in order to enhance validity by providing more equal representation among the initial groups selected for the study.

Data analysis

Coding of transcripts was completed in the order of the interviews conducted. Codes were created during the research process (Urquhart, 2013). Coding was conducted both manually by the lead researcher, and through computer-assisted qualitative data analysis software (NVivo 12). To test the reliability of the coding process, we utilized an inter-rater reliability check; the co-researcher coded a subset of the interviews (18 of the 62 total; 6 from each participant sample group) to compare to the lead researcher's codes. The process of analyzing, reanalyzing, and comparing new data to existing data is known as constant comparison (Birks & Mills, 2011; Urquhart, 2013). As each phase of coding began, the lead researcher reviewed the data collected in previous phases in order to see when saturation might be reached. Coding terminology followed the three-stage protocol developed by Glaser and Strauss (2009); open, axial, and selective/theoretical.

In the first phase of open coding, each line of interview text was transcribed resulting in numerous descriptive categories of response. Axial coding was then used when there were no new open categories, or when responses related only to the core categories that emerged in the interviews. Finally, selective/theoretical coding was conducted, comparing codes and categories that emerged during open coding and axial phases, where relationships were found among the previously established categories (Urquhart, 2013).

An example of this coding process is as follows for the first research question, "*What factors allow phishing to exist as a long-term, successful crime type?*" First, lines of dialog pertaining to *phishing* attack type were open-coded using respondents' own words, such as "simple/smart," "old/new," and "net/spear." Next, axial coding collapsed these related terms into concepts, "wide" (simple, old & net) and "narrow" (smart, new & spear). Finally, selective/theoretical coding integrated these conceptual codes to the "core concepts" of Routine Activity Theory, in this case *access*, an attribute of the *suitable target*. Though this process allows for new theoretical creation, our aim was to relate any relevant codes back to the established Routine Activity Theory.

Another example using the second research question, "*What technological solutions are viable now; and in the future?*" illustrates how some codes did not change through the coding process and were difficult to link back to theoretical "core concepts." Dialog mentioning "deepfakes" did not vary in the same way that dialog describing *wide* or *narrow* attack vectors did; the term *deepfake* is specific and does not cover a range of inter-related concepts. The axial code *phishing tool* does not add explanatory power, as no other *phishing tools* were mentioned by respondents. Likewise, neither code (*deepfake* nor *phishing tools*) provided a logical connection to a theoretical "core concept" of Routine Activity Theory, as the theory describes what factors may produce crime, but not how.

Findings

The findings to the questions are reported in the order they were presented to the interviewees, and include all the discovered codes for each question. The resulting codes were: (1) *wide* and *narrow attacks*; and *motivation*; (2) *technological proficiency differential* (TPD): and (3) *target value* (TV) for **RQ1**. For **RQ2**, they were: (1) *machine learning* and *multi-factor authorization*; (2) *human weakness*, and (3) *ransomware* and *deepfakes*. (1) *Target training* and (2) *target testing* were the only two relevant codes for **RQ3**.

RQ1: *What factors allow phishing to exist as a long-term, successful crime type?*

Nearly all participants (87%, N = 54) bifurcated *phishing* attacks, though the verbiage varied. These were coded as "*wide*" and "*narrow*," and had been labeled by the respondents in similar terms: "simple/smart," "old/new," and "net/spear."

"Wide" attacks

Wide attacks target large swathes of potential victims using low-effort and easily-defeated forms of *phishing*, primarily via e-mail, but increasingly via text (*smishing*) or phone (*vishing*). These attacks aim for the most easily gullible victims and the expected return rate is in decimal percentages. A consensus emerged from the interviews around the idea that these techniques are antiquated and unlikely to work well in most markets (79%, N = 49). One IT professional's response exemplified this view:: "*We all still get the occasional SPAM text and some of those SPAM texts are phishing attempts. But even my mom knows not to click on unsolicited links anymore, let alone give away the information phishers are looking for*" (IT#8).

"Narrow" attacks

Narrow attacks target specific groups or individuals using high-effort and complex forms of *phishing*, still primarily via e-mail, but incorporate relevant information to make the source of the attack more believable and the likelihood of success higher. Data from the FBI's Internet Crime Complaint Center (IC3) in 2019 reveals 23,775 complaints about Business E-Mail Compromise (BEC), which resulted in more than 1.7 USD billion in losses (Gorham, 2020).

A hacker's response regarding experiences with friends who have used BEC in the past said: "*These scams typically involve someone spoofing or mimicking a legitimate e-mail address. For example, you'll get a message that appears to be from an executive within your company or a business with which that person has a relationship. The e-mail will request a payment, wire transfer, or gift card purchase that seems legitimate but actually funnels money directly to a hacker*" (H#23).

Spear phishing and *whaling* attacks are also narrow attacks, though they are deployed with the less frequency than BEC because they require more up-front effort from attackers. Most "whales," such as CEOs, are insulated to e-mails from the general public; their e-mail addresses typically are not publicized, customizable software filters stop whatever is undesired, and many of these intended victims have an assistant to deal with their e-mail for them. However, a phishing attempt that can circumvent or penetrate these conditions may lead to a very large payout. As one academic respondent (AR#4) noted: "*You have to assume these are happening more than we hear about. What CEO wants to admit they've been duped?*" This in turn affects the issue of "non-issue making," (Crenson, 1972) or the tendency for corporations and governments to hide criminality *and their victimization* for fear of appearing weak, organizational sanctions against them, and, necessarily, increases their risk future victimization.

While earlier studies have utilized Routine Activity Theory (RAT) to identify factors causing a target's victimization, none have analyzed why those factors persist through time. In the categorization created in this study (wide vs. narrow), we can see that *phishing* has not remained the same and that the crime has changed, in both method and target.

When asked **RQ1** directly, the answers all took the wide vs. narrow distinction into account, producing three additional factors, coded as: *motivation, technological proficiency differential (TPD)*, and *target value (TV)*.

Motivation

Profit, or stealing things of monetary value, is the overwhelming motivational factor for *phishing* attacks (Egan, 2020; Gorham, 2020) and although the number of targets and means of targeting may change, this economic motivation has remained constant. Every respondent (100%, N = 62) cited money as the primary motivation for *phishing*. Beyond this, a number of participants mentioned non-monetary targets that produce motivation, such as nude photos of celebrities, a topic which will be covered in more depth under *target value*.

One hacker (H#18) made a novel comparison concerning relative risk for various cyber-crimes: "*Back in the day, you could deface websites for fun. They'd notice and fix it. You had your fun and maybe ruined a guy's afternoon, but no one was out millions of dollars and you're not looking at a possible felony charge. Now, if you're committing a crime online, you're doing it for a reason. And what better reason is there than money?*"

Technological proficiency differential

There remains a large difference in the technical capabilities between the average hacker and the average internet user. As respondents noted: "*Who is better with a computer, you or your mom? You, younger by definition. Who is more likely to be doing the phishing? The younger person. And who is targeted? The older one,*" (H#13) and "*It's the difference between pro-MMA (mixed martial arts) and backyard boxing. The guy coming at you does this for a living and you use your computer for fun*" (H#6).

This *technological proficiency differential* (TPD) is always present, even if it varies between offenders and victims. One academic researcher (AR#1) points to this as one of the defining problems for victims of *phishing*: "*No one secured their Wi-Fi. Wireless routers used to ship without encryption on by default, and no amount of public service announcements or scary news stories got anyone to change their behavior. So, the router companies just started shipping them with encryption on. Now the problem is that no one changes the default password. We've kicked the can down the road. Solved the first problem, but people are always going to be lazy.*"

Target value

Though *wide attacks* are still most prevalent, the increased use of *narrow attacks* presents an opportunity to analyze a new type of *suitable target*. In order for one victim to "replace" many, the target has to be worth more in order to provide comparative rewards to criminals. If a net catches hundreds of "salmon" for a worthy payout, one *whale* needs to be comparable in size. The reward does not necessarily need to be monetary; more than half of the participants (53.2%, N = 33) drew attention to the widely-publicized 2014 *phishing* case known colloquially as "Celebgate."

On August 31, 2014, a collection of approximately 500 nude pictures of various celebrities, mostly women, were posted to an online imageboard (Ohlheiser, 2016). The pictures were initially believed to have been obtained via a breach of Apple's cloud services suite iCloud, or from a security issue in the iCloud API that allowed attackers to make unlimited attempts at guessing victims' passwords. However, access was later revealed to have been gained via *spear phishing* attacks. Court documents from the case explain that the perpetrator created a fake e-mail account called "appleprivacysecurity" to ask celebrities about their security information (Ohlheiser, 2016). This further underscores a long-standing finding from major studies that the easiest way into a computer is usually the "front door" (Rosoff et al., 2014).

Participants stated that this case, represented a "perfect storm" for a *spear phishing* attack. That is, the suitable target is extremely rare (compromising photos of a particular celebrity), the capable guardian is at a technological disadvantage, and the offender is able to collect public data about the celebrity's life in order to craft a targeted e-mail that is believable.

Many of the factors described above are present in other forms of cyber-crime and are not unique to *phishing*, for example, *motivation* and *target value* are both present for website defacement. In these cases, the *motivation* is non-monetary, usually fame, and *target value* is based on visibility (Howell et al., 2019). Assuming more people are motivated by money than fame, or are more willing to risk a prison sentence for money than fame, we expect crimes such as *phishing* to out-pace crimes such as website defacement.

RQ2: *What technological solutions are viable now; and in the future?*

There were only two relevant solution codes for this research question, both of which had near complete (96.7%, N = 60) or complete frequency (100%, N = 62), respectively: *machine learning (ML)* and *multi-factor authentication (MFA)*. Another code had complete frequency (100%, N = 62), though it is not a solution, but rather a condition: *human weakness*. A follow-up question asked the interviewee to anticipate any growing problems for victims of *phishing*; two prominent codes emerged, *ransomware* and *deepfakes*.

Machine learning

The majority of participants (96.7%, N = 60) mentioned "AI" (artificial intelligence) or "ML" (machine learning, a subset of AI) as both an immediate and long-term solution. Studies on machine learning and phishing report a 97.98% accuracy rate for detection of phishing URLs for real-time and language-independent classification algorithms (Sahingoz et al., 2019). The major caveat, however, is that this type of detection only works on *wide attack* campaigns that are being replaced by the hard to humanly or machine-detect, *narrow attack* campaigns, such as Celebgate.

Just as unsolicited, bulk e-mail ("spam") has largely been defeated by automated inbox filters, participants believed ML algorithms would solve the *wide attack* vector of *phishing*. As one academic respondent described, *"Spam filters are garbage disposals. ML is 'The Terminator'"* (AR#10). There were far fewer participants (%/N) who believed machine learning would be a panacea for more sophisticated attacks. *"Nothing has passed the Turing Test, as far as I'm aware, and if [AI] can't fool us, why shouldn't we expect to fool it?"* (H#19) and, while that logic might not be sound, the sheer complexity of the issue remains valid. Machine learning depends on "big data" (patterns derived from large datasets) and *spear phishing* attempts are relatively rare for reasons discussed earlier.

Multi-factor authentication

Multi-Factor Authentication (MFA) is a secure identification method by which a computer user is granted access only after successfully presenting two or more pieces of evidence (or factors) to an authentication mechanism, such as knowledge (something only the user knows), possession (something only the user has), or inherence (something only the user is). *Phishing* attempts can only extract *knowledge*, not *possession* nor *inherence*. By enabling MFA, all participants claimed successful *phishing* attempts can be significantly negated or detected.

Human weakness

It is important to note that while most interviewees agreed that machine learning (96.7%, N = 60) and multi-factor authentication (100%, N = 62) were solutions for most *wide*, and some *narrow* vectors, all participants (100%, N = 62) repeated a variation of "there is no technical solution for every *human weakness*." Those weaknesses make even the best technological solutions incomplete and are covered in more depth under the findings for the next research question.

Two codes emerged suggesting present and future technological problems as well; these are *ransomware* and *deepfakes*.

Ransomware

Ransomware is a type of malware that threatens to perpetually block access to a user's data unless a ransom is paid (Brewer, 2016). It uses a technique called "cryptoviral extortion," in which malware encrypts the victim's files making them inaccessible; the offender then demands a ransom payment, usually in the form of untraceable cryptocurrency, such as Bitcoin, to decrypt the files for user-access (Mansfield-Devine, 2016a). The most frequent delivery method for *ransomware* is *phishing* (Egan, 2020; Gupta et al., 2018).

Ransomware is not a new problem, but one that many participants (66.1%, N = 41) believed was not part of the *phishing* discussion and should be. One IT specialist (IT#15) noted, *"According to the best data out there, ransomware costs corporations in one year what phishing costs them in three. The phishing costs don't include ransomware costs, even though phishing is the most common attack vector for ransomware.*" Others expressed similar thoughts, with varying levels of exasperation: "*Tell me how someone gets ransomware without clicking something they shouldn't have. Phishing is all about getting people to do just that*" (H#6).

Deepfakes

Deepfakes are synthetic media in which a person in an existing image, video, or audio file is replaced with someone else's likeness (Stupp, 2019). While the act of faking content is not new, deepfakes leverage powerful techniques from machine learning to manipulate or generate visual and audio content with a high potential to deceive. About half the interviewees (51.6%, N = 32) mentioned deepfakes as a possible *phishing* issue. One IT professional (IT#10) said, "*Can you imagine getting a realistic-sounding and angry-seeming voicemail from your 'boss'? The success rate on that type of attack would be near one-hundred.*"

Other researchers (91.9%, N = 57) were quick to offer an alternative future (AR#3): "*They fool people better than machines. This is an example where machine learning will help as much as hurt. The most popular technique for detection is to use algorithms similar to the ones used to build them to detect them. By recognizing patterns in how they are created, the algorithm is able to pick up subtle inconsistencies. People have developed automatic systems that examine videos for errors such as irregular blinking patterns of lighting already.*"

RQ3: *What human-focused prevention strategies are viable now; and in the future?*

Continuing the theme from the previous research question, one hacker (H#15) mused, "*You have to be vigilant every time you open an e-mail, fill out a form, or click a link. I just need you to mess up once.*" Technological solutions, interviewees agreed, can stop most *wide* attacks and, perhaps, some of the *narrow* ones as well, but there will invariably be ones that get through to the targeted end-user. The suggested *human-focused* solutions were coded as *target training* and *target testing.*

Target training

Research shows that people can be trained to recognize phishing attempts, and to deal with them through a variety of approaches (Arachchilage & Love, 2013, 2014). Such education can be effective, especially where training emphasizes conceptual knowledge and provides direct feedback (Arachchilage & Love, 2013, 2014). The problem, many (88.7%, N = 55) participants noted, is that most corporations treat "*cyber security like a joke and want to spend as little as possible on it, including optional trainings they know will be ignored*" (IT#2) and "*there's no cyber security training at all for people outside of Fortune 500 companies*" (IT#17). As a result, a number of respondents (69.3%, N = 43) believe cyber security education is currently inadequate. Some interviewees (45.1%, N = 28) noted that nearly all legitimate e-mail messages from companies to their customers contain an item of information that is not readily available to *phishers*, but that "no one" knows this. Again, this solution is of limited effectiveness against *spear phishing* attempts where attackers research their targets well and can utilize the collected information accordingly.

Interestingly, about half of the respondents (48.3%, N = 30) noted two subsets of end-users where training would be "worthless." First, end-users that were so technologically proficient that they were functionally "immune" to *phishing* and did not need additional training. Second, end-users that were so technologically inept that they were "immune" to training and would fall victim to attacks no matter what.

A number of interviewees (32.2%, N = 20) shared personal anecdotes such as, *"The people I know who are best about this stuff are the people who were previously victimized"* (AR#13) and *"The ones who never speed are the ones who got caught speeding before ... "* (H#20). These off-hand comments stress the importance of the next code, *target testing.*

Target testing

Many organizations run regular simulated phishing campaigns targeting their own staff to measure the effectiveness of their training (Whitaker & Newman, 2006; Wilhelm, 2013). Those that fall for the simulated attempt are given additional training, with anecdotal evidence that repeat offenders sometimes have e-mail access temporarily revoked. A few hackers (20%, N = 13) semi-joked that *target testing* could be improved by adding an element of shame: *"This problem would fix itself real [sic] quick if Jerry in accounts receivable was put on a public Hall of Shame list each time he clicked on a fake link"* (H#11). Interestingly, research on other white-collar crimes, such as embezzlement, demonstrates public shaming can have an effect on *offenders* (Braithwaite, 1989; Kahan & Posner, 1999; Murphy & Harris, 2007). Whether or not it would have an effect on victims remains to be seen. Even if it proved to be an effective solution, the morality of it is questionable at best.

Discussion

The goals of this study were to provide an overview of *phishing* in the present, reveal the factors that allow it to persist, suggest solutions to combat it, and to update the application of Routine Activity Theory to cyber-crimes.

Wide-net *phishing* remains the most common form of *phishing*, but *spear phishing* has grown in popularity since approximately 2010, especially against extremely high *target value* infrastructure. In 2011, staff at defense contractor RSA were successfully phished, which lead to the master key for all "RSA SecureID" security tokens being leaked (Richmond, 2011). These security tokens are utilized by all officials at the U.S. Department of Defense for multi-factor authentication. Two years later, all U.S. Target stores fell victim to an attack that occurred after a successful phishing attempt against the company's contracted heating and ventilation supplier (Kassner, 2015). There are numerous examples of similarly costly phishing attacks: Ubiquiti Networks lost 46.7 USD million in 2015 (Krebs, 2015), FACC Aerospace lost 55 USD million in 2016 (Nasralla, 2016), Crelan Bank lost 75.8 USD million also in 2016 (Schneider, 2016), and Google and Facebook lost a combined 100 USD million in 2017 (Romo, 2019).

These recent cases demonstrate a need for studies such as this one, which attempt to answer questions about the current state of *phishing* attacks, what can be done to increase security, and provide a guide for future theoretical development.

Phishing evolves and survives

This responses to our first research question suggest that the factors that allow phishing to adapt as a crime type and persist through time are *motivation, technological proficiency differential (TPD)*, and *target value*. Routine Activity Theory (RAT) assumes there is always a *motivated offender*. Past cyber-crime studies (Grabosky, 2001) have likened connecting to the internet to "opening a front door," (Rosoff et al., 2014) as it allows access to both legitimate and criminal parties. Our study did not attempt to answer the question "Why utilize *phishing* over other types of cyber-crime?" rather, what allows *phishing* to persist. The answers provided by our respondents fit within established Routine Activity literature (Clarke et al., 1999; Cohen & Felson, 1979; Leukfeldt & Yar, 2016; Yar, 2005) given they believe shifting *motivations* have resulted in a growth of *phishing* attack types, such as *spear phishing* and BEC. If these new types become less successful, as has happened for *wide* "net" attacks, we expect the *motivational* calculus to change and offenders to move to "greener pastures," possibly other types of cyber-crime.

As the primary *motivation* is monetary, successful attacks are those that adapted appropriately to follow the money; technological advances have more or less solved the *wide* approach, making these attacks less successful, so the motivated adapt and try the *narrow* approach instead. To justify the greater investment of time involved, targets are hand-picked. If there is potential financial gain through some form of *phishing*, there will be hackers willing to do it.

This study also suggests that a *technological proficiency differential* (TPD) may allow *phishing* to continue to succeed as a form of cybercrime through relative diminution of the *capable guardian* condition of RAT. For an attack to succeed against a corporate target, the *phisher* must make it past a number of industry-standard protections, including ISP-level filtering and custom corporate firewalls, plus the detection of the (likely trained, to some degree), targeted user. In this corporate case, ultimate detection is up to the end-user, but an attacker must first successfully navigate the protections installed by IT professionals that are likely to have a low TPD in relation to the offender. The IT department is close in abilities to whichever hacker may target the corporation and it ordinarily takes *target hardening* steps to protect the corporation from its employees and others. For an attack to succeed against a home user, however, the *phisher* must only make it past the number of protections the end-user is aware of and able to implement. As noted earlier, Wi-Fi encryption illustrates this point. Corporations were aware of and implemented Wi-Fi encryption early in its introduction, while individual households only began to adopt the protection when router companies turned the measure on by default (Gold, 2011).

For end-users to adequately protect themselves against *phishing* at home, they must be aware of and capable of properly configuring the following: a modem, a router, a firewall, an adblocker, a password manager, and multi-factor authentication. Moreover, they must know what *phishing* is and be able to detect it, in order to avoid victimization. As one interviewee (AR#17) put it, *"It's not even a manner of being lazy or ill-informed, how do you possibly keep up with the rate of advancement?"*

Phishing has evolved to the point where successful attacks are those that can circumvent the target hardening technology of corporations, as in carefully-tailored *whaling* messages, or that can evade the detection of uninformed users, such as in the case of business e-mail compromise (BEC).

Again, the goal of this research question was not to provide reasons *phishing* is utilized over other cyber-crimes, but the discussion with respondents suggests *phishing* might be a simple way of achieving their goals, which may be why some offenders use it. In the 2014 "Celebgate" case, for example, journalists originally assumed the hack was done through API vulnerabilities (Ohlheiser, 2016). This is a more complex task, requiring a hacker to test their abilities against Apple engineers instead of end-users, a situation where the offender may have a TPD deficit in relation. Ultimately, it was discovered that Celebgate was a "simple" *spear phishing* attack (Ohlheiser, 2016).

The final factor that our study suggests allows *phishing* to persist as a successful crime type is *target value*. Past studies have operationalized the *suitable target* portion of RAT using acronyms to describe accessibility: VIVA (Value, Inertia, Visibility, Access) (Cohen & Felson, 1979) and CRAVED (Concealable, Removable, Available, Valuable, Enjoyable, Disposable) (Clarke et al., 1999). Our research indicates digital accessibility is similar to physical accessibility, at least for *phishing*. Though we only received responses addressing the *target value* portion of VIVA and CRAVED, it is apparent that digital data is also easily concealable, easily removable, widely available, and easily disposable. As ISP-level e-mail filtering has become standard, the low-hanging fruit have been lessened, and the *phishing* community has responded by targeting things of ever-increasing value. Participants mentioned the 2014 "Celebgate" case, but the 2017 "Vault7" hack provides a more illustrative example of this phenomenon.

Vault7 is a series of documents that WikiLeaks began to publish in March of 2017, that detail the activities and capabilities of the United States' Central Intelligence Agency to perform electronic surveillance and cyber warfare (Barnes, 2020). The files, dated from 2013–2016, include details on the agency's software capabilities, such as the ability to compromise cars, smart TVs, web browsers, and the operating systems of most smartphones.

A CIA internal audit identified 91 out of more than 500 malware tools in use in 2016 being compromised by the Vault7 release (Barnes, 2020). The report detailed a wide range of security flaws that lead to the leak, mainly, that the intelligence community has yet to protect its.gov domain names with *multi-factor authentication*; and, the CIA, National Reconnaissance Office, and National Intelligence office have yet to enable *DMARC*[1] *anti-phishing protections.*

In both the Celebgate and Vault7 cases, the target *suitability* is determined almost exclusively by the *target value*. There is presumably a larger market for stolen nude photos of women than men, as during the initial release of stolen Celebgate photos, there were approximately 100 female victims and less than ten male ones. Likewise, while all major governments presumably have hacking tools that criminals desire, the U.S. is widely-known to have the world's largest collection of zero-day exploits (Smith, 2013; Zetter, 2014).

The Target retail store phishing example also demonstrates allowances can be made for inertia, visibility, and access, so long as the target is of high enough value. The heating and ventilation company that fell victim to the initial attack and provided a vector into Target's larger network is relatively small and only licensed to work in five states (Harris, 2014; Kassner, 2015).

The findings regarding *target value* suggest they may dictate which form of cyber-attack the offender chooses to utilize. The Celebgate example mentioned by about half of the participants (53.2%, N = 33) is not easily achievable via other means. A man-in-the-middle attack would have required the target images to be caught during transmission, something which is not guaranteed to occur (Hutchings et al., 2015). Ransomware does not work if the victim is willing to lose the data encrypted by the attack (Malecki, 2019). A brute-force attack on Apple's iCloud API may have worked, and was originally assumed to be how the hack occurred, but would have been more time- and skill-intensive than *phishing* (Ohlheiser, 2016).

Technological solutions are effective, yet imperfect

Our second research question addresses the ability of technology alone to act as a *capable guardian*. There are a wide range of solutions that have been implemented to varying success through the past two decades, most recently: Google's Safe Browsing URL blacklist (used by Chrome, Safari, and Firefox) and DMARC (used by Bank of America, Fidelity Investments, and JPMorganChase, among others). These can currently block many, but not all *phishing* attempts. Our research suggests two technologies can further protect average end-users. First, studies repeatedly demonstrate *machine learning* has a 95+% success rate at blocking *wide attacks* (Sahingoz et al., 2019). Second, *multi-factor authentication* offers not only additional protection against being successfully *phished*, but also notifies potential victims of *phishing* attempts (Kennedy & Millard, 2016).

Neither of the above solutions, however, protect against *spear phishing*. Though still less-frequent than traditional *phishing, spear phishing* attacks are increasing in popularity. One reason relates to the idea of *system capacity*, which is undoubtedly at play, as the types of crimes that succeed are those to which the current enforcement apparatus is unable to effectively respond (Pontell, 1982; Pontell et al., 1994). Routine Activity Theory suggests that *ML* and *MFA* are valid *target hardening* techniques for *wide*, but not *narrow* attacks. Unlike non-digital crimes, where potential victimhood occurs simply by being in contact with others, the technology necessary to adequately harden against *spear phishing* must also be able to save an end-user from themselves.

Our analysis produced two important related factors, which various people believed are current and growing problems emanating from phishing: *ransomware* and *deepfakes*. *Ransomware* is an immediate financial issue as it is currently the source of billions of dollars of damage to corporations yearly (O'Neill, 2020) and there remains no lasting technological solution. Ransomware has been widely researched as a cyber-crime, but there remain few studies that analyze links between ransomware and phishing, even though official statistics show ransomware is most commonly delivered as a *phishing* payload (Egan, 2020). *Deepfakes* appear to be a growing problem as well (Pantserev, 2020; Wojewidka, 2020), but most interviewees (91.9%, N = 57) believed the technology to detect deepfakes was progressing at much the same rate as the technology to produce them. Deepfakes as a crime tool have also been widely researched, primarily in relation to the production of fraudulent political videos and pornography, including fake celebrity sex videos (Maddocks, 2020; Öhman, 2020). There remain no studies of the interrelationships between deepfakes and phishing to date, although this may be due to the relative infancy of the combination of these cybercrimes, and a corresponding lack of data.

Regarding end-users and current solutions, our respondents believed that those most informed on *phishing*, and most *technologically proficient*, are the end-users that are in least need of technological solutions. For example, advanced computer users are both more likely to run adblockers and more likely to avoid clicking on any ads that might slip past the blocker.

The study results suggest that the types of *phishing* that have grown in popularity (*spear*, *whale*, BEC, etc.) are those that primarily bypass the human element of *guardianship*. Though these tend to also bypass technological solutions, they are designed with the end-user in mind and continue to succeed as a result. For example, SPAM has been almost entirely solved through the blocking of automated mass-e-mail (slowing the outward flow of SPAM) and shared blacklists (culling the inward flow of SPAM) (Crawford et al., 2015). Both of these are technological solutions with no level of human involvement. Likewise, direct human involvement was removed from the Wi-Fi encryption process when manufacturers started shipping routers with the protection on by default (Gold, 2011).

There currently is no effective way to entirely remove the "human" part of replying to an e-mail, text message, or phone call. Attacks that are personalized are especially likely to succeed by lowering user inhibitions through faux familiarity. And, though there is no way to entirely remove this human part of the risk, the final research question suggests ways to ameliorate it.

Teach, then test, and repeat, if necessary

The final research question addresses the measures necessary to produce the *capable guardian* as a human element. "Education" is a frequently offered, nebulous solution to complex issues such as cyber security, and it very well may be, but the finer details are often absent from the discussion (Arachchilage & Love, 2013, 2014). Respondents in this study agreed that proper training could reduce the vast majority of successful *phishing* attacks. The types of training suggested varied, but typically included "awareness" (what *phishing* is) and "prevention" (how to recognize it). The participants with industry experience did not generally believe that current programs were adequate (69.3%, N = 43).

Vulnerability assessment is the process of identifying, quantifying, and prioritizing the weaknesses in a system. They are performed on systems of information technology, energy supply, and communication, among others. The General Services Administration (GSA) has standardized "Risk and Vulnerability Assessments" (RVA) as a pre-vetted support service. This service conducts assessments of threats and vulnerabilities, determines deviations from acceptable configurations, and develops and/or recommends appropriate mitigation countermeasures in operational and non-operational situations. This standardized service offers many pre-vetted support services, but relevant to this discussion are Network Mapping, Vulnerability Scanning, and Phishing Assessment.

As part of these assessments, corporations or agencies are tested with a penetration test. A "pen test" is an authorized, simulated cyberattack on a computer system, performed to evaluate the security of that system, which can include *vishing*, *smishing*, and *phishing* attempts. As these are customized to the corporation or agency being tested, they accurately mirror real-world *spear phishing* attempts. Our study found that these are widely believed to be successful and worthwhile. It is a pro-social way of simulating victimhood that promotes learning and an adaption of future behavior. Some of the participants (20.9%, N = 13) also argued that they believed these assessments would be more effective with an element of shaming. This is beyond the scope of Routine Activity Theory and, thus, this study, but might be worthy of future research.

A final noteworthy result is that about half of the interview subjects (48.3%, N = 30) believed that certain end-users, perhaps the interviewee themselves, were functionally immune to *phishing*. They believed that these users were *technology proficient* enough that the *differential* was in favor of the target and not the *phisher*. Likewise, these participants felt that a countervailing population of end-users were immune to *training* and were almost guaranteed victims, if they were to be targeted. The remaining majority of people presumably fall somewhere in-between these two extremes, where the need for training and the benefits from it intersect.

Limitations

This study includes a number of limitations due to its nature as an interview-based, qualitative, and cyber-focused research project. Interviews are costly, time-consuming, and vulnerable to interviewer bias. These issues were addressed by conducting all interviews via voice or video, limiting sessions to roughly 45 minutes, and fully informing interviewees of our positions, affiliations, study aims, and general methodology. Qualitative research is also more vulnerable to sampling and self-selection biases. While it is possible our purposive sample has produced erroneous results, the resulting data saturation in this study leads us to believe that the information is accurate barring the rather unlikely prospect that the IT professionals, hackers, and academic researchers all offered intentionally false, yet overlapping responses. The possibility remains, however, that the interview subjects who participated (72.9%, N = 62) are significantly less-informed than those who did not (27.1%, N = 23). A demographic background study of all potential participants could address this, but was not feasible in this research, and self-selection bias existing to any significant degree is highly unlikely in any case. Lastly, while data availability for cyber-crime are increasing, there remains a noticeable lack compared to other subfields of criminology. Other studies on *phishing*, for example, have many of the same limitations listed here, or worse (Yang et al., 2015). For example, samples drawn from a population consisting entirely of college students are common (Bossler & Holt, 2009; Downs et al., 2006; Sun et al., 2016).

Future research

Our results suggest a number of avenues for future research. First, we believe *motivation, technological proficiency differential (TPD)*, and *target value* warrant more operationalization and quantitative study. TPD, in particular, is a factor that has potential explanatory power for a wide variety of cyber-crimes beyond phishing, including malware and ransomware victimization. Second, additional studies need to be conducted on the efficacy of *training* and *testing*. To date, there are no studies that we were able to locate on *phishing* education that use an experimental methodology. Third, Braithwaite's (1989) reintegrative shaming has been shown to be effective in the case of petty crimes, and past studies suggest shame also works for white-collar offenders as well (Kahan & Posner, 1999; Murphy & Harris, 2007), so the suggestion offered by respondents in this study for training that involves "shaming" for victims may also merit further study in the field of cybercrime in general.

Conclusion

Respondents in this study generally agreed with the notion that technological advances increase the proliferation of phishing attacks, but also aid in their detection. It has never been easier to conduct a simple attack, but a good attack requires more effort than ever before. Second, while phishing was viewed as directly responsible for a significant amount of financial fraud, it causes even more damage indirectly, as the primary attack vector for ransomware. Third, newer types of attacks utilizing technology such as deepfakes may make the problem worse in the short-term (Stupp, 2019). Fourth, prevention and enforcement will be derived primarily though machine learning and public education.

In sum, simpler forms of *phishing* have been relatively contained through technological efforts, similar to the removal of SPAM through filtering and the forced-adoption of Wi-Fi encryption. More targeted forms of phishing are unlikely to be halted by technology, and will continue to succeed if human-focused efforts, such as education, are lacking or non-existent.

Finally, the results show the utility of Routine Activity Theory as applied to *phishing* and cyber-crime analysis more generally with some modification, including the *technological proficiency differential* as a factor in cybercrime victimization. We believe the critiques of the application of Routine Activity Theory are valid (Leukfeldt & Yar, 2016; Yar, 2005), but perhaps overstated. The asynchronous nature of cyber-crime, for example, is not theory-breaking if we allow the "convergence" to be between victim and *phishing* e-mail, rather than between victim and the offender themselves. Likewise, we do not believe "location" and "distance" translate perfectly from real-world to digital, but do believe treating a user's e-mail inbox as the "scene of the crime" is appropriate.

Policy implications

The policy implications of this study are helpful, if bleak. The responses to the first research question, "What factors allow phishing to exist as a long-term, successful crime type?" provide meaningful guidance for future policy. The primary *motivation* for *phishing*, money, has remained constant, even as the targets have shifted from *wide* to *narrow*. Corporations and individuals cannot reduce the "benefit" (payout) of a successful *phishing* attempt, but it can increase the "cost" (security) of doing so. Increased security measures in the form of firewalls or multi-factor authentication, for example, are not guaranteed to keep an intruder out of a target system, but may deter them enough that they search for more easily-breached infrastructure. A few respondents (14.5%, N = 9) mentioned old joke-turned-security-adage: *"You don't have to swim faster than the shark, you just have to swim faster than your friend."* While we believe these deterrence measures would be effective at the individual level, studies have demonstrated increasing legal penalties at the governmental level may not have a similar effect (Forst, 1983; Herath & Rao, 2009; Scholz, 1997). In fact, the U.S. governmental response to cyber-crime, the Computer Fraud and Abuse Act of 1986, is routinely criticized for being too punitive already (Green, 2013; Wu, 2013).

Related to *motivation* is *target value*. As our lives have become more digitized, the likelihood that a compromised computer or account contains something of value has increased. Until the advent of the smartphone, photographs, including scandalous ones, were physical, likely hidden, and difficult to steal. The "Celebgate" case of 2014 is not only an example of a widely successful *phishing* attack, but also an example of a new type of *valuable target*. In the United States, there have been no policy proposals to protect these new types of data, and over the past decade, governments worldwide have decried the increased use of encryption by the public for fear of "going dark" and losing access to devices which may contain evidence of criminal activity (Bellaby, 2018; Weimann, 2016). Policy proposals to deal with "going dark," including the Lawful Access to Encrypted Data Act (LAEDA), seek to provide "backdoor" access potentially opening a new avenue of attack for savvy *phishers* (Crocker, 2020).

Addressing the *technological proficiency differential* is one area we believe public policy may have a large effect. In response to the third research question, "*What human-focused prevention strategies are viable now and in the future?*" many respondents (88.7%, N = 55) called for increased educational efforts or *training*. Many public schools require "typing" courses; including a unit on cyber security best practices could have wide-reaching and long-lasting effects. There has also been a concerted effort to include computer coding as part of school curriculum, which would reduce the *technological proficiency differential* between offenders and the general population, so addressing security in this context also makes sense.

The responses to the third research question also included references to *testing* and *shaming*. Under current U.S. law, most corporations are not required to conduct security audits, report breaches, or follow best practices. Three industries are currently regulated under federal law: healthcare organizations (via the 1996 Health Insurance Portability and Accountability Act), federal agencies (via the 2002 Homeland Security Act), and financial institutions (via the 1999 Gramm-Leach-Bliley Act). In 2012, two U.S. senators proposed the Cybersecurity Act, which failed to pass (Rizzo, 2012). Supported by the military and the president, the bill would have required creating voluntary "best practice standards" for protection of key infrastructure from cyber-attacks, which businesses would be encouraged to adopt through incentives such as liability protection. The opposition claimed the bill would introduce regulations that would not be effective and could be a "burden" for businesses (Rizzo, 2012). Nearly all respondents (69.3%, N = 43) mentioned a necessity for best practices, including *testing*, and some wondered about the efficacy of *shaming* (20.9%, N = 13). Though governments have used shaming in the past, historical examples include stocks and pillory, we do not believe this is something governments will (or should) do.

Lastly, returning to the second research question, "*What technological solutions are viable both now and in the future?*" we expect technological solutions will be created and willingly adopted by actors with vested interests in security. For example, Google's Safe Browsing URL blacklist (used by Chrome, Safari, and Firefox) and DMARC (used by Bank of America, Fidelity Investments, and JPMorganChase), allow corporations to provide increased security with low barriers to entry. In the future, government bans on *deepfakes*, at least within the political realm, seem likely, and technology will be the most efficient way to detect these fake videos.

We believe our findings show any and all technological solutions should be implemented; best practices would include filters that implement *machine learning* and the use of *multi-factor authentication*, with planned responses to *ransomware* and *deepfakes*. Future *phishing* attempts are likely to be become increasingly targeted and immune to these measures, so technological solutions must be supplemented with human-focused policy as well. Our findings strongly suggest both *training* and *testing* are necessary, but that these efforts still will not produce complete protection.

Note

1. DMARC (Domain-based Message Authentication Reporting and Conformance) is an e-mail validation system designed to protect an e-mail domain from being used for e-mail spoofing, phishing scams and other cybercrimes. DMARC leverages the existing e-mail authentication techniques, such as SPF (Sender Policy Framework) and DKIM (Domain Keys Identified Mail).

Acknowledgments

We would like to thank our interview respondents.

Disclosure statement

No potential conflict of interest was reported by the author(s).

ORCID

Adam Kavon Ghazi-Tehrani http://orcid.org/0000-0001-5750-0901
Henry N. Pontell http://orcid.org/0000-0003-2487-4581

Data availability

Data available upon request.

References

Alsharnouby, M., Alaca, F., & Chiasson, S. (2015). Why phishing still works: User strategies for combating phishing attacks. *International Journal of Human-Computer Studies*, *82*(October), 69–82. https://doi.org/10.1016/j.ijhcs.2015.05.005

Arachchilage, N. A. G., & Love, S. (2013). A game design framework for avoiding phishing attacks. *Computers in Human Behavior*, *29*(3), 706–714. https://doi.org/10.1016/j.chb.2012.12.018

Arachchilage, N. A. G., & Love, S. (2014). Security awareness of computer users: A phishing threat avoidance perspective. *Computers in Human Behavior*, *38*(September), 304–312. https://doi.org/10.1016/j.chb.2014.05.046

Barnes, J. (2020, June 16). C.I.A. failed to defend against theft of secrets by insider, report says. *The New York Times*.

Barratt, M. J., Ferris, J. A., & Lenton, S. (2015). Hidden populations, online purposive sampling, and external validity: Taking off the blindfold. *Field Methods*, *27*(1), 3–21. https://doi.org/10.1177/1525822X14526838

Bellaby, R. W. (2018). Going dark: Anonymising technology in cyberspace. *Ethics and Information Technology*, *20*(3), 189–204. https://doi.org/10.1007/s10676-018-9458-4

Birks, M., & Mills, J. (2011). *Grounded theory: A practical guide*. Sage.

Bossler, A., & Holt, T. (2009). On-line activities, guardianship, and malware infection: An examination of Routine Activities Theory. *International Journal of Cyber Criminology (IJCC)*, *3*(1), 974–2891. http://www.cybercrimejournal.com/bosslerholtijcc2009.pdf

Braithwaite, J. (1989). *Crime, shame, and reintegration*. Cambridge University Press.

Brewer, R. (2016). Ransomware attacks: Detection, prevention and cure. *Network Security*, *2016*(9), 5–9. https://doi.org/10.1016/S1353-4858(16)30086-1

Charmaz, K. (2006). *Constructing grounded theory*. Sage Publications.

Clarke, R. V. G., Great Britain, Home Office, & Policing and Reducing Crime Unit. (1999). *Hot products: Understanding, anticipating and reducing demand for stolen goods*. Home Office, Policing and Reducing Crime Unit, Research, Development and Statistics Directorate. http://books.google.com/books?id=-iEEAQAAIAAJ

Cohen, L. E., & Felson, M. (1979). Social change and crime rate trends: A routine activity approach. *American Sociological Review, 44*(4), 588. https://doi.org/10.2307/2094589

Cook, D. L., Gurbani, V. K., & Daniluk, M. (2009). Phishwish: A simple and stateless phishing filter. *Security and Communication Networks, 2*(1), 29–43. https://doi.org/10.1002/sec.45

Corbin, J. M., & Strauss, A. L. (2008). *Basics of qualitative research: Techniques and procedures for developing grounded theory* (3rd ed.). Sage Publications, Inc.

Crawford, M., Khoshgoftaar, T. M., Prusa, J. D., Richter, A. N., & Al Najada, H. (2015). Survey of review spam detection using machine learning techniques. *Journal of Big Data, 2*(1), 23. https://doi.org/10.1186/s40537-015-0029-9

Crenson, M. A. (1972). *The un-politics of air pollution: A study of non-decisionmaking in the cities*. Johns Hopkins Pr.

Creswell, J. W. (2014). *Research design: Qualitative, quantitative, and mixed methods approaches* (4th ed.). SAGE Publications.

Creswell, J. W., & Poth, C. N. (2018). *Qualitative inquiry and research design: Choosing among five approaches* (4th ed., international student edition). SAGE.

Crocker, A. (2020, June 24). *The Senate's new anti-encryption bill is even worse than EARN IT, and that's saying something*. EFF. https://www.eff.org/deeplinks/2020/06/senates-new-anti-encryption-bill-even-worse-earn-it-and-thats-saying-something

Dhamija, R., Tygar, J. D., & Hearst, M. (2006). Why phishing works. *Proceedings of the SIGCHI conference on human factors in computing systems - CHI '06*, 581. https://doi.org/10.1145/1124772.1124861

Downs, J., Holbook, M., & Cranor, L. (2006). Decision strategies and susceptibility to phishing. *Symposium on usable privacy and security*, 79–90.

Egan, G. (2020). *State of the Phish*. Proofpoint. https://www.proofpoint.com/us/security-awareness/post/2020-state-phish-security-awareness-training-email-reporting-more-critical

Etikan, I. (2016). Comparison of Convenience Sampling and Purposive Sampling. *American Journal of Theoretical and Applied Statistics, 5*(1), 1. https://doi.org/10.11648/j.ajtas.20160501.11

Forst, B. (1983). Capital punishment and deterrence: Conflicting evidence? *The Journal of Criminal Law and Criminology (1973-), 74*(3), 927. https://doi.org/10.2307/1143139

Glaser, B. G., & Strauss, A. L. (2009). *The discovery of grounded theory: Strategies for qualitative research* (4. paperback printing). Aldine.

Gold, S. (2011). Cracking wireless networks. *Network Security, 2011*(11), 14–18. https://doi.org/10.1016/S1353-4858(11)70120-9

Gorham, M. (2020). *2019 Internet crime report*. Federal Bureau of Investigation. https://pdf.ic3.gov/2019_IC3Report.pdf

Grabosky, P. N. (2001). Virtual criminality: Old wine in new bottles? *Social & Legal Studies, 10*(2), 243–249. https://doi.org/10.1177/a017405

Green, A. (2013, January 16). *"Aaron's Law" suggests reforms to computer fraud act (but not enough to have protected Aaron Swartz)*. Forbes. https://www.forbes.com/sites/andygreenberg/2013/01/16/aarons-law-suggests-reforms-to-hacking-acts-but-not-enough-to-have-protected-aaron-swartz/#44845bf66649

Gupta, B. B., Arachchilage, N. A. G., & Psannis, K. E. (2018). Defending against phishing attacks: Taxonomy of methods, current issues and future directions. *Telecommunication Systems, 67*(2), 247–267. https://doi.org/10.1007/s11235-017-0334-z

Harris, E. (2014, April 29). After data breach, target plans to issue more secure chip-and-PIN cards. *The New York Times*. https://www.nytimes.com/2014/04/30/business/after-data-breach-target-replaces-its-head-of-technology.html

Herath, T., & Rao, H. R. (2009). Encouraging information security behaviors in organizations: Role of penalties, pressures and perceived effectiveness. *Decision Support Systems, 47*(2), 154–165. https://doi.org/10.1016/j.dss.2009.02.005

Howell, C. J., Burruss, G. W., Maimon, D., & Sahani, S. (2019). Website defacement and routine activities: Considering the importance of hackers' valuations of potential targets. *Journal of Crime and Justice*, *42*(5), 536–550. https://doi.org/10.1080/0735648X.2019.1691859

Hutchings, A., Smith, R. G., & James, L. (2015). Criminals in the cloud: Crime, security threats, and prevention measures. In R. G. Smith, R.-C.-C. Cheung, & L. Y.-C. Lau (Eds.), *Cybercrime risks and responses: Eastern and Western perspectives* (pp. 146–162). Palgrave Macmillan UK. https://doi.org/10.1057/9781137474162_10

Hutchings, A., & Hayes, H. (2009). Routine Activity Theory and phishing victimisation: Who gets caught in the 'net'? *Current Issues in Criminal Justice*, *20*(3), 433–452. https://doi.org/10.1080/10345329.2009.12035821

Kahan, D. M., & Posner, E. A. (1999). Shaming White-Collar criminals: A proposal for reform of the federal sentencing guidelines. *The Journal of Law and Economics*, *42*(S1), 365–392. https://doi.org/10.1086/467429

Kassner, M. (2015, February 2). Anatomy of the target data breach: Missed opportunities and lessons learned. *ZDNet*. https://www.zdnet.com/article/anatomy-of-the-target-data-breach-missed-opportunities-and-lessons-learned/

Kennedy, E., & Millard, C. (2016). Data security and multi-factor authentication: Analysis of requirements under EU law and in selected EU Member States. *Computer Law & Security Review*, *32*(1), 91–110. https://doi.org/10.1016/j.clsr.2015.12.004

Kigerl, A. (2012). Routine Activity Theory and the determinants of high cybercrime countries. *Social Science Computer Review*, *30*(4), 470–486. https://doi.org/10.1177/0894439311422689

Krebs, B. (2015, August 7). Tech firm Ubiquiti suffers $46M cyberheist. *Krebs on Security*. https://krebsonsecurity.com/2015/08/tech-firm-ubiquiti-suffers-46m-cyberheist/

Leukfeldt, E. (2014). Phishing for suitable targets in The Netherlands: Routine Activity Theory and phishing victimization. *Cyberpsychology, Behavior, and Social Networking*, *17*(8), 551–555. https://doi.org/10.1089/cyber.2014.0008

Leukfeldt, E. (2015). Comparing victims of phishing and malware attacks: Unraveling risk factors and possibilities for situational crime prevention. *ArXiv:1506.00769 [Cs]*. http://arxiv.org/abs/1506.00769

Leukfeldt, E., Kleemans, E. R., & Stol, W. P. (2016). Cybercriminal networks, social ties and online forums: Social ties versus digital ties within phishing and malware networks. *British Journal of Criminology*, *57*(3). https://doi.org/10.1093/bjc/azw009

Leukfeldt, E., & Yar, M. (2016). Applying Routine Activity Theory to cybercrime: A theoretical and empirical analysis. *Deviant Behavior*, *37*(3), 263–280. https://doi.org/10.1080/01639625.2015.1012409

Maddocks, S. (2020). 'A deepfake porn plot intended to silence me': Exploring continuities between pornographic and 'political' deep fakes. *Porn Studies*, 1–9. https://doi.org/10.1080/23268743.2020.1757499

Malecki, F. (2019). Best practices for preventing and recovering from a ransomware attack. *Computer Fraud & Security*, *2019*(3), 8–10. https://doi.org/10.1016/S1361-3723(19)30028-4

Mansfield-Devine, S. (2016a). Ransomware: Taking businesses hostage. *Network Security*, *2016*(10), 8–17. https://doi.org/10.1016/S1353-4858(16)30096-4

Mansfield-Devine, S. (2016b). The imitation game: How business email compromise scams are robbing organisations. *Computer Fraud & Security*, *2016*(11), 5–10. https://doi.org/10.1016/S1361-3723(16)30089-6

Morrison, D. E., & Firmstone, J. (2000). The social function of trust and implications for e-commerce. *International Journal of Advertising*, *19*(5), 599–623. https://doi.org/10.1080/02650487.2000.11104826

Murphy, K., & Harris, N. (2007). Shaming, shame and recidivism: A test of reintegrative shaming theory in the White-Collar crime context. *British Journal of Criminology*, *47*(6), 900–917. https://doi.org/10.1093/bjc/azm037

Nasralla, S. (2016, May 25). *Austria's FACC, hit by cyber fraud, fires CEO*. Reuters. https://www.reuters.com/article/us-facc-ceo/austrias-facc-hit-by-cyber-fraud-fires-ceo-idUSKCN0YG0ZF

Ngo, F. T., & Paternoster, R. (2011). Cybercrime victimization: An examination of individual and situational level factors. *International Journal of Cyber Criminology*, *5*(1), 773–793. https://www.cybercrimejournal.com/ngo2011ijcc.pdf

O'Neill, P. H. (2020, January 2). Ransomware may have cost the US more than $7.5 billion in 2019. *MIT Technology Review*. https://www.technologyreview.com/f/615002/ransomware-may-have-cost-the-us-more-than-75-billion-in-2019/

Ohlheiser, A. (2016, May 24). The shockingly simple way the nude photos of 'Celebgate' were stolen. *The Washington Post*. https://www.washingtonpost.com/news/the-intersect/wp/2016/03/16/the-shockingly-simple-way-the-nude-photos-of-celebgate-were-stolen/

Öhman, C. (2020). Introducing the pervert's dilemma: A contribution to the critique of deepfake pornography. *Ethics and Information Technology*, *22*(2), 133–140. https://doi.org/10.1007/s10676-019-09522-1

Pantserev, K. A. (2020). The Malicious use of AI-based deepfake technology as the new threat to psychological security and political stability. In H. Jahankhani, S. Kendzierskyj, N. Chelvachandran, & J. Ibarra (Eds.), *Cyber defence in the age of AI, smart societies and augmented humanity* (pp. 37–55). Springer International Publishing. https://doi.org/10.1007/978-3-030-35746-7_3

Parmar, B. (2012). Protecting against spear-phishing. *Computer Fraud & Security*, *2012*(1), 8–11. https://doi.org/10.1016/S1361-3723(12)70007-6

Pontell, H. N. (1982). System capacity and criminal justice: Theoretical and substantive considerations. In H. E. Pepinsky (Ed.), *Rethinking criminology* (pp. 131–143). Sage Publications.

Pontell, H. N., Calavita, K., & Tillman, R. (1994). Corporate crime and criminal justice system capacity: Government response to financial institution fraud. *Justice Quarterly*, *11*(3), 383–410. https://doi.org/10.1080/07418829400092321

Pratt, T. C., Holtfreter, K., & Reisig, M. D. (2010). Routine online activity and Internet fraud targeting: Extending the generality of Routine Activity Theory. *Journal of Research in Crime and Delinquency*, *47*(3), 267–296. https://doi.org/10.1177/0022427810365903

Reyns, B. W., Henson, B., & Fisher, B. S. (2011). Being pursued online: Applying cyberlifestyle–Routine Activities Theory to cyberstalking victimization. *Criminal Justice and Behavior*, *38*(11), 1149–1169. https://doi.org/10.1177/0093854811421448

Richmond, R. (2011, April 2). The RSA hack: How they did it. *The New York Times*. https://bits.blogs.nytimes.com/2011/04/02/the-rsa-hack-how-they-did-it/

Rizzo, J. (2012, August 2). *Cybersecurity bill fails in Senate*. CNN. https://www.cnn.com/2012/08/02/politics/cybersecurity-act/index.html

Romo, V. (2019, March 25). *Man pleads guilty to phishing scheme that fleeced Facebook, Google of $100 Million*. NPR. https://www.npr.org/2019/03/25/706715377/man-pleads-guilty-to-phishing-scheme-that-fleeced-facebook-google-of-100-million

Rosoff, S. M., Pontell, H. N., & Tillman, R. (2014). *Profit without honor: White-collar crime and the looting of America* (6th ed.). Pearson.

Sahingoz, O. K., Buber, E., Demir, O., & Diri, B. (2019). Machine learning based phishing detection from URLs. *Expert Systems with Applications*, *117*(March), 345–357. https://doi.org/10.1016/j.eswa.2018.09.029

Schneider, O. (2016, January 19). Belgian bank Crelan hit by a 70 million Eur fraud. *The Brussels Times*. https://www.brusselstimes.com/news/belgium-all-news/36335/belgian-bank-crelan-hit-by-a-70-million-eur-fraud/

Scholz, J. T. (1997). Enforcement policy and corporate misconduct: The changing perspective of deterrence theory. *Law and Contemporary Problems*, *60*(3), 253. https://doi.org/10.2307/1192014

Smith, M. (2013, May 12). U.S. government is "biggest buyer" of zero-day vulnerabilities, report claims. *CSO Online*. https://www.csoonline.com/article/2224620/u-s–government-is–biggest-buyer–of-zero-day-vulnerabilities–report-claims.html

Stake, R. E. (2010). *Qualitative research: Studying how things work*. Guilford Press.

Stalans, L. J., & Donner, C. M. (2018). Explaining why cybercrime occurs: Criminological and psychological theories. In H. Jahankhani (Ed.), *Cyber Criminology* (pp. 25–45). Springer International Publishing. https://doi.org/10.1007/978-3-319-97181-0_2

Stembert, N., Padmos, A., Bargh, M. S., Choenni, S., & Jansen, F. (2015). A study of preventing email (spear) phishing by enabling human intelligence. *2015 European intelligence and security informatics conference*, 113–120. https://doi.org/10.1109/EISIC.2015.38

Stupp, C. (2019, August 30). Fraudsters used AI to Mimic CEO's voice in unusual cybercrime case. *The Wall Street Journal*. https://www.wsj.com/articles/fraudsters-use-ai-to-mimic-ceos-voice-in-unusual-cybercrime-case-11567157402

Sun, J. C.-Y., Yu, S.-J., Lin, S. S. J., & Tseng, -S.-S. (2016). The mediating effect of anti-phishing self-efficacy between college students' internet self-efficacy and anti-phishing behavior and gender difference. *Computers in Human Behavior*, *59*(June) 249–257. https://doi.org/10.1016/j.chb.2016.02.004

Thomas, K., Li, F., Zand, A., Barrett, J., Ranieri, J., Invernizzi, L., Markov, Y., Comanescu, O., Eranti, V., Moscicki, A., Margolis, D., Paxson, V., & Bursztein, E. (2017). Data breaches, phishing, or malware?: Understanding the risks of stolen credentials. *Proceedings of the 2017 ACM SIGSAC conference on computer and communications security*, 1421–1434. https://doi.org/10.1145/3133956.3134067

Urquhart, C. (2013). *Grounded theory for qualitative research: A practical guide*. SAGE.

Van Wilsem, J. (2011). Worlds tied together? Online and non-domestic routine activities and their impact on digital and traditional threat victimization. *European Journal of Criminology*, *8*(2), 115–127. https://doi.org/10.1177/1477370810393156

Van Wilsem, J. (2013). "Bought it, but never got it" assessing risk factors for online consumer fraud victimization. *European Sociological Review*, *29*(2), 168–178. https://doi.org/10.1093/esr/jcr053

Verizon. (2019). *2018 data breach investigations report*. https://enterprise.verizon.com/resources/reports/DBIR_2018_Report_execsummary.pdf

Weimann, G, (2016). Going dark: Terrorism on the Dark Web. *Studies in Conflict & Terrorism*, *39*(3), 195–206. https://doi.org/10.1080/1057610X.2015.1119546

Whitaker, A., & Newman, D. P. (2006). *Penetration testing and network defense*. Cisco Press.

Wilhelm, T. (2013). *Professional penetration testing* (2nd ed.). Syngress, an imprint of Elsevier.

Wojewidka, J. (2020). The deepfake threat to face biometrics. *Biometric Technology Today*, *2020*(2), 5–7. https://doi.org/10.1016/S0969-4765(20)30023-0

Wortley, R., & Tilley, N. (2014). Theories for situational and environmental crime prevention. In G. Bruinsma & D. Weisburd (Eds.), *Encyclopedia of criminology and criminal justice* (pp. 5164–5173). Springer New York. https://doi.org/10.1007/978-1-4614-5690-2_548

Wu, T. (2013, March 18). Fixing the worst law in technology. *The New Yorker*. https://www.newyorker.com/news/news-desk/fixing-the-worst-law-in-technology

Yang, W., Chen, J., Xiong, A., Proctor, R. W., & Li, N. (2015). Effectiveness of a phishing warning in field settings. *Proceedings of the 2015 symposium and bootcamp on the science of security - HotSoS '15*, 1–2. https://doi.org/10.1145/2746194.2746208

Yar, M. (2005). The novelty of 'cybercrime': An assessment in light of Routine Activity Theory. *European Journal of Criminology*, *2*(4), 407–427. https://doi.org/10.1177/147737080556056

Zetter, K. (2014, November 17). U.S. gov insists it doesn't Stockpile zero-day exploits to hack enemies. *WIRED*. https://www.wired.com/2014/11/michael-daniel-no-zero-day-stockpile/

Appendix. Interview Schedule

RQ1: What factors allow *phishing* to exist as a long-term, successful crime type?
RQ1A: How is *phishing* different now than 5 years ago? 10 years? 20 years?
RQ1B: You have mentioned (MOTIVATION, COSTS, RISKS, REWARDS, OFFENDER, VICTIM) but what about (ADDRESS ANY MISSING)?
RQ1C: Do you know of any exemplary cases of *phishing* (noteworthy targets, methods, or offenders)?

RQ2: What *technological* solutions are viable now; and in the future?
RQ2A: Conversely, are any *technological* problems on the horizon?
RQ2B: Which solutions do not work and why?

RQ2C: How should *technological* solutions be implemented (personal choice, corporate responsibility, or via government regulation)?

RQ3: What *human-focused* prevention strategies are viable now; and in the future?
RQ3A: Conversely, are any *human-focused* problems on the horizon?
RQ3B: Which solutions do not work and why?
RQ3C: How should *human-focused* prevention strategies be implemented (personal choice, corporate responsibility, or via government regulation)?

Online Fraud Victimization in China: A Case Study of Baidu Tieba

Claire Seungeun Lee

ABSTRACT

When it comes to online populations and markets, China has some of the largest in the world. As a result, Chinese cybercriminals have more opportunities to target and access victims. While extant research in Western countries has examined online fraud victimization and offenses in virtual communities, a relatively small body of research on these phenomena has been conducted in non-Western societies. This study attempts to address this gap by analyzing online fraud victimization in Chinese online communities. Routine activity theory is applied to understand the patterns and dynamics of victimization. Data were collected from Baidu Tieba (a Chinese version of Craigslist), a prominent Chinese online platform for reporting victimization. This study highlights the range of services, types, and methods along which victimization occurs. The results, which reflect China's rapid pace of technological development, show that different types of fraud are perpetrated online and that victimization methods are associated with particular types of media. This study also identifies implications for China and other countries where similar crimes and instances in cyberspace occur.

Introduction

The Internet creates countless venues and opportunities for crime and deviance in cyberspace. Online fraud is not only documented as one of the most frequently occurring crimes on the Internet, but it is also well known as one of the varieties of crime in which non-reporting victimization often occurs (Cross, 2016). Online communities serve as a platform to enable an understanding of victimization. In other words, victims share information, maintain solidarity, and often prepare for further collective actions together in virtual communities. Therefore, studying an online platform enables clear access to observe instances of victimization.

China has the largest connected population in the world. In March 2020, desktop and mobile Internet users in China numbered 904 million and 897 million, respectively (China Internet Network Information Center [CNNIC], 2020). As a platform similar to Craigslist, Baidu Tieba, which is lesser known in other parts of the world, is one of China's three largest social media platforms along with WeChat and Weibo – the Chinese counterparts to WhatsApp and Twitter. Its primary function is to facilitate access to interest groups online (Liu & Lu, 2018; Stockmann & Luo, 2017). Like other social media networks, WeChat and

Weibo have become particularly popular outlets for and facilitators of cybercrime in recent years (Gao & Zhang, 2015). In contrast, Baidu Tieba has become established as a platform on which victims can share their experiences of being victimized and warn other potential victims.

Previous studies of China's emergent Internet focus mostly on online communities, online spaces and society (Herold & Marolt, 2011; Marolt & Herold, 2015), online parody (Meng, 2011), contentious politics and online activism (Sullivan & Xie, 2009; Yang, 2011), and censorship (King et al., 2013, 2014; Liang & Lu, 2010), as well as Internet sovereignty (Jiang, 2010). Despite the Chinese Internet and cyberspace being an accumulative presence in the existing literature, any academic focus on crime and deviance and victimization in China is scarce, in both English and Chinese. Although online communities and platforms generally garner attention as sources of and venues for research in communication, sociology, and criminology, much of this line of inquiry explores U.S.-centered or English-language platforms, such as the original Craigslist (e.g., Frederick & Perrone, 2014; Garg & Nilizadeh, 2013; Grov, 2012; Lair & Andrews, 2018; Lair et al., 2016; Moskowitz & Seal, 2010; Oliveri, 2010; Park et al., 2014; Robinson & Vidal-Ortiz, 2013; Rosenbaum et al., 2013; Tofighi et al., 2016). Not only are English-language studies on China's cybercrime scarce (Liang & Lu, 2010, p. 111), but the intentional exploration of online web forums to understand Chinese cybercrime dynamics is also limited, unlike cases in other countries (Holt et al., 2016). More critically, from a theoretical standpoint, cybercrime from a cyber-victimization perspective is a well-established field of research in the United States, whereas cybercrime is still an understudied area in China; only recently and slowly has attention to it increased. In particular, research that draws from social media is even more limited: only a few studies published in Chinese discuss the various types of WeChat fraud (Xu, 2016; Yuan & Ye, 2016). Likewise, cybercrime, having emerged relatively recently compared with other crime typologies, has not yet become a major research area in Chinese criminology or related fields.

This study extends the extant literature by examining a Chinese online platform as an arena for reporting online fraud victimization, looking in particular at victims' behavioral traits that may poise them as targets (i.e., patterns of online fraud in China) and inside the patterns of victimization reporting (e.g., frequently described victimization methods and media types). The present study explores whether a type of media (i.e., online presence) leads to divergent patterns of online fraud victimization by laying a foundation of routine activities theory. This study shows that Baidu Tieba is used in China as a platform both to report online fraud victimization and to mediate online fraud. Analyzing these contingencies, the Chinese context of cyberspace, social media, and online fraud enables the study to make a contribution not only to broader online fraud literature but also to offset the Western bias of that literature. In doing so, this paper enhances our understanding of the online fraud literature that is cultivated predominantly from Western contexts by investigating online fraud in relation to the social media types and victimization methods in China, one of the world's largest markets of Internet users and, arguably, cybercrime as well. Due to China's unique background regarding online fraud, cyberspace, social media, and the historical, legal, and institutional contexts in relation to these landscapes, understanding online fraud victimization in the Chinese setting also highlights the lack of research with a non-Western focus. Finally, this study has political and practical implications. Since cyberspace is boundaryless, and access to China's Internet users and online platforms offer a unique opportunity for cybercriminals to utilize such conditions, an exploration of understudied Chinese cybercrime markets may identify new avenues for other countries to review their cybercrime prevention policies.

This paper is organized as follows: The first section reviews the conceptual and empirical background of online fraud and its extant literature. Next, the paper presents the relevant data, research methodology, and research findings. The final section summarizes the conclusions of the research and identifies practical and policy implications. This study also addresses implications of online fraud victimization for wider audiences.

Literature review

Online fraud victimization

The term "online fraud" refers to "the experience of an individual who has responded through the use of the internet to a dishonest invitation, request, notification or offer by providing personal information or money which has led to the suffering of a financial or non-financial loss of some kind" (Cross, 2016; Cross et al., 2014, p. 1). Online fraud intends to exploit people by using online platforms to gain access to them (Buchanan & Whitty, 2014). Online fraudsters utilize a wide range of methods to infringe upon victims' personal information and typically lure and persuade them to do certain things that will result in financial damages (Pratt et al., 2010; Reyns, 2013; Zahedi et al., 2015). Current scholarship on online fraud tends to focus largely on archetypes of these crimes, including "'get rich quick frauds' (e.g., the advance-fee fraud, lottery frauds, fake prize frauds)" (Buchanan & Whitty, 2014, p. 263), online dating romance scams (Buchanan & Whitty, 2014; Rege, 2009; Whitty & Buchanan, 2012), online consumer fraud victimization (Van Wilsem, 2013), online auction fraud (Conradt, 2012; Dolan, 2004), and phishing (Lee, 2020; Leukfeldt, 2014). Other scholars have studied the psychology and trauma experienced by elderly fraud victims (Cross, 2016, 2017; Mears et al., 2016), prevention strategies and approaches to online fraud (Cross, 2016; Cross & Kelly, 2016), reporting fraud (Cross, 2016, 2018), refund fraud (nonpayment fraud), and return fraud (non-delivery fraud) (Maimon et al., 2019).

While scholars acknowledge that online fraud is not a particularly new phenomenon but rather one augmented by the evolution of technology (Yar, 2013), a few issues exist within the growing body of literature. First, what is still left relatively unknown are common features among fraud victims (Buchanan & Whitty, 2014); specifically, little research has focused on particular technologies, online platforms, media, and tactics that feature in victimization via online fraud. Second, the existing literature is geographically focused predominantly on Western countries. Given China's lucrative and vibrant Internet environment, it is surprising to see that research emphasis exists only on China's online services (banking, e-commerce, shopping), particularly related to positive growth, economic perspectives and consumer satisfaction (Laforet & Li, 2005; D. Li et al., 2008; Lin & Li, 2005; Yang et al., 2009; Yoon, 2010), ignoring crime and deviance. In fact, the body of literature on cybercrimes in China is relatively limited (exceptions include Chang, 2012; Liang & Lu, 2010; Lu et al., 2010). Among the studies of Chinese cybercrime that do exist, very few have explored fraud. Instead, the existing research covers, for example, online shopping from the perspective of consumer risk (Ye, 2004), financial fraud in online markets and e-commerce (Guo et al., 2018; Zhang et al., 2013), risk assessment of financial frauds and fraud cases on the Chinese online shopping site Alibaba (Chen et al., 2015; Song et al., 2014; Zhang et al., 2013), and corporate fraud in China (Chen et al., 2016; Conyon & He, 2016).

Online communities as venues for online fraud: Baidu Tieba

A wide range of topics and activities are present on Craigslist, one of the most widespread virtual spaces in the United States since its launch in 1995, and it has been studied as a significant site for social and cultural activities (Hanson & Hawley, 2011; Kroft & Pope, 2014; Lair et al., 2016; Oliveri, 2010; Robinson & Vidal-Ortiz, 2013). Its innovative and far-reaching characteristics have attracted researchers who dive into its details as points for data analysis. Specific themes have emerged from this literature, including the notion of virtual communities as gated communities (Schackman, 2010), and research on housing (Hanson & Hawley, 2011; Oliveri, 2010), nanny advertisements (Lair & Andrews, 2018; Lair et al., 2016), same-sex partner matching, romantic relations, and other consequences (Frederick & Perrone, 2014; Moskowitz & Seal, 2010; Robinson & Vidal-Ortiz, 2013; Rosenbaum et al., 2013), HIV (Grov, 2012), substance use (Tofighi et al., 2016), and legal matters (Radbod, 2010). Despite the extensive existing research on Craigslist, there are only a few studies of the platform as a venue and source for understanding victimization and criminal cases (e.g., online fraud victimization [Garg & Nilizadeh, 2013; Park et al., 2014). Garg and Nilizadeh (2013) used the 30 largest metropolitan areas represented on Craigslist to examine automobile fraud using a macro-level approach and OLS regression analyses, finding that the characteristics of cities (e.g., racial homogeneity, per capita income) are associated with the exposure of fraud. Park et al. (2014) explored cases of advance-fee fraud – also known as Nigerian fraud – and characteristics of the fraudsters by using magnetic honeypot advertisements. Their findings showed that most fraudsters are located in Nigeria and that the accounts of 10 groups were highly involved in attempts to defraud others.

Baidu Tieba, a platform similar to Craigslist that operates in China, was launched in 2003. Like its U.S. counterpart, Baidu Tieba is a virtual community featuring classified advertisements that offer a single place for sharing information, goods, and services in multiple cities without the need to switch between websites. Baidu Tieba is more of an interest-based online community than a location-based one. One might assume that researchers would be drawn by the popularity and potential value of Baidu Tieba to look deeply at the site as both an online service provider and a community in China; however, given that it has already existed for more than 15 years but garnered little scholastic notice, this does not appear to be the case. Scholars have paid only limited attention to this platform, focusing on public opinion and fandom (L. Li et al., 2013; Stockmann & Luo, 2017), word-of-mouth effects on films (Godes & Mayzlin, 2004; Liu, 2006), and HIV-positive users (Liu & Lu, 2018). Also, Wu et al. (2014) have studied Baidu Tieba web forums in comparison with platforms Delicious and Flickr, to identify networks and dynamics of clickstreams. Perhaps a level of inaccessibility in terms of language barriers and censorship has prevented the Chinese Internet from becoming an attractive site for the study of criminal activities.

A few Craigslist studies show that cases of victimization through advertisements and threads posted on the site can provide important insights into cyberspace (e.g., Lair & Andrews, 2018; Lair et al., 2016; Park et al., 2014; Radbod, 2010). In a similar vein, some scholars point to Baidu Tieba as a venue for Chinese cybercrime and hacking (Fang et al., 2016; Yip, 2011). However, less is known about victimization on the same platform.

In an attempt to fill the gaps left by previous studies and to collect primary data innovatively in conducting cybercrime research (Bossler & Berenblum, 2019), this study analyzes Baidu Tieba as a venue for discussing and reporting cases of victimization from crimes related to a technology-based device or technological element. The following section describes the data, measures, and methodology used in this analysis.

Routine activity theory as an analytical framework

The routine activity theory (RAT) explains the frequency of criminal opportunities at the macro-level and the micro-level (Clarke & Felson, 1993). Its main propositions are that crime occurs as a result of the convergence of three elements – a suitable target, a motivated offender, and the lack of capable guardian – in space and time (Cohen & Felson, 1979). The RAT was initially proposed to explain a specific category of crime known as "direct-contact predatory violations" (Cohen & Felson, 1979, p. 589), which consists of crimes that involve direct physical contact during which one party takes or damages the other party or their property (Cohen & Felson, 1979, p. 589). Cohen and Felson (1979) propose that the occurrence of these violations is affected by the spatial and temporal components of community structure, which is composed of human interactions and relationships. The spatial component refers mainly to the physical locations in which the interactions and relationships occur. The temporal components are divided into three aspects: rhythm, tempo, and timing. These aspects of RAT's temporal components address the regularity and the frequency of crime occurrences and the activities that result from the interactions of that regularity and frequency (Clarke & Felson, 1979).

In the original conception of the RAT, motivated offenders were seen as the least important of the theory's three elements because the presence of individuals with criminal inclinations is taken for granted (Cohen & Felson, 1979). This is understandable as the purpose of the RAT is to understand the role of community structures and activities in crime patterns and occurrences. The other two components of the framework – a target's suitability and a lack of guardianship – explain the role of the immediate environment.

In general, at the macro-level, the RAT argues that macro-level crime results from major shifts in routine activities, as criminal act depend upon the spatial and temporal aspects of routine legal activities (Clarke & Felson, 1979; Felson & Cohen, 1980). The locations of bars and thier happy hour schedules, for instance, can predict to an extent the frequency, timing, and sites of assaults with that locale. Cohen and Felson (1979) have also discovered that frequency of household bulglaries during the daytime is directly proportional to the ratio of absent households during that window of time

At the micro-level, the RAT has been applied to explain the effect of individual behaviors on the nexus of the three crime-conducive elements in physical proximity (Cohen & Felson, 1979). The theory assumes that offenders are intrinsically motivated to commit crime. Therefore, RAT provides a useful framework for exploring victims' behavioral traits in relation to victimization. First, it addresses victims' use of the Internet. That is, a researcher can include in their model whether and how frequently a victim uses the Internet; the more often one uses the Internet/social media, the more likely they are to be victimized by online crime writ large resulting from greater exposure to motivated offenders. Second, it explores the particular types of social media that victims use and how that differentially affects victimization. Third, the relationship between victims and offenders can be used as a proxy for target suitability; that is, one's proximity to another person may be increased depending on the type of relationship they have with that person. Taken together, RAT is a useful framework for examining online fraud victimization in China through the use of Baidu Tieba.

Data, measures, and methods

Procedure

The data analyzed in this study were collected and derived from publicly accessible web forums based in China. The web forum Baidu Tieba, on which information, goods, and services are exchanged, was started in 2003. Baidu Tieba caters to interest groups and often features specialized thematic forums that are open to public comment. Figure 1 depicts the homepage of Baidu Tieba and Figure 2 shows a thread titled "Forum on Fraudsters" on the site.

This data was obtained between June and November 2017. To choose which online forums to include in this study, the author specifically searched Baidu Tieba for active *tiebas* (web forums) with a large number of posts and users who are reporting scams and scammers linked to the platform. Then, the author selected one such *tieba*, named *Dapianzi ba* (Forum on Fraudsters), a specialized forum for reporting scams; it included 265 cases between January 2010 and May 2017. In the period before 2010, Baidu Tieba allowed anonymous posting, displaying only the IP address of each poster.

Figure 1. Baidu Tieba.
Source: Baidu Tieba (2018). https://tieba.baidu.com/index.html.

Figure 2. "Forum on fraudsters" thread on Baidu Tieba.
Source: Forum on Fraudsters (*Dapianzi ba*), 2018. Baidu Tieba. http://tieba.baidu.com/f/good?kw=%B4%F3%C6%AD%D7%D3&fr=ala0&tpl=5

The author created a *tieba* database using both manual collection and a crawling method, in part using R. All threads that are publicly accessible were saved as web pages. These threads were initially examined in their original language and then translated into English in later analyses. Two Chinese research assistants reviewed all of the threads carefully and identified terms that were slang, Internet-specific terms, or new words meant to evade any policing by the web platform and the authorities. A dictionary of such terms was prepared for further analysis in order to capture the dynamics of the Chinese Internet.

In addition to identifying important terms for the study, the author coded key themes and keywords for further analysis. The author and the research assistants also coded and cross-checked themes and the information on the forum to create a higher-quality database. The research assistants' coding was then compared with the author's coding using 10% of the sample. Using this method, the inter-coder reliability was found to be 0.79, demonstrating that the codes identified between the coders were reliable (Landis & Koch, 1977).

As a result of such procedures, a total of 265 threads were collected; however, many of the threads either did not contain enough information for analysis or had overlapping information. For example, if a thread mentioned a specific person who was fraudulent but did not include specific information, which occurred frequently, it was deleted due to gaps that made it insufficient for data analysis. In addition, some threads did not pertain to technology-facilitated and online fraud cases and thus were not relevant to this research.

The threads span a seven-year period from 2010 to 2017, but the majority of threads were posted in 2017 (approximately 43.8%). Although the earliest year of posting was 2010, several threads were about incidents that had occurred prior to the year in which they were posted. For example, users posted about incidents from 2008 in four threads and 2009 in two threads. Ultimately, the data availability of all information in this research resulted in fewer than 300 cases used for analysis.

Because of the characteristics of the Baidu Tieba platform, the data utilized in this research may not reflect all technology-facilitated fraud cases in China as a whole or paint a general picture of such crime scenes. Like other online platforms, Baidu Tieba is largely dominated by younger users who are likely to use the Internet and smartphones in their everyday lives (Liu & Lu, 2018). Furthermore, platforms for exchanging information about fraud cases and victimization are not always open to the public. Baidu Tieba, the platform utilized in this research, is only one of the public places that has not been well explored by criminology researchers – unlike Craigslist, into which recent criminology research has delved in detail. Similar platforms in other countries have also not been researched adequately. Therefore, an investigation of this platform is meaningful. The findings of this study can document an early online venue for sharing information about cybercrime victimization and can also offer a potential direction for future research. By becoming aware of and reading details about previous fraud cases, individuals who may be targeted by similar fraudsters can prevent their potential victimization, and law enforcement agencies can better investigate such cases based on the available online information.

Methods

This study uses multiple correspondence analysis (MCA) and chi-square tests to understand patterns of online fraud on China's Baidu Tieba. MCA and chi-square tests are useful for studying categorical variables. Furthermore, MCA is powerful in revealing groupings and memberships of variable categories in dimensions (Costa et al., 2013).

Measures

This research uses MCA to understand victimization by online fraud and, in particular, explore what types of media, methods, and resources are used to commit such crimes as well as identify which types of victimization they intersect with.

Variables

Table 1 presents the descriptive statistics of relevant variables used in this research.

Variables identified from the database include crime incidents and the methods behind carrying them out. The contents of each variable are as follows: (1) *Type of media*, which includes Alipay, Phone, QQ, Taobao, and WeChat; (2) *Type of victimization method*, including card fraud, fake contacts, phone bill fraud, refund fraud (nonpayment fraud), or return fraud (non-delivery fraud); (3) *Year* indicates year of victimization; and (4) *Victimized money* (*victimization*) represents the amount of money each victim lost in their victimization (in Chinese Renminbi [¥]). Of all the victims in the dataset (N = 265), only 48.3% of the cases (N = 128) reported the amount of money involved in their victimization. Although in these cases there is no clear evidence of how much they lost, failure to report the amount of money does not necessarily mean that there was no financial loss. Following this logic, the first category starts from ¥1 and the last category ends with ¥200,000, which was the highest victimized amount in the dataset. With a high degree of

Table 1. Descriptive analysis.

Variable	N	%
Year (N=265)		
2008	4	1.5
2009	2	0.8
2010	4	1.5
2011	8	3.0
2012	6	2.3
2013	17	6.4
2014	14	5.3
2015	22	8.3
2016	55	20.8
2017	133	50.2
Type (N=265)		
Alipay	8	3.0
Phone	58	21.9
QQ	151	57.0
Taobao	27	10.2
WeChat	21	7.9
Method (N=265)		
Card fraud	5	1.9
Fake contact	10	3.8
Phone bill fraud	5	1.9
Refund fraud	160	60.4
Return fraud	85	32.1
Victimized money (in ¥) (N=128)		
0–122	32	12.1
123–500	34	12.8
501–3,000	35	13.2
3,001–15,000	14	5.3
15,001-200,000	13	4.9

variability, the amount of victimized money was coded into five categories by using its distribution, for the purpose of statistical testing: ¥1–¥122, ¥123–¥500, ¥501–¥3,000, ¥3,001–¥15,000, and ¥15,001–¥200,000.

Analytic strategy

To explore the patterns and characteristics of online fraud victimization in China, this study uses a mosaic plot - which is a visualization technique arranging the results of a crosstab analysis – and a multiple correspondence analysis (MCA). Mosaic plots, which were developed by Hartigan and Kleiner (1981), are designed to present and explore categorical data in a graphic manner. Each cell of a contingency table is represented by a tile. "The tile's size is directly proportional to the number of cases in this cell." To interpret a mosaic plot's results, the concept of a one-dimensional spineplot, which sheds light on proportions, is useful (Hofmann, 2000).

MCA is used in social sciences as an extended version of correspondence analysis. It systematically explores the patterns of associations between more than two categorical dependent variables (Abdi & Valentin, 2007) and "translates deviations from the independence model in the contingency table into distances" (Blasius & Thiessen, 2001). The general principles of MCA include a proportional relationship between the distance and volume of categories from the center of an axis and their impact on the axis' shape. On an MCA plot, short distances between data points represent high similarity, whereas long distances imply dissimilarity (Blasius & Thiessen, 2001, p. 7). In other words, the purpose of an MCA is to locate individuals or items by using similarity-based distance in dimensional spaces. The distances between different variables indicate whether these variables are highly correlated with one another. In criminology, MCA has not yet been widely adopted, but existing research has used this method to explore the internal dynamics of non-organized crime and organized crime in groups such as the mafia (Calderoni et al., 2016) and cyberterrorism (Choi et al., 2018). For non-organized criminal efforts, this analytical plan is also useful in understanding associations of different variables in the research. Thus, it is an effective means of understanding the dynamics of victimization in fraud cases.

Results

Trends in online fraud victimization in China

Before presenting our key research findings, this section briefly describes the context, dataset, and sample characteristics. China's vast number of Internet users and vast volume of social media and online platforms allow a unique opportunity for cybercriminals looking to utilize such conditions. In Chinese cyberspace, online gambling, pornography, and online fraud are the most frequently observed crimes (China Internet Network Information Center, 2018, 2020) (Internet Crime Reporting Center, 2015, 2016, 2017, 2018, 2019, 2020). The major techniques used to facilitate online fraud crimes in China – information that the Internet Crime Reporting Center no longer makes available to the public – include fake websites; fake trade; establishing friendships with victims through fake contacts on instant messaging service Tencent QQ (commonly known as QQ); selling exam answers or "cheat sheets"; recruitment fraud; and pyramid schemes (Internet Crime Reporting Center, 2016, 2017).

This study observed trends in China's online fraud victimization in the current data, which is presented in Figure 3. In this dataset, only four cases were documented in 2008. However, the number of cases grew rapidly and a total of 129 cases, or 49% of the whole dataset, were reported in 2017. Fewer than 10% of the cases were reported from 2008 to 2012. With the further penetration of technology and use of Baidu Tieba as a platform, more than 90% of cases were documented from 2013 to 2017.

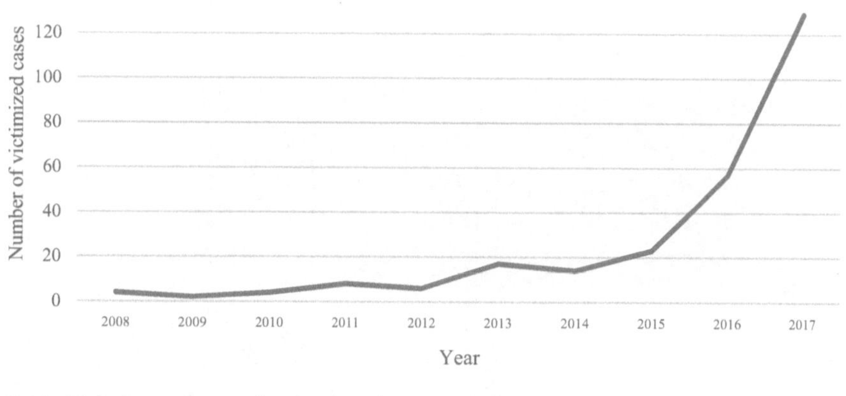

Figure 3. Baidu Tieba's yearly trends of online fraud victimization.

Examining the relationship between media types and victimization methods

As described earlier, mosaic plots represent a graphical way of visualizing contingency tables (Hartigan & Kleiner, 1981). The sizes and the positions of each rectangle (or tile) depict the cells in a contingency table (Hofmann, 2008) and the sizes of tiles are proportional to the cell count (Hu, 2004). Figure 4 above shows a mosaic plot of the criminological types and methods, based on the findings of a contingency table. Two types of online fraud show particularly interesting results. Refund fraud (i.e., an online non-delivery fraud) is one type of crime in which customer payments are made without the delivery of goods and services (Internet Crime Reporting Center, 2017; Maimon et al., 2019). Return fraud (i.e., an online nonpayment fraud), on the other hand, is a type of fraud in which goods and services are delivered without payment being made, and then fraudulently requesting money. Only one type of fraud was linked to online payment system Alipay, which is refund fraud (100.00%), while phones were used to commit four different types of fraud; proportionally speaking, the most common were return fraud (61.54%), followed by fake contact (19.22%), card fraud (9.63%), and phone bill fraud (9.61%). Phones were not used in refund fraud victimization. To carry out refund frauds, fraudsters typically advertise an item, product, or service on a classified-advertisement website and contact potential targets via e-mail or phone (Button & Cross, 2017; Maimon et al., 2019). QQ was used predominantly in refund frauds (70.08%), but also in return frauds (29.92%). As one of the largest online shopping and auction websites in China, with an enormous number of users, Taobao was also used predominantly in refund frauds (77.77%) as well as return frauds to a lesser extent (22.23%). WeChat was used predominantly in refund frauds (85.71%), followed by return frauds (14.29%). The resulting chi-square test results were statistically significant (x^2 = 123.091, $p < .00$).

Victimization patterns: media types, methods, and years (MCA)

This section describes the kinds of media utilized to contribute to victimization in Chinese cyberspace. MCA methods associate different categorical variables in order to fully comprehend the dynamics of online fraud victimization in China.

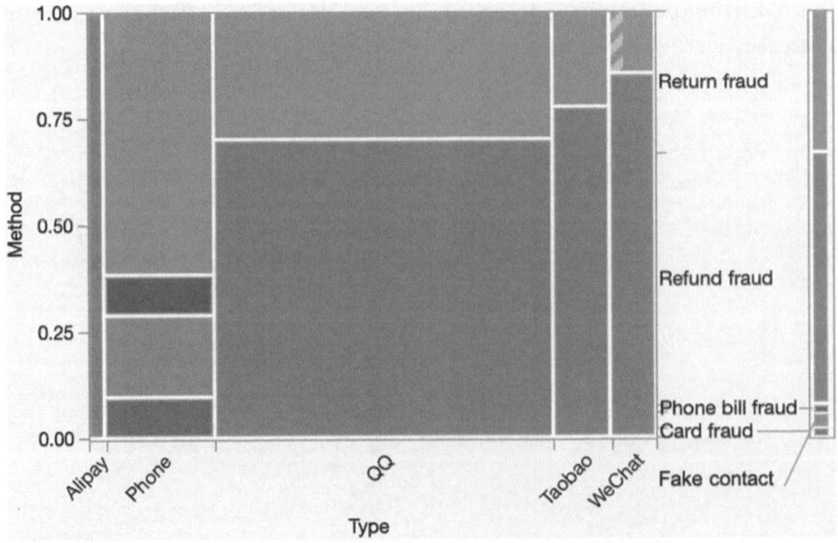

Figure 4. Mosaic plot.

Figure 5 shows the MCA results: i.e., the relationship between types of media, methods of victimization, and years on a joint plot of all these categorical variables along two dimensions. The MCA plot created by juxtaposing media and year had statistically significant results (p <.00). The following three clusters were found through MCA. The first cluster ("Phone frauds") is all about phones (media). Phones were used for and were highly associated with phone bill fraud, fake contacts, and card fraud (in line with the results shown in the mosaic plot). The second cluster ("Social media/Internet with refund frauds") shows that these types of new media are well clustered with refund fraud. Alipay, an electronic payment service, WeChat, and Taobao are highly associated with refund frauds, particularly in the years 2014, 2016, and 2017. QQ is also associated with refund frauds, but in different years, namely, 2012 and 2015. In the third cluster ("Return frauds"), return

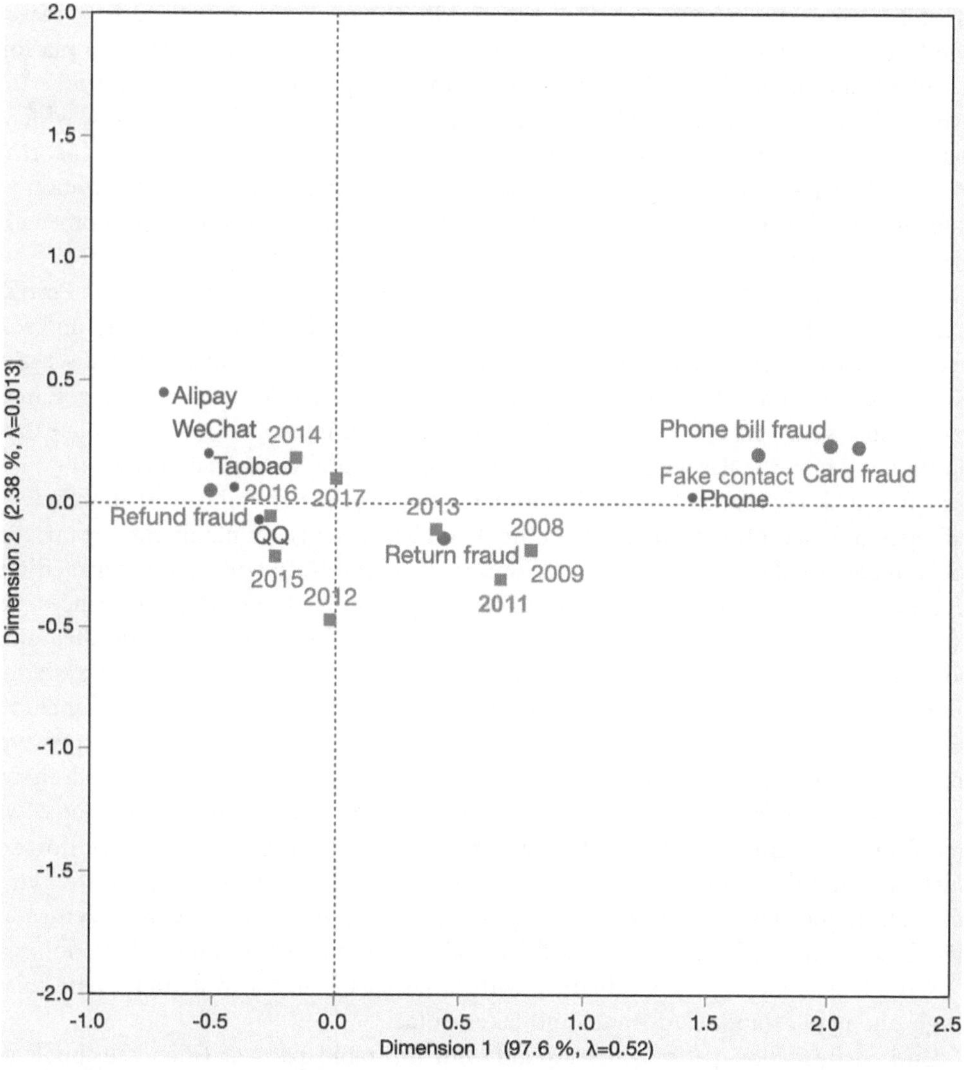

Figure 5. MCA map of method by type.

frauds are associated with 4 years: 2008, 2009, 2011, and 2013. Dimension 1 explains 97.62% of all cases.

QQ, an instant messenger used on phones and PCs, accounts for the majority of cases (57.1%), followed by calls and SMSs via smartphones (21.9%) and Taobao (10.2%), a leading Chinese online auction company; online payment system Alipay and instant messenger WeChat (with WeChat pay) together comprise 7.9% of the dataset. In this dataset, it was found that in cases of wireless and online messengers and online payment systems, phone numbers are used by perpetrators for keeping in touch with victims. This is particularly interesting because it shows that traditional methods of crime were coupled with new and emerging methods, reinforced by technology and the Internet (Button & Cross, 2017).

Discussion and conclusion

This study examined China's uncharted but rapidly growing cyberspace and how cases of online fraud victimization are being discussed and shared online. Baidu Tieba, a platform much like Craigslist in the United States, was chosen largely because it is a Chinese (and non-English language) community, and located in Asia – particularly China – which is understudied in research on online criminality because of language barriers and censorship.

While extant research in Western countries has examined online fraud victimization and offenses in virtual communities, a relatively small body of research on these phenomena has been conducted in non-Western societies. An emerging body of literature takes this into account and examines online data markets where stolen data was available (Franklin, Paxson, Perrig, & Savage, 2007; Holt, 2012; Holt et al., 2016; Motoyama et al., 2011; Wehinger, 2011), and some cybercrime research uses innovative methods such as analyses of online forum discussions (Bossler & Berenblum, 2019; Holt & Bossler, 2016). In an attempt to bridge the gap in the literature, this study explored the Chinese online community to understand online fraud victimization – in particular, to explore patterns in online fraud victimization cases.

The present study revealed several key research findings. First, while the relation between fraud types and victimization methods in the Baidu Tieba dataset is highly significant, types of social media shed light on different victimization methods. In addition, other mediums, except for phones, are known as new media/social media. Interesting differences exist between old and new media that are used for targeting victims in China. Specifically, refund frauds were primarily perpetrated through Alipay, which is a very popular system of e-payment. Online and mobile messengers that have e-payment functions, including WeChat and QQ, and the online shopping website Taobao are associated with two types of fraud techniques: return fraud and refund fraud. While return fraud is the predominant type for these three online venues, these mediums were also apparently associated with refund frauds. Exchanging goods and services online is done on the basis of trust; however, fraudsters exploit this basic tenet of online services to victimize targets. The fraudsters either do not return goods or services or do not pay the amount due; therefore, both return and refund frauds can be achieved rather easily. Another key research finding is that phones are still used either alone or in combination with other social media to defraud, particularly through phone bill fraud, card fraud, and fake contacts.

Second, victimization patterns correspond with the rapid pace of China's technological development, while a combination of online and traditional methods of perpetrating fraud still exist. This clearly indicates that not only does technology provide spaces for Chinese criminals to develop their skills in victimizing innocent people, but also the Internet in particular can be used as a tool by victims who wish to share information with the public about criminals they have encountered. Both parties – those committing crimes and those reporting victimization – take advantage of anonymity online (Bouchard, 2016; Grant & Lavery, 2017). While fraud is certainly not a new phenomenon (Grabosky & Smith, 1998), the extent to which fraud has evolved and changed in recent years is significant. In particular, the evolution of the Internet and other digital technologies has drastically changed the ways in which fraud is perpetrated (Yar, 2013). Fraud is still committed in traditional, offline contexts, yet the Internet now facilitates a globally connected network of both victims and offenders who can potentially interact with each other (Button & Cross, 2017).

Third, a combination of mosaic plot, chi-square test, and MCA results indicate that Baidu Tieba functions as a common space for victims to report victimization and interact with other victims. The results show that the use of a particular type of social media, such as QQ or WeChat, significantly predicts the occurrence of specific types of online fraud. Exploring victims' behavioral traits for victimization, those who are more exposed online and in social media are also more suitable targets of online fraud. Expanding the risk of users being targeted, QQ – traditionally a PC-based messenger – now also has a mobile app. Together with QQ, Taobao – arguably the most famous and popular online shopping website in China – is used primarily for return and refund fraud owing to its predominant function being the exchange of messages and payments. Compared with these sites, the smartphone-based messenger and payment apps WeChat and Alipay are typically used for refund frauds.

This research contributes to the field by examining an understudied topic within existing literature on cybercrime, drawing from an underutilized data source. The current literature on cybercrime, especially regarding online fraud, tends to concentrate on specific countries and/or regions. The present study adds a different perspective to our understanding of online fraud by examining the relationships between various online platforms in China and online fraud methods.

This research is not without limitations, but the limitations could also be potential avenues for future research. This research is an important step forward in examining China's largest cybercrime-reporting markets. However, the sample size was rather small due to the availability of analyzable information in the data. Although the forum that was chosen was the largest possible arena to study, future research should consider combining different forums into a single dataset to be explored and analyzed. In future research, detailed qualitative content analysis of Baidu Tieba forums can also be studied to understand nuanced meanings and procedures of victimization online. With more longitudinal data and the reduction of missing information, other rigorous statistical methods – such as event history analysis – can be used to create extended datasets that cover longer periods of time.

This study presents the following implications for the future. First, users' characteristics are related their likelihood of being victims. From the demographic features of social media users, victims are usually young, and young users typically use social media such as QQ and WeChat. This has further implications for social media-related victimization and social media policing. Second, the current law regarding online frauds in China is often applicable only to cases where a victim has lost more than 2,000 RMB, or about 296 USD (Standing Committee of the National People's Congress, 2016). There is no systematic legal recourse for victims who have been scammed out of a smaller amount of money. Thus, it is especially important for people to be vigilant and careful when making any contracts or transactions for goods and services online. Third, this research opens a research avenue and shows that innovative data collection methods can be used to examine cybercrime even in an under-studied country, such as China. In conclusion, these findings provide not only theoretical and methodological implications, but also practical implications for online fraud in China and elsewhere.

This study identifies implications and policy measures, along with the significance of cybercrime, for authorities and citizens to address issues of digital media environments and cyberspace. Finally, authorities and citizens should understand the significance of cyber-crime to address issues related to the environments of virtual communities and digital media and should take this data into account in forming future policy.

Disclosure statement

No potential conflict of interest was reported by the author(s).

ORCID

Claire Seungeun Lee http://orcid.org/0000-0002-0355-8793

References

Abdi, H., & Valentin, D. (2007). Multiple correspondence analysis. In N. J. Salkind (Ed.), *Encyclopedia of measurement and statistics* (pp. 650–657). Sage.

Baidu Tieba. (2018). Retrieved March 10, 2020, from https://tieba.baidu.com/index.html

Blasius, J., & Thiessen, V. (2001). Methodological artifacts in measures of political efficacy and trust: A multiple correspondence analysis. *Political Analysis*, *9*(1), 1–20. https://doi.org/10.1093/oxfordjournals.pan.a004862

Bossler, A. M., & Berenblum, T. (2019). Introduction: New directions in cybercrime research. *Journal of Crime and Justice*, *42*(5), 1–5. https://doi.org/10.1080/0735648X.2019.1692426

Bouchard, K. L. (2016). Anonymity as a double-edge sword: Reflecting on the implications of online qualitative research in studying sensitive topics. *The Qualitative Report*, *21*(1), 59–67. https://nsuworks.nova.edu/tqr/vol21/iss1/5/

Buchanan, T., & Whitty, M. T. (2014). The online dating romance scam: Causes and consequences of victimhood. *Psychology, Crime & Law*, *20*(3), 261–283. https://doi.org/10.1080/1068316X.2013.772180

Button, M. & Cross, C. (2017). Technology and fraud: The 'fraudogenic' consequences of the Internet revolution. In T. J. Holt & M. R. McGuire (Eds.), *The Routledge handbook of technologycrime and justice (Routledge International Handbooks)* (pp. 78–95). Routledge.

Calderoni, F., Berlusconi, G., Garofalo, L., Giommoni, L., & Sarno, F. (2016). The Italian mafias in the world: A systematic assessment of the mobility of criminal groups. *European Journal of Criminology*, *13*(4), 413–433. https://doi.org/10.1177/1477370815623570

Chang, L. Y.-C. (2012). *Cybercrime in the greater China region: Regulatory response and crime prevention across the Taiwan strait*. Edward Elgar.

Chen, J., Cumming, D., Hou, W., & Lee, E. (2016). Does the external monitoring effect of financial analysts deter corporate fraud in China? *Journal of Business Ethics*, *134*(4), 727–742. https://doi.org/10.1007/s10551-014-2393-3

Chen, J., Tao, Y., Wang, H., & Chen, T. (2015). Big data based fraud risk management at Alibaba. *Journal of Finance and Data Science*, *1*(1), 1–10. https://doi.org/10.1016/j.jfds.2015.03.001

China Internet Network Information Center. (2018). *Statistical Report on Internet Development in China (January 2018)*. CNNIC.

China Internet Network Information Center. (2020). *Statistical Report on Internet Development in China (March 2020)*. CNNIC.

Choi, K.-S., Lee, C. S., & Cadigan, R. (2018). Spreading propaganda in cyberspace: Comparing cyber-resource usage of al Qaeda and ISIS. *International Journal of Cybersecurity Intelligence & Cybercrime, 1*(1), 21–39. https://vc.bridgew.edu/ijcic/vol1/iss1/4/

Clarke, R. V., & Felson, M. (1993). Introduction: Criminology, routine activity and rational choice. In R. V. Clarke & M. Felson (Eds.), *Routine activity and rational choice: Advances in criminological theory* (Vol. 5). Transaction Publishers, 1–14.

Cohen, L., & Felson, M. (1979). Social change and crime rate trends: A routine activity approach. *American Sociological Review, 44*(4), 588–608. https://doi.org/10.2307/2094589

Conradt, C. (2012). Online auction fraud and criminological theories: The Adrian Ghighina case. *International Journal of Cyber Criminology, 6*(1), 912–923.

Conyon, M. J., & He, L. (2016). Executive compensation and corporate fraud in China. *Journal of Business Ethics, 134*(4), 669–691. https://doi.org/10.1007/s10551-014-2390-6

Costa, P. S., Santos, N. C., Cunha, P., Cotter, J., & Sousa, N. (2013). The use of multiple correspondence analysis to explore associations between categories of qualitative variables in healthy ageing. *Journal of Aging Research, 2013*, 1–12. https://doi.org/10.1155/2013/302163

Cross, C. (2016). Using financial intelligence to target online fraud victimisation: Applying a tertiary prevention perspective. *Criminal Justice Studies, 29*(2), 125–142. https://doi.org/10.1080/1478601X.2016.1170278

Cross, C. (2017). I've lost some sleep over it: Secondary trauma in the provision of support to older fraud victims. *Canadian Journal of Criminology and Criminal Justice, 59*(2), 168–197. https://doi.org/10.3138/cjccj.2016.E11

Cross, C. (2018). (Mis)Understanding the impact of online fraud: Implications for victim assistance schemes. *Victims & Offenders, 13*(6), 757–776. https://doi.org/10.1080/15564886.2018.1474154

Cross, C., & Kelly, M. (2016). The problem of 'white noise': Examining current prevention approaches to online fraud. *Journal of Financial Crime, 23*(4), 806–818. https://doi.org/10.1108/JFC-12-2015-0069

Cross, C., Smith, R. G., & Richards, K. (2014). Challenges of responding to online fraud victimisation in Australia. *Trends and Issues in Crime and Justice*, (474), 1–6.

Dolan, K. M. (2004). Internet auction fraud: The silent victims. *Journal of Economic Crime Management, 2*(1), 1–22.

Fang, Z., Zhao, X., Wei, Q., Chen, G., Zhang, Y., Xing, C., Li, W., & Chen, H. (2016, September 28–30). *Exploring key hackers and cybersecurity threats in Chinese hacker communities*. 2016 IEEE Conference on Intelligence and Security Informatics (ISI), Tucson, Arizona, USA. https://ieeexplore.ieee.org/abstract/document/7745436/authors#authors

Forum on Fraudsters (*Dapianzi ba*). (2018). *Baidu Tieba*. Retrieved November 21, 2018, from http://tieba.baidu.com/f/good?kw=%B4%F3%C6%AD%D7%D3&fr=ala0&tpl=5

Franklin, J., Perrig, A., Paxson, V., & Savage, S. (2007). An inquiry into the nature and causes of the wealth of internet miscreants. In *ACM Conference on Computer and Communications Security* (pp. 375–388). Association for Computer Machinery.

Frederick, B. J., & Perrone, D. (2014). "Party N play" on the internet: Subcultural formation, craigslist, and escaping from stigma. *Deviant Behavior, 35*(11), 859–884. https://doi.org/10.1080/01639625.2014.897116

Gao, S., & Zhang, X. (2015). Understanding the use of location sharing services on social networking platforms in China. International conference on E-business and telecommunitions (ICETE 2015). *E-Business and Telecommunications*, 124–136.

Garg, V., & Nilizadeh, S. (2013). *Craigslist scams and community composition: Investigating online fraud victimization*. 2013 IEEE Security and Privacy Workshops, San Francisco, California, USA.

Godes, D., & Mayzlin, D. (2004). Using online conversations to study word-of-mouth communication. *Marketing Science, 23*(4), 545–560. https://doi.org/10.1287/mksc.1040.0071

Grabosky, P. N., & Smith, R. (1998). *Crime in the digital age:Controlling telecommunications and cyberspace illegalities*. Transaction Publishers.

Grant, H., & Lavery, C. (2017). Masquerading sanity: Crimes, violence and victimization on the internet. *Acta Psychopathologica*, *3*(3), 1–4. https://doi.org/10.4172/2469-6676.100098

Grov, C. (2012). HIV risk and substance use in men who have sex with men surveyed in bathhouses, bars/ clubs,and on Craigslist.org: Venue of recruitment matters. *AIDS and Behavior*, *16*(4), 807–817. https://doi.org/10.1007/s10461-011-9999-6

Guo, Y., Bao, Y., Stuart, B. J., & Le-Nguyen, K. (2018). To sell or not to sell: Exploring sellers' trust and risk of chargeback fraud in cross-border electronic commerce. *Information Systems Journal*, *28*(2), 359–383. https://doi.org/10.1111/isj.12144

Hanson, A., & Hawley, Z. (2011). Do landlords discriminate in the rental housing market? Evidence from an internet field experiment in US cities. *Journal of Urban Economics*, *70*(2–3), 99–114. https://doi.org/10.1016/j.jue.2011.02.003

Hartigan, J. A., & Kleiner, B. (1981). *Mosaics for contingency tables*. Computer Science and Statistics: Proceedings of the 13th Symposium on the Interface (pp. 268–273), Pittsburgh, Pennsylvania, USA.

Herold, D. K., & Marolt, P. (Eds.). (2011). *Online society in China: Creating, celebrating, and instrumentalising the online carnival*. Routledge.

Hofmann, H. (2000). Exploring categorical data: Interactive mosaic plots. *Metrika*, *51*(1), 11–26. https://doi.org/10.1007/s001840000041

Hofmann, H. (2008). Mosaic plots and their variants. In C.-H. Chen, W. K. Haerdle, & A. Unwin (Eds.), *Handbook of data visualization* (pp. 617–642). Springer.

Holt, T. J. (2012). Examining the forces shaping cybercrime markets online. *Social Science Computer Review*, *31*(2), 165–177. https://doi.org/10.1177/0894439312452998

Holt, T. J., & Bossler, A. M. (2016). *Cybercrime in progress: Theory and prevention of technology-enabled offenses*. Routledge.

Holt, T. J., Smirnova, O., & Chua, Y. T. (2016). Exploring and estimating the revenues and profits of participants in stolen data markets. *Deviant Behavior*, *37*(4), 353–367. https://doi.org/10.1080/01639625.2015.1026766

Hu, M. Y. (2004). Line mosaic plot: Algorithm and implementation. In J. Antoch (Ed.), *COMPSTAT 2004 — proceedings in computational statistics* (pp. 277–285). Physica. https://doi.org/10.1007/978-3-7908-2656-2_22

Internet Crime Reporting Center (*Wangluo weifa fanzui jubao wangzhan*). (2015). Retrieved June 5, 2020, from http://www.cyberpolice.cn/wfjb/html/index.shtml

Internet Crime Reporting Center (*Wangluo weifa fanzui jubao wangzhan*). (2016). Retrieved June 5, 2020, from http://www.cyberpolice.cn/wfjb/html/index.shtml

Internet Crime Reporting Center (*Wangluo weifa fanzui jubao wangzhan*). (2017). Retrieved June 5, 2020, from http://www.cyberpolice.cn/wfjb/html/index.shtml

Internet Crime Reporting Center (*Wangluo weifa fanzui jubao wangzhan*). (2018). Retrieved June 5, 2020, from http://www.cyberpolice.cn/wfjb/html/index.shtml

Internet Crime Reporting Center (*Wangluo weifa fanzui jubao wangzhan*). (2019). Retrieved June 5, 2020, from http://www.cyberpolice.cn/wfjb/html/index.shtml

Internet Crime Reporting Center (*Wangluo weifa fanzui jubao wangzhan*). (2020). Retrieved June 5, 2020, from http://www.cyberpolice.cn/wfjb/html/index.shtml

Jiang, M. (2010). Authoritarian informationalism: China's approach to internet sovereignty. *SAIS Review of International Affairs*, *30*(2), 71–89.

King, G., Pan, J., & Roberts, M. E. (2013). How censorship in China allows government criticism but silences collective expression. *American Political Science Review*, *107*(2), 1–18. https://doi.org/10.1017/S0003055413000014

King, G., Pan, J., & Roberts, M. E. (2014). Reverse-engineering censorship in China: Randomized experimentation and participant observation. *Science*, *345*(6199), 1–10. https://doi.org/10.1126/science.1251722

Kroft, K., & Pope, D. G. (2014). Does online search crowd out traditional search and improve matching efficiency? Evidence from Craigslist. *Journal of Labor Economics*, *32*(2), 259–303. https://doi.org/10.1086/673374

Laforet, S., & Li, X. (2005). Consumers' attitudes towards online and mobile banking in China. *International Journal of Bank Marketing*, *23*(5), 362–380. https://doi.org/10.1108/02652320510629250

Lair, C. D., & Andrews, C. K. (2018). Advertising a particularly precarious occupation: Nanny ads on Craigslist. *Sociological Spectrum*, *38*(2), 69–85. https://doi.org/10.1080/02732173.2018.1430636

Lair, C. D., MacLeod, C., & Budger, E. (2016). Advertising unreasonable expectations: Nanny ads on Craigslist. *Sociological Spectrum*, *36*(5), 286–302. https://doi.org/10.1080/02732173.2016.1169236

Landis, J. R., & Koch, G. G. (1977). The measurement of observer agreement for categorical data. *Biometrics*, *33*(1), 159–174. https://doi.org/10.2307/2529310

Lee, C. S. (2020). A crime script analysis of transnational identity fraud: Migrant offenders' use of technology in South Korea. *Crime, Law, and Social Change*, *74*(2), 201–218. https://doi.org/10.1007/s10611-020-09885-3

Leukfeldt, E. R. (2014). Phishing for suitable targets in the Netherlands: Routine activity theory and phishing victimization. *Cyberpsychology, Behavior and Social Networking*, *17*(8), 551–555. https://doi.org/10.1089/cyber.2014.0008

Li, D., Li, J., & Lin, Z. (2008). Online consumer-to-consumer market in China – A comparative study of Taobao and eBay. *Electronic Commerce Research and Applications*, *7*(1), 55–67. https://doi.org/10.1016/j.elerap.2007.02.010

Li, L., Chen, Y.-W., & Nakazawa, M. (2013). Voices of Chinese web-TV audiences: A case of applying uses and gratifications theory to examine popularity of prison break in China. *China Media Research*, *9*(1), 63–74.

Liang, B., & Lu, H. (2010). Internet development, censorship, and cyber crimes in China. *Journal of Contemporary Criminal Justice*, *26*(1), 103–120. https://doi.org/10.1177/1043986209350437

Lin, Z., & Li, J. (2005, August 15–17). *The online auction market in China: A comparative study between Taobao and eBay*. Proceeding ICEC '05 Proceedings of the 7th International conference on Electronic commerce (pp. 123–129), Xi'an.

Liu, C., & Lu, X. (2018). Analyzing hidden populations online: Topic, emotion, and social network of HIV-related users in the largest Chinese online community. *BMC Medical Informatics and Decision Making*, *18*(2). https://doi.org/10.1186/s12911-017-0579-1

Liu, Y. (2006). Word of mouth for movies: Its dynamics and impact on box office revenue. *Journal of Marketing*, *70*(July), 74–89. https://doi.org/10.1509/jmkg.70.3.074

Lu, H., Liang, B., & Taylor, M. (2010). A comparative analysis of cybercrimes and governmental law enforcement in China and the United States. *Asian Journal of Criminology*, *5*(2), 123–135. https://doi.org/10.1007/s11417-010-9092-5

Maimon, D., Santos, M., & Park, Y. (2019). Online deception and situations conducive to the progression of non-payment fraud. *Journal of Crime and Justice*, *42*(5), 516–535. https://doi.org/10.1080/0735648X.2019.1691857

Marolt, P., & Herold, D. K. (2015). *China online: Locating society in online spaces*. Routledge.

Mears, D. P., Reisig, M. D., Scaggs, S., & Holtfreter, K. (2016). Efforts to reduce consumer fraud victimization among the elderly: The effect of information access on program awareness and contact. *Crime and Delinquency*, *62*(9), 1235–1259. https://doi.org/10.1177/0011128714555759

Meng, B. (2011). From steamed bun to grass mud horse: E Gao as alternative political discourse on the Chinese internet. *Global Media and Communication*, *7*(1), 33–51. https://doi.org/10.1177/1742766510397938

Moskowitz, D. A., & Seal, D. W. (2010). "GWM looking for sex—serious only": The interplay of sexual ad placement frequency and success on the sexual health of "men seeking men" on Craigslist. *Journal of Gay & Lesbian Social Services*, *22*(4), 399–412. https://doi.org/10.1080/10538720.2010.491744

Motoyama, M., McCoy, D., Levchenko, K., Savage, S., & Voelker, G. M. (2011, November 2–4). *An analysis of underground forums*. IMC'11, Berlin, Germany.

Oliveri, R. C. (2010). Discriminatory housing advertisements on-line: Lessons from craigslist. *Indiana Law Review*, *43*, 1125–1183.

Park, Y., Jones, J., McCoy, D., Shi, E., & Jakobsson, M. (2014). *Scambaiter: Understanding targeted Nigerian scams on craigslist*. NDSS Symposium 2014, San Diego, California, USA.

Pratt, T. C., Holtfreter, K., & Reisig, M. D. (2010). Routine online activity and internet fraud targeting: Extending the generality of routine activity theory. *Journal of Research in Crime and Delinquency*, *47*(3), 267–296. https://doi.org/10.1177/0022427810365903

Radbod, S. T. (2010). Craigslist - A case for criminal liability for online service providers? *Berkeley Technology Law Journal*, *25*, 597–615.

Rege, A. (2009). What's love got to do with it? Exploring online dating scams and identity. *International Journal of Cyber Criminology*, *3*(2), 494–512.

Reyns, B. W. (2013). Online routines and identity theft victimization: Further expanding routine activity theory beyond direct-contact offenses. *Journal of Research in Crime and Delinquency*, *50* (2), 216–238. https://doi.org/10.1177/0022427811425539

Robinson, B. A., & Vidal-Ortiz, S. (2013). Displacing the dominant "down low" discourse: Deviance, same-sex desire, and Craigslist.Org. *Deviant Behavior*, *34*(3), 224–241. https://doi.org/10.1080/01639625.2012.726174

Rosenbaum, M. S., Daunt, K. L., & Jiang, A. (2013). Craigslist exposed: The internet-mediated hookup. *Journal of Homosexuality*, *60*(4), 505–531. https://doi.org/10.1080/00918369.2013.760305

Schackman, D. (2010). Commons or gated community? A theoretical explication of virtual community and the example of Craigslist. *Journal of Community Informatics*, *6*(2).

Song, X.-P., Hu, Z.-H., Du, J.-G., & Sheng, Z.-H. (2014). Application of machine learning methods to risk assessment of financial statement fraud: Evidence from China. *Journal of Forecasting*, *33*(8), 611–626. https://doi.org/10.1002/for.2294

Standing Committee of the National People's Congress. (2016). *Cybersecurity law of the People's Republic of China*. Effective date: June 1, 2017.

Stockmann, D., & Luo, T. (2017). Which social media facilitate online public opinion in China? *Problems of Post-Communism*, *64*(3–4), 189–202. https://doi.org/10.1080/10758216.2017.1289818

Sullivan, J., & Xie, L. (2009). Environmental activism, social networks, and the internet. *The China Quarterly*, *198*, 422–432. https://doi.org/10.1017/S0305741009000381

Tofighi, B., Perna, M., Desai, A., Gorv, C., & Lee, J. D. (2016). Craigslist as a source for heroin: A report of two cases. *Journal of Substance Use*, *21*(5), 543–546. https://doi.org/10.3109/14659891.2015.1090495

Van Wilsem, J. (2013). 'Bought it, but never got it' assessing risk factors for online consumer fraud victimization. *European Sociological Review*, *29*(2), 168–178. https://doi.org/10.1093/esr/jcr053

Wehinger, F. (2011). The dark net: Self-regulation dynamics of illegal online markets for identities and related services. *Intelligence and Security Informatics Conference*, 209–213.

Whitty, M. T., & Buchanan, T. (2012). The online romance scam: A serious cybercrime. *Cyberpsychology, Behavior and Social Networking*, *15*(3), 181–183. https://doi.org/10.1089/cyber.2011.0352

Wu, L., Zhang, J., & Zhao, M. (2014). The metabolism and growth of web forums. *PLoS One*, *9*(8). https://doi.org/10.1371/journal.pone.0102646

Xu, Y. (2016). Research on the application of informational investigation to WeChat fraud case (*Xinxihua zhencha zai weixin zhapian anjian zhong de yingyong tanxi*). *Journal of Hunan Police Academy*, *28*(3), 35–40.

Yang, G. (2011). *The power of the internet in China: Citizen activism online*. Columbia University Press.

Yang, J., Cheng, L., & Luo, X. (2009). A comparative study on e-banking services between China and USA. *International Journal of Electronic Finance*, *3*(3), 235–252. https://doi.org/10.1504/IJEF.2009.027848

Yar, M. (2013). *Cybercrime and society*. Sage.

Ye, N. (2004). Dimensions of consumer's perceived risk in online shopping. *Journal of Electronic Science and Technology of China*, *2*(3), 177–182.

Yip, M. (2011, June 14–17). *An investigation into Chinese cybercrime and the applicability of social network analysis*. ACM WebSci '11, Koblenz, Germany. https://eprints.soton.ac.uk/272351/2/yip_poster_2011.pdf

Yoon, C. (2010). Antecedents of customer satisfaction with online banking in China: The effects of experience. *Computers in Human Behavior, 26*(6), 1296–1304. https://doi.org/10.1016/j.chb.2010.04.001

Yuan, J., & Ye, Z. (2016). Causes of WeChat fraud crime and countermeasures (*Weixinzhapianfanzui de zhenchakunjing he pojieduicefenxi: Jiyu weixinzhapianfanzuianjiande xianshikaocha*). *Journal of Hebei Vocational College of Public Security Police, 16*(2), 21–26.

Zahedi, M. Z., Abbasi, A., & Yan, C. (2015). Fake-website detection tools: Identifying elements that promote individuals' use and enhance their performance. *Journal of the Association for Information Systems, 16*(6). https://aisel.aisnet.org/jais/vol16/iss6/2

Zhang, Y., Bian, J., & Zhu, W. (2013). Trust fraud: A crucial challenge for China's e-commerce market. *Electronic Commerce Research and Applications, 12*(5), 299–308. https://doi.org/10.1016/j.elerap.2012.11.005

Interrelationship between Bitcoin, Ransomware, and Terrorist Activities: Criminal Opportunity Assessment via Cyber-Routine Activities Theoretical Framework

Hannarae Lee and Kyung-Shick Choi

ABSTRACT

In recent years, a new form of cyber-extortion called ransomware is baffling the world with the speculation of connection to terrorist activities. Since cybercriminals usually demand their ransom using Bitcoin, Bitcoin has also become a part of this speculation. Unfortunately, however, all of the stories are based on anecdotal evidence. Therefore, the current study explores the dynamic properties of ransomware attacks, Bitcoin prices, and terrorist activities by connecting two opportunity-based theory frameworks: The Routine Activity Theory (RAT) and Cyber-Routine Activity Theory (Cyber-RAT). The findings of the study indicated unidirectional ties between the prevalence of ransomware and Bitcoin as well as ties between the prevalence of ransomware and terrorist activities. Several policies and prevention strategies from the overall findings of interrelated relations among three events are also presented.

Introduction

In recent years, a new form of cyber-extortion known as ransomware continues to leave the world feeling perplexed. Unlike most traditional forms of cybercrime, which thrive off operating undetected, ransomware demands the victim's attention and requires action. This often leaves the victim feeling extremely vulnerable and personally attacked. There are two main forms of ransomware in circulation: Locker-ransomware and Crypto-ransomware (Savage et al., 2015). Locker ransomware will lock computers by denying access to the computer or device, while crypto ransomware prevents access into the files or data.

Kharraz et al. (2015), who studied a collection of ransomware samples between 2006 and 2014, divided 1,359 ransomware samples into 15 different ransomware families based on distinct encryption, deletion, and communication techniques of each ransomware. Apart from locking or preventing access into the victims' computers and/or networks, some ransomware families encrypt the data and demand a decryption key in order to access computers or networks. Other ransomware families steal user information or change the browser settings while performing multiple malware installations. In addition, several ransomware families are even capable of deleting existing data (Kharraz et al., 2015). Generally, regardless of different forms and approaches, ransomware is designed to deny access to valuable information while holding the decryption key to extort millions and billions of dollars from individuals, businesses, and even governments.

According to Zetter (2015), ransomware has been around for more than two decades, but the development of ransom encryption software and Bitcoin have greatly facilitated the scheme. Bitcoin, which was introduced by Satoshi Nakamoto in 2008, is a fast, open-source, peer-to-peer cryptocurrency that relies on public-private key technology and a decentralized electronic clearing system (Choi, 2015; Kristoufek, 2015; Luther & Olson, 2014). Since online payment methods were not so readily available until the mid-2000s, cybercriminals received ransom using several different payment methods. For instance, victims transferred money using SMS text messages to premium numbers or by mailing prepaid cards (Richardson & North, 2017). Once the online payment system was available, victims sent ransom using Moneypak, Paysafecard, and Ukash cards (Kharraz et al., 2015). There were also reported cases where victims were forced to buy software packages in order to unlock their compromised computers, which provided limited possibilities to trace the money (Kharraz et al., 2015).

The invention of Bitcoin in 2008, however, has shifted the ransom payment methods due to its unique technical and privacy advantages, which allow criminals to hide behind their ransomware attacks (Zetter, 2015). The blockchain, the backbone of Bitcoin technology, serializes a record of all confirmed transactions through a distributed public ledger, which is irreversible (Liao et al., 2016). A decentralized feature of Bitcoin guarantees no ties to any nation's currency or economy, enabling pseudonymous transactions with low or no fees (Luther & Olson, 2014). Thus, even compared to the existing financial system, Bitcoin leverages users, including cybercriminals, to engage in irrevocable and supposedly hard-to-trace financial transactions. Consequently, within the first quarter of 2016, damages from U.S. ransomware attacks were estimated at 29 USD million, with annual damage reaching 1 USD billion. Since then, ransomware has been surging and the estimated cost of ransomware to global markets is forecasted up to 20 USD billion by 2021, up from 11.5 USD billion in 2019, 5 USD billion in 2017, and 325 USD million in 2015 (Morgan, 2019).

The proliferation of ransomware can also be connected to terrorist activities. An example of terrorist activity and its connection to ransomware would be the Albanian Hacker case. According to Johnson (2016), in August 2015, a ransomware attack under the username of Albanian Hacker demanded payment of two Bitcoin, which accounted for 500 USD at the time, from an Illinois Internet retailer in exchange for removing bugs from their computer. While seizing control of computers, Albanian Hacker generated a kill list used as one of the first kill lists issued by the Islamic State of Iraq and Syria (ISIS). The WannaCry attack and its relationship with the Lazarus Group, sponsored by the North Korean intelligence agency, is an additional bona fide example of terrorist activities against another nation utilizing a new technology. The WannaCry outbreak had shut down computers in more than 80 National Health Service organizations in England alone, resulting in, 600 general practices having to return to pen and paper, and five hospitals simply diverting ambulances to handle more emergency cases (Hern, 2017). The WannaCry 2.0 global ransomware attack also resulted in damage to massive amounts of computer hardware, the extensive loss of data, money, and other resources (U.S. Department of Justice, 2018).

Additionally, a report from CNN introduced a new funding mechanism (i.e., cyber-attacks) for the nation to supplement the defect from the traditional tools that have been blocked due to the international community's economic sanctions following its developing nuclear weapons (Berlinger & Cohen, 2017). Use of Bitcoin and other cryptocurrency by terrorist organizations and militant groups also have been identified. According to Encila (2019), Hamas, a Palestinian militant fundamentalist organization, had financed its operation using Bitcoin. The recent seizure of cryptocurrency from al-Qaeda, ISIS, and the al-Qassam Brigades, Hamas's military wing, by the U.S. Department of Justice (DOJ) also demonstrate how terrorist groups adopt the cyber age to finance their activities (U.S. DOJ, 2020). Lastly, the 2019 state and local government ransomware attacks in the United States may demonstrate a tie between ransomware and terrorist activities. All of these examples suggest that ransomware and Bitcoin are handy tools for meeting both the political and economic objectives of the government or terrorist groups.

Scholars have long debated the definition and scope of terrorism based on the specific purpose of the act, including political, religious, or economic gains (Bruce, 2013; Enders & Sandler, 2011; Juergensmeyer, 2017; Schmid & Jongman, 2017). In their seminal work, Enders and Sandler (2011) defined terrorism as "the premeditated use or threat to use violence by individuals or subnational groups to obtain a political or social objective through the intimidation of a large audience beyond that of the immediate victims" (p. 4). Juergensmeyer (2017) added the influence of religious belief on explaining terrorism as a symbolic expression of violence. While presenting the difficulty of defining the term terrorism, Schmid and Jongman (2017) provided their own definition of terrorism as "a method of combat in which random or symbolic victims serve as an instrumental *target of violence*" (p. 1) with further details regarding characteristics of victims. In addition, the U.S. legal code broadly defines both international and domestic terrorism to include violent acts or acts dangerous to human life that are a violation of the criminal laws of the United States or of any States (18U.S. Code § 2331).

As demonstrated, there is no universal definition of terrorism yet, and the debate over the meaning and scope of terrorism is beyond the scope of the current study. Instead, the current study explores the possible connections that terrorist activities carry with new technology-based crimes and financial sources; thus, we sought the definition that could capture a broad scope of acts in global terrain. To review the definition and the scope of terrorist activities, the authors examined seven different databases:

(1) the State Fragility Index and Matrix; (2) Armed Conflict and Intervention Dataset; (3) the American Terrorism Study; (4) the Extremist Crime Database; (5) the Global Terrorism Database (GTD); (6) European Values Study; and (7) RAND Database of Worldwide Terrorism Incidents. All seven datasets contain unique characteristics and distinct merits. Based on the inclusion of the global community, the length of data coverage, and coverages of violent acts, this study adopted the GTD data and its definition among other databases. According to the GTD from the National Consortium for the Study of Terrorism and Responses to Terrorism (START), terrorist activities are "the threatened or actual use of illegal force and violence by a non-state actor to attain a political, economic, religious, or social goal through fear, coercion, or intimidation" (National Consortium for the Study of Terrorism and Responses to Terrorism (START), 2019, p. 10).

Despite the growth and popularity of ransomware, Bitcoin, and potential links to terrorist activities, some scholars argued that there is little evidence that terrorists are utilizing ransomware or Bitcoin to finance their activities on a measurable scale (Baron, O'Mahony, Manheim, Dion-Schwarz, 2015; Goldman et al., 2017). Scholars argue that many known terrorist groups operate in areas with infrastructure too poor to utilize modern technology in efforts to launch their attacks or convert or trade Bitcoin to other resources (Goldman et al., 2017). Nevertheless, with existing loopholes in global regulatory standards along with readily available unlicensed and underserved money service businesses, cryptocurrencies may not be quite attractive enough to terrorists just yet (Baron et al., 2015; Goldman et al., 2017). These arguments would be correct for the early 2010s.

The speed of technology evolvement and adaptation by criminals, however, cannot be ignored. Cyber-terrorist attacks have been confirmed by security experts around the world over the past few years. The frequency of seeing terrorists using Bitcoin to finance their operations will not be diminished. Instead, it will be increased exponentially since ransomware and Bitcoin potentials are too great to ignore. The above examples of terrorist groups financing activities and government ransomware attacks would be great indicators to show how ransomware attacks and Bitcoin can be very useful tools in order to fulfill any objectives of government or illicit groups.

From this study, we are not arguing this new trend will fully replace the traditional financing tools. Instead, based on the Routine Activity Theory (RAT) from the Rational Choice framework and Cyber-Routine Activity Theory (Cyber-RAT), the authors assume that the opportunities arising from cyberspace provide a suitable environment (i.e., convergence of motivated offender, suitable target, and lack of capable guardianship) for ransomware, Bitcoin, and terrorist activities to simultaneously benefit and prosper.

To demonstrate and explore theoretical connections, the following section presents a theoretical overview and explains how prepositions of theories provide a reasonable opportunity structure for how ransomware, Bitcoin, and terrorist activities flourished in cyberspace. The next section presents the research methodology and data analysis. Finally, the study discusses the main findings along with potential policy and prevention strategies with study limitations and future implications.

Theoretical framework: RAT and Cyber-RAT

Technological advancement, especially the Internet, has transformed the social and economic processes of our daily lives. The Internet is global, instantaneous, intrinsically transborder, and digital while enabling automated information processing. Such positive characteristics of the Internet and technology advancement in the information age also create a unique opportunity structure for cybercrime. For instance, the global reach of the Internet with its deterritorialization capability, anonymity, and flexible network structure enables motivated offenders to plant the ransomware to victims' computers without direct interaction. Additionally, writing a code to infect one's computer no longer requires advanced computing knowledge. One can easily buy or copy a malignant code online and execute it by hitting the enter key. Besides, affecting one's computer with ransomware is not a one-on-one procedure. It is an automotive process that usually occurs in a massive and aggregative scale in the blink of an eye.

Based on these built-in opportunity structures from technical advancement, the authors draw on routine activity theory (RAT) and cyber-routine activity theory (C-RAT) to explore possible links among Bitcoin, ransomware, and terrorist activities. RAT, which has evolved from the rational choice framework, assumes a rational decision-making process by individuals seeking the most cost-effective means based on opportunities, costs, and benefits to achieve a specific goal (Cornish & Clarke, 1987). The theory predicts that changes in legitimate opportunity structures, such as technology innovation, can increase the convergence of motivated offenders and suitable targets in the absence of capable guardianship.

Reflecting the concepts of Cohen and Felson's RAT and Hindelang's Lifestyle Exposure Theory to individual victimizations of computer crimes called Cyber-Routine Activities Theory, Choi (2008) proposed an integrated theory, Cyber-RAT. While the original theory's focus is primarily on computer hacking, the theory has been applied to many different forms of cybercrimes, including ransomware (Choi et al., 2016). The unique characteristics of the Internet and opportunities driven from technological advancement provide the vast opportunity to the motived offenders and hinder law enforcement efforts to regulate or prevent the incidents from occurring.

To demonstrate the possible intertwined relationship among three variables of the study, we posit that the opportunity structure provided by cyberspace and theoretical explanations and tenets from RAT and Cyber-RAT are supplied to link ransomware attacks, terrorist activities, and the use of Bitcoin.

As Figure 1 demonstrated, this study assumes that addressed cyberspace characteristics provide a vast amount of opportunity to motivated offenders in cyberspace to target numerous suitable targets where capable guardianship, especially formal guardianship, is lacking. Since cyberspace enables the convergence of three tenets, the opportunity to commit crime also increases. By combining these assumptions with anecdotal speculation of ransomware, Bitcoin, and terrorist connections, this study explores possible intertwined relationships among three different events.

Motivated offenders and suitable targets in cyberspace

In their seminal work, Cohen and Felson (1979) assert that criminal inclination is a given thing, assuming all social actors carry no shortage of motivations. Such motivations are likely to convert to law-breaking acts when an appropriate opportunity arises (i.e., technological advancement). In terms of a suitable target, online users who connect to the Internet

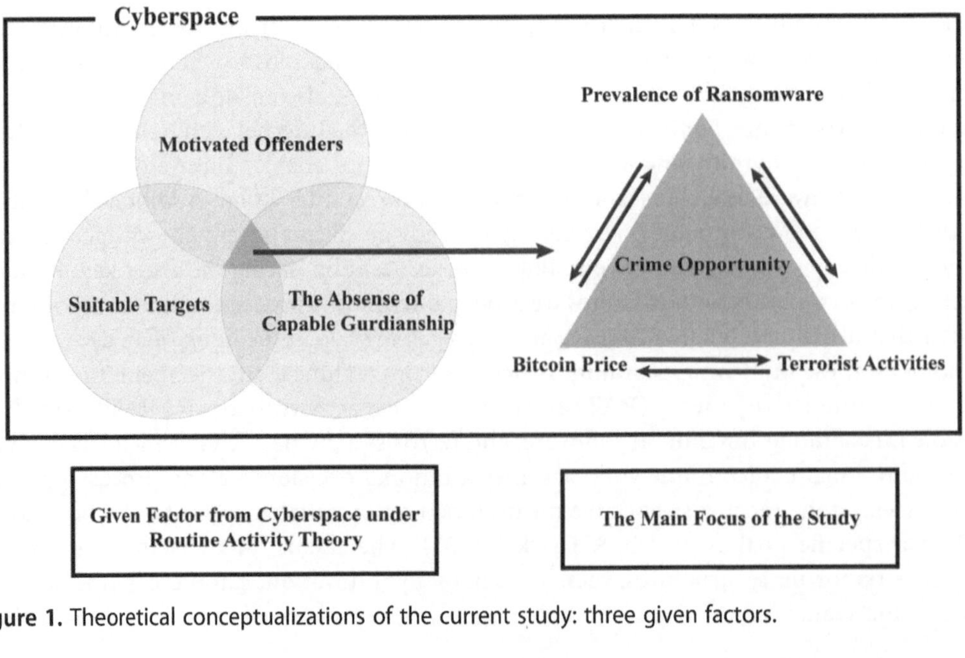

Figure 1. Theoretical conceptualizations of the current study: three given factors.

without precaution or equipping their machines with adequate computer security become easy prey for motivated offenders (Yar, 2005). To expand the explanation of target suitability, Felson and Boba (2010) stated that target suitability is likely to reflect four main criteria: The value of crime target, the inertia of crime target, the physical visibility of crime target, and the accessibility of crime target (VIVA).

In cyberspace, when an online user accesses the Internet, personal information in his or her computer naturally carries valuable information into cyberspace that attracts computer criminals. According to Symantec (2019), consumers were the main target of ransomware attacks, accounting for the majority of infections until 2017. Under the fear of losing their personal data and the lack of backup practices, individuals were willing to pay ransoms. Starting in 2017, businesses and government agencies have also become the top priority targets for ransomware attacks because they carry sensitive data, critical documents, and other pieces of vulnerable information (Symantec, 2019).

In the case of inertia, if criminals have sufficiently capable computer systems, the inertia of the crime target becomes almost weightless in cyberspace (Choi, 2008; Yar, 2005). Cybercriminals can easily find vulnerabilities to penetrate the entire network of agencies and departments that utilize out-of-date networks or servers without leaving a visible trace. Most institutions that contain costly data, such as financial institutions, educational institutions, political institutions, and religious institutions, are also vulnerable and are an easy target of ransomware if they do not have proper security mechanisms. Due to the addressed unique characteristics of the Internet that connects the world instantly, the target visibility and accessibility are also given features of the Internet and technical advancement. The prevalence and popularity of social media outlets are a great example that represents target visibility and accessibility in cyberspace.

Lack of capable guardianships in cyberspace

Regarding capable guardianship from RAT and Cyber-RAT, there is a conspicuous lack of capable formal guardianship in ransomware cases and the Bitcoin market. Even with the numerous countries' continuous legislative efforts, current legislation still lags behind the technical development. For example, the United Nations Office of Drugs and Crime's (UNODC) study (2013) on cybercrime indicated that while 80% of countries in Europe report sufficient criminalization of cybercrime acts, 60% of countries in other regions of the world report insufficiency of criminal code regarding cybercrime.

With substantive and procedural laws to regulate cybercrime, it must have proper enforcement strategies. Due to the volatile nature of data in cyberspace, officers who are investigating and collecting evidence require special knowledge and experience. According to Smith et al. (2004), a large number of cases referred for prosecution to U.S. federal authorities have been declined, primarily due to lack of evidence, which underlines the importance of resource allocation train officers. Due to the intrinsically boundary-transcending nature of cybercrime, mutual assistance in criminal matters by countries is vital. As indicated in the recent U.N. study (UNODC, 2013), many states agree to conform and cooperate, but the scope of its coverage is limited, and actual corporations are still questionable. The unique characteristics of the Internet and opportunities driven from technological advancement provide the vast opportunity to the motived offenders and hinder law enforcement efforts to regulate or prevent the incidents from occurring.

Besides, even with numerous countries' counterterrorism efforts, there are still loopholes in global regulatory standards (Goldman et al., 2017). Nonetheless, jurisdictional issues also contribute to a lack of capable guardianship in cases of ransomware, Bitcoin, and terrorist activities (Choi et al., 2016). Ransomware attacks that require payment in Bitcoin can be perpetrated by individuals, including terrorists, from anywhere in the world, including in areas outside the reach of one nation's jurisdiction. Therefore, investigations of ransomware or possible terrorist activities are incredibly challenging in the current stage.

Additionally, one can argue that having an anti-virus software might reduce the number of suitable targets in cyberspace while providing capable guardianship. It may be applicable to a particular type of cybercrime. However, in the case of ransomware, it is hard to protect one's computer from all the various ransomware families since they are capable of quickly transforming into another variety with a simple code change. An anti-virus software program cannot patch all ransomware varieties since the speed of new varieties usually exceeds the patching process of computer vaccine programs. Furthermore, it is also possible that a person's computer is already infected with malware, waiting for the cue sign by the offenders to execute the program.

Examples of RAT & Cyber-RAT convergence in cyberspace

As a result of the convergence of motivated offender, a suitable target, and lack of guardianship in cyberspace, many cybercrimes have been reported, including ransomware attacks. In 2019 alone, the U.S. experienced several government ransomware attacks, including Greenville, NC, Baltimore, MD, and 22 Texas State entities. Florida city case that paid 600,000 USD to the ransomware gang in order to take back their stolen data and Riviera City case that agreed to pay 941,000 USD to rebuild their entire computer network are other suitable examples (Cimpanu & Day, 2019).

Additionally, hospitals and other emergency services, such as law enforcement and fire departments, also contain valuable data. Especially in the case of a hospital, encrypting hospital data may quickly accelerate life or death situations, placing different levels of pressure to pay a ransom compared to average users. Other state agencies that use Multi-State Information Sharing systems are vulnerable and suitable prey for ransomware attacks (Mauraya et al., 2018). Furthermore, businesses and government organizations without adequate cybersecurity personnel were more susceptible to ransomware and likely to pay ransom to restore their networks and data (Mauraya et al., 2018).

Along with technical advancement, the recent COVID-19 pandemic also provides unprecedented opportunities to motivated offenders by making several critical infrastructures more visible than any other target during the pandemic. According to Grobman (2020) and European Union's Law Enforcement Agency's (2020), the recent Coronavirus pandemic has made several hospitals, governments, and universities more concerned and more likely to pay ransomware attacks. These crucial infrastructures and governments are more visible than any other target during the pandemic due to high monetary value, and high accessibility with no physical obstacles, since attacks happen within cyberspace.

Since utilizing cyber-resources is a low-risk strategy available to motivated offenders who plan to engage in criminal activities, we hypothesize that the prevalence of ransomware and the popularity of Bitcoin are interrelated and may connect to terrorist activities as possible financing sources. Even though the current study is not testing two theories directly using proposed data and methods, we formulated the following methodological frameworks to empirically assess criminal opportunities based on the insights from theories.

Methodological frameworks: criminal opportunity assessment

Ransomware and Bitcoin

One of Bitcoin's main features is guaranteeing pseudo-anonymity to its users. In other words, Bitcoin does not guarantee complete anonymity since the fundamental technology, blockchain, allows all the transaction records to be visible to the public. A person may hide his or her identity using pseudonyms, but his or her identity can be identified by public keys (i.e., Bitcoin addresses). While Bitcoin addresses alone are not explicitly tied to any real-world entities, a number of recent research efforts have shown that monetary movements and address links can be traced when real-world information and quasi-identifiers found on the Internet are imputed to users' Bitcoin addresses (Androulaki et al., 2013; Reid & Harrigan, 2013; Ron & Shamir, 2013). For example, addresses can be tied to forum usernames, anonymous online marketplaces, Bitcoin exchanges, and popular Bitcoin services (Liao et al., 2016).

If cybercriminals use Bitcoin, then it is possible to trace the transaction history using Bitcoin addresses and real-world information along with listed quasi-identifiers. It is possible, however, if and only if cybercriminals are using the same Bitcoin address for an extended period of time to collect large quantities of ransoms. In reality, however, cybercriminals are smart enough to conceal their tracks. According to Kharraz et al. (2015), who traced the transactions of 1,872 Bitcoin addresses that were used during the Cryptolocker attack, in order to better conceal the criminal activity, cybercriminals tend to use a short activity period, small Bitcoin amounts, and a small number of transactions. Since cybercriminals use multiple independent addresses with small amounts of Bitcoin, tracing the transaction history is considerably challenging.

Even though tracing all cybercriminals or cyberterrorists may not be plausible, from our theoretical connection to apparent ties between ransomware and Bitcoin, it is reasonable to assume that when ransomware is prevalent, Bitcoin transactions are also prevalent. Thus, the authors are assuming the following hypothesis:

H1: The ransomware prevalence affects the Bitcoin transaction, (i.e., Bitcoin prices).

Since there is no prior empirical study that demonstrates the causal relationship between ransomware and Bitcoin, there is also a possibility that Bitcoin prices influence ransomware prevalence; thus, we also examined bi-directional relationships between the two using the following hypothesis:

H2: Bitcoin prices affect the prevalence of ransomware.

Terrorist activities and technology

Due to stated distinct architectural advantages, ransomware and Bitcoin have become an attractive and lucrative revenue stream for cybercriminals and possibly for terrorists. The recent raid by the DOJ that confiscated cryptocurrency from three known terrorist groups would be a great example (U.S. DOJ, 2020). As Barratt (2012) indicated, distinct technical and systematic environments of ransomware and Bitcoin provide a new playground for organized crime and money laundering. Even with the evidence of terrorist activities that connect ransomware and Bitcoin use, there are a limited number of studies that examined such relationships. To fill these research gaps and provide empirical evidence of possible connections between terrorist activities and ransomware, along with Bitcoin, this study examines the following hypotheses:

H3: The ransomware prevalence affects the terrorist activities.

H4: Bitcoin prices affect terrorist activities.

To examine the causal relationship, we also examined bi-directional relationships of above hypotheses:

H5: Terrorist activities affect the prevalence of ransomware.

H6: Terrorist activities affect Bitcoin prices.

Figure 2 represents the six proposed relationships of the study to demonstrate the casual relationship among the prevalence of ransomware, Bitcoin price, and terrorist activities.

According to the anecdotal argument, the prevalence of ransomware is closely related to Bitcoin price (H1), which may fund terrorist activities (H4). This assertion, however, has never been empirically tested. Thus, it is also possible that other relationships (H2, H3, H5, and H6) can explain the interrelationship among three different events. Therefore, by exploring these six proposed hypotheses, the current study demonstrates possible causal relationships among three different events. All six hypotheses also represent one overall question: Whether ransomware and Bitcoin are salient factors that impact terrorist activities.

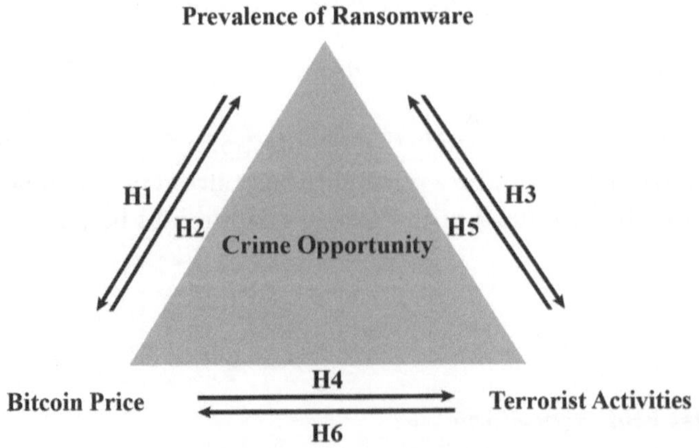

Figure 2. Hypotheses: interrelationships among ransomware, Bitcoin, and terrorist activities.

Data

To analyze the dynamic properties of ransomware prevalence, Bitcoin prices, and terrorist activities, three different data sources were utilized: Google Trends, Yahoo Financial data, and the Global Terrorism Database (GTD).

Google trends data: ransomware

Locating all varieties and occurrences of the exact dates and places of ransomware is impossible at the current stage. A computer or system may already be infected with ransomware varieties but in its dormancy until it receives the execution signal. In addition, technological development may generate new variations of ransomware that no one is aware of at the current stage. Therefore, instead of getting a direct measure of ransomware frequency, the authors utilized a proxy measure of prevalence by using search queries from a popular search engine: *Google Trend*. Another popular and well-known search website, Wikipedia, has a publicly available search query data. Unlike Google Trends, however, Wikipedia search queries do not provide worldwide search results. Therefore, the current study only examined Google Trends data.

The Internet search trends have been applied to demonstrate the public's interest and awareness in various areas (Drake et al., 2012; Glaser et al., 2014; Moat et al., 2013; Preis et al., 2010). In financial literature, researchers found a positive relationship between online search volumes and various financial indicators such as the attractiveness of a consumer consumption, trading stock, firm equity values, and the portfolio diversifications (Dimpfl & Jank, 2016; Drake et al., 2012; Moat et al., 2013; Preis et al., 2010; Vosen & Schmidt, 2011). Vosen and Schmidt (2011), who compared the online search queries and survey-based consumption indicators, found that search query data provide more predictive information compared to existing survey-based indicators.

The use of search query data also provides predictive information on the stock market. According to Dimpfl and Jank (2016), there is a strong co-movement of the Dow Jones' volatility and the volume of search queries for its name. Kristoufek (2013, 2015) also has demonstrated that Bitcoin's price correlates with conventional online behavioral metrics such as Google search. These findings represent that individuals' interest in a particular term, lead them to search for the inquiry, and such inquiry carries the power of predictability. Therefore, under the assumption that the frequency of search queries can gauge the prevalence of different types of ransomware, we utilized the Google Trends search queries of ransomware as a proxy measure of ransomware prevalence. Since the scope of Bitcoin prices and terrorist activities data capture worldwide incidents, the authors also utilized worldwide query results instead of results from a specific nation.

Figure 3 illustrated an overview of three events between August 2010 and December 2017. The prevalence of ransomware data from Google Trends indicated no search trends for ransomware for the first 18 months from August 2010 to January 2012, and the search reached its peak in May 2017. The study chose to analyze data between August 2010 and December 2017 to include the start point for Bitcoin data and to show the variation of ransomware prevalence, which includes its peak in mid-2017, (i.e., the case of WannaCry). Google Trends series are monthly normalized data that the maximum values

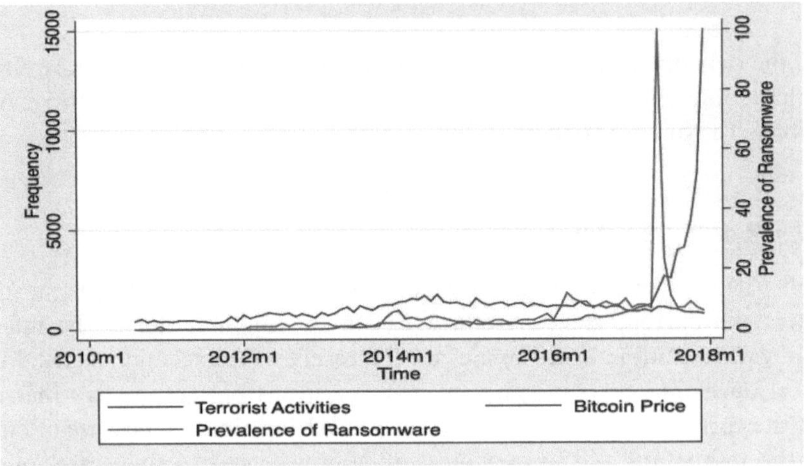

Figure 3. Ransomware, Bitcoin, and terrorist activities from 2010 to 2017.

of the series are equal to 100; thus, the daily terrorist activities data and daily Bitcoin price data were aggregated to monthly data.

Bitcoin data

To measure the changes in Bitcoin prices, we collected the daily Bitcoin trading data from the Yahoo Financial website: (https://finance.yahoo.com/quote/BTC-USD/history/) from August 2010 to December 2017; then, it was aggregated to a monthly format. Due to the skewness of the closing price of Bitcoin, we transformed the data using the natural log for the analyses.

Terrorism data

Among several publicly available terrorism databases, we chose the Global Terrorism Database (GTD) for several reasons. First, compared to other datasets such as the American Terrorism Study and the Extremist Crime Database, which covers the United States only, the GTD covers world-wide terrorist incidents.

Secondly, as indicated in the literature review section, the definition of terrorism varies, and so does coverage of existing databases. Many terrorism databases, such as the State Fragility Index and Matrix and Armed Conflict and Intervention Dataset, limit the scope of incidents related to political issues or agendas. According to the U.S. legal codes, however, the scope of terrorism can go above and beyond political issues. Lastly, the current study provides a preliminary analysis of relationships among ransomware, Bitcoin, and terrorist activities. Therefore, instead of limiting the scope of the terrorism activities to politically driven incidents, we chose the GTD, which includes both physical terrorist activities and various forms of cyberterrorism. For more details about the data and data collection methods, please visit the START website.

Table 1. Descriptive statistics.

	N	M	SD	Min	Max
Prevalence of Ransomware	89	4.33	10.95	0.00	100.00
Bitcoin Log Closing Price	89	4.99	3.01	−2.78	9.62
Terrorist Activity	89	927.57	331.47	336.00	1729.00

N represents a total of the number of months included in the data from August 2010 to December 2017.

Among various variables the GTD offers, the current study aggregated the frequency of daily incidents to monthly incidents. There was a total of 84,078 reported terrorist activities between August 2010 and December 2017.

Table 1 indicated the detailed descriptive statistics for each measure. A total of 101-month-data was utilized to analyze the relationship among the prevalence of ransomware, Bitcoin prices, and terrorist activities. As indicated, due to the skewness of the data, Table 1 showed the log of Bitcoin closing price rather than actual trading prices. The actual closing price of Bitcoin indicated a wide range of changes from less than a dollar in August 2010 to 15,034.53 USD in December 2017. For 89 months, there were a total of 84,078 reported terrorist activities between August 2010 and December 2017. The lowest number of terrorist activities were reported in August 2011 with 336 incidents, while the highest number of cases were reported in July 2014 with 1,729 incidents. According to the data, there was no single terror-free day for the given time period.

Analytic models

The aim of the analyses was two-fold. As Figure 2 demonstrated, the study explored a criminal opportunity assessment based on causal relationships among ransomware prevalence, Bitcoin prices, and terrorist activities. Thus, the current study required to run a model that allowed us to examine three recursive relationships between interdependent variables: (1) H1 and H2; (2) H3 and H5; and (3) H4 and H6. Each model needed to explore whether one variable's past behaviors are useful for predicting future behaviors of another variable (i.e., These models examined the bi-directionality of two variables). The second aim of the study was to explore the overall relationships of all three events during a seven-year frame. Thus, the study chose models that enable us to examine overall interrelation among three different events: The prevalence of ransomware, Bitcoin, and terrorist activities.

To fulfill two aims and four different relationships, rather than using more traditional multiple regression models, the authors ran the vector error correction model (VECM). VECM allows us to treat the variables as jointly endogenous, without creating an ad hoc model restriction by separating them as endogenous and exogenous variables among the non-stationary time series (Johansen, 1995). Since the VECM was estimated by OLS and test statistics may be prone to inconsistencies, a battery of diagnostic tests, including serial correlation, heteroscedasticity misspecification of functional form, and normality of residuals, were also performed.

Results

Conventional regression estimators encounter problems when applied to a non-stationary process since the regression of two independent random-walk processes would yield a spurious significant coefficient, even if they were not related (Granger & Newbold, 1974). To check the stationarity of the variable and the presence of unit-root, we performed the Augmented Dickey-Fuller test (ADF). ADF has a null hypothesis of a unit root, which indicates that the variables follow a non-stationary process. If the series is stationary after differencing once, it is integrated of order 1 or I (1). The alternative hypothesis is that the series was generated by a stationary process, which indicates that the series is integrated into an order of zero of I (0).

Table 2 demonstrated the outcomes of the stationary and unit-root test from the ADF test. All three variables exhibited the presence of a unit-root. Given non-stationary variables, we can model their relationship using a vector autoregressive model by taking the first difference of each time series. Nevertheless, this approach can suffer misspecification biases if cointegration is present. Thus, to analyze the dynamic properties and interconnections between the series, the author assumed a potential cointegration relationship. To test for the cointegration relationships, we utilized the trace and the likelihood tests of Johansen. The trace test indicated that there is one cointegration relation with a lag length of 8.

Table 3 and Figure 4 showed the outcomes of the first six hypotheses of the study. Table 3 provided the χ^2 statistics with the associated *p*-value, representing the joint significance of the dependent and independent variables.

According to Table 3 and Figure 4, we found the support for H1 (the impact of ransomware prevalence on Bitcoin price) and H3 (the impact of ransomware prevalence on terrorist activities), but failed to find support for H2 (the influence of Bitcoin price on ransomware prevalence), H4 (the influence of Bitcoin price on terrorist activities), H5 (the impact of terrorist activities on ransomware prevalence), and H6 (the impact of terrorist activities on Bitcoin price).

Table 4 provided the Johansen normalization restriction-imposed model, indicating the overall impact of all three measures of the study. It also provided the t-statistics associated with the error correction term (ECT) to demonstrate the long-run causality, (i.e., the overall interrelated impact of all three events over time). According to the ECT term, we found a salient impact of the prevalence of ransomware and Bitcoin prices on overall terrorist

Table 2. Stationary and unit-root tests.

	ADF	p-value	Stationary/Unit-root
Terrorist Activity	−0.524	> .05	Not stationary & Unit-root
Bitcoin Monthly Log Price	−1.677	> .05	Not stationary & Unit-root
Ransomware Google Trends Queries	2.215	> .05	Not stationary & Unit-root

Table 3. VECM short-run causality test: terrorist activity, Bitcoin, and ransomware.

	Independent Variables		
Dependent Variable	ΔRansomware	ΔLog of Price	ΔTerror
ΔRansomware	-	1.69	6.21
ΔLog of Price	19.99*	-	7.87
ΔTerror	16.51*	5.56	-

*** $p < .001$, ** $p < .01$, * $p < .05$
The model contains 1 cointegration, Lag length k = 8

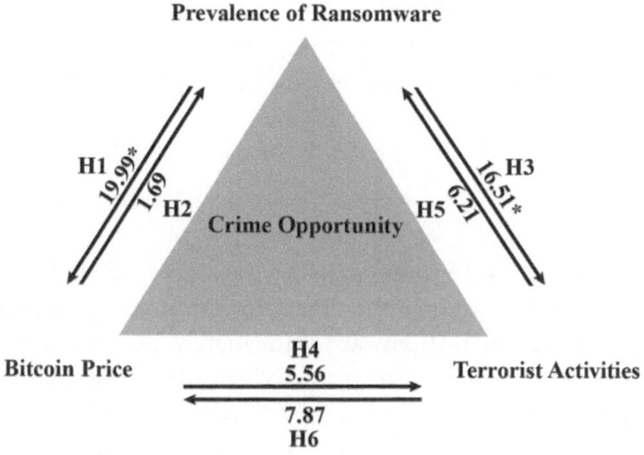

Figure 4. Results: interrelationships among ransomware, Bitcoin, and terrorist activities.
Notes: *** $p < .001$, ** $p < .01$, * $p < .05$

Table 4. VECM long-run causality test: terrorist activity, Bitcoin, and ransomware.

	Independent Variables			
Dependent Variable	ΔRansomware	ΔLog of Price	ΔTerror	ECT
ΔRansomware	-	−3.33**	0.02**	−0.02
ΔLog of Price	−0.30**	-	−0.01**	0.01**
ΔTerror	57.91**	−192.92**	-	−0.43**

*** $p <.001$, ** $p < .01$, * $p < .05$
The model contains 1 cointegration, Lag length k = 8

activities with the convergence speed of 43% from the previous month's error from terrorist activities within the current month. Since the current study is exploratory in nature, instead of specifying or weighting different types of terrorist activities, the authors utilized the frequency of the act. Therefore, the outcomes could not explain how funds generated from ransomware and Bitcoin were used for terrorist activities. Rather, the findings suggested the presence of interrelation.

Limitations and suggestions for the future study

As indicated in the theoretical framework section, instead of applying RAT and Cyber-RAT to examine the relationship among variables of interest, we posited the tenets of RAT and Cyber-RAT are provided based on the opportunity structure of the cyberspace and the current status of regulating systems. This is a strong assumption that may require further investigation.

Due to several limitations of data, the current study could not directly measure and assess the proposed relationships, especially the impact of actual ransomware. As previously stated, locating all varieties and occurrences of the exact dates and places of ransomware is impossible at the current stage. Therefore, instead of finding a direct measure, the authors utilized a proxy measure. Since the current study used the search query data as a proxy measure of ransomware for the first time, we invite other scholars to examine the quality and applicability of this proxy measure.

This study is an exploratory study examining the impact of ransomware and Bitcoin on a variety of terrorist activities without specifying types of terrorist activities. Therefore, it would be ideal if future scholars can differentiate the impact of ransomware on different types of terrorist activities.

Discussion

The current study assessed how terrorist activities are associated with ransomware attacks and Bitcoin prices for understanding the emerging criminal opportunity. The findings indicate that the prevalence of ransomware immediately influences both Bitcoin prices and terrorist activities. Additionally, terrorist activities are substantially impacted by both the prevalence of ransomware and Bitcoin prices, reflecting a 7-year cycle in the data. Reflecting rational choice theoretical concepts, utilizing cyber-resources is a low-risk strategy available to motivated perpetrators who plan to engage in terrorist activities (Guerette, 2010). In other words, as an offender encounters a higher level of the perceived risk of terrorism activity, the likelihood of achieving the goal will be reduced to reflect the potential costs involved. Furthermore, cyber-terrorist attacks have been confirmed by security experts around the world over the past few years. This shows that a ransomware attack is a very useful weapon for meeting both the political and economic objectives of the government. Furthermore, recent research also indicated that online lifestyle and cybersecurity have a direct influence on cyberterrorism activities, including ransomware victimizations (Choi, 2015; Choi et al., 2016).

In a similar vein, the overall influence of the prevalence of ransomware on Bitcoin prices and terrorist activities also suggests the anecdotal speculation of the ties between terrorist activities and sources of new funding mechanisms. Even though the current measure of ransomware does not directly measure the actual prevalence and frequency of ransomware, the findings should alert both law enforcement agencies and policymakers to be proactive toward enforcing and regulating the ransomware and Bitcoin.

Another interesting finding of the study is about ransomware and Bitcoin prices (H1 and H2). Since its debut in 2008, Bitcoin has been notoriously known for its volatility. According to the Bitcoin price index, the fluctuation of the Bitcoin market has been bearish to bullish and bullish to bearish. The cost of trading in August 2010 was below 1 USD per Bitcoin, which rocketed to 17,000 USD in December 2017 and dropped to 3,200 USD in December 2018. Therefore, the majority of Bitcoin literature discusses the monetary value of Bitcoin or the place of Bitcoin in the financial market (Böhme et al., 2015; Glaser et al., 2014; Yermack, 2015). There is, however, no consensus on how Bitcoin's monetary value should be determined nor where the Bitcoin fits in the financial market. These instabilities may drive some people out of the use of Bitcoin. Outcomes of the study, however, indicated that ransomware attacks influence Bitcoin prices while the changes in Bitcoin prices do not affect the ransomware attacks. This suggests that even with this vulnerability issue, most ransomware demands the ransom be paid using Bitcoin.

According to Goldman et al. (2017), following the money and blocking access to the formal financial system has been considered one of the most effective strategies to degrade terrorist activities. For example, by seizing suspected bank accounts, a government can cut the circulation of terrorists' financial funds. Currently, a government cannot block access to

Bitcoin by a particular user. This freedom of accessibility may also explain the use of Bitcoin as the primary source of ransom.

According to the U.S. Department of the Treasury's National Terrorist Financing Risk Assessment (NATFRA), the banking system and money are still the primary sources of finance for the terrorists who may target the United States, and Bitcoin does not present a significant threat at scale (U.S. Department of the Treasury, 2018). The findings of this current study, however, suggest reconsidering the importance of Bitcoin from illegal activities like a ransomware attack. The WannaCry incidents would be an ample set of cases. Thus, instead of waiting until the next big thing to happen, we should be proactive by imposing regulations and policies to control and prevent any future incidents. To accommodate the need, the authors recommend and propose policies and prevention strategies in the next section.

Policy and prevention strategies

Strategies for emerging threats

The findings indicate that ransomware attacks and Bitcoin price changes are interrelated with the overall terrorist activities, which broadly include both physical terrorist activities and various forms of cyberterrorism such as funding, recruitment, and propaganda indicated in the Global Terrorism Database. Particularly, this study is dedicated to the assessment of the suggested relationship and offers the trend of terrorism, which can facilitate government agencies and the public in order to have a better understanding of emerging threats, new trends of cyber-terrorism, and prevention strategies.

According to a 2017 CNN special report titled *The secrets behind Kim Jong Un's personal piggy bank*, North Korea has traditionally raised illicit funds to maintain its regime through counterfeiting, drug distribution, and money laundering (Berlinger & Cohen, 2017). However, North Korea has recently been struggling to raise funds smoothly due to the economic sanctions imposed by the international community following its development of nuclear weapons. The North Korean government's financial difficulties have led to a surge in cyber-attacks on banks and other companies within the United States and around the world. North Korea now generates between 500 USD million to 1 USD billion in illegal funds annually from criminal and illegal profits such as ransomware attacks, bank hacking, arms sales, drug handling, counterfeiting, and even trafficking of endangered species.

In order to decrease the effects of cyber terrorists, a deterrence strategy must be amended in efforts to impede the success of their terrorism plots strategically. Generally, cyber terrorists are widely successful not only because laws have not caught up to speed with the Internet, but also because of their advanced skills (Choi, 2015). As Choi (2015) suggested, because the cyberworld is ever-evolving, law enforcement in cyberspace lacks adequate training as well as staffing. Since most local and state law enforcement officers lack knowledge concerning the processing of computer data and related evidence, which would be necessary for effective cybercrime investigations, more specialized cybercrime investigation training programs are warranted to meet the needs of local and state law enforcement agencies.

In efforts to have the costs outweigh the benefits of cyberterrorism, governments around the world should implement an arms control policy within cyberspace. Though a policy like this can be beneficial, it can often be extremely complicated to establish within the cyberworld. According to Borghard and Lonergan (2018), who touched upon four main reasons as to why traditional arms control regimes are not appropriately pertinent to the cyberworld, implementing a policy like this into cyberspace can be difficult for several reasons. First, it can be challenging to measure how strong a country is, precisely its cyber capabilities. Second, due to technological innovations' rapid development, it can be challenging to predict cyber capabilities and complicate the process of establishing policies. Third, it can be strenuous when attempting to develop compliance amongst nations because it would require them to share private government information, which can exploit vulnerabilities and allow other countries to capitalize on said vulnerabilities. Lastly, it can be difficult to enforce as well as punish the breaking of established policies. Even if it may seem to be too challenging to construct a universal legal framework, establishing a cyber arms control regime can help to enforce, monitor, as well as mitigate the act of cyberterrorism. This requires international cooperation and constant efforts from government agencies, private sectors, and educational institutes.

As Nye (2015) indicated, implementing a policy like this can help to establish an agreement between nations in efforts to help diminish criminal acts within the cyberworld. For example, countries could agree not to target or attack certain sectors of civilian infrastructure. According to the UN (as cited in Nye, 2015), they recommended that each nation's government should accept responsibility when another nation seeks help due to an attack, nations should agree to not interfere with emergency response teams that are assisting other nations who fell victim to a cyber-attack, and lastly, to increase the amount of transparency between nations in regards to their cyber policies.

In tandem with an arms control policy, valuable in-depth training should be provided to governmental agencies. The USA v. Ardit Ferizi case revealed that military members' personal information was compromised due to their error of utilizing military e-mail addresses on websites that should not have been used. This would incorporate the improvement of their online lifestyles, which asserts the cyber-routine activities theory premise and would better decrease their chances of becoming victimized by cyberterrorists. In addition, the current study suggests that ransomware events fuel a significant increase in Bitcoin prices, potentially associated with terrorist activities. Monitoring changes in Bitcoin prices and ransomware attacks appears to be necessary in order for a potential diagnosis of other terrorist activities.

According to the FireEye report (2020), the median global dwell time of external and internal cyber-attacks is 141 days and 56 days, respectively. In the given time between the initial breach and detection, the major computer systems and data are compromised or encrypted. The report predicts that the significant threats of ransomware from established cybercrime groups will continue to monetize access to victim environments as a primary source of generating revenue.

The system and data backup are crucial, however, it may be a short term strategy considering extensive cleansing, recovery, and investigation time. Thus, organizations in both the public and private sectors need to rapidly respond to the impact of a cyber-attack. Constructing a robust incident response plan is vital to proactively prevent a catastrophic cyber-attack. Witty et al. (2019) suggest "Three Phases for Best-Practice Implementation". Phase 1 includes planning activities, which means organizations need to understand the characteristics of a cyber-attack and its potential organizational impact. Forming organizational cyber-attack response teams and establishing strong crisis management and communications processes are essential to boost the organization's capability to control the damage of a potential cyber-attack and ensure collaboration throughout all phases of the incident cycle. Phase 2 contains response and recovery activities, which requires the incident response team to advise the crisis management team lead, which designates an incident commander for the organization's overall management of the incident. Monitoring the timeline of the response and assessing the integrity of applications and data backups for recovery should follow with performing forensics check on all backups. The stand-down phase is the final stage of performing checkups to ensure the safe business and IT operations environment and conduct a review of the response and recovery processes for future improvement. Implementing the foundation of an effective incident response plan in organizations is one of the most viable action plans to keep the system and data safe, secure, and to remove the potential for future cyber terrorist attacks.

The most significant way to minimize cyber-threats within the state and local level would be through active community engagement to raise awareness of potential cybercrime activities on the Internet (Choi, 2010, 2015). Local and state law enforcement agencies should inform their citizens to be alert of suspicious online activity and to encourage them to report such behavior to a dedicated cybercrime investigation unit. Ideally, law enforcement agencies would train a community network on how to recognize potential cybercriminals and to report suspicious activities to law enforcement agencies. This type of effort would increase the reporting of cyber-attacks.

Educational strategies for public

Currently, there is no particular policy or detailed regulation that targets and/or enforces the issues regarding neither a ransomware attack nor Bitcoin. Instead, the U.S. government publishes recommendations when an incident occurs. For instance, right after the Texas Government Ransomware attack, U.S. Department of Homeland Security Cyber Infrastructure (CISA), Multi-State Information Sharing & Analysis Center (MS-ISAC), National Governors Association (NGA), and the National Association of State Chief Information Officers (NASCIO), generated the Federal Ransomware Tip Sheet (2019). This brief tip sheet reminds state and local government agencies to back-up the system daily, reinforce necessary cybersecurity awareness and education, and revisit and refine cyber incident response plans (2019). All these recommendations, however, assume that employees already know how to patch the system, back-up files, and are aware of cyber incident response plans. In addition, it implies that agencies have already implemented the training sessions or workshops to reassure the recommendations. It may be the case in state agencies, but may not be a standard in other segments of society. Therefore, the current paper emphasizes the importance of standardized, up-to-date, and regular training to educate everyone in an entity or an agency.

While governments are working toward making their efforts to impose regulations and policies, other entities and agencies can either initiate or reiterate prevention protocols through the Security Education, Training, and Awareness (SETA) program. According to D'Arcy et al. (2009), who studied the number of security breaches that involved internal misuse of information systems, if users are aware of the consequences of misuse with certainty and severity, especially sanctions, through the SETA program, it reduces the misuse incidents. The content of SETA programs can be modified to fit the missions and goals of any entity as long as the essential basic aspects of training are included. If entities or agencies already implemented a training program, they need to revisit the current programs and offer standard up-to-date training and workshops on a regular basis rather than once or twice a year recommended training. The SETA programs have to, at minimum, remind and teach all participants on how to keep the antivirus software up to date by patching the system whenever the new patches are available, teach them how to back-up files and make them do it almost daily, and teach them how to filter a possible spam mail with malware.

Some may argue that updating the current security system to the state-of-the-art level would reduce both prevalence and frequency of ransomware attacks. Since criminals can circumvent the most modern systems, it is almost impossible to prevent incidents solely by relying on technology. Also, updating to the new system can be quite costly, especially if individuals or entities do not have a spare budget. Therefore, investing money in the new system would not solve the problem. Instead, we should pay attention to continued and rigorous training and educational programs (Choi, 2010, 2015). Another aspect of civilian education is concerned with providing general knowledge of cybersecurity. Informing the public of the importance of securing home wireless networks the most straightforward way – by employing strong passwords protection for Internet access – can potentially minimize the risk of cybercrime victimization.

Conclusion

There is continued speculation about the relationship between technological advancement and terrorist activities. Notably, a wide range of ransomware attacks and Bitcoin use has been speculated to finance terrorist activities. In addition, ransomware victimization examples from individuals to basic infrastructures to businesses to government agencies indicate that danger can escalate from paying the ransom to restoring the crucial data to affecting basic infrastructures and possibly national security issues. Unfortunately, however, all of the stories are based on anecdotal evidence.

Thus, using the VECM, which allowed us to model the bidirectional causality between pairs of variables and long-term dependencies between variables, the current paper explored the possible association among ransomware prevalence, Bitcoin prices, and terrorist activities. Due to several limitations of data, we could not directly measure and assess the proposed relationships. The current exploratory approach, however, provides valuable insight for future studies.

As assumed from the anecdotal evidence, findings indicated a unidirectional tie from ransomware prevalence to terrorist activities and another tie from ransomware prevalence to Bitcoin price. In addition, a salient impact of the prevalence of ransomware and Bitcoin prices on overall terrorist activities also warrant the need for policies that can regulate ransomware and Bitcoin. Thus, the authors assert the need for an arms control policy, an effective incident response plan, and valuable in-depth training to protect and prevent emerging threats. The authors also suggest a semi-mandatory training and workshops of the best practices by cybersecurity professionals who are up to date on the new varieties of ransomware and recommend strengthening the human firewall aspects of any organizations or agencies. The outcome of these approaches will not be instant but will gradually pay off the efforts and money invested.

Disclosure statement

No potential conflict of interest was reported by the author(s).

References

Androulaki, E., Karame, G. O., Roeschlin, M., Scherer, T., & Capkun, S. (2013). Evaluating user privacy in bitcoin. In A. R. Sadeghi (Ed.), *Financial cryptography and data security* (pp. 34–51). Springer.

Baron, J., O'Mahony, A., Manheim, D., & Dion-Schwarz, C. (2015). *National security implications of virtual currency: Examining the potential for non-state actor deployment.* Rand Corporation. https://www.rand.org/content/dam/rand/pubs/research_reports/RR1200/RR1231/RAND_RR1231.pdf

Barratt, M. J. (2012). Silk road: Ebay for drugs. *Addiction*, *107*(3), 683. https://doi.org/10.1111/j.1360-0443.2011.03709.x

Berlinger, J., & Cohen, Z. (2017, July 20). *The secrets behind Kim jong un's personal piggy bank.* CNN. https://www.cnn.com/2017/06/20/politics/north-korea-illicit-money/index.html

Böhme, R., Christin, N., Edelman, B., & Moore, T. (2015). Bitcoin: Economics, technology, and governance. *Journal of Economic Perspectives*, *29*(2), 213–238. https://doi.org/10.1257/jep.29.2.213

Borghard, E. D., & Lonergan, S. W. (2018, January 16). *Why are there no cyber arms control agreements?* Council on Foreign Relations.

Bruce, G. (2013). Definition of terrorism social and political effects. *Journal of Military and Veterans Health*, *21*(2), 26–30. https://jmvh.org/article/definitionof-terrorism-social-and-political-effects/

Choi, K. S. (2008). Computer crime victimization and integrated theory: An empirical assessment. *International Journal of Cyber Criminology*, *2*(1), 308–333. https://www.cybercrimejournal.com/Choiijccjan2008.htm

Choi, K. S. (2010). *Risk factors in computer crime victimization.* LFB Scholarly Publishing.

Choi, K. S. (2015). *Cybercriminology and digital investigation.* LFB Scholarly Publishing.

Choi, K. S., Scott, T. M., & LeClair, D. P. (2016). Ransomware against police: Diagnosis of risk factors via application of cyber-routine activities theory. *International Journal of Forensic Science & Pathology*, *4*(7), 253–258. https://doi.org/10.19070/2332-287X-1600061

Cimpanu, C., & Day, Z. (June 19, 2019). *Florida city pays $600,000 to ransomware gang to have its data back.* ZD Net. https://www.zdnet.com/article/florida-city-pays-600000-to-ransomware-gang-to-have-its-data-back/

Cohen, L. E., & Felson, M. (1979). Social change and crime rate trends: A routine activity approach. *American Sociological Review*, *44*(4), 588–608. https://doi.org/10.2307/2094589

Cornish, D. B., & Clarke, R. V. (1987). Understanding crime displacement: An application of rational choice theory. *Criminology*, *25*(4), 933–948. https://doi.org/10.1111/j.1745-9125.1987.tb00826.x

D'Arcy, J., Hovav, A., & Galletta, D. (2009). User awareness of security countermeasures and its impact on information systems misuse: A deterrence approach. *Information Systems Research*, *20*(1), 79–98. https://doi.org/10.1287/isre.1070.0160

Dimpfl, T., & Jank, S. (2016). Can internet search queries help to predict stock market volatility? *European Financial Management*, *22*(2), 171–192. https://doi.org/10.1111/eufm.12058

Drake, M. S., Roulstone, D. T., & Thornock, J. R. (2012). Investor information demand: Evidence from Google searches around earnings announcements. *Journal of Accounting Research*, *50*(4), 1001–1040. https://doi.org/10.1111/j.1475-679X.2012.00443.x

Encila, J. (August 19, 2019). Terror groups use Bitcoin, instead of traditional cash, to fund their operations. Business Times. https://en.businesstimes.cn/articles/117276/20190819/hamas-terror-groups-Bitcoin-crypto.htm

Enders, W., & Sandler, T. (2011). *The political economy of terrorism* (2nd ed.). Cambridge University Press.

European Union's Law Enforcement Agency. (2020). *Covid-19: Ransomware.* EUROPOL. https://www.europol.europa.eu/covid-19/covid-19-ransomware

Federal Ransomware Tip Sheet. (2019). *CISA, MS-ISAC, NGA & NASCIO recommend immediate action to safeguard against ransomware attacks.* Texas Department of Information Resources. https://pubext.dir.texas.gov/portal/internal/resources/DocumentLibrary/Federal%20Ransomware%20Tip%20Sheet.pdf

Felson, M., & Boba, R. (2010). *Crime and everyday life* (4th ed.). SAGE Publications.

FireEye. (2020, February). *FireEye mandiant m-trends 2020 report reveals cyber criminals are increasingly turning to ransomware as a secondary source of income.* https://investors.fireeye.com/news-releases/news-release-details/fireeye-mandiant-m-trends-2020-report-reveals-cyber-criminals

Glaser, F., Zimmermann, K., Haferkorn, M., Weber, M. C., & Siering, M. (2014, June). Bitcoin-asset or currency? revealing users' hidden intentions. *Revealing users' hidden intentions. Proceedings of the 22nd European Conference on information systems,* Tel Aviv. https://pubs.aeaweb.org/doi/pdfplus/10.1257/jep.29.2.213?utm_source=dlvr.it&utm_medium=twitter&

Goldman, Z. K., Maruyama, E., Rosenberg, E., Saravalle, E., & Solomon-Strauss, J. (2017). *Terrorist use of virtual currencies: Containing the potential threat.* Center for a New American Security. http://www.lawandsecurity.org/wp-content/uploads/2017/05/CLSCNASReport-TerroristFinancing-Final.pdf

Granger, C. W., & Newbold, P. (1974). Spurious regressions in econometrics. *Journal of Econometrics, 2*(2), 111–120. https://doi.org/10.1016/0304-4076(74)90034-7

Grobman, S. (2020). *McAfee surveys cyber-threats in the age of coronavirus.* McAfee. https://www.mcafee.com/blogs/other-blogs/executive-perspectives/mcafee-surveys-cyber-threats-in-the-age-of-coronavirus/

Guerette, R. T. (2010). *Understanding crime displacement: A guide for community development practitioners. Local Initiatives Support Corporation (LISC), Crime Safety Initiatives (CSI) and the Metlife Foundation.* http://archive.instituteccd.org/-How-To-Do-It-/6-4-Community-Safety.html

Hern, A. (2017, December 30). *WannaCry, Petya, NotPetya: How ransomware hit the big time in 2017. The Guardian.* https://www.theguardian.com/technology/2017/dec/30/wannacry-petya-notpetya-ransomwarehttps://www.theguardian.com/technology/2017/dec/30/wannacry-petya-notpetya-ransomware

Johansen, S. (1995). *Likelihood-based inference in cointegrated vector autoregressive models.* Oxford University Press.

Johnson, T. (July 20, 2016). *Computer hack helped feed an Islamic State death list.* McClatchy DC Bureau. http://www.mcclatchydc.com/news/nation-world/national/article 90782637.html.

Juergensmeyer, M. (2017). *Terror in the mind of God: The global rise of religious violence* (4th ed.). University of California Press.

Kharraz, A., Robertson, W., Balzarotti, D., Bilge, L., & Kirda, E. (2015, July). Cutting the gordian knot: A look under the hood of ransomware attacks. In *International Conference on detection of intrusions and malware, and vulnerability assessment* (pp. 3–24). Milan, Italy: Springer Berlin Heidelberg.

Kristoufek, L. (2013). Bitcoin meets Google trends and wikipedia: Quantifying the relationship between phenomena of the internet era. *Scientific Reports, 3*(1), 3415. https://doi.org/10.1038/srep03415

Kristoufek, L. (2015). What are the main drivers of the Bitcoin price? Evidence from wavelet coherence analysis. *PloS One, 10*(4), e0123923. https://doi.org/10.1371/journal.pone.0123923

Liao, K., Zhao, Z., Doupé, A., & Ahn, G. J. (2016, June). Behind closed doors: Measurement and analysis of cryptolocker ransoms in Bitcoin. In *2016 APWG symposium on electronic crime research (eCrime)* (pp. 1–13). Toronto, Canada: IEEE.

Luther, W. J., & Olson, J. (2014). Bitcoin is memory. *Price & Markets, 3*(3), 22–33. http://dx.doi.org/10.2139/ssrn.2275730

Mauraya, A. K., Kumar, N., Agrawal, A., & Khan, R. A. (2018). Ransomware: Evolution, target and safety measures. *International Journal of Computer Sciences and Engineering, 6*(1), 80–85. https://doi.org/10.26438/ijcse/v6i1.8085

Moat, H. S., Curme, C., Avakian, A., Kenett, D. Y., Stanley, H. E., & Preis, T. (2013). Quantifying Wikipedia usage patterns before stock market moves. *Scientific Reports, 3*(1801), 1–5. https://doi.org/10.1038/srep01801

Morgan, S. (2019). Global cybersecurity spending predicted to exceed $1 trillion from 2017-2021. *Cybercrime Magazine.* https://cybersecurityventures.com/cybersecurity-market-report/#:~:text=Ransomware%20damage%20costs%20are%20predicted,than%20they%20were%20in%202015.&text=Global%20ransomware%20damage%20costs%20are,2015%2C%20according%20to%20Cybersecurity%20Ventures.

National Consortium for the Study of Terrorism and Responses to Terrorism (START). (2019). *Global terrorism database [data file].* https://www.start.umd.edu/gtd

Nye, J. S. (October 1, 2015). *The World needs an arms-control treaty for cybersecurity. Harvard Kennedy School Belfer Center.* https://www.belfercenter.org/publication/world-needs-arms-control-treaty-cybersecurity

Preis, T., Reith, D., & Stanley, H. E. (2010). Complex dynamics of our economic life on different scales: Insights from search engine query data. *Philosophical Transactions of the Royal Society A: Mathematical, Physical and Engineering Sciences, 368*(1933), 5707–5719. https://doi.org/10.1098/rsta.2010.0284

Reid, F., & Harrigan, M. (2013). An analysis of anonymity in the bitcoin system. In Y. Altshuler, Y. Elovici, A. B. Cremers, N. Aharony, & A. Pentland (Eds.), *Security and privacy in social networks* (pp. 197–223). Springer.

Richardson, R., & North, M. M. (2017). Ransomware: Evolution, mitigation and prevention. *International Management Review, 13*(1), 10–21. http://americanscholarspress.us/journals/IMR/pdf/IMR-1-2017.%20pdf/IMR-v13n1art2.pdf

Ron, D., & Shamir, A. (2013). Quantitative analysis of the full bitcoin transaction graph. In A. R. Sadeghi (Ed.), *Financial cryptography and data security* (pp. 6–24). Springer.

Savage, K., Coogan, P., & Lau, H. (2015). The evolution of ransomware. Symantec. https://docs.broadcom.com/doc/the-evolution-of-ransomware-15-en

Schmid, A. P., & Jongman, A. J. (2017). *Political terrorism: A new guide to actors, authors, concepts, data bases, theories, and literature.* Routledge.

Smith, R., Grabosky, P., & Urbas, G. (2004). Cyber criminals on trial. *Criminal Justice Matters, 58*(1), 22–23. https://doi.org/10.1080/09627250408553240

Symantec. (2019, February). *Internet security threat report.* https://docs.broadcom.com/doc/istr-24-2019-en

U.S. Department of Justice. (2018, September). *North Korean regime-backed programmer charged with conspiracy to conduct multiple cyber attacks and intrusions.* https://www.justice.gov/opa/pr/north-korean-regime-backed-programmer-charged-conspiracy-conduct-multiple-cyber-attacks-and

U.S. Department of Justice. (2020, August). *Global disruption of three terror finance cyber-enabled campaigns: Largest ever seizure of terrorist organizations' cryptocurrency accounts.* https://www.justice.gov/opa/pr/global-disruption-three-terror-finance-cyber-enabled-campaigns

U.S. Department of the Treasury. (2018). *National terrorist financing risk assessment 2018.* https://home.treasury.gov/system/files/136/2018ntfra_12182018.pdf

United Nations Office on Drugs and Crime. (2013). *Comprehensive study on cybercrime.* United Nations. https://www.unodc.org/documents/organized-crime/cybercrime/CYBERCRIME_STUDY_210213.pdf

Vosen, S., & Schmidt, T. (2011). Forecasting private consumption: Survey-based indicators vs. Google trends. *Journal of Forecasting, 30*(6), 565–578. https://doi.org/10.1002/for.1213

Witty, R., Hoeck, M., & Gregory, D. (2019, August 14). How to prepare for and respond to business disruptions after aggressive cyberattacks. Gartner. https://content.fireeye.com/assets/rpt-gartner-how-to-prepare-and-respond-to-cyber-attacks

Yar, M. (2005). The novelty of cybercrime: An assessment in light of routine activity theory. *European Journal of Criminology, 2*(4), 407–427. https://doi.org/10.1177/147737080556056

Yermack, D. (2015). Is Bitcoin a real currency? An economic appraisal. In D. Lee & K. Chuen (Eds.), *Handbook of digital currency* (pp. 31–43). Academic Press.

Zetter, K. (2015, September 17). *Hacker lexicon: A guide to ransomware, the scary hack that's on the rise.* Wired. https://www.wired.com/2015/09/hacker-lexicon-guideransomware-scary-hack-thats-rise/

The Use of Military Profiles in Romance Fraud Schemes

Cassandra Cross and Thomas J. Holt

ABSTRACT
Romance fraud occurs when offenders use the guise of a genuine relationship to defraud a victim, typically via online communications. Research has focused on the general structure of romance frauds, but few scholars have considered the potential link between victimization and specific narratives employed by offenders. This article explores the reported romance fraud victimizations of a group of Australians and explores similarities and differences in how a military narrative is involved compared to other genres. Limited differences were observed between those frauds using military narratives, highlighting the need for broader consideration of fraud prevention and disruption measures.

Introduction

Fraud is a global problem, which has expanded dramatically since the mid-1990s due to the rise of various forms of communications technologies (Button & Cross, 2017; Yar & Steinmetz, 2019). Fax machines, e-mail, websites, and social media increased the number of potential targets available to offenders and simplified the process of connecting with potential victims (J. Buchanan & Grant, 2001; Button & Cross, 2017). Fraud is largely defined by the use of deception to gain a financial advantage (Baker & Faulkner, 2003; Fletcher, 2007). Historically, fraud occurred through the direct transfer of money, but more recently it can involve the use of identity credentials and money muling as a means of obtaining money (J. Buchanan & Grant, 2001; Cross, 2019).

The global scope of fraud has massive economic impacts, particularly in western nations. In the United States of America, the Internet Crime Complaint Center reported losses of US $2.7 billion to cybercrime in 2018 up from US$1.4 billion in 2017 (Internet Crime Complaint Centre (IC3), 2019; Internet Crime Complaint Centre (IC3), 2018). Further, Canadians reported CAD$97 million (Competition Bureau, 2019), the United Kingdom reported over £1.2 billion (UK Finance, 2019, p. 4) and Australians reported AUD$487 million lost to fraud in 2018 (Australian Competition and Consumer Commission, 2019). Fraud losses are not restricted to Western countries, with Hong Kong, Singapore and South Africa also recording substantial fraud losses of their citizens (Leung, 2019; Mahmud, 2018; South African Banking Risk Information Centre (SABRIC), 2019).

Criminological inquiry on fraud over the last two decades focused heavily on the categorization and quantification of various fraud types as presented online, whether by offenders or victims (Holt & Bossler, 2015; Maimon & Louderback, 2019). In the early

2000s, scholars examined the prevalence and vagaries of advance fee fraud (AFF), which occurs when a victim is asked to send a small amount of money with the promise of receiving a larger amount of money in the future (Chang, 2008; Holt & Graves, 2007; Ross & Smith, 2011). Over the last decade, there has been a transition to explorations of romance fraud schemes (Cross, 2020; Rege, 2009), defined as instances where "criminals pretend to initiate a relationship via an online dating site or social networking site with the intention to defraud their victims" (Whitty, 2013, p. 666). Researchers also consider romance fraud to involve activities "where a person is defrauded by an offender/s through what the victim perceives to be a genuine relationship" (Cross et al., 2018, p. 1304).

While researchers emphasize the emotional and economic harm romance fraud schemes pose to victims, it is important to note that they are functionally equivalent to other online frauds in that they all involve the pursuit of financial gain for the offender. In fact, some argue that romance fraud can be viewed as a form of advance fee fraud due to common aspects of the approach (Ross & Smith, 2011). For instance, AFF narratives involve language suggesting the offender is in the military as a pre-text to elicit a response from potential victims (Holt & Graves, 2007; Nhan et al., 2009). Recent media reports suggest romance fraud offenders increasingly pose as US military personnel to target victims (Hafner, 2020; Leffler, 2018; Nicas, 2019; Rubinsztein-Dunlop, 2019), to the point where the US Army has warnings on its webpage (US Army Criminal Investigation Command, 2018). Offenders have also taken on military identities across all branches of armed services, as well as peacekeeping agencies and law enforcement to a lesser degree.

Despite the anecdotal prevalence of this narrative used by romance fraud offenders globally, to date there has been no known empirical examination of this particular approach to romance fraud. It is also unknown if military narratives in romance fraud have distinct characteristics, or mirror many of the known characteristics of other well-established fraud schemes. To address this gap in the literature, this study utilized a mixed methods analysis of 3,259 reports made to Scamwatch, an Australian online reporting mechanism for fraud, between July 2018 and July 2019. This analysis examined the ways in which the military narrative was employed through quantitative analyses of complainant reports to assess risk factors for fraud targeting and economic loss. Additionally, a qualitative thematic analysis was conducted to highlight the practices of offenders using a military narrative and their relationship to fraud types generally. The implications of this analysis for our understanding of the similarities and differences in military schemes relative to other AFF fraud types are discussed in detail.

Contextualizing online fraud schemes and advance fee fraud (AFF)

Romance fraud has largely been examined by criminologists as a distinct genre of fraud, due to the substantial dollar losses reported by victims, as well as the serious emotional harm they suffer (e.g., Cross et al., 2018; Whitty, 2013; Whitty & Buchanan, 2012). Many report a sense of profound personal loss due to the psychological ramifications of being defrauded by a perceived romantic or emotional partner (Cross et al., 2018; Whitty, 2013). In fact, many victims report that the violation and betrayal in the breakdown of the relationship is much harder to cope with than the sole loss of funds (Cross, 2020).

At the same time, the nature of the fraud and the methods employed by the offender can also be situated it in the context of advance fee fraud (AFF). Victims of AFF are typically asked to send a small amount of money with the promise of receiving a larger amount of money in the future (Chang, 2008; Holt & Graves, 2007; Ross & Smith, 2011). These approaches are not new (Nikiforova & Gregory, 2013, p. 393), arguably finding their origins in the "Spanish prisoner" scheme dating back to the sixteenth century, which as the name suggests, asked letter recipients for funds to be released from prison (Nikiforova & Gregory, 2013). Evidence suggests AFF schemes were delivered via postal mail and faxes throughout the 20th century (Holt & Graves, 2007; Smith et al., 1999). The evolution of technology, particularly e-mail and the Internet, established opportunity for offenders to target a much larger group of potential victims (Button & Cross, 2017; Yar & Steinmetz, 2019). Typical AFF schemes occur under the pretenses of investment schemes, lottery entries, unclaimed inheritances, and employment schemes (Ross & Smith, 2011; Cross & Kelly, 2016).

AFF is a global phenomenon, with both victims and offenders residing in many countries (Internet Crime Complaint Centre (IC3), 2019). There is a strong association with AFF offenses to West Africa, particularly Nigeria, due to the prevalence of fraud involving narratives of Nigerian royalty seeking to move funds out of their nation (Nhan et al., 2009; Salifu, 2008). Several scholars have examined the characteristics of AFF messaging to understand how offenders effectively target and defraud victims (Schoenmakers et al., 2009). This body of research presents an overall understanding of the ways in which these approaches are constructed and the techniques used to solicit success. While arguably all approaches are unique in some ways (Cross & Kelly, 2016), there are distinct characteristics and commonalities evident across many of the AFF schemes. In general, they contain a promise of financial gain for the recipient (Dion, 2010; Onyebadi & Park, 2012). There are some variations in structure, but many take an authoritative tone with the recipient and blend truth and fictions in the narrative to increase the perceived legitimacy of their requests (Dion, 2010; Holt & Graves, 2007). Many also contain grammatical errors and may not actually address the recipient by name (Holt & Graves, 2007; Onyebadi & Park, 2012).

A key element to all AFF approaches also involves engendering trust in the recipient so as to promote distribution of funds (Chang & Chong, 2010; Nikiforova & Gregory, 2013). In most cases of AFF, this needs to be done without the "usual body language, tonal cues and relational references that are consciously and unconsciously used to judge a person in the flesh" (Nikiforova & Gregory, 2013, p. 395). Individuals are likely to respond to those who assert themselves to be in positions of authority, even when the individual is not physically present (Cialdini & Goldstein, 2002). In this way, offenders often take on the identity of an expert or someone in authority, as a means to increase their likelihood of success (Chang, 2008, p. 76).

Research has also put forward several classifications of AFF approaches, based on the context and scenario of the financial request (Dion, 2010; Ofulue, 2010). Many of these involve some type of business opportunity, misused or unclaimed funds, estate settlement, or lottery winnings (Dion, 2010; Holt & Graves, 2007; Ofulue, 2010). The details surrounding each of these requests are likely to change and be tailored specifically to an individual victim's circumstances, to increase the likelihood of success with their approach.

Therefore, it is "no surprise that fraudsters usually take on identities such as lawyers, doctors and other professions that are more likely to be trusted, and furnish character and scenario details in a way that can be judged more favourably" (Chang & Chong, 2010, p. 342). In the case of many AFF narrative approaches, offenders will typically state their occupation in the first few sentences of the message (Nikiforova & Gregory, 2013, p. 396). In their research, Nhan et al. (2009, p. 463) found that fraudsters used a variety of occupations in the AFF e-mail communications studies, which included bank officers, lawyers, politicians, clergy, military officers, and doctors. The concluded that "fraudsters often attempted to gain trust by representing themselves as reputable individuals within respected companies and organisations" (Nhan et al., 2009, p. 468).

In addition to their identity selection, offenders often use details of actual events to support their scenarios and financial requests. As an example, both Holt and Graves (2007) and Chang and Chong (2010, p. 344) note the use of the Iraq war in their research as one event which was used several times by offenders in targeting victims with AFF approaches. The use of real events to support their storylines infers to the (potential) victim that there is some element of truth, and this may also extend to any promises of financial reward in the future (Nikiforova & Gregory, 2013, p. 397)

Contrasting AFF and romance fraud

In looking at the relationship between these traditional AFF approaches and romance fraud, there are both similarities and differences to consider. There are scholars who categorize romance fraud as a sub-set of AFF (Ross & Smith, 2011, p. 1). However, Cross, 2020 argues that the motivations driving AFF and romance fraud are different and "target distinct vulnerabilities of victims." From a victim perspective, the motivations to respond to AFF and romance fraud approaches are distinct. Chang (2008, p. 77) asserts that "all forms of advance fee fraud offer an incentive to the recipient in the form of monetary reward". While it is clear that many of the traditional AFF approaches focus heavily on the monetary reward to the recipient in order to solicit involvement, it is arguable that the shift to romance fraud, and using the guise of a genuine relationship to ensnare victims, appeals to the reward of companionship or love, rather than a focus on the money. The requests for money are almost a secondary outcome from the victim's perspective, whose primary focus is on fostering and nurturing their relationship.

Romance fraud first came to global attention as a crime between 2007 and 2008 (T. Buchanan & Whitty, 2014). In this way, the use of a relationship to defraud individuals can be understood as an evolution in methods used by offenders to gain financial advantage. Romance fraud was not evident in the early classifications of AFF, but has clearly become a dominant approach in recent years. In fact, romance fraud is now one of the highest categories of financial loss associated with fraud across many countries (Australian Competition and Consumer Commission, 2019; Internet Crime Complaint Centre (IC3), 2019).

While the motivations and anticipated rewards for romance fraud victims may be different compared to traditional AFF approaches, the goal of the offender is exactly the same: financial gain (Cross, 2020). Romance fraud simply changes the way in which fraud is operationalized. Both romance fraud and AFF contexts are important to the current article. The aim of the current analysis is to determine the ways in which offenders are using military profiles as a key element to their offending. It is not known whether the use of a military profile is unique in its application to romance fraud, or whether it displays the same characteristics of other more traditional AFF approaches.

Research aims and methodology

As noted above, military profiles and narratives were evident in previous AFF research (see Chang & Chong, 2010; Holt & Graves, 2007; Nhan et al., 2009; Nikiforova & Gregory, 2013).

There has been no research to date specifically exploring the use of military profiles as part of AFF, and additionally, how military profiles and narratives have been employed in the context of romance fraud. The current article seeks to address this gap by assessing the frequency and ways offenders utilize profiles and narratives based around military identities to deceive victims through romance fraud schemes. This study sought to address this knowledge gap by addressing the following four research questions:

(1) Who is targeted by romance fraud offenders using a military narrative?
(2) Is this group different to other categories of fraud victims?
(3) How is the military narrative used by offenders to defraud victims?
(4) Is this the same and/or different to what is currently known about romance fraud and AFF?

In order to answer these questions, a mixed methods analysis was performed using romance fraud reports provided by the Australian Consumer and Competition Commission (ACCC). These questions combine a quantitative and qualitative approach to data analysis. The first two are focused largely on demographic variables, and the third and fourth research questions focused on complainant narratives.

The inclusion of both quantitative and qualitative data in the current analyses provides a means of better understanding the use of military profiles and narratives. The quantitative analysis focused on largely demographic factors that may differentiate those who are both targeted and fall victim to the military narrative. The analysis of the comments provided by complainants give a richness to the analysis that the numbers alone cannot provide. Further, it provides a more thorough and nuanced understanding into the ways in which offenders used the military identity and narrative as a deliberate strategy to increase their success of victimization.

Data

The data for this analysis was obtained from the Australian Consumer and Competition Commission (ACCC) on reports of romance fraud lodged to them between July 2018 and July 2019 (inclusive). The authors submitted a written request to the Australian and Competition Consumer Commission (ACCC) for data relating to romance fraud reports. An ethics exemption was granted by Queensland University of Technology Human Research Ethics Committee (#1,900,000,738) for this data request. In response, the ACCC provided data for those who had reported romance fraud to Scamwatch during the period 1 July 2018 and 31 July 2019 (inclusive). As noted earlier, Scamwatch is an online reporting mechanism for fraud within Australia. While targeted at Australian victims, the online nature of the portal means that victims across the globe can lodge a report on an incident which may or may not have an alleged Australian link. There were 4,354 reports filed during this timeframe, with 3,463 (80%) reports indicating that they were willing to share the contents of their report for scam awareness. Scamwatch is not a law enforcement agency and cannot investigate or take action on individual fraud complaints. Rather, the information gathered by Scamwatch is used for intelligence purposes to drive consumer awareness and education across Australia.

The self-reported nature of this data limits its generalizability as Scamwatch is an online reporting mechanism with no screening or human interaction in the reporting process. It is similar in structure to the US Internet Crime Complaint Center's reporting mechanism which creates issues for victims and complainants when trying to provide their information (see Holt & Bossler, 2015). Those reporting may have found the website through internet searches or in some cases, it is evident they were directed to report by third parties, such as police and banks. As a result, the experiences reported by complainants may not be reflective of the experiences of all romance fraud victims generally. The difficulties inherent in accessing fraud victim populations (see Cross, 2020), coupled with the general absence of quantitative data sources to assess victimization and experiences with fraud (Holt & Bossler, 2015) make this data invaluable to understand the contours of various fraud schemes.

The ACCC provided a de-identified excel spreadsheet containing the details of these 3,463 reports. Each report included the following information: demographic details of the complainant (gender, age, and jurisdiction both within Australia and overseas), details about the fraud (how the approach was received, the location of the alleged offender), and any losses incurred (amount, payment methods, sensitive details lost). Vulnerability indicators of the complainant were also included, particularly around age, disability, sickness, financial hardship, and location. The de-identified free text field where each complainant wrote a summary/description of what happened was also made available to the researchers.

Upon review of the data, 204 duplicate entries were removed, leaving a final total of 3,259 distinct reports available for analysis. There is, however, some degree of missing information across these remaining reports since respondents may not have provided responses to all demographic questions or excluded details from their narrative. As a result of listwise deletion for quantitative analyses, the full sample of complainants was 2,478. Of these, a military narrative was used in 375 total individual complaints. This data set was used for the construction of quantitative variables for statistical analyses.

Key variables for the quantitative analysis

The key measure of interest for this analysis was whether the offender employed a *military profile* in their fraud scheme. This measure was developed through reading the free text sections of each report, as well as a key word search for the following terms: military, army, navy, marine, soldier, deploy, sergeant (sargent, SGT), general, officer, peace, force, major, UN, defense (defense), Afghan (Afgan), Syria, NATO. Any report where complainants indicated the person was in the military, army, airforce, navy, marines, or police was coded to reflect a military narrative (1), while all others were treated as no (0). References to peacekeeping, the United Nations and NATO were also included, although those that referenced UNICEF or other humanitarian agencies were excluded. As such, 15% of complainants reported an incident where the complainant indicated the offender employed the use of a military profile in the scheme (see Table 1). The overwhelming majority of reports explicitly mentioned the traditional military identities of army, marines or navy in a predominantly USA focused context. The majority of complainants reporting military schemes were older females (90%).

A binary variable for *financial loss* (0 = no; 1 = yes) was created to reflect those complainants who either noted in a checkbox that they suffered a financial loss, or indicated in the free text section of the report that they had sent money to the offender(s).

Table 1. Descriptive statistics of quantitative measures.

	Full Sample (n = 2,478)		Military Narrative Only Sample (n = 375)			
Variable	Mean	S.D.	Mean	S.D.	Min	Max
Military	.15	.358	–	–	0	1
Financial loss	.41	.492	.41	.492	0	1
Abuse evident	.12	.322	.09	.288	0	1
Social networks	.353	.478	.522	.500	0	1
Bank details	.10	.297	.09	.284	0	1
Personal Details	.31	.464	.40	.490	0	1
Foreign nation	.65	.478	.56	.497	0	1
Disability Status	.09	.282	.07	.263	0	1
ESL	.09	.282	.07	.263	0	1
Financial Hardship	.18	.382	.22	.412	0	1
Remote community	.05	.224	.07	.254	0	1
Illness	.04	.203	.04	.190	0	1
Indigenous	.03	.179	.03	.183	0	1
Age	4.03	1.250	3.81	1.110	1	6
Gender	.61	.489	.90	.299	0	1

Reading the free text section was essential to determine monetary loss, as well as gain a more comprehensive understanding of who sent money as a result of a specific fraudulent approach. Since the ACCC was not able to verify all reported complainant losses, a binary variable was used in lieu of the reported dollar figure. Such a conservative measure allows for an assessment of factors associated with monetary loss without being impacted by complainant over or under-reporting of dollar value. With that in mind, a total of 41% of all complainants reported losses, as did 41% of those reporting military schemes.

A binary variable was also created around whether abuse was evident in the complainant narrative (Cross et al., 2018). This was created through reading the free text section of the report. Abuse in this context was broad in scope and encompassed incidents where the complainant talked about anger and nastiness, through to explicit threats or incidents of harm (physical and emotional), blackmail and extortion. It did not differentiate the point of time in which it was experienced, therefore including offenders who used this language in either the start, middle, or end of the scheme when the individual realized it was fraud and attempted to cease communications (12% of all respondents; 9% of military narrative complainants).

When filing a complaint, respondents were also presented with various drop-down menus and options related to both their personal demographic characteristics and the nature of the offense. For instance, complainants could identify the way in which they were initially contacted by the offender, including: 1) e-mail; 2) fax; 3) internet; 4) in-person; 5) mail; 6) mobile apps; 7) phone (voice); 8) social networking/online forums; or 9) text message. Only one category could be selected by a complainant, and the majority identified being contacted via social networking sites or forums. Thus, a binary measure was created to reflect contact via *social networks* (35.3% of all complaints fell into this category; 52.2% of military narrative complaints)

Respondents were also asked to identify what sorts of information they lost in the course of the offense. This analysis focuses on two specific items: the reported loss of *bank details* (10% all complaints; 9% military narrative complaints) and *personal details* (31% all complaints; 40% military narrative complaints). There was no additional information provided to complainants so that they could better understand what these terms meant. As a result, the self-report nature of these measures should be viewed with caution.

Complainants were also asked whether they resided in Australia or a *foreign nation* (0 = Aus; 1 = foreign). The majority of complainants were in Australia, though the percentage drops to a simple majority when only examining military complaints (65%; 56%). Additional demographic variables were captured in reports to better understand the extent to which victims may fall into protected or vulnerable populations. Specifically, complainants were presented with a series of checkboxes to indicate their: 1) *disability status* (9%; 7%); whether English is their primary language *ESL* (9%; 7%); if they are living in *financial hardship* (18%; 22%); reside in a *remote community* (5%: 7%); have a chronic/serious *illness* (4%; 4%); and identify with *Indigenous* status (3%; 3%). Similar to the loss variables noted above, no additional information was provided to respondents to explain these terms or authenticate their claims. While it is hoped that any complainant would correctly identify that they fall into one of these categories, there is the potential they may have been selected in error. As a result, they should be treated with caution.

Two additional control variables were included in the analyses. First, a categorical variable for complainant age was included (1 = 18–24; 2 = 25–34; 3 = 35–44; 4 = 45–54; 5 = 55–64; 6 = 65 and over). Second a binary variable was created to reflect complainant gender (0 = male; 1 = female). Complainants were given the opportunity to not report a gender, so those cases were excluded from the quantitative analyses presented below.

Quantitative findings

In order to answer the first two research questions of this study, the following section used the demographic data to examine who was targeted by an offender using a military identity and compares this with the broader sample of complainants. Subsequent multivariate analyses were discussed in detail below.

A binary logistic regression model was estimated to assess any factors associated with reporting that a military narrative was used in the course of a romance fraud (see Table 2 for detail). There were no issues observed with respect to multicollinearity as no VIF was higher than 1.162, and no tolerance was lower than.860. There were multiple significant predictors identified for reporting a military narrative, including being female (OR = .6.897, $p < .001$), being younger in age (OR = .785, $p < .01$), being an English speaker (.630, $p < .05$), and not living in Australia (OR = .790, $p < .05$). The significance of gender and age fits with prior research on the risks of fraud victimization generally, and is somewhat similar to observed work on romance frauds which may be more comparable to these military schemes.

Complainants who lost their personal details (OR = 1.359, $p < .05$) were also more likely to involve military narratives. Additionally, those schemes that began via a social networking site (OR = 1.843, $p < .001$) and did not indicate signs of abuse (OR = .650, $p < .05$) were more likely to involve military narratives. The relationship to social networking sites was expected as they provide offenders with immediate access to victim populations. The significance of abuse is also sensible as these schemes do not necessarily require the same emotional and romantic manipulations expected with romance fraud (e.g., Cross, 2020). In effect, the characteristics of the fraud scheme itself seem to be more significant predictors of military schemes, than those of the complainant.

Table 2. Binary logistic regression models estimated for military fraud structures (n = 2,478).

Variables	b	S.E.	Exp(B)
Financial loss	.128	.132	1.137
Abuse evident	−.431	.202	.650*
Social networks	.611	.119	1.843***
Bank details	−.340	.223	.712
Personal Details	.306	.129	1.359*
Foreign nation	−.236	.124	.790*
Disability Status	−.153	.224	.858
ESL	−.462	.225	.630*
Financial Hardship	.158	.155	1.171
Remote community	.230	.246	1.259
Illness	−.200	.307	.819
Indigenous	−.013	.323	.987
Age	−.242	.052	.785**
Gender	1.931	.183	6.897***
Constant	−2.413	.279	.090***

-2LL = 1843.579; Chi square = 262.781***, Nagelkerke R2 =.176

An analysis examining the factors associated with economic loss with the full sample demonstrated that the use of a military narrative was not significant (see Table 3 for detail). No evidence of multicollinearity was present as no VIF was higher than 1.226 and no tolerance was lower than was .816. Male complainants (OR = .681, p < .001) were significantly associated with financial loss, as were those who reported financial hardship status (OR = 3.726, p < .001). This is sensible as higher rates of economic loss have been reported by males and those in lower socio-economic status groups in prior studies (see Harrell, 2015 for review).

Those who did not report abuse in their narrative (OR = .662, p < .01), did not lose personal details (OR = .357, p < .001), but lost their banking details (OR = 5.150, p < .001) were also more likely to report financial losses. Again, these findings seem logical as the loss of personal information such as home address does not readily enable individuals to engage in specific forms of economic fraud. Instead, the loss of banking details, such as one's account numbers or pin details, would readily enable fraudsters to access victims' finances

Table 3. Binary logistic regression model estimating correlates of reported financial loss by complainants.

	Full Model (n = 2,478)			Only Military (n = 375)		
Variables	b	S.E.	Exp(B)	b	S.E.	Exp(B)
Military	.122	.130	1.130	–	–	–
Abuse evident	−.413	.149	.662**	−.024	.402	.976
Social networks	.119	.095	1.126	−.063	.233	.939
Bank details	1.639	.167	5.150***	1.789	.483	5.983***
Personal Details	−1.030	.110	.357***	−.761	.259	.467**
Foreign nation	−.029	.095	.971	−.091	.243	.913
Disability Status	.277	.158	1.320	.585	.456	1.796
ESL	−.011	.162	.989	−487	.505	.614
Financial Hardship	1.315	.120	3.726***	1.292	.289	3.639***
Remote community	−.169	.201	.845	−.483	.506	.617
Illness	.111	.227	1.117	.017	.645	1.017
Indigenous	−.044	.249	.957	.608	.611	1.837
Age	−.001	.037	.999	.052	.107	1.053
Gender	−.383	.095	.681***	.711	.418	2.037
Constant	−.235	.181	.791	−1.300	.595	.273*

Model 1:-2LL = 2989.139; Chi square = 368.984***, Nagelkerke R2 =.186; Model 2: 2LL = 446.188; Chi square = 60.148***; Nagelkerke R2 =.200

and move funds with or without their consent. Similarly, emotional or other abuse would not be required to defraud victims in many fraud schemes, such as 419 or other advance fee fraud methods (e.g., Holt & Graves, 2007; Nhan et al., 2009).

Within the sample of respondents who reported a military scheme was involved in their experience (n = 375 due to missing data), those who lost money were more likely to have reported financial hardship status (OR = 3.639, $p < .001$), lost their bank details (OR = 5.983, $p < .001$), but less likely to have lost their personal details (OR = .467, $p < .01$) (see Table 3 for detail). Again, the significance of personal information and financial details may reflect an offender's ability to gain direct access to victim finances to engage in fraud. The relationship between one's level of income and military fraud is not immediately clear, though it may be in part associated with an increased potential for having served in the military or have close associates who served. Consequently, economic losses among military scheme victims are more generally difficult to predict on the basis of demographic characteristics alone.

Qualitatively exploring the military narrative in complainant reports

Having explored the quantitative risk factors associated with military fraud and financial loss, the following section examines how an offender uses this storyline to defraud individuals. As detailed earlier, the free text section of all complaints was made available to the researchers. In order to answer the third and fourth research questions as to how offenders used a military narrative in their romance fraud approaches, a thematic analysis was undertaken. From the original excel spreadsheet, the 463 reports which used a military narrative were cut and pasted into a new excel spreadsheet and subsequently imported into NVivo version 12 (qualitative software analysis tool). Importantly, this analysis assesses all reports where a military identity was employed, which covers those with and without financial losses. This number differs from the number of cases in the quantitative analyses since this analysis focused on the free text narrative section of complaints. No cases were deleted for analysis on the basis of missing quantitative data, making it a larger overall sample.

Once in NVivo, a node was created called "reason for money" (n = 280). This captured all the details provided in the complainant's text as to why they were asked for money from an offender (noting that offenders may request money on multiple occasions for multiple reasons). From this one node, distinct themes were identified to form the basis of the following analysis. In particular, this node captured reports where the military narrative of the offender appeared to be incidental to the overall justification for funds, compared to those where the unique characteristics of the military narrative were central to the overall storyline. The ways in which both narratives played out will be explored in detail in the following sections.

There was varying quality and content provided by complainants in each of the free text fields across the reports containing a military narrative. In some circumstances, there was limited or no information outlining the reason given by the offender for requesting money. Alternatively, there were many reports where the complainant wrote a detailed summary or outline of events. The numbers given below indicate the reports where a theme was evident. The absence of detail from other reports simply reflects what was available in the current dataset. It does not necessarily reflect that a theme was not present in their experience. If all complainants were specifically asked details on the reasons behind their requests for money, the prevalence of some of these themes (military or otherwise) may in fact be much higher. The reports may not be representative of all individuals who are targeted and/or experience romance fraud by offenders who adopt military identities.

Overall, the qualitative data provided by complainants demonstrates two distinct categories of approaches. In the first instance, the military narrative did not appear to be employed by the offender as a context to request money. Rather it appeared that the selection of a military identity was chosen to attract a connection with a potential victim in the first place. In these cases, the military identity was neither part of the storyline the offender employed nor a justification for money. In the second, there were many cases (n = 137) where the military profile was crucial to both the identity and the storyline of the offender. The unique characteristics of military personnel and military service were core to the requests for money and the ways in which the offender communicated with the (potential) victim. Both forms provide insights into the relationships military narrative-driven romance fraud have with AFF and other fraud types. The following sections explore both approaches in more detail, providing examples to support the use or nonuse of the military identity within the offender narrative to effect romance fraud victimization.

Military identity as incidental to the romance fraud narrative

Examining the qualitative complainant report data demonstrated that the use of a military profile was not always central to the offender's overall storyline or request for money. Rather, it appeared to only be evident in the profile, and an offender could have easily substituted the military profile and instead used a different trusted profession, such as engineer, architect, or doctor, to achieve their desired means. In looking at the cases where the military profile was not central to the overall narrative, requests for money were categorized as fees for consignments/inheritances; health emergencies; criminal justice emergencies; assistance for family members; and a combination of these reasons. In most cases, these requests were not in any way related to their military identity, or active service. Examples of each of these categories and how they presented, are detailed below.

Fees for consignments and inheritances

The majority of complainants suggested the offender requested funds in order to pay for fees associated with the sending and receipt of consignments, as well as the processing of inheritance funds (n = 49). These events did not focus on emergencies such as with medical care or arrests, but still contain the same sense of urgency in requesting money for other purposes. They also focused on the individual offender and sought to include the (potential) victim in the future benefits of their actions, as observed in various AFF schemes (Chang & Chong, 2010; Holt & Graves, 2007). In these cases, while the promise of benefits may not be explicit, it is caught up in assurances of the ongoing nature and future of their relationship. The victim considers an action in light of, and in the context of, the benefit to their overall relationship. This can be highlighted in the request for funds related to the release of gold bars.

> [Offender] said he was going to retire from the army and open a business in California selling gold. He needed help because his gold shipment got stuck in customs and he needed money to get it out of the country. I paid cash to his "agent" up to 20 000 (case 351)

> She claimed to have 40 gold bars she got paid for her work with the UN and was now trying to get the gold bars out of the country to the US. She claimed that she needed a load ok 56K to pay for her gold license gold seals security costs and other local government related taxes (case 2583)

Second, there were also instances where the requested fees related to expenses derived from an inheritance.

> After a few weeks of conversing she requested a small amount of money to assist. Money was transferred to her grandfather's bank account which was an Australian Defence Force account. Then she urgently needed to travel to South Africa to settle inheritance from her father before laws changed due to the political unrest. After months of messaging started requesting money to assist with settlement of inheritance with promise of sharing a % of the inheritance (case 49)

> The 3rd was to become his beneficiary to his 5Mil estate the 4th for his trip back from Pakistan to Texas as he was on a UN mission. I queried all these amounts and why he couldn't pay them. He told me he wouldn't get paid until he finished his mission with the UN he had no money. He promised gifts and the [$}5M[illion] (case 2855)

There were also cases where the offender simply requested funds to enable the processing or release of a package.

> Been speaking for a year have sent cards and money to him while he claims to be deployed now he is sending a cash box of money to me that I need to pay 1500 to receive (case 3370)

> He said he was due to retire and needed help to get a suitcase containing personal paperwork out of the country. He asked me to make several payments on average of 1 000 (case 1836)

The cases above illustrated several reasons given by the offender in justifying financial requests to the victim. Many of the reasons outlined in these examples mirror prior research into AFF (Dion, 2010; Ofulue, 2010), and use very existence of a relationship and the promise of a future together as a means to garner support from the victim.

Health emergencies

It was common for offenders to request money in response to a health emergency (Dion, 2010; Ofulue, 2010). In these cases (n = 18), the offender asserted that they were ill, or involved in an accident such as a car crash. They required immediate medical assistance, such as surgery at a hospital, which they could not afford. The offenders used this to elicit sympathy and action from the victim. This is evident in the following cases.

> He surposedly [sic] had to have a back operation so I sent money to pay for it as he said he was unable to access his funds or his travel insurance provider (case 999)

> He also told me that he had to have surgery because he had bleeding ulcers (case 1118)

> The taxi driver had a wreck and died. [Offender] was injured in head and unconscious and supposedly taken to [redacted] Hospital in Santo Domingo. A Doctor ... supposedly did head surgery then another head surgery within a week. Needed 48,000. Then while in hospital he got a blood clot and they took test and also he needed a coronary bipass [sic] surgery. He needed sixty six thousand dollars all medical money (case 3263)

In some of the above cases, victims paid what was requested, in the hope that their "partner" would recover and continue their relationship.

Criminal justice emergencies

Similar to the health emergencies, offenders often used incidents associated with the criminal justice system to justify requests for money (n = 10). The contacts usually focused on costs associated with their arrest and/or prosecution and asserted the need for funds to release them from jail.

> He was supposes [sic] to come back on the 6th Feb but never did. His story now is that he has been held in South Africa because someone stole his passport identity and is on the run with some heavy charges. He now need [sic] 76K for the bail .... (case 2081)

> Right now he is supposedly in Barcelona Spain. He has been accused of being a spy/terrorist. If I send his lawyer 2 000.00 he can get him out of jail and he can fly here to be with me (case 2375)

In these cases, the need for funds is coupled with a promise for the future, to enable release to be with the (potential) victim. Failure to send the money as requested will supposedly leave the offender in jail in an overseas country for an unspecified period.

Family assistance

In addition to requests for money that focused on the individual offenders themselves, offenders also often made requests based on the need to financially assist a family member (n = 23). In some cases, this was for medical emergencies like those observed above:

> After about 1 month of chatting he asked me to help transfer money for his daugther's [sic] heart surgery into his daughter's nanny's account (case 958)

> After about a month he started mentioning his daughter being sick with skin cancer. A week after that asked for money to pay for medical bills since he was allegedly on duty in Afghanistan and his credit card "was stolen by terrorists" (case 1093)

They can also be for other reasons that do not have an immediate heath implication, most of which focused on school fees, as noted below:

> He stated he had a daughter aged 10 named [redacted] who lives in a boarding school in Germany. He said he owned money on her boarding fees (case 460)

> After several days he says he has an economic problem with his son at school and needs him to say that I am his wife and send an email to [redacted] and say that he needs me to say that I am his wife. And have money sent to my account to fix the whole situation (case 551)

The above cases demonstrate that the request for money was not always focused on the individual offender themselves, but was also justified in assisting others. In addition, the need for money did not always center around an emergency (medical or otherwise). Instead, they could take a much more mundane route of assisting with daily living costs, in this case, school fees.

Combination of the above reasons

It was also not unusual for offenders to weave a storyline that included a combination of these above justifications for the request for money. This was demonstrated in the quote below.

> This story I was told that they got a gold inheritance when there [sic] mother died in England. They went to the funeral then inherited the gold they were herding back to Australia and got caught in at customs and needed money for bail and then for a lawyer (case 302)

In this case, the need for funds to process an inheritance was combined with a criminal justice emergency (in this case, money to make bail and pay for subsequent legal fees). Another example is found below.

> Then said he needed to get home as he had to obtain his inheritance or he would lose it. Sent money for a ticket and then supposedly was involved in an accident and stuck in an Afghanistan hospital. Couldn't get home so wanted me to receive the inheritance on his behalf so once received I could send him the money to pay for his hospital fees and to get home (case 271)

Again, the above example combined an inheritance storyline with a personal health emergency justification. This is further illustrated below.

> Then said they needed money for business deposit and they had no access to their bank account whilst overseas in Syria on deployment. This amount was 2500 USD (AUD$3578.25) on [date]. Then I was told their aunt was sick in hospital and needed money for deposit for that so I obliged again (amount was for 2500 USD [or] AUD$3944.69). Wanted more money for sick aunt (case 3013)

The above example illustrated how the first request for money was for a business transaction. However, the second request moved away from this business narrative and instead focused on the health of a family member.

Having examined the instances where offenders use a military identity but have not integrated this across the context for money transfers, the following section contrasts this against cases where offenders used the military narrative as both an identity and a justification for financial requests.

Harnessing the full potential of a military identity

A much larger proportion of requests (n = 137) involved an offender utilizing a military narrative not only in terms of their identity and establishing an initial connection, but was also the main premise underpinning their requests for money. Invoking the full power of a military narrative was evident in three distinct themes: leave requests, resources and security. Each of these will be explored in detail.

Leave requests

The military profile provided unique characteristics to justify financial requests to (potential) victims, with a distinctive focus on leave (n = 78). This accounted for the largest number of cases where the military context was central to the request for money. Some of these requests focused on assistance with obtaining early retirement.

> She said she will apply for a special exit to leave the army to move to Australia to be with me. She said it will cost a bit of money and could I support her. She asked if I could make a payment directly to the US Embassy (case 1094)

> [The offender] now wants me to supposedly help him to get early retirement 10.500.00. Have letter to send to General for this (case 2161)

Other requests for leave were not as permanent, and focused on gaining vacation leave, or simply permission to leave the base, which all required a fee.

> He told me he was going to be deployed and needed to pay the US government 4200 to leave the base (case 3329)

> He then began asking for money so he can take leave from the US army so he can come to Australia to meet me (case 477)

In addition to paying for leave, there were instances where the offender requested funds to pay for costs associated with leave such as travel and medical needs.

> Said he was with NATO in Syria. Needed forms with identity so that he could have leave. He then had someone supposedly from NATO contact me by phone requesting my details plus a signature. He said that I would be required to pay all airfares of 11 070 as he ... could not access any money while he was in Syria (case 2386)

> He then asked to speak with his commander to get leave to come home which I did. In short after some conversation with this Commander they told me I needed to register my number which cost 75. Which I transferred to speak with [offender] further. Then I was told it would cost me 400 for flights and a medical check up which I transferred 320(case 2573)

The issue of safety was also present in relation to the request to assist with leave. The immediate need to access leave and avoid continued service was premised on that fact that further deployment represents a risk of death and heightens the likelihood of injury (n = 18). Therefore the request to assist with leave in some cases was framed as a life or death choice for the conscience of the victim.

> He said he is with the US military and in Afghanistan. He wanted to get out of Afghanistan before he & his men get sent to Pakistan on a War zone. He's asked me to write email to [redacted] asking permission to come to Australia to marry me. I've got a reply from the email above asking me for money to pay airfare for [redacted]. I message [redacted] saying I can't send cash but I'm willing to pay his airfare using my credit card. [redacted] said that I need to send cash to U.N and they are buying his airfare. No I said. He then said that I'm allowing him to go to Pakistan to die (case 63)

> Later on he said that he was there for 5 months and was supposed to be 7 but he didn't want to die there because the war was getting close to his camp and he wanted to go home to his son and meet me and that he had to pay for his earlier release U$5 500.00 and urge me to send it but before that he was like desperate calling me (case 1422)

The above examples all focused on the desire to take leave from the military as a way of justifying financial requests. In some cases, this was argued to enable a permanent departure from the military, whereas other circumstances were more transient and focused on vacation leave. Requests were also premised on the immediate need to avoid life threatening situations. All were founded upon a promise of being together in the future, and in many cases, of being physically together .It is clear from the data that offenders invoked other aspects related to the experience of deployment to justify their monetary requests. This was evident in those who were seeking a variety of resources (n = 22). In particular, schemes focused around an inability to access appropriate levels of food.

> Then he need a Military Care Package which cost 450.54 US for [redacted] deployed to Africa. He was without enough food he said (case 113)

> But after few days of talking ... he started asking me if I can send him some assistance because such as food clean water and medicine because he said his running out supply in Syria. Because

> he was starving in there as their supply is running out and they have to wait for months for it to arrive (case 1655)

As evident in this last quote, in some cases, offenders also extended their requests for personal items and medical supplies.

> Became suspicious when he needed money for his medication (case 2333)

> We talked for months as a good friend then suddenly again no communication because she got sick and she was asking money for toiletries (case 1128)

In addition to the food and medicine requests, the narrative also included assistance with communications (such as telephone and internet).

> He asked me if I could help him pay for his internet that the Army was going to turn him off (Case 408)

> Claimed to be a military person and needing help to pay for her internet (case 1679)

The above examples all couch the legitimacy of their financial requests in the very nature of deployment, adding a potential air of legitimacy for someone in a military context.

Security

While the two previous themes focused on the reasons for requesting money in the first place, the military narrative was also invoked as a justification underpinning the offenders actions and requests while on deployment (n = 23). For example, offenders provided ample reasons as to *why* they were unable to access their own banks accounts and funds, and instead, needed money from their (potential) victim. The security requirements of being in the military on deployment were argued to restrict individual's access to banks and other resources.

> In one week [he] started to be asking for money because as he said "According to the protocol from the start they didn't let them have access to their banking account in need of some money and pay you back as soon as he gets home" (case 1064)

> He is pretending to be an American soldier over in Iraq or wherever and his excuse is he can't access his own bank accounts until he gets back to America (case 1455)

Clearly, there were security requirements which were legitimate in any military context, though offenders drew on these concepts as justifications for why the victim must pay on their behalf. Further, offenders argued that there were regulations that prohibited the individual from using cameras or communicating in certain ways. These conditions limited the ability of the offender to openly communicate with their victims. Additionally, this scheme aided the ability of offenders to continue their deception for the duration of the relationship.

> He always refused video call or call, say[s] that it is forbidden for a soldier to make contact during their duty. And he mentioned that he used the military device to contact me with a consequences loosing [sic] of his job (case 80)

> He couldn't speak via phone or send videos also because of "security reasons" (case 1627)

This aspect of security was further extended to the level of information offenders were able to provide during any communication. Offenders emphasized the need for secrecy that justified them not being able to share specific details with their partners about their circumstances, what was happening, or the reasons behind any requests.

> Says he can't give me information and to not speak of him to anyone (case 2593)

> He is claiming he is in army or National Guard in Afghanistan. He will tell u [sic] he is covert and can't speak that he is on duty (case 2794)

These examples illustrated that the offender's need for secrecy was usually framed in terms of security for themselves and the special missions they were purportedly involved with. The known level of security and secrecy that surrounds many military operations seeks to normalize this behavior to the (potential) victim.

Discussion and conclusions

This article examined the use of military profiles and narratives in romance fraud approaches. Romance fraud affects millions globally and results in substantial losses to victims, across both financial and non-financial harms. Despite the popularity of military profiles being used within romance fraud and AFF approaches by offenders, there has been no specific examination of how military profiles and military narratives have been used to target potential victims in the context of romance frauds alone.

This article set out to answer four research questions: to determine who is targeted by military approaches; to determine whether or not this group is different to other fraud victims; to understand how the military identity is employed by offenders in their narratives; and to understand how the military narrative is the same and/or different to existing romance fraud and AFF approaches. A mixed methods analysis framework was employed to address each of these questions.

In terms of the first two research questions and understanding who is targeted by romance fraud approaches that use a military narrative, the quantitative analyses demonstrated that there are few significant victim characteristics that predict the response to military schemes. While women were more likely to respond, gender was non-significant with respect to economic loss within this fraud type. As a result, this gender function may be more a reflection of the demographics of romance frauds generally (Australian Competition and Consumer Commission, 2019).

The characteristics of the scheme instead appeared as salient drivers for the risk of experiencing military schemes generally. The consistent relationship between loss of banking details and the risk of victimization is particularly important as it predicts both reporting a military theme and economic losses. The loss of financial information could easily facilitate identity crimes and fraudulent transactions, regardless of the nature of the scheme (Holt & Graves, 2007; Ofulue, 2010). The potential for secondary victimization therefore poses a distinct threat to this group of romance fraud victims.

Similarly, the pattern of risk associated with individuals reporting a financial hardship status cannot be underestimated. The fact that victims who fall into low income groups were more likely to experience military schemes and report economic loss also reflects some of the literature on economic identity theft (Copes et al., 2010; Harrell, 2015; Holt & Bossler,

2015). In addition, the mixed nature of the narratives observed in the qualitative analysis highlight the challenge victims may have in reporting their experience. Fraud types may generally fall into simple categories, though there are nuances in the nature of the scheme that may make it more difficult to consistently predict loss. As a result, it is imperative that fraud awareness campaigns be targeted toward all income groups, but with particular emphasis on those among lower income communities to increase resiliency.

The lack of significance for military schemes in models for economic loss as a function of fraud victimization are particularly salient as it supports previous research which notes the difficulties in attempting to differentiate victims from non-victims (Button & Cross, 2017). In some ways, this affirms the vulnerability of all individuals to these approaches (Cross & Kelly, 2016), and the ways in which offenders manipulate and exploit individual weaknesses. Vulnerability to fraud is not necessarily fixed in terms of demographics or other characteristics but may be more telling of the circumstances that individuals find themselves in on the day they receive the initial fraudulent communication or invitation.

In answering the last two research questions, the use of the free text comments generated some new insights into how this identity and narrative is used by offenders. For those offenders who use a military identity, but do not integrate this into their overall story or justification for money, requests which focus on consignments and inheritances are similar to what is established in existing AFF research (Ofulue, 2010; Dion, 2010). However, there were also additional categories evident, which align with the existing research on romance fraud (Whitty & Buchanan, 2012). These include reasons relating to individual health, criminal justice emergencies, or those related to family members. These emergency narratives transcend the type of identity used by an offender, and instead seek to evoke empathy in the victim more broadly.

There were also several examples where the offender not only used a military identity, but infused all contextual elements of their scheme with military references, particularly characteristics of military service and deployment in their requests for money. The strong focus on military leave was unique to this sector and effective in soliciting money from victims. Other aspects of resources and security were both drawn specifically from the deployment experience and are unique to the military context. The nature of military service and deployment, and the known conditions for deployments to war and peacekeeping missions globally, support some of these assertions. It also drew upon an assumed lack of knowledge of actual conditions and the care and provisions afforded to those in the military. Many of these requests seemed reasonable in the context of military deployment, rather than excessive or outrageous outside of this context.

Overall, there were two distinct ways in which military identities and narratives were employed by offenders. It is arguable that both are deliberate strategies, either in establishing an initial connection through the use of a military identity, or through continuing this storyline into financial requests. There was also evidence of the incorporation of elements known across existing AFF and romance fraud research in the justification for money. In this way, the distinction between these categories of fraud does not seem to be important. Rather, it can be argued that fraud is fraud, and the offenders will use whatever means necessary to gain a financial advantage from their victims (Cross, 2019). Their use of a military identity and accompanying narratives (where relevant) to solicit money are used deliberately on the part of the offender to target their individual victims, but the ways in which they employ this appears to be at the discretion of each offender.

Taken as a whole, the mixed methods findings of this analysis demonstrate the relatively persistent and overlapping nature of fraudulent schemes regardless of their orientation and the difficulties in seeking to group these into distinct categories. The military narrative, while enabling several unique contexts for requesting money and justifying the need for these funds, also demonstrated the use of more traditional AFF approaches that have been documented in previous research, as well as research undertaken in a broader context of romance fraud. While offenders may creatively ensnare victims using different pre-texts for contact (military or otherwise), there appear to be few consistent drivers for the loss of money. Further, the similarities in the nature of fraud schemes generally highlight that segmentations of victim populations and fraud schemes do not inherently improve our capacity to reduce the risk of victimization (Cross & Kelly, 2016). In effect, victimization may be more diffuse and less subject to nuanced risk factors than previously thought.

This article provided some initial insights into the ways in which military identities and narratives are used by offenders in the targeting of romance fraud approaches. This analysis demonstrated the commonalities evident between romance fraud and AFF generally. In this way, while the military identity and narrative is able harness unique justifications for requesting money, there is no evidence to suggest that it can be understood as a stand-alone category of romance fraud. Rather, it appears to embrace characteristics of both AFF and romance fraud at the discretion of the offender. In particular, the inability to distinguish key variables to predict financial loss across this genre of romance fraud, and the similarities demonstrated to other known fraud types, highlights the challenges evident in preventing romance fraud. This is consistent with the difficulties in seeking to counter romance fraud as a whole.

Taking this into consideration, the best ways to reduce victimization may already exist via continuous messaging to reduce victims' likelihood of responding in the first place. One key strategy would be to implement technological solutions to minimize victims' receipt of first contacts from offenders to generally reduce the risk of victimization (Holt & Bossler, 2015; Holt & Graves, 2007). For instance, targeted e-mail server filtering has helped reduce the overall number of AFF and phishing messages received in large organizations and corporate environments (Holt & Bossler, 2015). Similar strategies designed to automatically detect, quarantine, filter, or delete social media profiles and private messaging by profiles that are suspicious or fraudulent may be essential to reduce offenders' opportunities to potentially engage with victims (Holt & Bossler, 2015). While many online dating website and social media platforms have processes in place to identify and remove fraudulent profiles, it is a constant challenge for both the platforms and victim populations.

Romance fraud targets an emotional response from victims and seeks to manipulate and exploit the feelings of love and compassion for an offender. The deliberate use of a military profile exploits the inherent trust and other positive character attributes associated with this profession. Prevention messaging needs to continue to focus attention to the fact that not all profiles are genuine, and that not all persons are who they say they are. There needs to be a healthy amount of skepticism and critical thinking employed when using dating websites and other social media platforms that facilitate the establishment of relationships.

Finally, there is a continued need to promote a consistent message on not sending money in response to an online request. Offenders use the guise of a genuine relationship to overcome potential suspicion and use emotional triggers to persuade victims to comply. Further work is needed to promote the techniques used by offenders on these sites and the brutal ways that they seek to target unsuspecting victims. The current article has demonstrated that offenders will use the good will afforded to military personnel without hesitation, and in a variety of ways, to gain their financial advantage.

Acknowledgements

This work has been supported by the Cyber Security Research Centre Limited whose activities are partially funded by the Australian Government's Cooperative Research Centres Programme. The authors would like to thank the Australian Competition and Consumer Commission (ACCC) for their provision of data and their ongoing support of research in this area. The authors would also like to thank Helen Berents, Bridget Harris, Bridget Lewis and Fiona McDonald for their helpful comments on earlier drafts.

The views expressed in this article are those of the authors alone, and do not necessarily represent those of the Australian Government. All errors and omissions are the sole responsibility of the authors.

Disclosure statement

No potential conflict of interest was reported by the author(s).

Funding

This work was supported by the Cybersecurity Cooperative Research Centre.

ORCID

Cassandra Cross http://orcid.org/0000-0003-0827-3567

References

Australian Competition and Consumer Commission. (2019). *Targeting scams: Report of the ACCC on scam activity 2018*. https://www.accc.gov.au/publications/targeting-scams-report-on-scam-activity/targeting-scams-report-of-the-accc-on-scam-activity-2018

Baker, W., & Faulkner, R. (2003). Diffusion of fraud: Intermediate economic crime and investor dynamics. *Criminology*, *41*(4), 1173–1206. https://doi.org/10.1111/j.1745-9125.2003.tb01017.x

Bhugra, D., & De Silva, P. (1996). Uniforms—fact, fashion, fantasy and fetish. *Sexual and Marital Therapy*, *11*(4), 393–406. https://doi.org/10.1080/02674659608404453

Buchanan, J., & Grant, A. J. (2001, November). Investigating and prosecuting Nigerian fraud. *United States Attorneys' Bulletin*, *49*, 29–47.

Buchanan, T., & Whitty, M. (2014). The online dating romance scam: Causes and consequences of victimhood. *Psychology, Crime and Law*, *20*(3), 261–283. https://doi.org/10.1080/1068316X.2013.772180

Button, M., & Cross, C. (2017). *Cyberfraud, scams and their victims*. Routledge.

Chang, J. (2008). An analysis of advance fee fraud on the internet. *Journal of Financial Crime*, *15*(1), 71–81. https://doi.org/10.1108/13590790810841716

Chang, J., & Chong, M. (2010). Psychological influences in e-mail fraud. *Journal of Financial Crime*, *17*(3), 337–350. https://doi.org/10.1108/13590791011056309

Cialdini, R. B., & Goldstein, N. J. (2002). The science and practice of persuasion. *The Cornell Hotel and Restaurant Administration Quarterly*, *43*(2), 40–50. https://doi.org/10.1177/001088040204300204

Competition Bureau. (2019). *Competition Bureau launches the 15th edition of education and awareness campaign.* https://www.canada.ca/en/competition-bureau/news/2019/02/fraud-prevention-monthhelping-canadians-stand-up-to-scammers.html

Copes, H., Kerley, K., Huff, R., & Kane, J. (2010). Differentiating identity theft: An exploratory study of victims using a national victimization survey. *Journal of Criminal Justice, 38*(5), 1045–1052. https://doi.org/10.1016/j.jcrimjus.2010.07.007

Cross, C. (2019). Online fraud. In *Oxford research encyclopedia of criminology and criminal justice.* Oxford University Press. https://doi.org/10.1093/acrefore/9780190264079.013.488

Cross, C. (2020). Romance fraud. In T. Holt & A. Bossler (Eds.), *Palgrave handbook of international cybercrime and cyberdeviance.* London, UK: Palgrave.

Cross, C., Dragiewicz, M., & Richards, K. (2018). Understanding Romance fraud: Insights from domestic violence research. *British Journal of Criminology, 58*(6), 1303–1322. https://doi.org/10.1093/bjc/azy005

Cross, C. & Kelly, M. (2016). The problem of 'White noise': Examining current prevention approaches to online fraud. *Journal of Financial Crime, 23*(4), 806–828. https://doi.org/10.1108/JFC-12-2015-0069

Dion, M. (2010). Advance fee fraud letters as Machiavellian/narcissistic narratives. *International Journal of Cyber Criminology, 4*(1&2), 630–642. http://www.cybercrimejournal.com/micheldion2010ijcc.pdf

Fletcher, N. (2007). Challenges for regulating financial fraud in cyberspace. *Journal of Financial Crime, 14*(2), 190–207. https://doi.org/10.1108/13590790710742672

Hafner, K. (2020). *No, this sailor doesn't want your love or money. It's a scam, and he's a victim too.* https://www.military.com/daily-news/2020/05/12/no-sailor-doesnt-want-your-love-or-money-its-scam-and-hes-victim-too.html

Harrell, E. (2015). *Victims of identity theft, 2014. 1-26/NCJ 248991.* U.S. Department of Justice, Office of Justice Programs, Bureau of Justice Statistics.

Harris, K., Gringart, E., & Drake, D. (2013). Military retirement: Reflections from former members of special operations forces. *Australian Army Journal, 10*(3), 97–112.

Holt, T. & Bossler, A. (2015). *Cybercrime in progress: Theory and prevention of technology-enabled offenses.* New York: Routledge. https://doi.org/10.4324/9781315775944

Holt, T., & Graves, D. (2007). A qualitative analysis of advance fee fraud e-mail schemes. *International Journal of Cyber Criminology, 1*(1), 137–154. http://www.cybercrimejournal.com/thomasdanielleijcc.pdf

Internet Crime Complaint Centre (IC3). (2018). *2017 internet crime report.* https://pdf.ic3.gov/2017_IC3Report.pdf

Internet Crime Complaint Centre (IC3). (2019). *2018 internet crime report.* https://pdf.ic3.gov/2018_IC3Report.pdf

Küster, D., Krumhuber, E., & Hess, U. (2019). You are what you wear: Unless you moved—effects of attire and posture on person perception. *Journal of Nonverbal Behavior, 43*(1), 23–38. https://doi.org/10.1007/s10919-018-0286-3

Leffler, D. (2018). *This army veteran become the face of military romance scams. Now he's fighting back. Task & Purpose.* https://taskandpurpose.com/news/military-romance-scams-bryan-denny

Leung, C. (2019). *Hong Kong crime rate lowest in 48 years but social media scams almost double, police report. South China Morning Post.* https://www.scmp.com/news/hong-kong/law-and-crime/article/2184114/hong-kong-crime-rate-lowest-48-years-social-media-scams

Mahmud, A. (2018, March 26). *Internet love scams" 'I got carried away with his words' says victim as police strengthen task force. Channel News Asia.* https://www.channelnewsasia.com/news/singapore/internet-love-scams-police-transnational-commercial-crime-mule-10077380

Maimon, D., & Louderback, E. R. (2019). Cyber-dependent crimes: An interdisciplinary review. *Annual Review of Criminology, 2*(1), 191–216. doi:10.1146/annurev-criminol-032317-092057

Nhan, J., Kinkade, P., & Burns, R. (2009). Finding a pot of gold at the end of an internet rainbow: Further examination of fraudulent email solicitation. *International Journal of Cyber Criminology, 3* (1), 452–475. http://cybercrimejournal.com/nhanetalljan2009.htm

Nicas, J. (2019, July 28). 5 Things to know about military romance scams on Facebook. *The New York Times*. https://www.nytimes.com/2019/07/28/technology/military-romance-scams-facebook.html

Nikiforova, B., & Gregory, D. (2013). Globalization of trust and internet confidence emails. *Journal of Financial Crime*, *20*(4), 393–405. https://doi.org/10.1108/JFC-05-2013-0038

Ofulue, C. (2010). A digital forensic analysis of advance fee fraud (419 scams). In *Handbook of research on discourse behavior and digital communication: Language structures and social interaction: Language structures and social interaction, IGI Global: Hershey, PENN* (pp. 296–318). https://doi.org/10.4018/978-1-61520-773-2.ch019

Onyebadi, U., & Park, J. (2012). 'I'm Sister Maria. Please help me": A lexical study of 4-1-9 international advance fee fraud email communications. *The International Communication Gazette*, *74*(2), 181–199. https://doi.org/10.1177/1748048511432602

Rege, A. (2009). What's love got to do with it? Exploring online dating scams and identity. *International Journal of Cyber Criminology*, *3*(2), 494–512.

Rohall, D., Prkopenko, O., Ender, M., & Matthews, M. (2014). The role of collective and personal self-esteem in a military context. *Current Research in Social Psychology*, *22*(2), 10–21. https://crisp.org.uiowa.edu/sites/crisp.org.uiowa.edu/files/2020-04/art4.17.14_2.pdf

Ross, S., & Smith, R. G. (2011). Risk factors for advance fee fraud victimization. *Trends and Issues in Crime and Criminal Justice*, *420*, 1–6. https://www.aic.gov.au/publications/tandi/tandi420.

Rubinsztein-Dunlop, S. (2019, November 26). Sydney woman Maria Exposto wins appeal against conviction on drug traffkicking charges in Malaysia. *ABC News*. https://www.abc.net.au/news/2019-11-26/sydney-grandmother-facing-death-learns-fate-in-malaysian-court/11738850

Salifu, A. (2008). The impact of internet crime on development. *Journal of Financial Crime*, *15*(4), 432–443. https://doi.org/10.1108/13590790810907254

Schoenmakers, Y., de Vries, R. & van Wijk, A. (2009). *Mountains of Gold: An exploratory research in Nigerian 419 Fraud*. Netherlands: SWP.

Smith, R. G., Holmes, M., & Kaufman, P. (1999). Nigerian advance fee fraud. *Trends and Issues in Crime and Criminal Justice*, *121*, 1–6. https://www.aic.gov.au/publications/tandi/tandi121

South African Banking Risk Information Centre (SABRIC) (2019). *SABRIC annual crime stats 2018*. https://www.sabric.co.za/media-and-news/press-releases/sabric-annual-crime-stats-2018/

Topor, L. (2008). *War and fashion: Political views and how military styles influence fashion* [Masters Thesis]. Eastern Michigan University.

UK Finance. (2019). *Fraud the facts 2019*. https://www.ukfinance.org.uk/system/files/Fraud%20The%20Facts%202019%20-%20FINAL%20ONLINE.pdf

US Army Criminal Investigation Command. (2018) *Online romance scam information*. http://www.cid.army.mil/romancescam.html

Whitty, M. (2013). The scammers persuasive techniques model: Development of a stage model to explain the online dating romance scam. *British Journal of Criminology*, *53*(4), 665–884. https://doi.org/10.1093/bjc/azt009

Whitty, M., & Buchanan, T. (2012). *The psychology of the online dating romance scam*. University of Leicester.

Yar, M., & Steinmetz, K. (2019). *Cybercrime and Society* (3rd ed.). Sage.

The Distillation of National Crime Data into A Plan for Elderly Fraud Prevention: A Quantitative and Qualitative Analysis of U.S. Postal Inspection Service Cases of Fraud against the Elderly

Donald Rebovich and Leslie Corbo

ABSTRACT

The following article represents the product of a research study funded by the United States Postal Inspection Service (USPIS) and conducted by researchers from the Identity Management and Information Protection Center (CIMIP) of Utica College. The study focuses on frauds committed against victims aged 55 years and older. The primary objective was to uncover as much key empirical information on characteristics of victims of elderly fraud, those who commit these crimes, and the methods they employ to commit these fraudulent acts. For this study, researchers were afforded the opportunity to examine criminal case investigation data from the USPIS national criminal case database on elderly frauds. The data that supplies the foundation for this study relies on information from criminal case investigators transposed to a national database reflecting critical characteristics of cases of fraud against the elderly. Recommendations are offered as to how the analysis of this information can be beneficial in the development of effective public awareness campaigns for helping to prevent elderly fraud victimization.

Background

Statement of the problem and research questions

This article focuses on frauds committed against victims aged 55 years and older. This age group is often referred to by terms like senior citizens, the aged, and the elderly. The primary objective was to uncover as much key empirical information on characteristics of victims of elderly fraud, those who commit these crimes, and the methods they employ to commit these fraudulent acts. Much of the prior research conducted on this area has been in the form of surveys of those 55 years and older. These surveys have provided useful insights regarding victims of elderly fraud and the types of frauds committed against them. The study that this article is based on takes a much different research tack. For this study, researchers examined criminal case investigation data from the USPIS national criminal case database on elderly frauds. The study represents one of the few empirical studies of fraud against the elderly that examines and analyzes fraud cases relying on the impressions and experiences of criminal case investigators who worked these cases and reported on them. The data that supplies the foundation for this study relies, in large part, on the actual words of criminal case investigators transposed to a national database reflecting critical characteristics of cases of fraud against the elderly/financial exploitation of the elderly, which has become, undeniably, one of the most serious problems facing the nation's aging population.

The elderly are particularly vulnerable to financial exploitation, due to several interrelated factors. First are those factors directly related to the aging process, specifically the decline of cognitive and physical abilities. This decline often reduces the elderly to being dependent on others and/or making decisions the quality of which are compromised by cognitive/physical impairments. These impairments, in turn, heighten the chances of financial exploitation. Compounding this are personal financial factors. Con artists will often target the elderly due to their supposition that a large percentage of the elderly have accumulated significant wealth over the years, and are likely bearing the responsibility of managing those funds (Burnett, 2019; Deane, 2018). It is difficult to ascertain the actual monetary cost of elder fraud in the U.S. The question that is often posed is "What is the annual total dollar amount of the losses suffered by victims of elder financial exploitation?" The 2011 MetLife Study of Elder Financial Abuse has been cited most often in an attempt to answer this question and had estimated the annual cost at close to 3 USD billion although many have claimed that this figure grossly underestimates the actual amount lost.

What empirical evidence is there on the extent of elder fraud victimization across the U.S? The U.S. SEC Office of the Investor Advocate's 2018 report, entitled *Elder Financial Exploitation Why it is a concern, what regulators are doing about it, and looking ahead* summarizes prominent elder studies over a six-year period (Deane, 2018). Each of the studies' findings accentuate the growing problem of financial exploitation of the elderly. As an example, The 2010 National Elder Mistreatment Study examined past year prevalence of incidents of elder financial mistreatment perpetrated by family members discovering a prevalence rate of 5.2% (Acierno et al., 2009; Amstadter et al., 2011). The Laumann national survey, found a past year prevalence rate of 3.5% for financial mistreatment by a family member. The Peterson (2014) study conducted in New York State in 2014 found rates of 2.7% for past-year prevalence and 4.7% for lifetime prevalence (since age 60) of elder financial exploitation. The most common form of such exploitation consisted of the stealing or misappropriation of elderly victims' money or property, accounted for more than three-fourths of past-year and lifetime prevalence (Laumann et al., 2008). In 2017, a collaborative effort by three federal entities–the Consumer Financial Protection Bureau, the U.S. Department of Treasury, and the Financial Crimes Enforcement Network (FinCEN) – concluded that elder financial exploitation is the most common form of elder abuse in the United States. The Acierno study resulted in the significant finding that financial exploitation had a higher prevalence than for any other forms of elder abuse including emotional, physical, sexual mistreatment and general. Mirroring this research finding, the Self-Reported Study component of the Under the Radar study in New York found that financial exploitation was the most common type of elder mistreatment that respondent had experienced in the preceding year (Lachs & Berman, 2011).

More recent patterns of elderly fraud victimization have been notable. Despite the fact that the elderly account for only a third of the U.S. population, they accounted for half of all fraud complaints for the period of January through March of 2020. Monetary amounts lost to elderly fraud have risen. In the U.S., amounts of loss attributed to fraud perpetrated against individuals 80 and older more than doubled from 11 USD million for the first three months of 2019 to 23 USD million for the first three months of 2020. By age of victims, the greatest percentage increases were for those in their 50s and 60s (50% increases for both age brackets). In addition, the elderly were more likely than younger persons to report being targeted for technological-related crimes like cybercrime and tech support scams and the recent COVID-19 pandemic was found to have given rise to related schemes targeting the elderly involving Social Security Administration Fraud personal care scams and "grandparent scams" (Mangalonzo, 2020).

Introduction

The original goal of the USPIS support for this research endeavor was to utilize the study results to construct an evidence-based public awareness program directed at the elderly population in the United States in an attempt to help prevent such crimes from occurring in the future. Researchers were able to extract and analyze general demographics on those victimized and the interactions that they engaged in with those who victimized them. In some cases, the empirical data supported findings of past surveys. In other cases, results of the present study conflicted with the findings those surveys. In general, though, study results highlighted the manner in which offenders targeted their victims and how victims succumbed to the efforts of their fraudsters. The results offer a unique perspective of how fraudsters selectively prey upon those whom they believe to have diminished cognitive abilities and may be more trusting of strangers than the average individual.

For this research study, a total of 23,731 victims, associated with 374 separate cases, were made available for data collection/analysis in two database files provided by the USPIS. The two separate data files were cross referenced and integrated to construct a broader dataset for analysis. This allowed for additional cross-tabulation between data elements to pinpoint characteristics which aided in constructing more in-depth fraud scheme profiles for each scheme type. Researchers conducted a comprehensive analysis of a sample of 177 cases and available characteristics of 8,911 victims associated with these cases. Cases were grouped by the following categories established by the USPIS in the databases: Advance Fee Fraud; Boiler Room Fraud; Charitable Solicitation Fraud; Investment Fraud; Lottery Fraud; Sweepstakes Fraud; Fiduciary Fraud; Confidence Swindles; and Miscellaneous Fraud.

In the study, researchers were allowed to analyze a sample of elderly fraud cases covering a span from 2003 through 2015. For that period of time, researchers extracted and analyzed characteristics of 177 cases and the 8,911 victims associated with these cases. The cases were categorized into nine discrete crime categories including investment fraud, charitable solicitation fraud, lottery fraud, and sweepstakes fraud (see Table 1, Number of cases and victims in each fraud scheme category). In every situation examined in these cases, offenders employed techniques that exploited vulnerabilities in their victims, resulting in a "blind trust" of those who would defraud them. In some instances, the fraudsters would rely on "get- rich" quick schemes. Others would tempt potential victims through the sense of a false kinship connected with what was believed to be a common religion or age group shared between victim and offender (i.e., "affinity fraud"). Sometimes fraudsters would try to recruit local community leaders to vouch for them in an effort to substantiate a sense of trust for those who might be more suspicious of their motives. Other schemes included capitalizing on a sense of benevolence by ensuring victims that their funds would be used to help the poor and sick. In more extreme cases, fraudsters would use coercive tactics if initial strategies proved to be unsuccessful. Figure 1 provides a depiction of the "affinity fraud" exploitation phases.

A common thread connecting the cases examined is that victims were not likely to conduct due diligence on the backgrounds of those perpetrating the criminal acts. These are crimes of misplaced trust. Similar to fraudsters who might target younger age groups just starting their adult lives because of perceived naïveté, these fraudsters understand the opportunities presented to them by those who are moving closer to the end of their adult lives. The cases examined demonstrate that whether it is a senior citizen mourning the loss of a spouse, suffering a serious illness, or dealing with the side effects of treatments of the illness, individuals with criminal motives will be there to take advantage. These are the victims, the offenders, and the criminal offenses committed. It is hoped that the findings of the present study and the conclusions drawn from them can be of great use to preventing future frauds against the elderly.

Project design/implementation methods

The primary aim of the project was to perform both a quantitative and qualitative analysis of a sample of United States Postal Inspection Service (USPIS) closed consumer fraud cases to detect and synthesize case patterns as they relate to elderly fraud. The project is exploratory, in that the researchers entered the endeavor without pre-conceived notions, or with the intent of testing hypotheses. This inductive approach was employed to allow patterns and trends to emerge without being artificially encumbered by pre-designed restrictive parameters. The research was guided by USPIS database categories for victims, offenses, and offenders and followed a three-step process of:

- Initial Exploratory Analysis of Cases;
- Iterative Collection/Analysis of Cases; and
- Intensive Analysis of Case Data for Pattern Detection

(1) Initial Exploratory Analysis of Cases

The first step was to analyze investigations closed no earlier than 2003 and no later than 2015. Electronic copies were analyzed. Special attention was paid to the categorical collection/analysis of victim, offenses and offender data. Such information included data on gender and geographic location and methods used by offenders to defraud the victims (Including original offender- victim contact information [e.g., mail, telephone, Internet], social engineering techniques employed, frequency/duration of offender contacts with victims and amount of loss).

(2) Iterative Collection/Analysis of Cases

The second step involved the collection of quantitative and qualitative data from the USPIS closed cases. Special attention was paid to the critical dimensions of the cases, the official processing of them, and an assessment of the overall influence of organizational and systemic variables in the cases. The data collection instruments focused primarily on the collection of nominal level data as it related to the case narrative information and ratio level data as it relates to quantitative case related information. Researchers employed qualitative content analysis techniques specifically designed for use in the cross-case comparison of qualitative data. An "iterative model" for qualitative data was utilized in which the researchers shuttled among four modes of: data collection, data reduction, data display, and drawing and verifying conclusions. To avoid data overload and lack of comparability across cases, researchers developed strong conceptual data collection frameworks that are receptive to case idiosyncrasies, but are supportive of common, general parameters for comparison of cases. The researchers used the case-ordered implementation matrix and the predictor-outcome analysis matrix conceived by qualitative analysis scholars like Patton (2002).

(3) Intensive Analysis of Case Data for Pattern Detection

In the third step, the case-ordered data collection matrix was used to construct the most economical display of qualitative and quantitative data that allowed the analysts to work with the full set of cases on one or several variables at a time to understand case content patterns. Scoring was done to draw overall comparisons and weighting was be used when particular factors were seen by analysts as strong "facilitators" to the act of successfully defrauding elderly victims and to criminal relationships within and between cases.

The total number of Fraud against Consumer (FC) cases contained in the *MF Closed Consumer Cases* file received from the USPIS was 1,598. After eliminating those Fraud against Consumer cases that were not categorized as one of the 12 Fraud Scheme categories of interest and those that fell outside of the target time period (2003–2015), a total of 666 cases remained for examination. Three scheme categories contained no cases. Table 1 below is a tabulation of the number of cases and the corresponding number of victims available for analysis based on the case numbers included in the *MF Closed Consumer Cases* file. The number of cases available is significant and will facilitate the targeted analysis.

Table 1. Number of cases and victims in each fraud scheme category.

Fraud Scheme	Number of Cases	Number of Victims
Investments	158	42,326
Miscellaneous	150	122,623
Lottery	158	767,894
Sweepstakes	85	1,786,281
Fiduciary	38	1,513
Advance Fee	33	63,953
Charitable Solicitations	19	16,488
Boiler Room	18	114,688
Confidence Swindles	7	67
Admin Action	0	0
Precious Metals, Gemstones, Hard Assets, Etc.	0	0
Contest/Sweepstakes	0	0
Totals	666	2,915,833

There was extensive viable information available regarding the commission of the crime including the *Victim Loss, Amount of loss for Scheme, Number of Victims, Scheme Type, Original Offender-Victim Contact, Made Wire Transfers, Sent Monetary Instruments through the Mail, Other Items of Value Relinquished, Number of Times Defrauded, Social Engineering Techniques Employed, Frequency of Offender Contact with Victim*, and *Duration of Offender Contact with Victim* variables. The *Amount of loss for Scheme* data, or the cumulative amount of money defrauded from all victims as a result of the scheme, was accessible from the *MF Closed Consumer Cases* file. The total *Number of Victims* affected by the scheme and the *Scheme Type* was also found in the *MF Closed Consumer Cases* file. The *Scheme Type* was clearly defined as one of the nine remaining Fraud Scheme Types of interest in the study in both data sources. The more specific *Victim Loss* data, or the amount of money that was stolen from the individual victim as a result of the fraud scheme, was not available within the ISIIS/CM system, but was sometimes found within the text of the victim Memorandum of Interviews, upon review of such documents for each individual victim of every case.

The *Original Offender-Victim Contact* was found in the narrative of the MOI along with whether the victims *Made Wire Transfers, Sent Monetary Instruments through the Mail*, or there were *Other Items of Value Relinquished*. The *Number of Times Defrauded, Social Engineering Techniques Employed, Frequency of Offender Contact with Victim*, and *Duration of Offender Contact with Victim* were also available in the text of the MOI. The *Original Offender-Victim* Contact, or the means of communication used by the offender to initiate contact with the victim including by mail, telephone, Internet, or otherwise was accessible through the MOI. The Case Summary also provided good information on variables related to the commission of the frauds.

The original 2 million+ victims in 666 cases were identified by the USPIS as being available for analysis at the onset of the project. After having difficulty with accessing the ISIIS system to collect data, we moved to the idea of the agency performing a data extraction of a more manageable size. The data extraction file contained information on approximately 54,000 victims, but had to be filtered to remove cases involving fraud scheme types other than the nine targeted by our parameters. The filtering process resulted in the 23,731 victims in the 374 cases.

Researchers began by including the first three scheme types in their entirety, but proved to be too large of a sample to analyze efficiently. Researchers then moved on to selecting a proportional sample from the remaining six scheme types.

Scheme Types Completed in Entirety:

- Advance Fee Fraud
- Boiler Room Fraud
- Charitable Solicitations Fraud

Remaining Scheme Types:

- Confidence Swindles (1.9% of the total number of victims)
- Fiduciary Fraud (4.3% of the total number of victims)
- Investment Fraud (25.2% of the total number of victims)
- Lottery Fraud (2.7% of the total number of victims)
- Miscellaneous Fraud (14.4% of the total number of victims)
- Sweepstakes Fraud (7.0% of the total number of victims)

The study sample drawn excluded cases in which victims did not fit the study parameters (e.g., businesses) or in which critical data elements were unknown, a proportional sample was drawn which included 816 victims from the remaining scheme types. The 816 victims in the sample of the six scheme types above is representative of the percentage of the entire population ascribed to each scheme type. For this sample of 816 victims, a systematic method of sampling was employed in which intervals were determined by the ratio of the population size to the sample size. This resulted in every 16th victim being systematically assigned to the study sample. Combining the entire population of Advance Fee Fraud, Boiler Room Fraud and Charitable Solicitations Fraud with samples from the remaining six crime categories, the entire sample studied was comprised of 8,911 victims associated with 177 criminal cases. The following presents an overview of general observations followed by more specific observations by offense category.

Summary of results

Overview

In a majority of the cases studied, two or more fraudsters conspired together to defraud elderly victims (57.25%). In the remaining cases (34.75%), fraudsters acted alone in the perpetration of their fraudulent schemes. Fraudsters found it highly productive to initially engage potential victims through mailed information presenting a fictitious opportunity or award for potential victims. The vast majority of cases used the mail as the primary means of communication with elderly victims, accounting for a little over 74% of the communication types employed. A distant second was communication by telephone which accounted for approximately (8%).

In 59.1% of the cases examined, some form of misrepresentation was used to victimize elderly individuals. Within that category, close to 30% of the cases involved misrepresentation and misappropriation of funds received from victims. Entities misrepresented to elderly victims ranged from municipal bonds, to real estate, to hunting tours. A common element among most of these cases was that victims conducted little background investigations on their own of the offers/opportunities presented, instead placing their trust in the hands of strangers who would cheat them out of their funds. In 21.3% of the cases, fraudsters misrepresented types of "services" that they sold to elderly victims (e.g., work at home schemes, fraudulent business ventures).

In the cases examined, fraudsters were found to use one or more "social engineering" manipulation techniques to capitalize on victims' diminished capabilities of mental processes of perception, memory, judgment, and reasoning (Techniques employed were grouped into 15 different categories for the study).In 43.1% of the cases (the plurality), the social engineering technique used was a "promise" of high earnings or large rewards to potential victims. Many of these social engineering efforts involved the description of high earnings or awards to be expected from "investments." Some of the techniques used included encouragements to take advantage of "limited time" opportunities to help enrich not only the victims themselves, but also descendants of the victims (e.g., grandchildren).

In 13.4% of the cases, a form of "affinity" fraud was employed by fraudsters; a method in which the criminal ingratiates himself within a particular demographic "group" in order to gain trust through a false "kinship." Within the affinity fraud sub category the plurality

(39.5%) were cases where the "affinity" was "age" in which the fraudster was in the over-55 age bracket or pretended to be to bolster an age-related "connection" between the victim and the fraudster. This connection would be instrumental in causing the victim to let down his/her "guard" such that false trust would result. In other cases, the "affinity tool" could be one of a "pretended" common religion between the fraudster and victim. In some cases, fraudsters would seek out community leaders to vouch for them, serving as "trust catalysts" to potential victims facilitating further victimizations. Consequently, the targeted group will tend to experience "transference distortion"; an embedded transference of trust with the leaders to the scam artist, paving the way for successful deception of the victims. In situations with elderly victims, where cognitive perception can be diminished, this can lead to cognitive distortions. In cases like this, victims can experience repetitive compulsions to identify with the offender and fall victims to the same offender over time, making it increasingly difficult for effective law enforcement intervention. The next figure is a graphical representation of this sequential relationship.

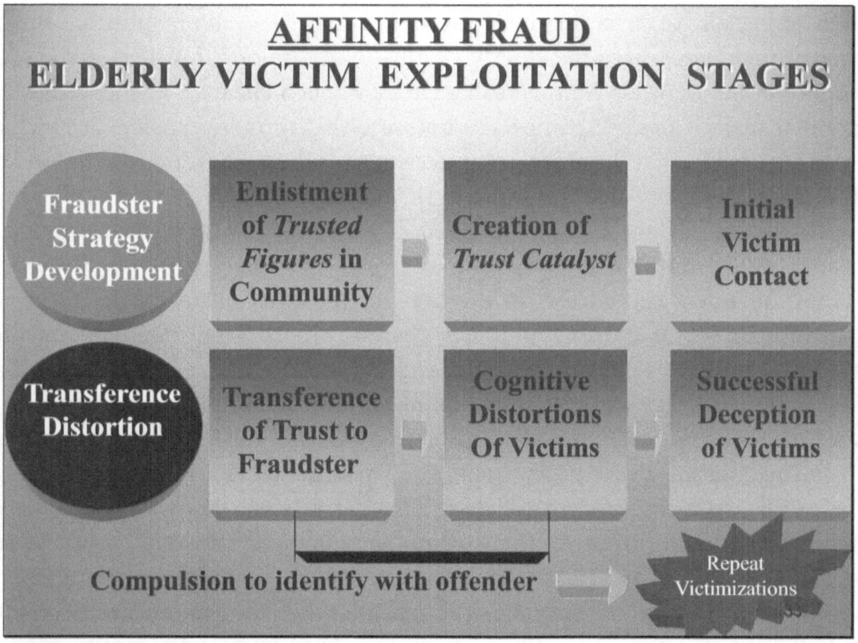

Figure 1. Affinity fraud exploitation stages.

In some cases, shrewd fraudsters exploited limitations on senior citizens' knowledge of how computers can be used as a 'tool" by fraudsters to advance their criminal schemes. In many of the frauds examined, offenders used the Internet to distribute wide-spread fake e-mails to dupe their victims and then turn to wire transferring to complete their "deals". In the most damaging confidence swindle examined, criminals from the Netherlands perpetrated a massive international scheme. The "con artists" sent spam e-mail to thousands of potential victims in which they falsely claimed to have control of millions of dollars located in a foreign country that belonged to an individual with a terminal illness. The scammers solicited the help of the potential victims to collect and distribute the funds to charity. In exchange for the victims' help, the offenders promised the victims a share of a large inheritance, and informed the victims that they had to pay a variety of fees for legal representation, taxes or bogus documentation.

With this starting point using the Internet, the fraudsters then attempted to confuse their victims and conceal their identities. They did this by using a variety of e-mail addresses, aliases, and phone numbers. In one scenario, the defendants sent e-mails purporting to be from an individual suffering from terminal throat cancer who needed assistance distributing approximately 55 USD million to charity. In exchange for a victim's help, the defendants offered to give a 20% commission to the victim or a charity of his or her choice. To help "authenticate" the swindle, the offenders offered "documents of proof" through the Internet that the scam was legitimate.

To finalize their scams of the elderly, the fraudsters then took advantage of a lack of technological knowledge of victims' familiarity with the ramifications of the wire transfers of funds. Because of EFAA regulations, most bank-to-bank wire transfers between accounts are completed within 24 hours. Some banks make wired funds available to recipients immediately, especially on transfers between accounts at the same institution. In the cases examined, scammers pressured the elderly victims to use money transfers so the scammers obtain the money before their victims realized they've been cheated. In short, they counted on the fact that many elderly victims were unaware that money transfers are virtually the same as sending cash in that there are no protections for the sender; there is no way one can reverse the transaction or trace the money. In the cases studied, after the victims wired funds, the fraudsters did not deliver the funds as promised. Total losses to the victims in these cases was more than 1.2 USD million.

Sometimes, offenders capitalized on the draw of the Internet to create "targeted" fake websites to lure in senior citizens and then defraud them. The offenders went to great lengths to make these sites appear authentic and tailor them to specific elderly subgroups, hoping that potential victims would not go to the trouble of conducting background checks on the sites. In some of these cases, fraudsters "zoned in" on individuals of a particular religion who had recently lost his/her spouse. These schemes involved fictitious online dating sites. The target group of one of these schemes was widows/widowers who were of the Roman Catholic faith. Promises made were that clients, for a price, would be matched with others of the same faith. It was found that fraudsters operated more than 200 of these websites for a period of 4 years, victimizing thousands who fell for the scam; accounting for over 1 USD million in victim loses. The victims were "matched" with imaginary people. At one offender's sentencing, the judge characterized the scheme as being particularly "cruel" and adding, "You stole the victims' money, you stole their hope and dignity, for the most base of reasons: money." At the sentencing, a senior citizen victim remarked, that the dating service "raised my hopes, and then they dashed them. I felt foolish, embarrassed and depressed. They preyed on me and others when we were at our most vulnerable, all for the sake of their own greed."

Advance fee fraud

Advance fee fraud is a type of fraud in which the fraudster makes some sort of offer to the individual he targets as a potential victim on the condition that the target provides the fraudster with some sort of up-front fee. The study found that 1,546 were victimized by advance fee frauds. Overall, the gender distribution was fairly even (Female – 51.4%, Male – 48.6%). California and Illinois data showed a higher rate of victimization of females (California – 63.8% female, 36.2% male; Illinois – 54.1% female, 45.9% male). The breakdown for Pennsylvania departed markedly from this pattern with male victims accounting for 66.8% and female victims at 33.2%.

In some cases, fraudsters were found to target elderly victims who had experienced financial difficulties. One such scheme offered a false credit repair service for those with poor credit records. Another offered a service that claimed to identity sources guaranteeing automatic loans. Others overlapped with "sweepstakes fraud" and "lottery fraud" schemes (two other fraud categories studied) maintaining that victims could not claim their "awards" without first paying an up-front fee. Regardless of the approach, victims, paid "advanced fees" for misrepresented services/awards, leaving them with nothing.

Boiler room fraud

The study database separated certain cases under the category entitled "Boiler Room." This is a specific subcomponent of a category of offenses in which telemarketing direct mail or Internet practices are used to perpetrate frauds against senior unsuspecting individuals. Review of the Boiler Room cases revealed data available for 2,799 victims. The state with the largest frequency of victims was Arizona 71.5%. Unlike, advance fee fraud cases, there was a higher percentage of victims who were male (53.3%) than females (46.7%). 84.2% of the Boiler Room Fraud cases were perpetrated through fake telemarketing telephone calls to elderly victims. The remainder involved contacting through direct mail. The more criminally successful schemes were those that combined one communication method (e.g., telephone) with others (e.g., Internet, direct mail) to perpetrate the frauds. One criminal group was brazen enough to draw victims to, unwittingly, recruit other senior citizens into the boiler room scheme, indirectly leading to their victimization.

Charitable solicitation fraud

An effective ploy of fraudsters seeking to exploit senior citizens is to persuade them that they have an opportunity to dedicate a portion of their funds to a "good cause" through a charity. A total of 4,004 known victims comprised the Charitable Solicitations category. The state with the largest frequency of victims was Nevada (68.3%). 51.0% of this type of fraud was male and 49.0% female. It is of interest to note that the gender breakdown of the top two states were somewhat different. In Nevada, 53.8% of the victims were male, and 46.2% were female. In California, the gender distribution was reversed. There, 55.5% of the victims were female and 44.5% were male.

A common pattern found in the USPIS database, were cases in which the "charity" solicits donations from the general public using the mail, telephone or the Internet to convey misleading or completely false information. The "causes" can be ones to, in general, battle disease, physical or mental. Fraudsters in this category were careful to give their fake charities official sounding names to help lure in unsuspecting citizens with good hearts. Donors were often told that their donations would be used to help law enforcement officers and firefighters who were killed or injured in the line of duty, and their families, as well as needy veterans. Some of the Charitable Fraud cases in the USPIS database involved the creation of "charitable trusts" by the victims. In the United States, many individuals use charitable trusts to leave all or a portion of their estate to charity when they die, both for philanthropic purposes and, sometimes, for tax benefits. In some cases, offenders had legitimate credentials to create such trusts, but had records of unethical behavior unknown to the victims.

Investment fraud

For the study, researchers analyzed a sample of 372 USPIS cases in which the primary criminal action was Investment Fraud. This type of fraudulent activity is a deceptive practice in stock or other commodities that induces investors to make purchase or sale decisions on the basis of false information, frequently resulting in losses, in violation of the law. Frauds in this category span many states in the USPIS database (24 states). In terms of victimization, the top three states were Montana (15.3%), Minnesota (14.8%) and New York (14.2%). A major difference from other fraud categories in victim characteristics for Investment Fraud was the victim gender distribution. This proved to be more of a male dominated victim group, with just under 60% being male. An interesting point is that, while females represented a minority of victims, they represented almost 52% of the total monetary loss resulting from these frauds.

By far, the commodities victims "invested" in were stocks (71.2%). Investments in precious metals/gemstones/hard assets accounted for 28% of the purported investments. In typical investment fraud cases, investors were duped by financial advisors or those pretending to be financial advisors who falsely advised clients that their funds were being invested in conservative securities.

In the sample, a common tactic used by investment fraudsters would be to lure them in with promises that their money would be used to invest in stocks in companies owned by the offenders that would return handsome profits. The promotion of promising business opportunities was another tactic that fraudsters used to victimize their customers. One such fraud involved a male - female team that solicited investors to fund a project for a senior citizen living development. Another promised investment in innovative technology to efficiently dispose of hazardous waste. A common investment fraud tactic found in the USPIS database was the Ponzi scheme; a situation in which the fraudster collects money from new investors and uses it to pay purported returns to earlier-stage investors instead of investing funds properly. Some Ponzi schemes were found to target pension funds of senior citizens who had retired. One such Ponzi scheme lasted for over 15 years and focused on retirees and a particular occupational grouping; retired bus drivers.

Lottery fraud

With this type of fraud, fraudsters used the element of surprise to disarm their senior citizen victims into believing that they had won a monetary prize through a lottery with some important strings attached (e.g., paying "taxes" on the award, providing personal information that can be used for identity fraud).In the sample examined, cases in which the fraudsters were from the U.S. were rare. Approximately 80% originated from other countries like Myanmar and Java. Some of the cases were found to have originated in Jamaica. It was not unusual to see cases in which "go-betweens" in the United States were used by Jamaican fraudsters to further the schemes.

The state with the largest frequency of victims was Florida with 37.5%, followed by California with 27.5% and South Dakota with 15.0%. By percentage, males tended to be victimized more - male –55%; female –45%. Once again, females suffered larger total monetary losses making up 54.8% of the combined loss total compared to 45.2% for males.

Sweepstakes fraud

A major difference between a lottery and a sweepstakes is that with the former, a participant makes a monetary purchase to enter the lottery and, with a sweepstakes, there is no purchase to enter the contest. Illegal sweepstakes are ones in which "handling fees" or "taxes" are required to be paid prior to receiving the monetary prize. In these scams, claims that there are actual prizes are false. The number of victims affected by the sample of sweepstakes fraud cases examined was 112. Utah had the largest percentage of victims (58%) and the total distribution by gender was even (i.e., half male, half female). Females, as a group, suffered 3% more of monetary losses than did males.

Sweepstakes fraudsters were found to use entity names similar to legitimate sweepstakes entities to confuse elderly victims. Other fraudsters would represent themselves as part of government agencies "sponsoring" the sweepstakes (e.g., the U.S. Internal Revenue Service) to lend an air of "authenticity" to the gambit. In one case, based upon the fraudsters' determination that certain elderly groups would be more susceptible to certain language, original contact letters would be tailored accordingly. In other cases, fraudsters would prey upon victims' sense of altruism by attesting that up-front fees to claim the sweepstakes awards would be used for benevolent causes like cancer research. In some cases, those representing sweepstakes entities tried to bilk elderly victims by upping the ante and the fees associated with procuring the fictitious monetary awards. Some fraudsters would resort to forms of coercion by threatening to refer the victims to law enforcement agencies for arrest if they did not pay "taxes" on the "winnings."

Fiduciary fraud

For the study fiduciary fraud was defined as illegal practices committed by financial institutions and financial professionals that constitute a breach of trust between the financial agent and the client. Cases sampled for this category covered 53 victims. By gender, females were found to account for a majority of the victims (56.6%) and made up a much greater percentage of total monetary loss than males (females - 60.3%; males - 39.7%). The plurality of victimizations took place in Virginia (47.2%).

The most egregious case examined in this category involved fraudsters who conspired to misrepresent a tax-deferral program that diverted victim funds to areas not fully explained to them. Victims thought they were using a risk-free service, as opposed to investing. The firm's owners used customer deposits to invest in real estate and to buy personal items. Over 300 individuals were cheated out of a total of 125 USD million.

Confidence swindles

A confidence swindle is the intentional misrepresentation of existing fact or condition, or the use of some other deceptive scheme or device, to obtain money, goods, or other things of value.

The number of victims studied in this category totaled 30, the majority residing in Illinois (86.7%). While females made up 66.7% of the victims, males accounted for 75% of total monetary loss. In the most damaging confidence swindle examined, criminals from the Netherlands perpetrated a massive international scheme sending thousands of e-mails to potential victims. In total, the victims lost over 1 USD million.

The elderly community demonstrate a higher susceptibility to confidence swindles, particularly with phishing e-mails and ransomware, where the computer owner's files are locked until the victim pays a ransom (Sannd & Cook, 2018). An Australian study discovered adults over the age of 60 ignored significant indicators of phishing e-mails (e.g., spelling and grammatical errors) if the scammer used a well-known logo. In fact, even when the participants recognized the syntax errors, the e-mail still felt "safe" because of the trusting branding.

Miscellaneous fraud

Miscellaneous Fraud was embodied by cases that did not fit into any of the previously described categories. In total, 209 victims were studied for this category, the plurality of them coming from Virginia (47.4%). The sample had a slightly greater percentage of males (50.2%) and males made up an even greater percentage of total monetary loss (56.3%). In one case, retirees were a target of fraudsters perpetrating a "work at home" scheme to purportedly train senior citizens to successfully invest in the stock market. Another case involved a fraudulent online dating service targeting individuals of a particular religion who had recently lost his/her spouse.

Discussion

Being an empirical study of official criminal investigation data of frauds against the elderly, this study is a notable departure from previous studies on the same topic that have relied on survey results. One such study that gained much public attention was conducted by the AARP foundation in March of 2011. This study surveyed 1,509 individuals in the general population and 723 victims. Some key findings of the survey were that investment fraud victims were more likely to be male and have a higher average age than the general population, more likely to expose themselves to sales situations, and less upset at the prospect of losing money. Business opportunity fraud victims were also likely to be male, but more likely to take preventive actions. Lottery fraud victims were more likely to be single and have a higher average age of than the general population. This victim group also was taking fewer prevention actions, fell victim to a greater number of persuasion techniques and more likely to expose themselves to sales pitches. Across the fraud types studied, senior citizen fraud victims were more likely than the general public to expose themselves to risky situations for potential victimization even if they previously lost money to fraudsters (Pak & Shadel, 2011).

While the results of surveys like this can be insightful, such surveys are prone to suffer limitations due to the research method used. There is evidence that a key limitation is that they depend upon self-reports subject to issues like respondents being unaware of being defrauded, forgetting the encounter, or simply not preferring to reveal the victimization. Surveys that are conducted by identifying victims through complaint agencies and victim lists tend to overcome such limitations. But, they suffer from different limitations. One of those limitations is that these studies tend to survey smaller samples and, therefore, become less representative of the general population of victims (Ross et al., 2014; Grossman et al., 2013; Loftus et al., 1985; Ross & Mirowsky, 1989; Ross et al., 2014; Schwarz, 1999).

Criminal case data analysis studies have some limitations as well. One is that by only concentrating on closed criminal case data, comparisons to the general population of those not victimized can be difficult. However, the authors of the present study feel that a primary strength of this type of approach is that the analysis of data related to the criminal cases can supply reliable first-hand information on victim, offender characteristics and, most notably, can be instrumental in re-creating the environment of a criminal act including the types of exchanges between victims and offenders. One of the greatest values of the present study is that it reveals the methods and strategies employed by the fraudsters, how they manipulate their targets, and adjustments and adaptions that they make in the course of their involvement with the victims. From a criminological standpoint, the study results vividly portray the type of person that noted criminologist Robert Merton would characterize as a "criminal innovator." Were they to use their skills in a legitimate way, these individuals could likely be successful systems analysts, because they seem to be adept at analyzing actions and reactions of their targets and" innovating" as they go along. Most of the offenders from the study worked together in conspiracies taking advantage of their individual skills working toward a collective goal; defrauding the unsuspecting elderly victim.

Offenders proved to be skilled in exercising social engineering techniques on their victims, the plurality of which were promises of high earnings or large rewards. Many of these fraudsters were knowledgeable of ways to disarm their victims by pretending to form a psychological bond with the victims through expressing some type of affinity by religion, by age, or by some other means of an invented connection. Successfully manipulating the victims in this way, fraudsters were able to successfully develop a false sense of trust that proved to be the key to obtaining targeted funds from their victims. The offenders were not easily dissuaded, proving to be criminally resourceful by soliciting the knowing or unwitting endorsement of trusted members of the community, thus heightening the chances of cultivating a false impression of credibility.

In terms of specific crime categories examined, findings support some of the results of the AARP survey. For instance, investment fraud victims were more likely to be male than female. However, if the victim of investment fraud was a female, she was more likely to be victimized for a higher monetary loss. In general, victims of investment fraud were duped into investing in misrepresented or nonexistent stocks. In some cases, offenders coupled the promises of high returns with a false sense of altruism by noting that stocks invested in would help those in need, especially those in the over 55 year age bracket. For some fraudsters, raiding elderly victims' pension funds was a primary goal. Females were victimized at a higher rate than males for Advance Fee Fraud. This proved to be a pattern in several other crime categories. And, even when female victims were in the minority, they lost more on average. This was particularly pronounced in Sweepstakes Fraud cases (i.e., females accounting for over 60% of total monetary loss).

Similar to "spear phishing", a type of identity theft tactic in which certain demographic types are targeted (e.g., the wealthy) through e-mail, advance fee fraudsters targeted elderly victims with financial problems to offer them fake credit repair services or "instant loans.". Of particular note were instances in which fraudsters took advantage of elderly victims' limited knowledge of computer technology and how their technological naivete could make them more susceptible to falling victim to offenders' scams. In a 2019 report, the Federal Trade Commission (FTC) reported "tech support" scams as the leading scam category.

Individuals allowing unknown "tech support" to gain access to their computer open themselves to far more than financial losses. Access gained in this manner allows scammers access to personal and sensitive information, as well as opportunities to introduce various types of malware. The malware remains undetected long after scammer has ended their call and purported "assistance". The malware permits scammers to see personally identifiable information, such as log in credentials to bank and credit card accounts, and medical history.

A 68-year-old man suffering from dementia lost 356,000 USD (Johnson, 2019). When the fraudsters purporting to be from tech support continued to call, he continued to pay them to keep his computer "safe". Another victim, a 74-year-old man, continued to make payments to update his security software. Over two years, the victim paid over 500,000 USD to the fraudsters.

The COVID-19 pandemic almost immediately ushered in a variety of Internet scams involving fake personal protection equipment (PPE), fake treatment options, fraudulent COVID-19 tests and vaccines, and charity related scams for pandemic *victims* and their families (U.S. Department of Justice, 2020). The most susceptible and scared citizens, primarily those 65 years of age and older, sought information from the Internet. From February through September 2020, financial institutions in the United States filed 91,000 Suspicious Activity Reports (SARS) pertaining to suspected illicit payments associated with the coronavirus pandemic.

The pandemic not only created health related swindles, but scams that focused upon the isolation and loneliness of seniors. The significant increase of "romance scams" has been attributed to the restricted access to friends and family by elderly victims. Seniors are often contacted via online dating sites or social media platforms by scammers posing as interested romantic contacts. Once they gain the victim's trust, the fraudster convinces the target to send money. Senior citizens have refinanced their homes, depleted their 401 K, bank accounts, and in some instances, life savings.

In one such scam, a 67-year-old widow that had recently lost her husband met a seemingly perfect gentleman who described himself as a contractor from Connecticut on the website ChristianMingle.com (Jordan, 2014). After three months, she began wiring him money. Her "beau", whom she had never met, ran into one disaster after another. One story he told her was that he was in Nigeria working on a project and had ran out of money. His scam was so sophisticated that he even had an English-speaking "nanny" vouch for him. After she had sent him a total of 15,000, USD she realized he was a con artist. The woman, a businessperson, believed she was duped because she was so vulnerable.

In another case, a daughter discovered her father had depleted his life savings after meeting a woman online that needed "support" for her and her daughter (Dagher, 2016). When her 79-year-old father had a stroke and was hospitalized, she discovered he had lost his entire life savings. Still another of countless examples involved a 68-year-old social worker who thought she was in a relationship with an Air Force pilot serving in the Middle East (Span, 2020). Fortunately, her loss was only 1,200 USD.

Fraudsters have no bounds to their heinous imaginations when developing scams. The scam of a funeral home invoice or funeral notification is particularly callous. In the case of a funeral home invoice, the victim is sent an e-mail that contains a "funeral recovery notice". When the unsuspecting victim clicks the link that appears to be a legitimate funeral home or opens the attachment they believe to be a bill, their computer is taken over by malware. Consider that many transactions are conducted online, including life insurance policy payouts. That information can be easily discovered when the fraudster has access to the victim's computer.

In past instances, criminals have sent out a "funeral notification", many times exploiting vulnerabilities of a legitimate funeral home's website. Known as "watering hole" attacks, the fraudsters target funeral homes and e-mail addresses within similar geographical locations. Once the unsuspecting e-mail recipient clicks the link, they are brought to the compromised website where malware is dropped on the victim's computer.

Like Investment Fraud, Boiler Room Fraud also showed a preponderance of male victims, the majority of them located in Arizona. Telephonic communication was the predominant method used for Boiler Room Fraud, while more savvy fraudsters "compounded" crime methods (e.g., combining Internet and mail) for greater success. Fraudsters targeting the elderly used both the postal service and the victim's e-mail address to commit a crime. For example, the victim would receive a check in the mail to deposit as part of a work-from-home part-time employment position. After communicated with the fraudster online, the victim would pay a "fee"; however, once the bank discovers the check was fraudulent, the money had to be returned.

Many seniors participate in social media quizzes. In 2020, fraud prevention entities warned of so-called "Coronavirus Awareness Tests" that purported to evaluate the participant's knowledge of the pandemic (Hart, 2020). Actually, the test contained questions to reset passwords, including mother's maiden name, first pet's name, and the city where the victim met their spouse. This information was used, among other things, to reset back account passwords.

Other interesting findings included how victims appeared most susceptible to victimization when fraudsters used tactics that fostered a perceived aura of authority to cajole their targeted victims. A favorite tactic here was impersonation as agents of government agencies. In addition, fraudsters would engage in fraudulent "gamesmanship" with victims, by upping the "ante" through enticing the victims with ever-growing "riches" while incrementally increasing fees for obtaining greater amounts of money. Having already "hooked" their game, they continued to milk the ploy as long as the victim was willing to pay.

Given the results of this study (and those of previous studies by AARP), it would seem a logical conclusion that the elderly are targeted by fraudsters who understand the opportunity presented to them in the form of a potential victim base of individuals with diminished cognitive abilities, high "trust quotients" (i.e., projection of their sense of trust to others), desires for instant wealth and a high level of altruism. Despite this, there are some who would question the underlying hypothesis. In their article in the journal, *Perspectives on Psychological Science* (July, 2014), two scholars from the University of Waterloo do just that. In their article, *Contrary to Psychological and Popular Opinion, There Is No Compelling Evidence That Older Adults are Disproportionately Victimized by Consumer Fraud* (Ross et al., 2014), the authors present evidence that questions conventional wisdom, and prior study findings, that the elderly are more susceptible to being victimized by fraudsters. In their argument, they cite evidence that elderly victims actually may be more skeptical then those in other age groups.

However, other scientists, using brain scan research conclude the opposite. In *Neural and Behavioral Bases of Age Difference in Perceptions of Trust*, scholars from UCLA concluded that the elderly are, indeed, more susceptible to being defrauded (Castle et al., 2012). These psychologists from UCLA studied how individuals in two age groups perceived photographs of faces that had been pre-rated for trustworthiness and approachability. The researchers found that older adults between the ages of 55 and 84 rated untrustworthy faces as significantly more trustworthy than younger research subjects. The researchers also asked subjects to assess the faces for trustworthiness while undergoing functional magnetic resonance imaging (fMRI). Subjects in the study between the ages of 20 and 42, demonstrated a pronounced response in a region of the brain called the anterior insula. This part of the brain is responsible for controlling intuitive feelings that are instrumental in decision-making, particularly with regard to examining untrustworthy faces. In contrast, the elderly subjects demonstrated very little activation in this brain area. This would suggest that the warning signs for elderly subjects were either diminished or nonexistent. Shelley Taylor, one of the psychologists conducting the research, explained that the brains of the elderly are not saying "be wary." According to Dr. Taylor, the elderly are not getting the "uh-oh" signal that younger people get (Castle et al., 2012; Corbyn, December 2012).

The authors of the present study believe that the results of the UCLA study underscore the effects of aging particularly with regard to decision-making and reasoning. Time after time, USPIS cases examined demonstrated tendencies of victims to put "blind trust" in those they had never met. Combined with other features of the elderly highlighted in detailed descriptions of the cases examined (e.g., enhanced altruism, susceptibility to establishing a sense of false kinship with fraudsters), it is clear that fraudsters have a very accurate understanding of the vulnerabilities of the elderly. In this regard, they are quintessential criminal "opportunists." They see their opportunities clearly, and they take full advantage of them. It is hoped that this study and recommendations (below) on how the results can be applied to optimize the efforts to control and prevent fraud against the elderly in the future.

Recommendations

The distillation of this research study's findings provides robust empirical information on which the law enforcement community can base enhanced proactive elderly fraud control and prevention efforts. It is one of the few studies of its kind to provide to law enforcement agencies and fraud investigators empirical data concerning the key factors of fraud against the elderly and the conditions under which that behavior occurs. The recommendations presented here are based on the use of the study's findings. While conjecture and conventional wisdom may have led to some of the same conclusions in the past, this study allows law enforcement and policy makers to point to the data as a basis for applying them. These recommendations are an effort to ensure that the findings will be used to improve and increase proactive measures that law enforcement and fraud investigators use to combat fraud committed against the elderly. They fall into several categories:

- Public Awareness Development
- Proactive investigation, detection, prevention, and prosecution
- Enhanced law enforcement training
- Enhanced management of cases and resources
- Briefings for law enforcement executives so that they can develop policy, allocate resources, and advocate training based on empirical research
- Future research

Public awareness development

The findings of this research study should be converted into public awareness crime prevention programs aimed at the elderly.

Recommendation 1

Federal, state and local law enforcement leaders should collaborate in the effective development and implementation of elderly-oriented public awareness programs utilizing present study results as a starting point.

First and foremost, it is highly recommended that the findings of the present study be transformed into a most useful tool for the victim group spotlighted; the elderly. Of course, this would be an awareness program that is evidence-based and applicable to the needs of the elderly. Such a program should be one that serves as an "alert system" to the elderly, educating them in: 1) warning signs of potential victimization; 2) patterns of behavior in others to be wary of; 3) patterns of behavior in themselves they should avoid; 4) how to extricate themselves from potentially dangerous communications with suspicious types: and 5) what to do if they are victimized. It is critical that if the data here is to be used as a foundation of an awareness program, such a program should apply the findings sensibly, utilize proven methods of dissemination and implement the program in an effective manner, optimizing positive impact on crime prevention.

To ensure, the preceding objectives of an effective awareness are achieved, the program should follow the lead of experts in the field of crime awareness program implementation, like Barthe (2006), and follow proven methods of program development. Research has shown that there is limited effectiveness in developing and implementing general publicity campaigns aimed at victims. The studies indicate that if crime prevention methods are handled in a general fashion, the words of wisdom that are promulgated often fall on deaf ears. A common reason for this is that if the crime prevention awareness campaigns are too general, victims do not always feel that it concerns them (Barthe, 2006; Burrows & Heal, 1980). In some cases, this is because there may be a tendency to deny the possibility that they will fall victim to criminals (Barthe, 2006; Sacco & Trotman, 1990). Some other explanations for this phenomenon include a feeling of apathy toward the general message or embracing a mentality of "it will not happen to me."(Riley & Mayhew, 1980). It has been shown, however, that victim campaigns that tend to focus on specific crimes, like fraud, coupled with being implemented in small, independent geographic regions are more effective (Barthe, 2006; Johnson & Bowers, 2003). Such campaigns that include television public service announcements, crime prevention brochures, community bulletin boards, newsletters from mayors' offices, and local billboards have enhanced effectiveness. The role of the local police in such campaigns can be critical through local community functions in the dissemination of specific crime prevention information (Simmons & Farrell, 1998).

While the natural temptation is to reach as many as possible with a broad brush stroke, elderly audiences are more likely to respond to messages they perceive as being personal and relevant to their immediate surroundings (Holder & Treno, 1997). The failure of some law enforcement webpages directed at the elderly for fraud prevention purposes can be directly attributable to the fact that many are very general in tone, lacking essential details in what to be aware of, what to avoid, and how to avoid it. A clear understanding of local customs and cultural considerations is vital for awareness program efficacy. This is important, especially within the category of affinity fraud as it relates to religion, ethnicity and nationality, particularly with regard to newly emigrated populations.

Overall, the most important aspect of a successful awareness campaign is, naturally, the message content. Any public awareness content derived from this study on fraud against the elderly must stress the relevancy of the content and must be sensible to those it is aimed at. At all costs, a fraud awareness campaign for the elderly must avoid sending any direct or indirect message of "blame" as potential victims are not usually open to being reminded of personal shortcomings. It is also imperative that the agency identified as being responsible for the awareness campaign not present an air of superiority through delivery of its message, negating any possible positive effect for program delivery. It is critical that any awareness campaign directed at the elderly not appear condescending to them. Research has shown that awareness campaigns directed at potential victims should also not resort to "scare tactics", but rather simply provide education. So then, while it is important to convey "real life" situations in which the elderly may fall victim to fraudsters, it is not helpful, and could be counterproductive, if extreme examples emphasizing exorbitant monetary loss are used as examples. It is more important, and useful, to provide information on the steps that fraudsters usually take in their strategies, and the steps that potential victims can take to reduce their chances of victimization (Scottish Office Central Research Unit, 1995). In essence, it has been shown that the most effective campaigns have provided the target audience with as much practical detailed information as possible (Derzon & Lipsey, 2002). Thus, extrapolating case study information from the present study on elderly fraud, in terms of how the frauds were carried out and what part victims may have played in their own victimization, can be the most useful take away from findings that are converted into successful public awareness programs.

In devising a fraud awareness program for the elderly, the program developers must pay special attention to campaign durations. Research has shown that crime awareness programs that advertise crime prevention tips, usually run fairly long and raise the risk of boring their target audience or cultivating a sense of indifference (Riley & Mayhew, 1980). That is why it is more effective to publicize in "short bursts." These are short intense bursts of information that rely on repetition. In a sense, it would seem to be more productive for fraud awareness programs aimed at the elderly to conduct them keeping in mind the significance of repetition to enhance retention by the target audience (Hallahan, 2000). For reaching the elderly population, any fraud awareness program must take into account the media outlets that the elderly would be more inclined to have exposure to. While printed brochures have a degree of utility, local television campaigns have proven to be the most successful for elderly audiences. Some success with billboard advertising on highways and major roads help ensure visibility with their imposing letters. Location is critical in ensuring that elderly individuals have a higher likelihood of exposure to messages.

In summary, whatever strategies are used for a fraud awareness campaign for the elderly, based on present research findings, the methods used must be multifaceted and robust. Influencing audience behavior often rests with understanding the best ways to reach the targeted audience. Sometimes the best way is direct contact from local police to the audience, particularly for the elderly population. As put by Emmanuel Barthe, "If we know that elderly women living alone have a greater fear of crime, police should seek greater campaign efficiency by addressing this group more directly." This valuable advice should be kept in mind for any federally initiated crime awareness program; a most productive course of action is to engage local enforcement who can then act as agents for the program through direct contact with elderly groups.

Proactive measures

The findings of this research study should result in proactive measures, including improved investigative methods and enhanced prevention and detection strategies for federal, state, and local law enforcement.

Recommendation 2

Local and state law enforcement leaders should encourage more cooperation with federal law enforcement where it has begun and foster it where it is not occurring.

The manner in which the criminal justice system addresses the cases from the beginning underscores the instrumental role of local law enforcement in the referral of cases to the U.S. Postal Inspection Service. The referrals may result from victim reports of fraud to local law enforcement, but also may be the product of the alertness of local officials in recognizing telltale signs of elderly fraud while investigating unrelated crimes. Local police and sheriffs' departments often act as conduits to successful federal investigations and prosecutions of these cases. This trend shows a collaborative approach to investigating elderly fraud cases and should continue and increase. A task force/team mentality should be encouraged if fraudsters preying on the elderly are to be successfully thwarted.

Recommendation 3

Law enforcement at all levels should be aware of offender characteristics and changing trends in their strategies of victim targeting and manipulation and apply that knowledge to investigations. Law enforcement should share the information they find at all government levels, so that prevention and detection strategies can be enhanced.

The findings show that fraudsters who exploit the elderly are diverse in terms of the manner in which they choose social engineering strategies and targeting strategies to raise their odds of realizing handsome profits from their criminal endeavors. Law enforcement should not only integrate findings of victim characteristics into enforcement strategies, but should also be aware of the evolving methods used by fraudsters, and factor that information into proactive enforcement strategies.

Law enforcement training

Recommendation 4

The findings should be infused into existing training programs to move beyond assumptions and anecdotes and gain a greater understanding of fraud against the elderly.

The findings of this applied research bring to light a number of characteristics of elderly fraud offenders which can contribute to continued and improved investigation and prosecution. These include the offender demographics, the methods used in the commission of the crimes, the relationships between the offenders and their victims, and organized crime group activity since a majority of the cases involved criminal conspiracies of 2 or more fraudsters. As with public awareness program development, law enforcement training pertaining to elderly fraud response and enforcement, should not be treated in a "one size fits all" approach. Federal agencies should work with state and local agencies to foster an approach that recognizes differences in regional and local demographic makeup, such that training programs are tailored to the needs of special populations within the wider senior citizen domain.

Management of cases and resources

The results of this study allow law enforcement to see a spectrum of elderly fraud cases, rather than dealing with one at a time. Law enforcement managers can use this information to intelligently assign resources and prioritize cases.

Recommendation 5

The findings of this study should be reviewed by law enforcement executives to gain a broader picture of where and how to focus their resources to combat fraud against the elderly.

The findings show that the actual dollar loss of the cases was, generally high spanning a multitude of victims per case. In addition, the study revealed examples in which the same victims were victimized more than once. To no one's surprise, elderly fraud was found to take place throughout the U.S., but there was some evidence that certain types of fraud were more common in specific pockets of the nation, addressing victim groups with unique combinations of victim demographics. Connections between gender correlations with specific types of victim behaviors should be a part of determining where resources are assigned along with proportional amounts. Indeed, fraudsters proved to be careful in tailoring manipulation strategies to the types of potential victims they were targeting. Law enforcement should take note of these methods, and dedicate resources to areas in which this criminal "fine tuning" exists.

Executive briefings

In addition to the law enforcement training that is recommended here, the relevant findings should be disseminated to law enforcement executives so that they can develop policy, allocate resources, and advocate training based on empirical research.

Recommendation 6

A briefing on the research findings which will aid law enforcement executives in developing and implementing policies and procedures for investigation and prosecution of elderly fraud should be made available.

This briefing should focus on conclusions drawn from the findings in the areas of offender methods, points of compromise (i.e., social engineering), organizational crime activity, and the victims.

Future research

This research study should be used as a model for a series of studies. The multi-year study of closed USPIS elderly fraud cases resulted in a rich data set which can be used to assist law enforcement agencies in their fight against elderly fraud. However, the criminals are continually adapting to law enforcement investigative methods by designing new methods for committing such crimes. In order to combat these crimes, law enforcement needs up-to-date information on trends, patterns, and groups, both current and emerging, to move from a reactive posture to a proactive one. Building on the baseline created through this research, further longitudinal study of USPIS closed cases with an elderly fraud component should be undertaken to determine trends and patterns of the crimes in the near past and to anticipate future trends and areas of vulnerability. All of the recommendations posited here will be better served and implemented if more applied research studies, such as this one, are completed. The ultimate goal of this and future studies is increased proactive investigation, prevention, and prosecution of these crimes.

This study is significant because it did not depend on self-reported or survey data. USPIS cases provided reliable information which was collected objectively and analyzed to reach conclusions. The impact of these findings will be measured by the effective application of the recommendations concerning proactive law enforcement methods, enhanced law enforcement training, management of cases and resources, policy development, and future research.

Disclosure statement

No potential conflict of interest was reported by the author(s).

References

Acierno, R., Hernandez-Tejada, M., Muzzy, W., & Steve, K. (2009, March) *The national elder mistreatment study*. National Institute of Justice.

Amstadter, A., Zajac, K., Strachan, M., Hernandez, M., Kilpatrick, D., & Acierno, R. (2011). Prevalence and correlates of elder mistreatment in South Carolina: The South Carolina elder mistreatment study. *Journal of Interpersonal Violence*, *26*(15), 2927–2972. https://doi.org/10.1177/0886260510390959

Barthe, E. (2006). *Crime prevention publicity campaigns* (Response Guide No. 5. Center for Problem-Oriented Policing). University at Albany.

Burrows, J., & Heal, K. (1980). Police car security campaigns. In R. Clarke & P. Mayhew (Eds.), *Designing out crime* (pp. 99–111). Her Majesty's Stationery Office.

Carlson, E. (2007). Phishing for elderly victims: As the elderly migrate to the internet fraudulent schemes targeting them follow. *The Elder Law Journal*, *14*, 423–452.

Castle, E., Eisenberger, N., Seeman, T., Moons, W., Boggero, I., Grinblatt, M., & Taylor, S. (2012, October 24). Neural and behavioral bases of age differences in perceptions of trust. *Proceedings of the National Academy of Sciences*, *109*(51), 20848–20852. https://doi.org/10.1073/pnas.1218518109

Corbyn, Z. (2012, December). Older people are more susceptible to swindlers. *Nature*. https://doi.org/10.1038/nature.2012.11928

Dagher, V. (2016, June 12). When an elderly parent has been scammed. *The Wall Street Journal*. https://www.wsj.com/articles/when-an-elderly-parent-has-been-scammed-1465783683

Deane, S. (2018, June) *Elder financial exploitation why it is a concern, what regulators are doing about it, and looking ahead*. U.S. Securities and Exchange Commission, Office of the Investor Advocate.

Derzon, J., & Lipsey, M. (2002). A meta-analysis of the effectiveness of mass communication for changing substance-use knowledge, attitudes, and behavior. In W. Crano & M. Burgoon (Eds.), *Mass media and drug prevention: Classic and contemporary theories and research* (pp. 231–258). Lawrence Erlbaum.

Grossman, I., Na, J., Varnum, M. E., Kitayama, S., & Nisbett, R. E. (2013). A route to well-being: Intelligence versus wise reasoning. *Journal of Experimental Psychology, 142*(3), 944–953. https://doi.org/10.1037/a0029560

Hallahan, K. (2000). Enhancing motivation, ability, and opportunity to process public relations messages. *Public Relations Review, 26*(4), 463–480. https://doi.org/10.1016/S0363-8111(00)00059-X

Hart, K. (2020). *Coronavirus quiz data harvesting spreads through social media.* Chartered Trading Standards Institute.

Holder, H. D., & Treno, A. J. (1997). Media advocacy in community prevention: news as a means to advance policy change. *Addiction, 92*, S189–S199. https://doi.org/10.1111/add.1997.92.issue-s2

Johnson, K. (2019, March. 7). $356,000 to protect your computer? Feds promise 'all-out attack' on scams targeting the elderly. *USA Today.* https://www.usatoday.com/story/news/politics/2019/03/07/justice-department-pledge-attack-tech-support-other-scams-hitting-elderly/3091696002/

Johnson, S., & Bowers, K. (2003). Opportunity is in the eye of the beholder: The role of publicity in crime prevention. *Criminology and Public Policy, 2*(3), 497–524. https://doi.org/10.1111/j.1745-9133.2003.tb00011.x

Jordan, M. (2014, February. 7). Users of online dating sites fall victim to Fraud. *Wall Street Journal.* https://www.wsj.com/articles/SB10001424052702304851104579363024081588350

Lachs, M., & Berman, J. (2011) *Under the Radar: New York state elder abuse prevalence study* (Final Report. Prepared by: Lifespan of Greater Rochester, Inc). Weill Cornell Medical Center of Cornell University New York City Department for the Aging.

Laumann, E., Leitsch, S. A., & Waite, L. (2008). Elder mistreatment in the United States: Prevalence estimates from a nationally representative study. *Journals of Gerontology: Series B, 63*(4), 5248–5254. https://doi.org/10.1093/geronb/63.4.S248

Loftus, E., Feinberg, S. E., & Tanur, J. (1985). Cognitive psychology meets the national survey. *American Psychologist, 40*(2), 175–180. https://doi.org/10.1037/0003-066X.40.2.175

Mangalonzo, J. (2020, June 4). *ODU study explores growth of fraud and shifts in crimes against the elderly during the pandemic.* WYDaily.

Pak, K., & Shadel, D. (2011). *AARP national fraud victim study.* AARP.

Patton, M. Q. (2002). *Qualitative research and evaluation methods.* Sage Publications.

Peterson, J. C., Burnes, P., Caccamire, A., Henderson, C., Wells, M., Berman, J., Cook, A., Shukoff, D., Brownell, M., Powell, M., Salamone, A., Pillemer, K., & Lachs, M. (2014). Financial exploitation of older adults: A population-based prevalence study. *Journal General Internal Medicine, 29*(12), 1615–1623. https://doi.org/10.1007/s11606-014-2946-2

Riley, D., & Mayhew, P. (1980). *Crime prevention publicity: An assessment* (Home Office Research Study No. 63). Home Office.

Ross, C. E., & Mirowsky, J. (1989). Explaining the Social Patterns of Depression: Control and Problem Solving–or Support and Talking? Journal of health and social behavior, 206–219 2 30 doi:10.2307/2137014

Ross, M., Grossman, I., & Schryer, E. (2014, July). Contrary to psychological and popular opinion, there is no compelling evidence that older adults are disproportionately victimized by consumer Fraud. *Perspectives on Psychological Science, 9*(4), 427–442. https://doi.org/10.1177/1745691614535935

Sacco, V., & Trotman, M. (1990). Public information programming and family violence: Lessons from the mass media crime prevention experience. *Canadian Journal of Criminology, 32*(1), 91–105.

Sannd, P., & Cook, D. (2018). *Older adults and the authenticity of emails: Grammar, syntax, and compositional indicators of social engineering in ransomware and phishing attacks.* 2018 Fourteenth International Conference on Information Processing (ICINPRO) (pp. 1–5). IEEE: Bengaluru, Karnataka, India..

Schwarz, N. (1999). Self reports: How the questions shape the answers. *American Psychologist, 54*(2), 93–105. https://doi.org/10.1037/0003-066X.54.2.93

Scottish Office Central Research Unit. (1995). *Evaluation of the Scottish office domestic violence media campaign.* Author.

Simmons, T., & Farrell, G. (1998). *Evaluation of North Brunswick township police department's community-oriented policing project to prevent auto crime*. North Brunswick Township Police Department.

Span, P. (2020, March 27). When romance is a scam. *The New York Times*. https://www.nytimes.com/2020/03/27/well/elderly-romance-scam.html

U.S. Department of Justice. (2020, October 18). *Attorney general's annual report to congress on department of justice activities to combat Elder Fraud and abuse.*

Organized Crime as Financial Crime: *The Nature of Organized Crime as Reflected in Prosecutions and Research*

Jay S. Albanese

ABSTRACT

Organized crime is a financial crime because its objective is profit or other material gain. The provision of illicit goods and services dominates organized crime profit making. Sometimes an organized crime offense is directed at power or intimidation (in cases such as racketeering or extortion), but these actions are designed to ensure the survival and profitability of an ongoing criminal enterprise. Therefore, organized crime has important similarities to the white-collar forms of financial crimes. What has been lacking in organized crime research is a comparison of actual cases of organized crime (i.e., prosecutions and convictions) to determine the extent to which organized crime prosecutions correspond to the specific offenses being researched on organized crime. An entire calendar year of organized crime prosecutions and published research articles are examined to evaluate their similarities and differences. In addition, aspects of organized crime prosecutions reveal important similarities and differences from other forms of financial crime.

The problem

Organized crime is a generic term like pornography. It has an amorphous meaning and often is not defined clearly in law, if at all. The result is imprecision. What distinguishes organized crime from other crimes? What makes organized crime "organized"? How do we determine trends in organized crime?

A consensus definition of organized crime was derived from the work of multiple authors over the years. In succinct form, organized crime is a continuing criminal enterprise with several important elements (Albanese, 2015; Finckenauer, 2005; Hagan, 1983; Maltz, 1985; Von Lampe, 2000).

(a) Planned, rational acts committed by groups of individuals.
(b) The crimes committed often respond to public demand for illicit goods and services.
(c) The objective of the crimes is financial or material gain.
(d) Corruption and intimidation are used to protect ongoing criminal enterprises.

It is crucial to recognize that organized crime seeks financial gain as an objective, unlike terrorism, some hate crimes, or other forms of organized criminal behavior which is centered around ideology or political objectives. In this regard, organized crime and white-collar crimes are similar, given their financial objectives.

On the other hand, white collar and organized crimes have important differences. There are multiple definitions of white-collar crime, some including occupational settings, abuse of power, the offender's social status, and inclusion or exclusion of government misconduct (Albanese, 1995; Benson & Simpson, 2018; Friedrichs, 2010; Geis, 1992; Hirschi & Gottfredson, 1987; Steffensmeier, 1989; Sutherland, 1940). The term "economic crime" is used instead of white-collar crime by some investigators to focus more on the nature and objective of the crime, rather than by the nature of the perpetrator (Chambers, 2012; Edelhertz, 1980; Engdahl & Larsson, 2016; Kryvoi, 2018).

U.S. Attorney's Offices, under the supervision of the Department of Justice, are inclusive in the cases they consider part of the organized crime problem. These cases deal with both traditional and non-traditional organized criminal groups, as well as illegal drug trafficking prosecutions. Federal prosecutions focus particularly on the importation of illegal narcotics, interstate, large-scale or organized drug trafficking, or individuals or groups that use violence in the course of drug dealing, as well as other kinds of illegal or banned goods (U.S. Department of Justice, 2020). State and local jurisdictions prosecute the vast majority of drug offenders, so the U.S. Attorney's Offices focus their efforts on interstate, international, organized crime offenders, and cases involving the diversion of prescription drugs for illegal sale. Therefore, prosecutions of organized crime in the US are generated by both organized crime *group* activity, as well as by the nature of *crimes* committed (organized trafficking in illicit goods and services).

The literature

Organized crime has a folklore and mythology surrounding it, involving ethnicity, national origin, trafficking illicitly in goods and services, and extortion threats (Albini & McIllwain, 2013; Catino, 2019; Finckenauer, 2007; Nicaso & Danesi, 2017; Viano et al., 2004). These are terms not associated with white-collar crime or financial crimes in general, even though organized crime has the same objective of financial gain.

There has been much discussion and debate about the true nature and status of organized crime. Are organized crime activities shifting more toward economic crimes, such as cybercrime and fraud, or does it remain focused on illicit trafficking of goods and services? There are multiple known cases of transnational frauds committed by criminal groups or networks, but it has not been determined whether this is typical or aberrant behavior in the world of organized crime. Likewise, there is commentary on the rise (or fall) of mafia groups, street gangs, prison gangs, and transnational groups operating in the US. Many reports are based on anecdotal evidence, so it is difficult to distinguish particular incidents from actual trends (Asmann et al., 2020; Behar, 2020; Belger, 2019; Muggah, 2020). These are all empirical questions, which require evidence to support or refute. A lack of systematic data collection leaves researchers to generate data based on available information, resulting in many small-scale, and regional studies, and the speculation of experts (Kumar & Tidey, 2020; Mahadevan, 2020; Tilley & Hopkins, 2008; Weber & Kruisbergen, 2019). These studies are quite useful, but they cannot paint a big picture of trends across a large area. The result has been a reliance on organized crime research on official data or interviews with public officials and, less often, on offenders and victims. Windle and Silke (2019) found in their review of 160 published research articles on organized crime that "secondary analysis of open-access documents has overwhelmingly dominated the field" (p. 410). The reason for this situation, of course, is the lack of available funding in most locations around the world (including the US) to support original data collection on organized crime. This leaves researchers in the position of carrying-out small-scale empirical studies, or attempting larger studies based on existing data, usually using government sources for data.

The existing research on organized crime reveals that much attention is devoted to particular types of organized crime. This finding was empirically determined, after a review was undertaken (for this manuscript) of all the published articles (in English) in four research journals that focus primarily on organized crime issues, plus a broader search of journals indexed by EBSCO Academic Search Complete. Articles were evaluated for their central focus on specific types of organized crime activities (some articles focused on more than a single type). They are summarized in Figure 1.

Figure 1 indicates that 58 organized crime research articles were published in journals in 2019. These 58 articles focused on 11 different types of organized crime activity with racketeering/extortion being the most common and tobacco smuggling and retail theft the least. It is not surprising that so many articles focused on racketeering/extortion because the articles focused on how groups and networks organize, structure themselves, and operate. The remaining substantive crimes addressed in these various studies reveal that organized crime research is focused on a circumscribed list of offenses. The substantive crimes carried out vary widely across the six continents covered by these research studies

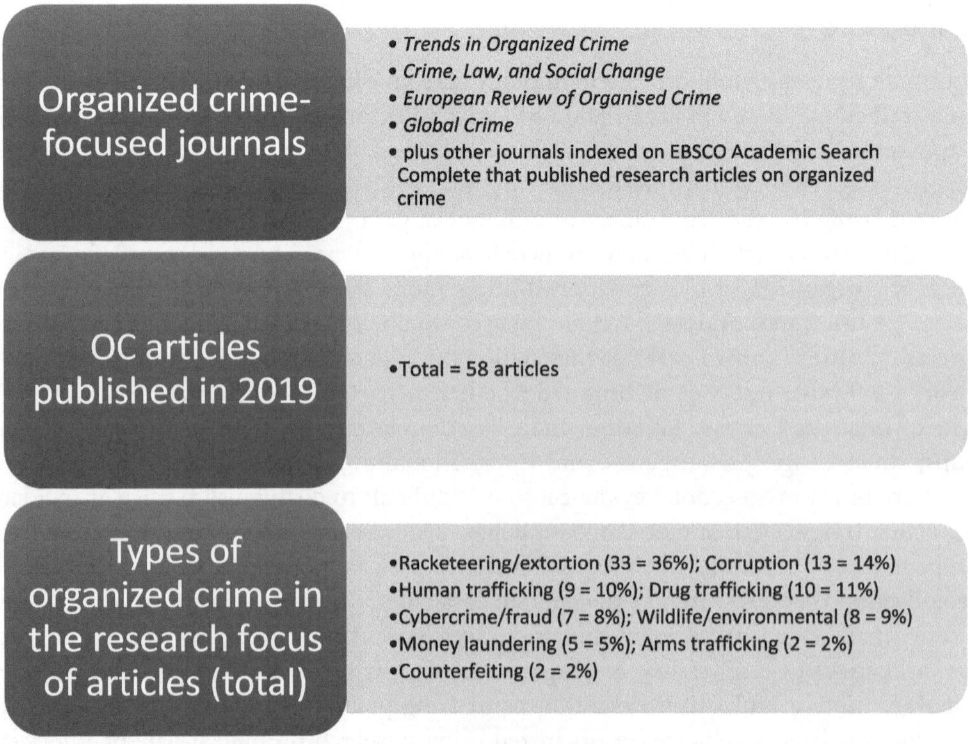

Figure 1. Types of organized crime found in research journals.

(the bulk of which are focused on a single country or region within a country). This summary paints a very broad picture of the nature of organized crime research published during 2019, understanding that some additional research articles may have appeared in other journals not indexed by the sources used.

The current study next attempted a large-scale examination of all organized crime criminal cases that occurred during 2019. These cases are empirically justified for inclusion in that they have all met a burden of proof (probable cause for arrest or indictment, and proof beyond reasonable doubt for conviction). Therefore, the cases in this sample reflect actual organized crime conduct, rather than opinions and speculations. Second, this study will compare its findings on the characteristics of specific cases to the nature of the research studies published in journals, and also the interviews and opinions with experts and others on the current state of organized crime.

Methods

This study is focused on determining the current characteristics of organized crime by evaluating actual criminal cases in which a burden of proof has been reached, which include organized crime as a central feature. Using the government's own classification in determining whether a case was related to organized crime, every press release issued by a U.S. Attorney's Office that contained anywhere the term "organized crime" was coded. This was a painstaking process that required a review of every document released that contained this phrase. Most of these documents reported on specific cases relevant to the current research. Others were announcements of new task forces, or other community or government initiatives that were excluded from this analysis. As a result, this sample includes only cases involving organized crime in some way that occurred over a single calendar year.

U.S. Attorney's Offices invariably issue a press release when an organized crime case results in an arrest, indictment, conviction, or sentence. Interviews with former career Department of Justice (DOJ) prosecutors confirmed that cases involving public corruption or organized crime result in wide dissemination (Albanese & Artello, 2019). This occurs for two primary reasons: the U.S. Department of Justice has specialized units dealing with organized crime, and there is great public interest in organized crime cases, so it provides the DOJ with an opportunity to demonstrate and publicize its work against organized crime.

Data are presented here to examine the extent to which research discussions about organized crime match the organized crimes found in practice. The U.S. government does not systematically make available charging documents, indictments, guilty pleas, or sentencing memos in systematic fashion. Details from available cases involving organized crime cannot be separated from other cases with any efficiency using government records. Similarly, news media reports are not comprehensive and their coverage varies widely around the country, making it an incomplete data source. The written releases from U.S. Attorney's Offices are a comprehensive alternative in that they include all organized crime cases, and they also include the names of principals in those cases. This enables the connecting of multiple defendants involved in a single criminal scheme, who are prosecuted, convicted, or sentenced at different times, avoiding double-counting.

There are 94 U.S. Attorney's Offices in the United States, distributed geographically across the country. Each office's output was reviewed for this study, resulting in 1,451 total reports involving organized crime cases identified in this analysis. The nature of the project is more complicated than it appears, given that an arrest, indictment, conviction, or sentence might result in separate press releases on a single case at different stages of the criminal process. In addition, organized crime cases usually involve multiple defendants. The scope of this effort involved careful review of a large number of cases, the descriptions and multiple locations of the criminal operations, and the need to combine individual defendants into distinct criminal schemes. For example, 10 defendants might be charged, arrested, indicted, or convicted at different times, but the review of documents reveals they were part of a single criminal scheme. In these cases, we merged the documents that referred to the same case, but simply reported on different stages of criminal procedure. We were interested in distinct cases (organized crime events or incidents), rather than individual defendants.

Given the large number of cases, only those that occurred over a single calendar year (2019) were analyzed for this study. Therefore, the research design is cross-sectional, although it includes every organized crime case occurring over 12 months.

Findings

Organized crime cases were brought in nearly every U.S. region in 2019, but the cases are not evenly distributed. Some regions had very few cases, while others had large numbers. Table 1 reveals that only 10 of the 94 federal judicial districts accounted for nearly half of all cases brought. In addition, the cases are not concentrated in large urban areas, as one might assume. Jurisdictions such as West Virginia, Western Pennsylvania, North Carolina, and New Hampshire were in the top 10 most active regions in generating organized crime cases. Therefore, factors other than urban environments play an important role in organized crime activity.

The cases discovered were at different stages of adjudication during 2019. Of the total 1,451 unique organized crime cases found during the calendar year, the vast majority were either indictments (formal charges) or sentences imposed (see Figure 2). Other cases were at the arrest stage, had resulted in convictions, or were awaiting adjudication or sentencing. By their nature, organized crime cases involve multiple defendants and victims, so it is common for a case to take several years from arrest through sentencing. The cross-sectional sample used here captures these cases at a single point in time, regardless of adjudication status. Other work on case trends over 30 years found that the federal government prosecutes two-thirds of investigative referrals in organized cases, and most

Table 1. Organized crime cases by federal district.

US district	Freq.	Percent
West Virginia-North	152	10.5
New York-South	101	7.0
Pennsylvania-West	94	6.5
North Carolina-East	55	3.8
New York-East	53	3.6
California-Central	52	3.6
Maryland	50	3.4
New Jersey	44	3.0
Massachusetts	40	2.8
New Hampshire	35	2.1
Total	676	46.6

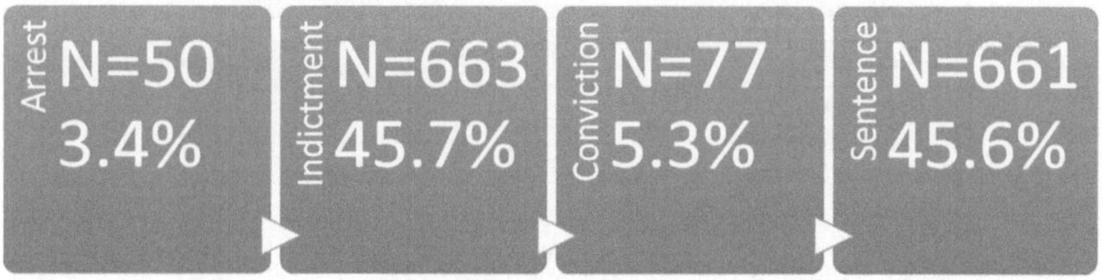

Figure 2. Organized crime cases by adjudication status.

of these adjudicated cases result in convictions (Artello & Albanese, 2019a). Once a case is initiated, therefore, it is likely to result in a successful prosecution.

Given the increasingly transnational nature of organized crime, an effort was made to determine the extent to which these cases, occurring in the US, had documented connections to other regions of the world. The connections usually involved the supply or demand for an illicit product or service. In other cases, the criminal scheme occurred on one continent with victims located elsewhere, or it moved transnationally.

As shown in Table 2, 17% of all cases (N = 241) prosecuted had proven connections outside the US. The largest percentage of cases (45.2%) involved North American connections outside the US (i.e., Mexico or Canada). The second largest group involved Central American countries (30.7%). These results are not surprising, because smuggling routes often take the closest, easiest, and most profitable path from supply to demand locations (Karson, 2014; Owens et al., 2014; Tinti, 2014; UNODC, 2018). Nevertheless, 13.7% of these cases that were prosecuted in the US had documented connections to Asia, and another 10.4% had connections to Europe, Africa, or the Middle East, illustrating the global reach of organized crime.

An important part of this project was to identify the nature of the organized crimes prosecuted, as a reflection of both their incidence and level of public/government concern. Table 3 summarizes the nature of the lead (primary) charges that resulted in prosecution. These charges are grouped into 10 substantive categories of illegal behavior. Drug trafficking was, by far, the most common charge (72.8%), followed by racketeering/extortion cases (13.3%). The other types of crimes occurred much less frequently, but there were significant numbers of cases involving human trafficking, fraud/counterfeiting, cybercrime, and money laundering.

Organized crime cases are often complex, because the offenses are occurring as part of an ongoing criminal enterprise. Therefore, multiple illicit activities often occur simultaneously and over time. Table 4 presents these data, illustrating that racketeering/extortion was the

Table 2. Transnational connections in organized crime cases.

Continents outside US	Number	Percent
North America	109	45.2
Central America	74	30.7
Asia	33	13.7
Eastern Europe	8	3.3
Africa	9	3.7
Middle East	4	1.7
Western Europe	4	1.7
Total	241	100

Table 3. Charges brought in US organized crime cases.

Lead Crime Type	Number	Percent
Drug trafficking	1,052	72.8
RICO/extortion/violence	192	13.3
Human trafficking	46	3.2
Fraud & counterfeit goods	39	2.7
Cybercrime	38	2.6
Money laundering	33	2.3
Corruption, bribery, obstruction	20	1.4
Firearms trafficking	14	1
Gambling bus./dog fighting	7	0.5
Wildlife, Environment crimes	5	0.3
Total	1,446	100

most common second- and third-level charge in organized crime cases. This finding indicates that the ongoing organization of the group or network behind the activity (racketeering) and the threats needed to enforce illicit authority and compliance (extortion) were also a focus of these organized crime prosecutions. In addition to prosecuting the substantive offense, it is clear that prosecutions also were directed at the organized crime group itself in operating an ongoing criminal enterprise.

It also is shown in Table 4 that money laundering is a commonly charged second or third-level offense (ranked #2 and #3, respectively). This suggests the placing and moving the profits from illicit enterprises is a focus of organized crime prosecutions (when such evidence is available). Similarly, cybercrimes are the #3 and #4 most commonly charged offenses in cases involving multiple crimes, suggesting a significant role of illicit cyber activity in contemporary organized crime cases. When considering the range of organized crime offenses, this empirical examination is similar in result in the hypothesized spectrum of organized crimes (Holmes, 2016; Sergi, 2017; Wright, 2006). Therefore, the types of organized crime cases prosecuted in practice are similar in content to those included by authors writing on the subject.

The nature and size of organized crime groups prosecuted vary considerably. The average number of defendants per case was six, although cases ranged from one defendant to several hundred. Organized crime groups with specific names also were captured in this search. Groups identified by name appeared in 297 cases with a total of 179 distinct groups named in the more than 1,400 total prosecutions. Table 5 identifies the top 14 groups identified by frequency of appearance in these criminal cases. These 14 groups include all those groups named in at least three criminal prosecutions, representing 41% of all groups identified by name during 2019.

Table 4. Second and third-level charges in organized crime cases.

Second & Third Level Charges	Number	Percent	2ndRank	3rdRank
Drug trafficking	16	17.6	3	2
RICO/extortion/violence	30	33	1	1
Human trafficking	6	6.6	6	5
Fraud & counterfeit goods	8	8.8	5	4
Cybercrime	13	14.3	4	3
Money laundering	13	14.3	2	3
Bribery, corruption, obstruction	2	2.2	8	6
Firearms trafficking	2	2.2	7	6
Gambling business/dog fighting	0	0	9	8
Wildlife, Environment crimes	1	1.1	10	7
Total	91	100		

Table 5. Organized crime groups named in criminal cases.

OC Groups & Gangs	N	% of all cases
Total groups identified	279	19.3%
Total different groups identified	179	
Top 14 Groups Involved:	***115 cases***	***41%***
MS-13 (La Mara Salvatrucha)	28	9.4
Greenway Boy Killas (GBK)	22	7.4
Gangster Disciples (GD)	9	3
Nine Trey Gangsters (Blood gang)	8	2.7
Almighty Latin Kings Nation	7	2.4
SCO gang	7	2.4
Kingsmen Motorcycle Club	6	2
Sinaloa Cartel, Mexico	5	1.7
Hillside Enterprise	5	1.7
Black *P*-Stones	4	1.4
Nuestra Familia prison gang	4	1.4
Trained to Go (TTG)	4	1.4
Murdaland mafia Piru Bloods gang	3	1
Colombo organized crime family	3	1

As Table 5 illustrates, a number of street gangs and drug trafficking organizations are represented in the top 14 groups identified, reflecting the strong concentration of drug trafficking cases prosecuted. Many are groups with Mexican or Central American origins. Only one traditional mafia group was in the top 14 list. Of course, many organized crime operations do not have identifiable names or affiliations, but it can be seen that such affiliations existed in nearly 20% of all organized crime cases prosecuted.

Limitations

This study reviews one calendar year of organized crime prosecutions in the United States. The primary limitations of this work are two: cross-sectional design and official data source. This project examined all cases (1,451) prosecuted during calendar year 2019 in the US. In order to examine trends over time, it would be necessary to review cases over multiple years, which requires greater resources than are currently available. Such a multi-year perspective would also have to account for other longitudinal factors, such as changing federal prosecution priorities over time, world events (e.g., COVID-19, economic recessions), and related factors that might also influence prosecution trends. These factors are amorphous in that their role in the causal chain of events is difficult to assess.

It is noted, however, that an earlier examination of organized crime cases found no significant increases in prosecution referrals over time (Artello & Albanese, 2019). Therefore, there have not been wide fluctuations year-to-year in the US, although the total number of organized crime cases has declined over the last 30 years in favor of other prosecution targets. For example, immigration cases now comprise the largest percentage of federal criminal prosecutions in the United States, due to a recent surge in prosecuting these cases as crimes beginning in 2017 (TRAC, 2020; U.S. Sentencing Commission, 2020).

A second limitation is the use of official data. Government prosecutions against organized crime reflect its priorities, and not necessarily changes in the nature of organized crime itself. As noted earlier, however, Windle and Silke (2019) review of 160 published research articles on organized crime found that the vast majority relied on official data, given the limits of funding, and the time and access required to conduct interviews of offenders, victims, or others.

Nevertheless, this study reflects the universe of organized crime cases prosecuted in the US over a full calendar year. This group of more than 1,400 cases reflects significant government investigative and prosecution effort against organized crime. It provides many insights into the nature of organized crime activity uncovered during this period.

Discussion & conclusions

A central aspect of the vast majority of organized crimes – financial gain – provides an anchor for directing future research and policy in the field in order to highlight the similarities, rather than the differences, among the various types of organized crime. Although white-collar financial crime often involves frauds in the legitimate sector to deceive victims, organized crime activities seek profit through provision of illicit goods and services for which the public is willing to pay (Friedrichs, 2010; Holmes, 2016; Marriott, 2020; Soltes, 2016). Therefore, the fraudulent methods and deviation from legitimate business activity, that characterize white-collar crimes, are replaced by trafficking and distribution of illicit products and services as part of an ongoing criminal enterprise that characterizes organized crime.

Comparing the current emphasis in organized crime research (see Figure 1) to actual cases prosecuted, there are both similarities and differences that emerge. The contemporary research literature focuses primarily on racketeering/extortion (36%), corruption (14%), human trafficking (10%) drug trafficking (11%), cybercrime/fraud (8%), and wildlife/environmental crimes (9%). Recent organized crime prosecutions, occurring during a similar timeframe, are dominated by drug trafficking, racketeering/extortion, human trafficking, fraud/counterfeit goods, cybercrime, and money laundering (see Tables 3 and 4). Therefore, research studies focus more on corruption and environmental crimes than do actual prosecutions, whereas criminal prosecutions focus on fraud/counterfeiting and money laundering more do than the research studies identified in this review.

On the other hand, both research and prosecution efforts devote significant effort to organized crime involving racketeering/extortion, human trafficking, and cybercrime, illustrating the dominance of these contemporary manifestations of organized crime. It remains to be seen whether actual prosecutions will follow the research lead to investigating corruption and environmental crimes (Chin & Murillo, 2020; Williams, 2019). In the same fashion, the future is uncertain whether more research will follow the prosecution focus on fraud/counterfeiting and money laundering offenses (see Jurva, 2018; Lallerstedt, 2018).

The differences between organized crime and white-collar crime are well documented, but their similar objectives often overlooked. This research offers insight into the nature of organized crime through an examination of a large number of prosecuted cases. The specific types of illicit activities, groups, and locations identified here offer insight into the nature of organized uncovered through prosecutions, how it is similar and different to the current research on the subject, and its similarity in motive to white-collar financial crimes. It is noteworthy that organized crime prosecutions are widely distributed geographically, and include many non-urban areas. In addition, most of the organized crime cases prosecuted occurred entirely within the US. It remains to be investigated whether this characterizes the true nature of organized crime activity occurring, or whether it reflects the difficulty in discovering and proving transnational crimes.

In a study of financing-related aspects of organized crime in 27 EU member states, it was found that "intelligence gathering by law enforcement agencies has typically been focused on identifying members of criminal groups and tracing illicit goods or services they sell, whereas their financial transactions have rarely been traced" (Center for the Study of Democracy, 2015, p. 419). An important finding of this research is how often the structure of an organized crime group or network is the focus of criminal prosecutions. This is revealed in the significant number of cases that involve prosecutions for racketeering/ extortion, money laundering, and corruption – -all crimes needed to *protect* an illicit enterprise and its profits, rather than as direct *income-producing* activity as an important source of revenue. It has also been observed that corruption "is one of the primary enabling activities" of organized crime that "make possible and/or facilitate the conduct" for the profit-making provision of illicit goods and services (Reed, 2009).

In 2011, The US National Security Council released its *Strategy to Combat Transnational Organized Crime*. Its recommended "priority actions" included two categories of substantive crimes: (1) disrupting drug trafficking due to its prevalence and high-level of profits which funds other criminal activities, and (2) protecting the financial system and strategic markets against transnational-organized crime. This emphasis included cybercrime, money laundering, and asset forfeiture (National Security Council, 2011). These two priority areas are clearly reflected in the prosecuted cases reported here with drug trafficking the most common substantive offense, and money laundering the most common second and third-level offense charged. Cybercrime cases closely followed money laundering as second and third-level charges. This finding suggests that public/government emphasis and attention given to specific types of crimes can result in shifting the targets of investigation and prosecutions. What remains to be seen is whether research findings can similarly be highlighted to draw attention to other kinds of serious organized crime that currently lack the same prosecution priority (i.e., corruption and environmental crimes).

The challenge for the future is to find ways to use more robustly funded research to highlight "emerging" or newly discovered crimes. A greater effort must then be made to disseminate these findings to a wider audience (that includes both the general public and government decision-makers) in an effort to move forward research findings about new kinds of criminal activity into public priorities that are acted upon, in order to reduce their incidence and harm. In this way, we can move away from finding the organized crime we're looking for, to finding newly discovered types of organized crime identified as emerging threats.

Disclosure statement

No potential conflict of interest was reported by the author(s).

ORCID

Jay S. Albanese http://orcid.org/0000-0003-4496-8147

References

Albanese, J. S. (1995). *White Collar crime in America*. Prentice Hall.
Albanese, J. S. (2015). *Organized crime: From the mob to transnational organized crime*. Routledge.

Albanese, J. S., & Artello, K. (2019). The behavior of corruption: An empirical typology of public corruption by objective & method. *Journal of Criminology, Criminal Justice, Law & Society*, *20*(1), 1–12.

Albini, J. L., & McIllwain, J. S. (2013). *Deconstructing organized crime*. McFarland & Company.

Artello, K., & Albanese, J. S. (2019). Investigative decision-making in public corruption cases: Factors influencing case outcomes. *Social Sciences*, *5*(1), 1–15. https://www.tandfonline.com/doi/full/10.1080/23311886.2019.1670510

Artello, K., & Albanese, J. S. (2019a). The calculus of public corruption cases: Hidden decisions in investigations and prosecutions. *Journal of Criminal Justice and Law*, *3*(1), 21–36. http://uhd.edu/academics/public-service/jcjl/Documents/Volume%203%20Issue%201%20Article%202%20Artello%20Albanese%202019.pdf

Asmann, P., Dalby, C., & Robbins, S. (2020, May 4). *Six ways coronavirus is impacting organized crime in the Americas*. Insightcrime.org. https://www.insightcrime.org/news/analysis/coronavirus-organized-crime-latin-america/

Behar, R. (2020, March 27). *Organized crime in the time of corona*. Forbes. https://www.forbes.com/sites/richardbehar/2020/03/27/organized-crime-in-the-time-of-corona/#2f5224150d5b

Belger, T. (2019, December 26). *The 11 richest countries with the biggest organized crime problems*. Yahoo Finance. https://finance.yahoo.com/news/best-worst-countries-organised-crime-ranked-world-economic-forum-davos-homicide-rate-054509313.html

Benson, M. L., & Simpson, S. S. (2018). *White-collar crime: An opportunity perspective* (3rd ed.). Routledge.

Catino, M. (2019). *Mafia organizations: The visible hand of criminal enterprise*. Cambridge University Press.

Center for the Study of Democracy. (2015). *Financing of organised crime*. European Commission.

Chambers, C. (2012). Can you ever regulate the virtual world against economic crime? *Journal of International Commercial Law & Technology*, *7*(4), 339–349. https://www.neliti.com/publications/28762/can-you-ever-regulate-the-virtual-world-against-economic-crime

Chin, S., & Murillo, Y. (2020). *Has environmental crime changed during the COVID-19 crisis?* Global Initiative against Transnational Organized Crime. https://globalinitiative.net/covid-environment/

Edelhertz, H. (1980). Transnational White-Collar crime: A developing challenge and need for response. *Temple Law Quarterly*, *53*(4), 1114–1148.

Engdahl, O., & Larsson, B. (2016). Duties to distrust: The decentering of economic and White-Collar crime policing in Sweden. *British Journal of Criminology*, *56*(3), 515–536. https://doi.org/10.1093/bjc/azv070

Finckenauer, J. O. (2005). Problems of definition: What is organized crime? *Trends in Organized Crime*, *8*(3), 63–83. https://doi.org/10.1007/s12117-005-1038-4

Finckenauer, J. O. (2007). *Mafia and organized crime*. Oneworld Publications.

Friedrichs, D. O. (2010). *Trusted criminals: White Collar crime in contemporary society* (4th ed.). Wadsworth.

Geis, G. (1992). White-Collar crime: What is it? In K. Schlegel & D. Weisburd (Eds.), *White-Collar crime reconsidered*. Northeastern University Press.

Hagan, F. E. (1983). 'Organized crime' and 'organized crime': Indeterminate problems of definition. *Trends in Organized Crime*, *9*(4), 127–137. https://doi.org/10.1007/s12117-006-1017-4

Hirschi, T., & Gottfredson, M. (1987). Causes of White-Collar crime. *Criminology*, *25*(4), 961. https://doi.org/10.1111/j.1745-9125.1987.tb00827.x

Holmes, L. (2016). *Advanced introduction to organised crime*. Elgar Publishing.

Jurva, G. (2018). *Five-part series — Counterfeit goods: Money laundering in plain sight*. Thomson Reuters Legal Executive Institute. https://www.legalexecutiveinstitute.com/counterfeit-goods-money-laundering/

Karson, L. (2014). *American smuggling as White Collar crime*. Routledge.

Kryvoi, Y. (2018). Economic crimes in international investment law. *International & Comparative Law Quarterly*, *67*(3), 577–605. https://doi.org/10.1017/S0020589318000131

Kumar, I., & Tidey, A. (2020, March 3). COVID-19: Organised crime groups 'adapting' with 'new crime trends', interpol warns. *Euronews.com*.

Lallerstedt, K. (2018). Measuring illicit trade and its wider impact. In V. Comilli (Ed.), *Organized crime and illicit trade*. Palgrave Macmillan.

Mahadevan, P. (2020). *Cybercrime threats during the COVID-19 epidemic*. Global Initiative Against Transnational Organized Crime. https://globalinitiative.net/wp-content/uploads/2020/04/Cybercrime-Threats-during-the-Covid-19-pandemic.pdf

Maltz, M. (1985). On defining organized crime. In H. Alexander & G. Caiden (Eds.), *The politics and economics of organized crime*. Lexington Books.

Marriott, L. (2020). White-Collar crime: The privileging of serious financial fraud in New Zealand. *Social & Legal Studies*, *29*(4), 486–506. https://doi.org/10.1177/0964663919883367

Muggah, R. (2020, May 8). *The pandemic has triggered dramatic shifts in the global criminal underworld*. Foreign Policy. https://foreignpolicy.com/2020/05/08/coronavirus-drug-cartels-violence-smuggling/

National Security Council. (2011). *Strategy to combat transnational organized crime*. Retrieved June 1, 2020, from https://obamawhitehouse.archives.gov/administration/eop/nsc/transnational-crime

Nicaso, A., & Danesi, M. (2017). *Made men: Mafia culture and the power of symbols, rituals, and myth*. Rowman & Littlefield.

Owens, C., Dank, M., Breaux, J., Bañuelos, I., Farrell, A., Pfeffer, R., & McDevitt, J. (2014). *Understanding the organization, operation, and victimization process of labor trafficking in the United States*. Urban Institute.

Reed, Q. (2009). *Squeezing a balloon? Challenging the nexus between organised crime and corruption*. U4 Anti-Corruption Resources Centre. Retrieved June 3, 2020, from https://www.u4.no/publications/squeezing-a-balloon-challenging-the-nexus-between-organised-crime-and-corruption-2.pdf

Sergi, A. (2017). Mafia and organised crime: The spectrum and the models. In Anna Sergi (Ed.), *From Mafia to organised crime. Critical criminological perspectives* (pp. 21–59). Palgrave Macmillan.

Soltes, E. (2016). *Why do they do it? Inside the mind of the White Collar criminal*. Public Affairs.

Steffensmeier, D. (1989). On the causes of White-Collar crime: An assessment of Hirschi and Gottfredson's claims. *Criminology*, *27*(2), 347. https://doi.org/10.1111/j.1745-9125.1989.tb01036.x

Sutherland, E. (1940). White-Collar criminality. *American Sociological Review*, *5*(1), 1–12. https://doi.org/10.2307/2083937

Tilley, N., & Hopkins, M. (2008). Organized crime and local businesses. *Criminology & Criminal Justice: An International Journal*, *8*(4), 443–459. https://doi.org/10.1177/1748895808096469

Tinti, P. (2014). *Illicit trafficking and instability in Mali: Past, present and future*. Global Initiative against Transnational Organized Crime.

TRAC. (2020). *Federal criminal prosecutions plummet in wake of COVID-19*. Transactional Records Access Clearinghouse. https://trac.syr.edu/tracreports/crim/609/

U.S. Department of Justice. (2020). *Narcotics and organized crime*. Retrieved May 15, 2020, from https://www.justice.gov/usao-edpa/divisions/criminal-division

U.S. Sentencing Commission. (2020). *Fiscal year 2019 overview of federal criminal cases*. Retrieved May 27, 2020, from https://www.ussc.gov/sites/default/files/pdf/research-and-publications/research-publications/2020/FY19_Overview_Federal_Criminal_Cases.pdf

UNODC. (2018). *Global study on smuggling of migrants 2018*. United Nations Office on Drugs and Crime.

Viano, E. C., Magallanes, J., & Brid, L. (2004). *Transnational organized crime: Myth, power, and profit*. Carolina Academic Press.

Von Lampe, K. (2000). *Definitions of organized crime*. Retrieved June 1, 2020, from www.organized-crime.de/organizedcrimedefinitions.htm

Weber, J., & Kruisbergen, E. W. (2019). Criminal markets: The dark web, money laundering and counterstrategies - An overview of the 10th research conference on organized crime. *Trends in Organized Crime*, *22*(3), 346–356. https://doi.org/10.1007/s12117-019-09365-8

Williams, D. A. (2019). *Understanding effects of corruption on law enforcement and environmental crime*. U4 Anti-Corruption Resource Centre. Retrieved June 3, 2020, from https://www.u4.no/publications/understanding-effects-of-corruption-on-law-enforcement-and-environmental-crime.pdf

Windle, J., & Silke, A. (2019). Is drawing from the state 'state of the art'? A review of organised crime research data collection and analysis, 2004–2018. *Trends in Organized Crime*, *22*(4), 394–413. https://doi.org/10.1007/s12117-018-9356-5

Wright, A. (2006). *Organised crime*. Willan Publishing.

Preventing Identity Theft: Perspectives on Technological Solutions from Industry Insiders

Nicole Leeper Piquero, Alex R. Piquero, Stephen Gies, Brandn Green, Amanda Bobnis, and Eva Velasquez

ABSTRACT

An estimated 26 million American citizens per year have been victims of an identity-based crime. This study contributes to the scholarship on financial crimes facilitated through identity-based criminal activity by examining the views on technological approaches to the prevention of identity theft among 50 professionals working in the identity-based crime victim services, including those from the public sector and private industry. The professionally diverse sample included private investigators, fraud examiners, victim service providers, and executives of firms offering victim services and protection services. Data were collected during a series of focus groups held at professional conferences. The paper reports on the views held by focus group participants on specific technological solutions to identity theft victimization, including biometric scanning, dark web scanning, subscription - based monitoring programs, and broader thematic observations about the current environment for protecting information, emerging sources of risk, and policy recommendations identified by focus group participants. Perspectives from insiders about the pros and cons of each approach can provide researchers and enforcement agencies with enhanced capacity to avoid empty technological promises that fail to protect victims from subsequent victimizations.

Introduction

Identity-based victimization continues to be a growing problem in terms of both the total number of victims and the amount of direct and indirect harm caused to those victims. Like other white-collar crimes, the victims are individuals as well as organizations. The costs of identity-based crimes often are believed to be easily calculated by simply assessing the amount of direct victimization or the amount of money that has been taken (Cohen, 2016). However, as many scholars who estimate the costs of crimes have found, the taxonomy of crime costs includes at least three major categories: 1) costs incurred in anticipation of the crime (i.e., prevention), 2) costs incurred as a consequence of the crime (i.e., victimization), and 3) costs in response to crime (i.e., criminal justice expenditures) (Brand & Price, 2000; Cohen, 2005, 2016). The focus of this paper is on understanding prevention efforts, particularly the technological approaches, to combating identity-based crimes. In order to do so, we asked industry insiders their views about existing and emerging threats to victims, both individual and organizational, their assessment of effectiveness and limitations to specific technological prevention solutions, and recommendations for improving systems and policies.

The prevention of identity theft (Gilbert & Archer, 2012; Milne, 2003) does not lie with only one entity but rather requires the responsibility, cooperation, and actions of three major groups: individuals, businesses, and government. Individuals have the information that must be protected and need to take care to guard their personally identifiable information (PII). To help them do so, agencies such as the Federal Trade Commission recommend a plethora of preventive measures, such as shredding sensitive documents and regularly reviewing credit reports and credit card statements, which individuals are encouraged to undertake for their own protection. Businesses are entrusted with consumers' PII, whether they require individuals to give it to them during business transactions or whether individuals freely share such information with them (e.g., on free social networking sites). Government or legislative bodies enact legislative measures that are designed either to deter the crime by creating tough punishments for those guilty of identity theft or to prod businesses into improving security measures for safeguarding the PII that individuals have entrusted to them. Actions taken in isolation by any one of the three entities (individuals, businesses, or government) will increase protection; however, as indicated by industry experts we spoke with, what really must occur is the collective cooperation and proactive engagement of all who bear responsibility for preventing identity-based crimes.

Background evidence

Identity theft and identity fraud, while connected, are not the same (Sullivan, 2009). Identity theft is often the first step in a two-step process by which specific types of personally identifiable information (PII) are stolen and used to commit identity fraud (Vieraitis et al., 2015).

Incidence of identity-based victimization

In 2016 the estimate for incidents of past-year identity-based victimization in the United States was at 26 million (Harrell, 2019). Identity-based crimes, including identity theft and fraud, are growing areas of crime (Center for Victim Research [CVR], 2019). Comparison studies of identity-based crime victims and victims of both violent and nonviolent crimes have concluded that victims of identity-based crimes are less likely to report an incident to law enforcement and are more likely to report it to non-law enforcement agencies than other types of victims (Copes et al., 2010; Harrell & Langton, 2013; Piquero, 2018; Reyns & Randa, 2017; Tcherni et al., 2016). Victims generally do not report the incidents of identity-based crime to law enforcement for one of two reasons: they have settled the issue with their financial institution, or they believe their losses are minor and have little hope that their personally identifiable information (PII) will be recovered (Tcherni et al., 2016). Remediation efforts vary greatly across different types of identity-based crimes. In addition, prior scholarship has noted that some personal data can be readily canceled (e.g., credit card numbers) whereas others (e.g., fingerprints) cannot (Solove & Citron, 2018).

Risk factors for identity-based victimization

Victimization research examining the relationship between activities taken by victims and exposure to the risk of identity theft has concentrated on online transactions (Lai et al.,

2012; Milne et al., 2004; Solove & Citron, 2018), the consequences of being the victim of a data breach (Solove & Citron, 2018), spending time in chat rooms and engaging in social networking (Holt & Bossler, 2014), and use of online security tools (Ricci et al., 2019). The consensus is that those who engage in routine computer communication and commerce supported by electronic transfers (e.g., credit cards) are at a slightly higher risk for identity-based crimes and that this risk is in contrast to the convenience electronic commerce creates for those who participate in modern business transactions (Chen et al., 2017; Payne & Kennett-Hensel, 2017; Reyns & Randa, 2017).

Adoption of technologies to prevent identity theft

As individuals spend more time online (e.g., checking e-mail, reading social media, ordering goods and services, banking), it is no surprise that there has been a concomitant increase in the risk of identity theft victimization, and in the range of services and technologies that people can use to help lower – but not eliminate – the risk of victimization. Unfortunately, not much is known about these services.

A recent study on fraud trends in the technology and payments industries offered recommended practices for individuals seeking to secure their PII, detect fraudulent activity, and obtain damages. Methods included using a digital wallet for instore and online purchases, setting up two-factor authentication for online accounts, adopting security measures for digital devices (e.g., screen locking, encrypting data, avoiding public Wi-Fi), placing security freezes on credit reports, and signing up for suspicious-activity monitoring of financial accounts (Tedder & Buzzard, 2020).

Zou et al. (2020) examined individuals' reasons for following or rejecting 30 expert-recommended security, privacy, and identity theft protection practices. A major concern associated with many of the recommended practices was their usability for the general public. Issues with set-up times, low quality of service, or barriers to implementation (such as lack of password managers, two-factor authentication, tools to limit tracking, e-mail encryption, or key management) affected the likelihood that individuals would continue these practices. Individuals were most likely to use security practices (e.g., evaluating the safety of links and attachments before accessing them, using good antivirus software) followed by privacy practices (e.g., hiding non-essential information in online transactions, using privacy-enhanced extensions for web browsers). The identity theft protection practice most used by individuals was regular checking of account statements. Interestingly, credit freezes and fraud alerts were among the top rejected identity theft protection practices, although they are two of the most commonly recommended practices for victims of data breaches.

Current study

Much has been learned about identity theft since it became a federal crime in 1998. Out of necessity, this body of work has expanded rapidly as more people move to doing daily tasks online, whether by computer, tablet, or, increasingly, cell phone. Identity theft research has helped to provide needed information on the characteristics of victims (Golladay & Holtfreter, 2017; Holtfreter et al., 2005; Rebovich, 2009), risks of exposure to victimization (Lai et al., 2012; Payne & Kennett-Hensel, 2017; Reyns & Randa, 2017), prevention strategies utilized (Lai et al., 2012), and understanding the motives of offenders (Copes &

Vieraitis, 2012) but much less effort has been devoted to understanding the technologies used to guard against victimization and the extent to which these technologies are useful.

This study is the outgrowth of a two-phase, mixed-methods project on the effects and quality of services available for victims of serious identity-based crime[1] in the United States. The project was funded through a grant awarded by the U.S. Department of Justice's National Institute of Justice to Development Services Group, Inc. In phase 1, the investigators integrated existing quantitative data from the U. S. Bureau of Justice Statistics' National Crime Victimization Survey with primary data collected from victims who used services provided by the Identity Theft Resource Center (Green et al., 2020). In phase 2, they collected qualitative data through interviews and focus groups with experts from public and private sector organizations engaged in preventing or remediating identity theft, and they analyzed these data (Green et al., 2020). For the analysis presented here, the key research questions were as follows: 1) How do identity theft industry professionals define the existing threats facing organizations and potential victims? 2) What are the emerging threats associated with serious identity-based crimes? 3) What proactive steps might individuals and organizations take to address the current and emerging threats for identity-based crimes?

Methodology

Participant recruitment

In coordination with the Identity Theft Resource Center (ITRC), the investigators prepared an initial list of 10 professional conferences that directly or indirectly address identity-based crime victimization. For each conference, ITRC's president or lead communications officer contacted the sponsoring organization's director or meeting planner to determine if the researchers could conduct focus groups during a regularly scheduled conference session. Two of the 10 organizations agreed to participate: the Association of Certified Fraud Examiners and the National Center for Victims of Crime. In addition to multiple focus groups at each of these two conferences, the investigators conducted focus groups of professionals who regularly engaged with the ITRC but were not ITRC employees. Advertisements for the focus groups were included with conference registration materials available before the meetings and were displayed at a vendor table staffed by the research team and ITRC personnel during the meetings. Potential participants were given the opportunity to join a focus group or complete a one-on-one interview. This recruitment process produced a total of 50 participants, including 45 people who were separated into 7 focus groups and 5 individuals who chose one-on-one interviews. To increase the comfort of focus group participants, no demographic or personal information was collected during these focus groups. All events occurred within the United States and all participants who shared details about their professional roles shared that they work primarily in the context of the United States.

Data collection

A focus group interview guide was developed by the research team, reviewed by ITRC personnel, and piloted with three individuals prior to use at the first focus group. The same interview guide was used for all focus groups. The focus group interview guide was semi-structured and the focus group facilitator prompted respondents to elaborate or provide more detailed information about their answers. Each focus group member was asked to sign a consent form before participating in the focus group.

The research team audio-recorded and transcribed all focus groups sessions and interviews. The research team members also took notes during each meeting and produced an initial set of field notes within 1 day after the completion of each focus group. Each focus group meeting or one-on-one interview was scheduled for 1 hour. All research protocols were reviewed and approved by the DSG Institutional Review Board, the ITRC, and the National Institute of Justice grant project officer.

Data analysis

An inductive, or open, coding scheme was developed by the principal investigator and reviewed by the research team (Creswell, 2017). The inductive coding scheme was informed by the existing literature on technological solutions for preventing or remediating identity-based victimization. The principal investigator and a research assistant coded all transcripts using NVivo to manage the coding process and to enable inter-rater reliability. To begin the analysis process, both coders coded two transcripts and discussed differences and similarities in their coding. This discussion led to some convergence of codes and a few adjustments to the coding scheme. After agreement was reached on the final coding scheme, each of the two coding team members coded all the transcripts. Using the coding comparison query in NVivo enabled the team to further examine intercoder reliability. When there was less than 80% agreement between the coders about the quotations associated with a particular code, the coders re-reviewed all quotations under that code, achieved consensus on the appropriate codes for each quotation, and recoded quotations as needed. All quotations presented in the Results section were lightly edited for clarity and de-identified to protect the study participants' anonymity.

Results

The coding of the data lead to the identification of three overarching themes each corresponding with a specific research topics: (1) context for countering identity theft and fraud, (2) new frontiers of risk for identity-based crimes, and (3) recommendations for improving systems and polices to help prevent identity-based crimes.

Research question 1: How do identity theft industry professionals define the existing threats facing organizations and potential victims?

Industry insiders who participated in the study shared several common perspectives on the current threats faced by organizations and, indirectly, by individual consumers whose information may be stolen and used to commit fraud. The environment is one of constant change, where organizations are playing cat-and-mouse with sophisticated criminal actors who, like the organizations they target, are staying abreast of the most up-to-date technological solutions for preventing and detecting identity theft and related fraud. One focus group member described the context as follows:

> Every time we put a protection in place, the bad guys figure out a way to leverage that and use that to their advantage. So, it's a constant game of whack-a-mole. And so, we're looking at analytics, we're looking at biometrics, we're looking at blockchain, we're looking at what advanced technologies we can use and leverage to help continue to stay in front of that game.

Focus group members emphasized that their goal is no longer to simply prevent the theft of PII, because it already has been stolen. There was a consensus among participants that criminal organizations are acutely aware of the value of information and that the financiers of identity theft operations range from international gang networks to nation–states. One focus group participant who provides businesses with information technology (IT) solutions highlighted some of the challenges associated with trying to stop criminal actors who are attempting to commit identity theft:

> The fundamental issue, particularly for large companies, is the massive investment that these criminal organizations are making to get into our systems. Part of the problem is these people aren't even located here in the U.S. They're located overseas. They're funded by nation–states and are looking to disrupt our country economically. So, to your point, I don't know how our Chief Information Officer sleeps.

The fact that individual organizations' IT departments may be engaging in cybersecurity against nation–states suggests a massive disparity in scale between the two sides regarding personnel and financial resources dedicated to fighting this battle. Advances in the technologies criminal actors use creates another vector of exposure for entities that hold PII. A focus group member who concentrates on services for financial institutions made this observation: *"From the financial industry's perspective there is no single bullet to stopping all this. That's why I mentioned the need for trying to keep pace with where the innovations are coming from the criminal side."*

Throughout the focus groups, participants reflected on the tradeoffs associated with particular technological solutions that are relatively widespread. Table 1 lists intervention mentioned by at least one focus group member and summarizes the groups' perspectives on the general advantages and limitations of each intervention. This table only captures statements made during the focus groups; it does not represent a complete analysis of the tradeoffs associated with each intervention. It does, however, provide insights about how industry professionals view each intervention within the context of identity theft protection services.

When making decisions about implementing an intervention, organizations seek to balance their own fiduciary interests with the public good. Industries sometimes agree to share the cost of a technological solution. The introduction of chip cards, which focus group participants considered an effective intervention, required an agreement between the banking industry and the retail industry to shift the liability for fraudulent activity to the points of sale, away from the banks that issue the credit cards, as articulated by a focus group participant with first-hand knowledge of that process:

> If you're liable for the losses, you're going to do something about it ... So the banks rolled out the EMV [Europay, Mastercard, and Visa]technology, the chip cards that you now have in your wallet to help reduce counterfeit fraud and it's very successful at doing that. But it came at enormous costs, right? ... and so in order to convince the banks to spend all this money to implement this new security technology the agreement was to shift some of the liability for fraud ... Now, if a ... physical chip card is used at the retailer, and it's fraudulent, the retailer has the fraud liability, the bank is off the hook. So, we've shifted the liability from the financial institution to the retail organization, sort of in exchange for the banks investing in this security technology.

Table 1. Summary of limitations and perceived effectiveness of specific technological interventions for preventing identity theft.

Intervention	Limitations	Perceived Effectiveness
Identity theft prevention software	• Is heavily marketed but claims of usefulness are exaggerated • Detects identity theft based on credit bureau monitoring but less than half of identity theft incidents include financial events that would result in reports to credit bureaus	• Ineffective
End-user agreements	• Are difficult for users to understand because the prose is highly technical rather than user friendly • Do not engage users as partners in protecting their PII • Fail to effectively anticipate future risks	• Ineffective
Knowledge-based authentication	• Has very limited utility because information used for authentication also has been stolen and can be used to commit identity theft	• Ineffective
Artificial intelligence- and machine learning-based authentication	• Is currently limited in its capacity to detect and prevent identity theft • Is costly and therefore inaccessible to smaller organizations • Is based on algorithms that may be derived from fraudulent or corrupted PII, given the pervasiveness of identity fraud	• Partially effective
Chip cards	• Are costly to manufacture	• Effective
Two-factor authentication	• Is easily manipulated by criminal actors • Does not protect against other vectors of risk, including insider threats	• Partially effective
Monitoring software	• Can be misused by the organization that installed the program	• Not rated
Biometric identifiers (e.g., fingerprints)	• Cannot be replaced with new identifiers if stolen	• Partially effective

In addition to identifying the limitations of particular interventions, focus group participants highlighted two other challenges: insider threats and outdated software. One focus group member commented on the prevalence of identity theft committed by insiders:

> Only 35 percent of all data breaches are related to IT and hacking. IT and hacking are the 'sizzle' that make the news headlines, but it's the insider threat, whether [the victim is] consumer[s] and seniors, insider threat. Or whether [the victim is] business, it's the insider threat.

Participants emphasized the need for a set of integrated risk management systems incorporating processes that help firms identify insider threats among employees who may be recruited to participate in identity theft activity. Insider threats are not new to the world of fraud protection, but they have increased in sophistication and number, as the theft and sale of PII has continued to grow in potential value.

Focus group members who worked with organizations ranging in size and technological sophistication also express concerned about the potential for IT systems to be hacked. One variable that heavily influences criminal actors' ability to access PII is the age, and therefore the security, of the IT systems and software programs businesses used to manage their budgets, human resources, and daily operations. A focus group member working in cybersecurity alluded to the vulnerability associated with outdated technology:

> ...from an IT perspective, from a cybersecurity perspective, we're still relying on 30-year-old technologies to protect us. As opposed to technologies that can prevent and detect the kinds of attacks that we've seen for 30 years.

The point was made that industries vary in the resources and capacity they have available for addressing these outdated systems. A focus group member indicated that larger banks are improving their technology for combatting identity theft, but smaller banks, which tend to be less sophisticated in this regard, are being targeted by criminal actors:

> ...the bigger banks are getting better at putting in controls. The smaller institutions or one-branch community banks ... there's a big vulnerability there. And I think part of the criminal elements are shifting focus now and trying to hit the smaller ones.

Other participants noted that all organizations remain at risk because of the ubiquity of the collection of personal information among business. One participant observed that data breaches persist even in industries with the most financial and IT resources:

> When I look at banking, healthcare, the three credit bureaus, and social media, they all collect more personal information than any other business sector, and they all have more financial and IT resources than any other business sector. Banking and healthcare and the three credit bureaus and social media continue to get breached.

Additionally, one focus group member stated that the window of opportunity has closed for preventing identity theft:

> All these conversations of identities being stolen are irrelevant. the data is already stolen. It's over, it's done with, you can't do anything about it ... it can't be mitigated anymore. The issue is, you have to change the processes ... companies need to be careful, government entities need to be careful, IRS has had a breach, SEC has had breaches, everyone has had breaches ... it's just the processes need to change.

When examining the context for combatting identity theft and fraud, our focus group participants described a constantly changing and rather bleak environment, noting that firms of any size or capacity are at risk, that most individuals already have had their PII stolen and distributed, and that firms have a default orientation toward deterrence and minimizing impact for eventual attempts at identity theft.

Research question 2: What are the emerging threats associated with serious identity-based crimes?

Focus group participants were quick to highlight some of the new frontiers of identity-based crime, many of which are unknown to the average consumer but are on the radar of experts in the fraud prevention industry. These frontiers include small and midsize businesses, synthetic identities, and a criminal middle-class.

Small and midsize businesses

A subset of focus group participants worked for a regional grain processor based in the midwestern United States. They shared a story about how as their business grew, they became the target of a wide variety of schemes to access and steal PII. The schemes ranged from phishing through e-mail and the telephone to multiple efforts to hack their database and IT infrastructure. One of these participants drew a correlation between the firm's size and the increased attempts at identity theft:

> I think, too, because we're not invisible now. Because we've grown so large ... if you Google grain processing and our name comes up right away. So ... our name is out there a lot more, we have a lot more exposure. So, then people can get our information a lot easier.[2]

After experiencing these threats, the company shifted policies and began to return to a previously used paper-based system for record keeping, verifying sales, and accomplishing transfers of funds. From this company's perspective, switching to a paper-based approach proved to be an effective solution. For businesses and consumers across most sectors, however, returning to paper-based recordkeeping is not an option because the convenience of seamless and quick transactions is so compelling.

As computer-based commercial transactions and social interactions have increased, so have opportunities for identity theft, and as identity theft has increased, federal and state policies have attempted to address the risks of, and liability for, stolen PII. One respondent noted that the risks small and midsize businesses represent may not be effectively addressed by major data protection legislation:

> I think the state and federal laws are important. But they really only apply to people, companies, big money ... the FTC [Federal Trade Commission] Red Flags Rule, has been in effect in this country for 8 years. And the majority of SMBs [small and midsize businesses] in the U.S. who have anything to do with FTC Red Flags Rule don't have a clue about it ... I think GDPR [the General Data Protection Regulation] is going to be the same way – unless you're a big company, the majority of the small to medium-sized businesses don't care. Unfortunately, the majority of the small to medium-sized businesses are a conduit.

Both smaller and larger businesses have been making progress in decreasing the points of risk and potential exposure, but the continued updating of software and systems needed to manage IT infrastructure creates additional and new opportunities for vulnerabilities. Focus group participants highlighted the Gordian knot of exposure that can arise not only with the use of antiquated systems but also with the adoption of new technology. One industry insider described the ongoing challenge of staying one step ahead of criminal actors as follows:

> We had network firewalls and we shrunk those down to application firewalls, it's the same technology shrunk down. We have squeezed all that we can out of that model, and we now have to look for different models of protecting software because software is even more ambiguous ... 111 billion new lines of code added every year. There aren't not enough fingers on keyboards to write correct code to deal with that volume.

A desire to increase the ease of interactions that result in financial transactions and purchases of goods and services drives smaller businesses to augment their computer capability and update their software. However, mixing legacy technology with contemporary technologies while trying to ensure continued ease of interactions creates opportunities for identity theft, and these opportunities are multiplying because more companies are collecting and reselling PII.

Questions arose among focus group participants about the long-term implications of data storage. The observation was made that no limitations have been set on the length of time firms can keep information. One participant noted that companies establish their own policies:

> What limits how long companies can keep data? Companies are putting in rules for record retention. So you might have to keep it for 5 or 10 years, but then you get rid of it when you don't have a legal need for it.

A separate paper (Green et al., 2020) examined in depth the interactive nature of identity theft, in which the behaviors of the organization holding an individual's PII, and the behaviors of the individual whose PII the organization is holding, affect both parties and influence the extent to which each becomes a victim of identity theft. Understanding the dynamic relationship between the organization and the individual is a key part of understanding emerging risks and how the risks vary by organizational size and IT capacity. This knowledge, in turn, is vital to the development of more targeted, and therefore more effective, interventions. One focus group member highlighted the fact that identity theft nearly always involves organizations:

> There's also an organization behind all of that data, for the most part. And those organizations also go through a process of learning. It's a painful learning experience and I can tell you from personal experience of having been there. But . . . at the end of the day, all of these crimes that we're talking about begin with someone extracting the data resources from an organization, by and large.

Synthetic identities

Focus group participants considered synthetic identities the most worrisome emerging threat to individuals who may be victimized by a serious identity-based crime. Unfortunately, not many people understand what this emerging crime is and how dangerous it can be. Synthetic identity theft requires that a criminal slowly and methodically create an artificial, or synthetic, person they can use to access capital. The process involves pairing a valid social security number with completely fictious personal information derived from one or more individuals such as name, address, date of birth, or any other information necessary to apply for any line of credit.

As one focus group participant ominously noted:

> If James is our bad guy. He will try to get his hands on a valid Social Security numbers and the key prize, the holy grail he's looking for, are SSNs of minors and kids.

Another important thing to note about creating a synthetic identity is that it takes time, patience, and an understanding of how lines of credit are established. The initial stages of forming a synthetic identity entail using the existing systems to check on an individual's credit history. The made-up name paired with the valid stolen social security number is not likely to immediately be granted any line of credit since there is no credit history. However, even though a credit application may at first be denied the attempt to create the synthetic identity has still been successful as it has put into motion the creation of a file at the credit bureau.

> And he will provide his made-up name, John Doe, paired with the valid SSN of a child and apply for a credit card. James' bank is going to go out, they've got an application, they're going to attempt to underwrite it, they will probably call out to a credit bureau to attempt to get a credit history. Well, that credit bureau will try to find a file associated with John Doe's valid SSN and other PI, and of course there's no file. So, they will return that response to James' bank, and James' bank more than likely is not going to take a risk and extend credit to John Doe and will just deny the application and go about their day. Now, what happens, is that inquiry from James' bank triggers the creation of a file at the credit bureaus, with John Doe and the kid's SSN and one denied credit by James' bank.

The focus group participant elaborated on the additional steps in the process:

> James is likely to go to an accomplice of his and do a practice that is legal, called piggy-backing, where they will then associate that synthetic file with their friend's valid credit card. And then make payments. Immediately that pairing of the two [i.e., the synthetic file and the valid credit card] transfers the presumably good credit of his accomplice onto the synthetic file itself. They'll spend some time making payments, buying things, paying it off on time, and over time you start to develop a tradeline on that synthetic file that starts to look OK. At some point James will then go to a new bank and apply for a credit card. Now, this second bank will put that through underwriting, and get a credit file back. It's not great, but it might be enough where [the second bank]doesn't know, it might be a new entry into the workforce, a college student, you never know, but maybe it's enough where you want to extend them a very modest credit line to allow them to get into the banking system. Now, the synthetic identity has credit. You do that multiple times, suddenly you've got a pretty nice chunk of change, and then you're going to bust out, where you max everything out and you disappear.

The preying upon minors' social security numbers likely ensures that the discovery of the identity theft crime is several years if not a decade or more off as it is unlikely that credit checks will be initiated until the victim is in their mid- to late-teens. Participants repeatedly emphasized their concern about the rise of synthetic identity theft and coupled lack of clear and effective prevention practices.

Criminal middle-class

The fact that synthetic identity theft is an emerging threat suggest a new class of criminal actors may be coming into being who have the financial capacity, knowledge, and patience to execute a multi-stage process that unfolds gradually over time.

This concern was echoed by several respondents, who spoke about the ways in which opportunities for identity theft and fraud may appeal to a "middle-class criminal." One participant referred to the "professionalization" of identity fraud:

> It's going to continue to increase as we have more people becoming connected, more people coming online, people realizing how lucrative this is. Right? Because this is the business model now. Fraud has been professionalized ... We will create a middle-class criminal culture, where education separates those who are street level from those who are not. I'm not positive we need a middle criminal class, but I think we're going to get one.

As many respondents noted, identity theft-based crimes include highly sophisticated operations that may be receiving financial support from nation–states. Coupled with this increased sophistication and support structure is the existence, according to respondents, of a simple and direct way to sell digital goods: the dark web. Echoing other focus group members, one of our participants emphasized the dark web's role in facilitating identity-based crime:

> And there is nearly unlimited consensus for the [criminal] groups, whether organized or unorganized, state actors or not state actors, there is basically a one-way economy that is super productive, and the dark web is going on to make this happen.

To summarize the new frontiers of risk, our industry experts agreed that the emergence of an increasingly sophisticated set of criminal actors and ever-changing techniques will create new challenges for law enforcement and for organizations seeking to protect the information held by companies. Of particular concern was the unique disadvantage of small and mid-size companies in keeping up with the barrage of new and constant risks, the growing use of synthetic identities as the reaches of which may not be known for quite some time, and the emergence of a new class of professional fraudsters.

> **Research question 3: What proactive steps might individuals and organizations take to address the current and emerging threats for identity-based crimes?**

During each focus group, participants were asked to identify how to address the myriad challenges they had outlined during the discussion. Respondents made a variety of recommendations aimed at different stakeholder groups, including companies, policy makers, victim services professionals and organizations, and law enforcement. In this paper we document the recommendations aimed at companies and policy makers. Recommendations for victim services and law enforcement have been presented elsewhere (Gies et al., 2020; Green et al., 2020).

Recommendations for companies

> But in the world today, with so much doubt of being exposed, the paradigms need to change and that's what we're focusing on as a business. Because at this point ... it's already done. All the data's stolen.

Companies need to continue upgrading and adapting the approaches they take to protect PII. Their strategies should include, according to focus group participants, extended vigilance to ensure effective mitigation of insider threats, a balance of easy transactions and safety, use of evolving technologies (specifically artificial intelligence and machine learning), and broader efforts to complete regular audits for potential fraud. The challenge participants noted lies in how best to motivate companies to expend the financial resources necessary to update systems and maintain surveillance and monitoring. The point was made that companies can be motivated by modifications or new laws within the regulatory structure established through new state and federal laws. One participant, who was echoed by many others, also highlighted the value of public–private partnerships where financial service industries take the lead:

> I think you're going to see models like that in a number of industries where we kind of come to the table and say, the financial institution may be the best kind of central entity to handle this type of transaction, or it's a healthcare organization or a retail organization or whatever it is, but we have to have some agreement and some process for sharing in this responsibility, this liability and the cost.

These partnerships are fundamentally about cost-sharing and distribution of risk. Multiple participants identified the need for better consumer-oriented protections and more consistency in norms and ethics related to data sharing, data storage, opt-out options for data agreements, expansion of open-sourced software, and adaptations of technological solutions to different types of vulnerable groups (e.g., seniors, teenagers). As the quote at the beginning of this section underscores, paradigm shifts may be needed to ensure the continued viability of electronic transmission and storage of PII in an environment where all the information already has been stolen. In the view of the study participants, within the current paradigm firms are struggling to keep up and already may have lost.

Recommendations for policy makers

The issue of identity theft will expand in importance as will the burden it places on the individuals and organizations that have been defrauded. One respondent highlighted the need for improved responses from the federal government:

> So, I believe the answer is a response from the government. I think companies need to focus on being resilient and compromise-ready. I think they need to focus on response and recovery.

The reason for this need is, as noted earlier, that prevention is no longer an appropriate conceptual framework for identity theft. Participants indicated that complicated questions must be addressed regarding policies associated with individuals' consent for firms to use their PII, for two reasons: first, few current user agreements are intelligible; and, second, it is possible that uses will be made of PII in the future that could not be anticipated at the time a user agreement was developed and signed.

Focus group members pointed out that the rise of synthetic identity theft is a complex phenomenon requiring the attention of experts in the domains of law, ethics, and policy. One industry professional observed that synthetic identity theft raises sweeping security questions:

> And I think people are beginning to understand how easy it is to compile an ID or to steal one or to exploit one. And so, I am seeing it start to move into some of the more kind of legal and risk and broader security questions people are asking.

Underscoring the importance of this issue, respondents described how children whose Social Security numbers have been attached to synthetic identities may not discover that they are victims of identity fraud until they become adults, potentially allowing for a decade or more of fraudulent activity to occur before the fraud comes to light.

A few respondents saw hope amidst the rapidly growing threat of identity theft that stems from the ways in which profits from the sale of PII can be linked to other types of crime. One of our focus group members pointed out that these links may result in better resource allocation to address identity theft:

> I am kind of backhandedly optimistic, because some of the people that I've talked to, particularly in international law enforcement, and at the NYPD [New York Police Department], are [aware of]the number of situations in which these kinds of [identity-based] crimes are being used to fund and facilitate broader crime rings. Right? So, street gangs are the ones who are using the stolen credit cards, and then they're using the stolen IDs to then go and fund gang activity. And so, this is actually – the line between kind of ID theft, cybercrime, ID theft, real-world crime – all of these things are coming together and that's merging. So, I think there's a possibility that there will be better resource allocation, because people will begin to recognize that these are not distinct instances or distinct types of crimes.

This observation also suggests that the funding of law enforcement divisions with the capacity to investigate identity theft-related crimes may be a growing area of need in all law enforcement departments.

Overall, experts who participated in these focus groups suggest the best way to improve systems and policies is to change the paradigm. Those groups responsible for PII, (i.e., individuals, businesses, and government) should stop independently seeking ways to prevent identity-based crimes because as most of our experts agreed PII is already out. Criminals already have access to the valuable information they need and are constantly finding new ways to use/abuse it. Thus, this is no longer a prevention or even a rescue operation but rather is a recovery operation. The path forward necessitates the groups work collaboratively together to remedy the harms already perpetrated on the victims.

Discussion

This study sought to address three questions: 1) How do identity theft industry professionals define the existing threats facing organizations and potential victims? 2) What are the emerging threats associated with serious identity-based crimes? and 3) What proactive steps might individuals and organizations take to address the current context and emerging threats for identity-based crimes? To investigate these questions, we collected and analyzed data from focus groups, and one-one-one interviews with 50 professionals in the field of identity-based crime victim services. The sample included private investigators, fraud examiners, victim service providers, and executives of firms offering victim services and protection services.

Our results led to three overall conclusions. First, in the context of a rapidly evolving criminal enterprise with deep pockets, firms of all sizes are striving to make technological adaptations that decrease risk from identity theft and ensure trust in their services. Second, study participants highlighted three new frontiers of risk that warrant continued attention: Small and midsize businesses, synthetic identity theft, and an emerging "criminal middle class." Third, focus group members highlighted strategies and adjustments to policies and procedures that could protect both firms and individuals. Most notably, there is a pressing need for many companies to update antiquated technology that may be 30 years old or older, and that often is mixed with new technology. More attention also must be paid to insider fraud (i.e., fraud committed by employees targeting the same organizations that are victims of fraud). Further, individuals and organizations should not presume that identity theft prevention software, end user agreements, or knowledge-based authentication will automatically safeguard one from identity theft victimization. Focus group members deemed these methods ineffective. Biometric identifiers, two-factor authentication, and artificial intelligence-based authentication were considered partially effective. Only chip cards were perceived as effective. At the end of the day, being careful is the essential mitigation strategy that should be practiced regardless of the technological interventions adopted.

These study results underscore the need for a paradigm shift to effectively and efficiently address, and prevent, identity-based crimes. This broad finding has major implications for how law enforcement, businesses and other organizations, and individual consumers conceptualize, manage, and use personally identifiable information (PII).

First, it is incumbent upon law enforcement and other criminal justice system actors to change underlying assumptions regarding identity-based crimes. Identity-based crimes traditionally have been low on the law enforcement priority list, for several reasons. There is a lack of knowledge regarding identity theft and fraud in general as well as a lack of understanding of how widespread the problem is. Further, many law enforcement agencies are not equipped or trained to address the problem because the tactical and strategic responses significantly differ from the enforcement of traditional crime the police were designed to address. Perhaps most important, despite the fact that identity-based crime can be a harrowing and devastating experience for victims (Golladay & Holtfreter,

2017; Reyns et al., 2019; Solove & Citron, 2018), there is an underlying belief that identity-based crimes are not serious because victims often recover the monetary losses through their financial institutions.

One of the consequences of this lack of knowledge and training is that law enforcement and other criminal justice actors have, in some respects, taken a backseat to the financial sector and its institutions when it comes to addressing identity-based crimes. The frontline defenders in this case are less likely to be criminal justice professionals and more likely to be software engineers in the cybersecurity industry and other financial sector entities. This tendency is even true regarding the scholarship on identity-based crimes. The number of manuscripts authored by financial experts exceeds those by criminologists, although we are encouraged by the fact that this trend is shifting, with more recent attention being paid to the issue by criminologists.

Without the invested involvement of the criminal justice system, the emphasis seems to be less on policing and prosecuting identity-based criminals and more on mitigating liability and monetary losses. This shift in the actors (away from law enforcement, toward the cybersecurity industry and financial sector entities) and the focus (away from policing and prosecuting, toward mitigating liability and monetary losses) may have a significant influence on offenders' decision to commit identity-based crimes. Deterrence theory and criminal justice policy hold that, under certain conditions, punishment can improve compliance and deter future criminal activity (Piquero et al., 2011). While the theory of deterrence relies on three individual components of punishment – severity, certainty, and celerity – Nagin (2013) points out that the evidence supporting the deterrent effect of punishment certainty is far more consistent than for punishment severity. Moreover, the evidence supporting the effect of certainty pertains almost exclusively to the probability of apprehension. This finding has important policy implications for identity-based crimes because the probability that perpetrators of identity-based crimes will be apprehended is exceedingly low, owing to the fact that the chief protagonists in the battle to protect PII are software engineers with no legal authority or interest in pursuing criminal sanctions and to the fact that many victims of identity theft do not realize they have been victimized until many months, or even years, later – if at all.

Identity-based crimes are not simply financial crimes that can be adequately addressed by financial institutions. Rather, they are a growing, complex, and often devastating problem for the victims, and they increasingly are being linked to traditional, organized, and transnational crimes. Moreover, identity-based crimes should be policed and prosecuted in an effort to deter future crimes. As noted in an earlier quote, one of our focus group participants expressed this view when asked what steps must be taken to address the current context and emerging threats for identity-based crimes:

> These kinds of [identity-based] crimes are being used to fund and facilitate broader crime rings ... real-world crime – all of these things are coming together and that's merging. S,o I think there's a possibility that there will be better resource allocation, because people will begin to recognize that these are not distinct instances or distinct types of crimes.

A second, related point is that the criminal justice system's response to identity-based crimes is disjointed and lacking in coordination (Wyre et al., 2020), which can be attributed to the fact that some of the criminal entities involved in these crimes are multi-jurisdictional and others, as one of our experts observed, are located abroad. The degree to which identity-based crimes are being committed by offenders situated in foreign countries is unclear, but the experts in our focus groups believe that foreign nationals are responsible for at least some of the identity-based crimes committed against United States citizens. Multi-jurisdictional identity-based crimes cannot be pursued through traditional law enforcement means and techniques. As such, we must rethink our approaches to combatting international identity-based crimes and consider what or which agencies are in the best position to handle such cases? One such approach would be to draw on existing efforts designed to address other types of multi-jurisdictional crime such as the fusion centers created to combat terrorism

Another notable observation made by more than one focus group participant is that efforts to prevent identity theft at this point actually may be futile because the PII already has been. While this perspective merits consideration, it may amount to throwing in the towel a bit too soon. If all the PII already has been stolen, one would think that data breaches would be on the decline. Yet, the available data, although probably incomplete, do not bear that out. According to the Identity Theft Resource Center annual data breach report, the number of U.S. data breaches tracked in 2019 (1,473) increased 17% from the total number of breaches reported in 2018 (1,257) (Identity Theft Resource Center, 2020).

Further, new individuals are added to the pool of potential victims every day in hospitals around the world. According to the Centers for Disease Control and Prevention (CDC), nearly 4 million births occur every year in the United States alone. While protecting these identities is likely fraught with difficulties, it seems prudent to try to protect, as much as possible, the PII of those who have not been exposed. Protecting this information starting at a person's birth can go a long way toward preventing the creation of synthetic identities.

Conclusion

Focusing on preventing identity theft without mitigating the harm caused by identity fraud would be naive. Any strategy for dealing with identity-based crimes must integrate prevention and mitigation. This integration will require that consumers, businesses, and governmental agencies change their approach to the conceptualization and use of PII, as some of our focus group participants noted.

The first step in effecting this change is to increase consumer education regarding how the online exchange of PII may increase the risk of identity-based crimes (Gilbert & Archer, 2012; Milne, 2003; Milne et al., 2009). In today's digital environment, consumers demand the freedom to do almost everything on their own terms – to open new financial accounts, to hail a car through ride-share services, to share vacation photos instantly on social media sites, to send highly confidential information by e-mail. Business entities in turn provide these services, sometimes without charging a fee, in exchange for the consumer consenting to an End User License Agreement (EULA). Because EULAs typically are lengthy, highly technical, and full of legal jargon, most people do not pay close attention to them. In terms of identity-based crimes, the problem with these agreements is that they often (but not always) expose a person's PII by giving the business entity the right to remotely, collect, process, use, share, and store information about the consumer, including PII. As people become increasingly connected across networks, they exponentially expand the footprints of their identities, and thus provide more ways for their identity to be exposed and put at risk.

To prevent, or at least safeguard, this exponential sharing of identity footprints, consumers and governmental entities, like law enforcement, must re-conceptualize PII as currency. In reality, the value of one's identity far exceeds the cost of the paper that it is printed on or the file space in which it is stored. A thief who steals the information can sell it to other criminals or use it himself or herself to fraudulently obtain hundreds or even thousands of dollars in products and/or services. A business entity can sell the information to another business for use in a direct marketing campaign. The important policy implication is that consumers and policymakers must begin to value PII as much as the businesses who legally collect it for legitimate businesses purposes and offenders who illegally steal it.

On the mitigation side of the equation, when identity-based crime occurs, systems and processes must be in place to give victims the comprehensive help they need. Although identity theft and fraud are crimes in every state, victims still often face a tremendous financial, physical, emotional, and social burden in repairing the harm committed against them. How can victims rectify these consequences? Currently, as noted above, financial institutions will typically reimburse fraudulent credit cards charges and certain other financial costs. Like the victims of other types of crime, victims of identity theft and fraud also may have access to counseling services to deal with the crime's emotional consequences. However, victims of identity-based crimes sometimes suffer from long-term, residual effects that are unique to fraud victimization. For example, if a perpetrator uses the victim's name or health insurance policy numbers to see doctors, obtain prescription drugs, or file insurance claims, the victim's health record is adulterated, which may negatively affect the victim's treatment, health insurance, payment record, and credit report. In addition, the victim may receive the wrong medical care based on the false medical history.

Currently, these adulterated records, be they medical, legal, or financial, are not easily corrected and cause constant problems for the victim. Governmental entities must realize that more and more people will require remediation for this growing problem. One potential solution would be to create a mechanism similar to a petition for expungement, the removal of records from public inspection. In Maryland, for example, records may be expunged from 1) Motor Vehicle Administration files, 2) police files, and 3) court and police files. Each process removes very specific files and must be accomplished through the proper agency. Precedent exists for such judicial action. Some safe harbor laws, for example, permit juvenile victims to vacate delinquency adjudications and criminal convictions for offenses arising from commercial sexual exploitation or sex trafficking (Gies et al., 2020). The aim is to mitigate the multifaceted, lasting impact of adjudications and conviction. A similar mechanism could be established to help victims of identity-based crimes address problems posed by adulterated financial and medical records.

We do not want to leave readers with a "doom-and-gloom" conclusion about identity theft victimization and prevention. While our experts were less than impressed with several commonly used prevention techniques (e.g., prevention software, end-user agreements, knowledge-based authentications), they did identify some promising avenues to be pursued such as the use of biometrics, two-factor authentication, and chip cards. These strategies need to be coupled with careful vigilance in order to safeguard PII. Our experts noted several times this is a constant game of "whack-a-mole" thus individuals and organizations must be aware, agile, and adapting to the latest updates and innovations to protect their identities. Much like we have become accustomed to updating our smartphones and changing our passwords, we must also get in the habit of regularly checking our credit reports and updating technology to try to stay at least one step ahead of identity thieves.

Notes

1. Serious identity-based crime is defined as any incident of identity theft and fraud other than those involving only the misuse of an existing credit card.
2. The type of business was modified slightly to protect the organization's anonymity.

Acknowledgments

We would like to express our appreciation to the staff of the ITRC, specifically Mona Terry and Charity Lacey, for assisting us with recruitment of interviewees. This study would also not have been possible without the willingness of interviewees to share their stories with us. Finally, the editorial and managerial staff at Development Services Group, Inc. provided support and review of the manuscript.

Disclosure statement

The authors of this study have no conflicts of interest that may shape or limit the study.

Funding

This project was supported by [grant number 2016-VF-GX-K006], awarded by the National Institute of Justice, Office of Justice Programs, U.S. Department of Justice.

References

Brand, S., & Price, R. (2000). *The economic and social costs of crime*. Home Office.

Center for Victim Research. (2019). *Research brief: Identity theft and fraud*. Office of Victim Services, U.S. Department of Justice. https://ncvc.dspacedirect.org/bitstream/item/1228/CVR%20Research%20Syntheses_Identity%20Theft%20and%20Fraud_Brief.pdf

Chen, H., Beaudoin, C. E., & Hong, T. (2017). Securing online privacy: An empirical test on internet scam victimization, online privacy concerns, and privacy protection behaviors. *Computers in Human Behavior*, *70*, 291–302. https://doi.org/10.1016/j.chb.2017.01.003

Cohen, M. A. (2005). *The costs of crime and justice*. Routledge.

Cohen, M. A. (2016). The costs of white-collar crime. In S. R. Van Slyke, M. L. Benson, & F. T. Cullen (Eds.), *The Oxford handbook of white-collar crime* (pp. 78–98). Oxford University Press.

Copes, H., Kerley, K. R., Huff, R., & Kane, J. (2010). Differentiating identity theft: An exploratory study of victims using a national victimization survey. *Journal of Criminal Justice*, *38*(5), 1045–1052. https://doi.org/10.1016/j.jcrimjus.2010.07.007

Copes, H., & Vieraitis, L. M. (2012). *Identity thieves: Motives and methods*. Northeastern University Press.

Creswell, J. W. (2017). *Qualitative inquiry and research design: Choosing among five approaches*. Sage Publications.

Gies, S., Healy, E., Green, B., & Bobnis, A. (2020). From villain to victim: The impact of safe harbor laws on minors involved in commercial sexual exploitation. *Criminology & Public Policy*, *19*(2), 73–95. https://doi.org/10.1111/1745-9133.12497

Gies, S. V., Piquero, N. L., Piquero, A. R., Green, B., & Bobnis, A. (2020). Wild, wild theft: Identity crimes in the digital frontier. *Criminal Justice Policy Review*, 1–26. https://doi.org/10.1177%2F0887403420949650

Gilbert, J., & Archer, N. (2012). Consumer identity theft prevention and identity fraud detection behaviors. *Journal of Financial Crime*, *19*(1), 20–36. https://doi.org/10.1111/j.1745-6606.2009.01148.x

Golladay, K., & Holtfreter, K. (2017). The consequences of identity theft victimization: An examination of emotional and physical health outcomes. *Victims & Offenders*, *12*(5), 741–760. https://doi.org/10.1080/15564886.2016.1177766

Green, B., Gies, S., Bobnis, A., Piquero, N., Piquero, A., Velasquez, E. (2020). Exploring identity-based crime victimizations: Assessing threats and victim services among a sample of professionals. *Deviant Behavior*, 1–20. https://doi.org/10.1080/01639625.2020.1720938

Harrell, E. (2019). *Victims of identity theft, 2016, Bulletin*. United States Department of Justice, Office of Justice Programs, Bureau of Justice Statistics. https://www.bjs.gov/content/pub/pdf/vit16.pdf

Harrell, E., & Langton, L. (2013). *Victims of identity theft, 2012, bulletin*. United States Department of Justice, Office of Justice Programs, Bureau of Justice Statistics. https://www.bjs.gov/content/pub/pdf/vit12.pd

Holt, T. J., & Bossler, A. M. (2014). An assessment of the current state of cybercrime scholarship. *Deviant Behavior*, *35*(1), 20–40. https://doi.org/10.1080/01639625.2013.822209

Holtfreter, K., Van Slyke, S., & Bloomberg, T. G. (2005). Sociolegal changes in consumer fraud: From victim-offender interactions to global networks. *Crime, Law, and Social Change*, *44*(3), 251–275. https://doi.org/10.1007/s10611-006-9006-8

Identity Theft Resource Center. (2020). *2019 end-of-year data breach report*. https://www.idtheftcenter.org/2019-databreaches/?utm_source=pressrelease&utm_medium=web&utm_campaign=Jan20_2019DataBreachReport

Lai, F., Li, D., & Hsieh, C. T. (2012). Fighting identity theft: The coping perspective. *Decision Support Systems*, *52*(2), 353–363. https://doi.org/10.1016/j.dss.2011.09.002

Milne, G. R. (2003). How well do consumers protect themselves from identity theft? *Journal of Consumer Affairs*, *37*(2), 388–402. https://doi.org/10.1111/j.1745-6606.2003.tb00459.x

Milne, G. R., Labrecque, L. I., & Cromer, C. (2009). Toward and understanding of the online consumer's risky behavior and protection practices. *Journal of Consumer Affairs*, *43*(2), 449–473. https://doi.org/10.1111/j.1745-6606.2009.01148.x

Milne, G. R., Rohm, A. J., & Bahl, S. (2004). Consumers' protection of online privacy and identity. *Journal of Consumer Affairs*, *38*(2), 217–232. https://doi.org/10.1111/j.1745-6606.2004.tb00865

Nagin, D. S. (2013). Deterrence in the twenty-first century. *Crime and Justice*, *42*(1), 199–263. https://doi.org/10.1086/670398

Payne, D., & Kennett-Hensel, P. A. (2017). Combatting identity theft: A proposed ethical policy statement and best practices. *Business and Society Review*, *122*(3), 393–420. https://doi.org/10.1111/basr.2017.122.issue-3

Piquero, A. R., Paternoster, R., Pogarsky, G., & Loughran, T. (2011). Elaborating the individual difference component in deterrence theory. *Annual Review of Law and Social Science*, *7*(1), 335–360. https://doi.org/10.1146/annurev-lawsocsci-102510-105404

Piquero, N. L. (2018). White-collar crime is crime: Victims hurt just the same. *Criminology & Public Policy*, *17*(3), 595–600. https://doi.org/10.1111/capp.2018.17.issue-3

Rebovich, D. (2009). Examining identity theft: Empirical explorations of the offense and the offender. *Victims & Offenders*, *4*(4), 357–364. https://doi.org/10.1080/15564880903260603

Reyns, B. W., Fisher, B. S., Bossler, A. M., & Holt, T. J. (2019). Opportunity and self-control: Do they predict multiple forms of online victimization? *American Journal of Criminal Justice*, *44*(1), 63–82. https://doi.org/10.1007/s12103-018-9447-5

Reyns, B. W., & Randa, R. (2017). Victim reporting behaviors following identity theft victimization: Results from the national crime victimization survey. *Crime & Delinquency*, *63*(7), 814–838. https://doi.org/10.1177/0011128715620428

Ricci, J., Breitinger, F., & Baggili, I. (2019). Survey results on adults and cybersecurity education. *Education and Information Technologies*, *24*(1), 231–249. https://doi.org/10.1007/s10639-018-9765-8

Solove, D. J., & Citron, D. K. (2018). Risk and anxiety: A theory of data-breach harms. *Texas Law Review*, *96*(4), 737–786. https://texaslawreview.org/wp-content/uploads/2018/03/Solove.pdf

Sullivan, C. L. (2009). Is identity theft really theft? *International Review of Law, Computers & Technology*, *23*(1–2), 77–87. https://doi.org/10.1080/13600860902742596

Tcherni, M., Davies, A., Lopes, G., & Lizotte, A. (2016). The dark figure of online property crime: Is cyberspace hiding a crime wave? *Justice Quarterly*, *33*(5), 890–911. https://doi.org/10.1080/07418825.2014.994658

Tedder, K., & Buzzard, J. (2020). *Javelin 2020 identity fraud study: Genesis of the identity fraud crisis*. Javelin, Inc. https://www.javelinstrategy.com/coverage-area/2020-identity-fraud-study-genesis-identity-fraud-crisis

Vieraitis, L. M., Copes, H., Powell, Z. A., & Pike, A. (2015). A little information goes a long way: Expertise and identity theft. *Aggression and Violent Behavior*, *20*, 10–18. https://doi.org/10.1016/j.avb.2014.12.008

Wyre, M., Lacey, D., & Allan, K. (2020). The identity theft response system. *Trends and Issues in Crime and Criminal Justice*, *592*, 1–18. https://www.aic.gov.au/sites/default/files/2020-05/ti592_the_identity_theft_response_system.pdf

Zou, Y., Roundy, K., Tamersoy, A., Shintre, S., Roturier, J., & Schaub, F. (2020). *Examining the adoption and abandonment of security, privacy, and identity theft protection practices*. CHI, Honolulu. https://yixinzou.github.io/publications/chi2020-zou.pdf

Forecasting Identity Theft Victims: Analyzing Characteristics and Preventive Actions through Machine Learning Approaches

Xiaochen Hu, Xudong Zhang, and Nicholas P. Lovrich

ABSTRACT

Researchers in criminology and criminal justice have been making increasing use of the machine learning approach to investigate questions involving large amounts of digital data. We make use here of survey data on over 220,000 respondents drawn from three waves of the National Crime Victimization Survey Identity Theft Supplement (NCVS-ITS) conducted by the Bureau of Justice Statistics (BJS) in 2012, 2014, and in 2016. We use three distinct machine learning algorithms to analyze these data: 1) logistic regression; 2) decision tree; and, 3) random forest. We assess the efficacy of these approaches against these evaluative criteria: the overall percentage of correct classification, receiver operating characteristics (ROC), the area under the ROC curve (AUC), and feature criticality. Our findings indicate that the logistic regression algorithm performs best in predicting overall identity theft victimization, misuse of credit cards, misuse of financial accounts of other types, and the opening of new accounts; the random forest algorithm performs best in predicting misuse of checking/saving accounts. Our findings suggest that the respondent's age, educational level, and online shopping frequency are significantly related to identity theft victimization. Additionally, frequently checking credit reports and changing passwords of financial accounts are strong predictors of identity theft victimization. We draw out the implications of our work for our collective understanding of identity theft, and for informing our judgment as to the potential utility of the use of machine learning approaches in criminology and criminal justice.

Introduction

The National Crime Victimization Survey (NCVS) started adding questions related to identity theft in 2004 as growing public concern began to be expressed (Baum, 2006). Baum (2007) reports that in 2005 about 5.5% of U.S. households reported experiencing identity theft. The NCVS began using an Identity Theft Supplement (ITS) in 2008, which was used again in 2012, 2014, and 2016. Using the 2016 ITS, Harrell (2019) estimates that about 1-in-10 U.S. adults (16+) have been victims of identity theft (26 million). The 2018 the Federal Trade Commission's *Consumer Sentinel Network* (Federal Trade Commission

(FTC), 2019) reported that almost every known type of identity theft has increased in recent years. Britain's National Fraud Authority similarly reports that about 1.8 million British citizens are affected by identity theft annually (Reyns, 2013). A multi-nation survey conducted in 2010 revealed that a majority of citizens (ranging from 50% to 85%) in Australia, Belgium, Brazil, Germany, New Zealand, the U.K., and the U.S. were of the belief that identity theft is a growing problem (Piquero et al., 2011).

Besides "traditional" identity theft approaches such as theft of wallets, dumpster diving, pretext calling, and skimming (Allison et al., 2005), new Internet-based approaches are arising. For example, e-mail users receive unsolicited junk e-mail messages daily, some of which contain hyperlinks used by identity thieves to steal personal information. Additionally, individuals may become victims of identity theft even though they do not engage in high-risk online behavior. Data breaches have occurred whereby the personal information of millions of corporate customers are stolen, such as the one wherein *Capital One* files on over 100 million persons were stolen (Chapple, 2019). A month earlier, the *American Medical Collection Agency* experienced a data breach that affected millions of their patients (Chapple, 2019). It has been reported that the *Equifax* credit bureau may pay out approximately 650 USD million in settlements for a data breach occurring in 2017 which impacted 147 million individuals (Cowley, 2019). Each such data breach involves unauthorized access to sensitive personal information such as social security numbers, bank accounts numbers, credit card information, and home and business addresses.

Identity theft commonly involves both substantial monetary consequences and noteworthy nonmonetary consequences alike, with significant emotional distress associated with a deep sense of violation of one's privacy and security (e.g., Golladay & Holtfreter, 2017; Harrell, 2019; Piquero et al., 2011; Randa & Reyns, 2019). Although it is nearly impossible to eliminate completely the risk of being victimized by identity theft, many people take precautions to reduce their risk (e.g., checking all credit card reports carefully, purchasing credit card monitoring services, using security software programs). Prior studies have focused primarily on the demographic characteristics and types of online behavior engaged in to predict identity theft victimization (e.g., Allison et al., 2005; Anderson, 2006; Golladay & Holtfreter, 2017; Reyns, 2013). It remains unknown if taking commonly used preventive actions is effective in reducing exposure to identity theft.

We make use of survey data on over 220,000 respondents drawn from three waves of the NCVS Identity Theft Supplement (ITS) to explore this very question. To forecast identity theft victimization, we make use of machine learning approaches to analyze this quite large dataset. Machine learning has been used in criminology to forecast recidivism (Barnes & Hyatt, 2012; Berk et al., 2009; Neuilly et al., 2011), incidents of misconduct among prison inmates (Berk et al., 2006), informing arraignment decisions in domestic violence cases (Berk et al., 2006), predicting the costs of criminal justice policy interventions (Manning et al., 2018), and in some areas of forensic science (Carriquiry et al., 2019). Among numerous machine learning algorithms, we assess the efficacy of three distinct machine learning algorithms: 1) logistic regression; 2) decision tree; and, 3) random forest. In this study we explore two principal research questions: 1) Can these three algorithms be used to forecast identity theft victims? and 2) Which algorithm performs best in forecasting different types of victimization? Limitations, research implications, and policy implications are also discussed.

Literature review

Identity theft and its impact

Identity thieves often use unlawfully obtained personal identities to commit financial crimes such as cash advances, taking out loans, applying for new credit cards, accessing government benefits, and even taking full control over another person's financial accounts (Allison et al., 2005; Reyns, 2013). Unfortunately, consensus does not yet obtain on a precise definition of identity theft. For example, some scholars use a more general term "identity fraud" (e.g., Pontell, 2002) in framing their work, but dissenting scholars object on the grounds that identity theft often does not meet one element of fraud pertaining to a direct communication between an offender and a victim (Golladay & Holtfreter, 2017; Reyns, 2013). Typically, contemporary victims of identity theft do not know who has stolen their identities (Allison et al., 2005). A second less broad definition of identity theft has been used by some scholars to refer to "the unlawful use of another person's personal identifying information" (Piquero et al., 2011, p. 438; also see Golladay & Holtfreter, 2017; White & Fisher, 2008).

This definition is perhaps useful, but it does not entirely solve the definitional problem. For instance, victimization surveys have typically included unauthorized use of an existing credit card as one measure of identity theft (Copes et al., 2010), but this act is generally not included in research involving offender interviews and the study of police archival records (e.g., Copes & Vieraitis, 2009; Rebovich, 2009). As Copes et al.'s (2010) correctly notes in this regard, counting misuse of an existing credit card as identity theft may "obscure the fact that those who are female, black, young, and low income are disproportionately victimized by existing bank account fraud" (p. 1045).

Whichever way it is defined, the impact of identity theft is undoubtedly massive. Official reports and academic studies have estimated the substantial monetary consequences of identity theft variously. For instance, the FTC estimates that in 2006 the direct costs of identity theft were about 15.6 USD billion (Piquero et al., 2011). Estimates derived from NCVS ITS surveys are 24.7 USD billion in 2012 and 15.4 USD billion in 2014 (Harrell, 2015; Harrell & Langton, 2013). The latest report by Harrell (2019) maintains that although over 85% of identity theft victims report minimal monetary loss, the total losses for those reporting serious financial damages are estimated at 17.5 USD billion in 2016. Victims who have experienced at least one identity theft involving substantial loss ($100+) average 850 USD in losses (Harrell, 2019). Victims whose identity theft leads to the opening of new accounts report losses averaging 3,460 USD (Harrell, 2019). In the U.K., Britain's National Fraud Authority estimates that annual aggregate identity theft losses are on the order of £2.7 billion, with around £1,000 in loss from each stolen identity (Reyns, 2013).

Regarding nonmonetary costs, the time spent on resolving issues brought on by identity theft ranges from hours to days, and even years in some cases (Copes et al., 2010; Golladay & Holtfreter, 2017; Piquero et al., 2011; Slosarik, 2002). Moreover, Harrell (2019) estimates that about 10% of identity theft victims experience severe emotional distress. Using the 2012 NCVS ITS data, Golladay and Holtfreter (2017) report that victims often experience serious physical and emotional symptoms, including insomnia and depression. They report that the aged and low-income people who are repeat victims tend to experience high levels of emotional distress from being victimized (Golladay & Holtfreter, 2017). Using the same data source, Randa and Reyns (2019) confirm Golladay and Holtfreter (2017) findings and note how the longer the period of correction of losses suffered the more severe the distresses experienced (Randa & Reyns, 2019).

Predictors of identity theft

Most research on identity theft focuses on demographic characteristics as predictors of the likelihood of identity theft victimization (Golladay & Holtfreter, 2017). One of the most frequently tested predictors is age. Prior research has shown that the victims of identity theft are usually older than victims of property and violent crimes (Golladay, 2017). Using NCVS data, Morgan and Oudekerk (2019) reported that in 2017 the highest rate of serious crimes (i.e., rape, sexual assault, robbery, aggravated assault, burglary, and motor-vehicle theft) occurs to people aged from 12 to 17 (about 2.15%) and the lowest rate occurs to people who are over 65 (about 1.05%). Regarding identity theft victimization, using the FTC's 2003 survey Anderson (2006) reported that individuals in the 25–54 age range are the most likely to experience identity theft while persons 75+ are least likely. This highest and lowest likelihood of victimization pattern was confirmed by Harrell's (2019) report using 2016 NCVS ITS survey data. The Federal Trade Commission's (2019) most recent report notes a similar pattern, adding that the age group reporting the most identity theft is the 30–39 group, followed by the 40–49 group.

Gender may be another predictor of identity theft, but findings from prior research are not consistent in this regard. Some research suggests that females are more likely to become a victim of identity theft than men (e.g., Allison et al., 2005; Anderson, 2006). But other studies suggest that males are more likely to become victims of identity theft than females (e.g., Reyns, 2013). Yet other studies conclude that there is no actual difference between males and females (e.g., Harrell, 2019; Harrell & Langton, 2013). Race may be another indicator of identity theft, but just as in as the case of gender the impact of race on identity theft remains to be determined. Some studies suggest that, compared to other races, Whites are more likely to become a victim of identity theft (Allison et al., 2005; Harrell, 2019); another major study, however, reports that race/ethnicity are not significant predictors of identity theft (Reyns, 2013).

Income and economic status are quite another matter. Numerous studies based on both regression analysis (e.g., Anderson, 2006; Reyns, 2013) and descriptive analysis (e.g., Harrell, 2019) document the association between economic well-being and identity theft victimization. Anderson (2006) reports that persons with incomes of 75,000 USD+ have a significantly higher risk of identity theft victimization compared to those of annual incomes of 25,000 USD or less. Harrell (2019) reports that about 14% of persons with 75,000 USD+ incomes report being victimized while only around 6% of individuals with incomes of 25,000 USD and less report victimization.

Family structure is another plausible predictor of identity theft (Golladay & Holtfreter, 2017). Persons residing in a one-adult household have about a 35% greater chance of being a victim than persons who co-habitat with multiple adults (Anderson, 2006). The number of children in households likewise may have an impact on identity theft victimization. Households with three or more children appear to be more likely to experience victimization than households with no children (Anderson, 2006). Likewise, marital status may be another predictor. Reyns (2013) reported that married persons are more likely to be victims than single persons, but this relationship is mediated by the character of routine activities done online.

Some scholars have argued that researchers ought to make use of prior research on fraud victimization to explore identity theft (Golladay & Holtfreter, 2017). For instance, prior studies on fraud have found that low self-control persons are disproportionately likely to become a victim of fraud schemes (Holtfreter et al., 2008; Reisig & Holtfreter, 2013). Using self-control as the theoretical framework, Holtfreter et al. (2015) report that older (60+) persons with low self-control are more likely than others to engage in risky remote purchasing, a behavior that can significantly increase the likelihood of identity theft victimization.

Previous studies on fraud targeting and victimization have shown that proclivity toward remote purchasing behaviors is a significant predictor of fraud victimization (Holtfreter et al., 2008; Pratt et al., 2010). Inspired by this finding, some research has focused on victims' routine online activities. For example, Reyns (2013) analyzed the 2008–2009 British Crime Survey and found that persons who do online banking and make heavy use of e-mail are more likely to be victims of identity theft than persons who do neither. Reyns (2013) also reports that persons who shop online and download frequently are most likely to be identity theft victims.

Risk perceptions may also come into play. Reisig et al. (2009) report that individuals who have a higher perceived risk of being an identity theft victim tend to spend less time online and make online purchases less frequently (Reisig et al., 2009). In theory, doing so may reduce the risk of being victimized. However, one empirical study indicates that individuals who perceive a high risk of being victimized are nearly three times more likely to become an identity theft victim than those who do not (Reyns, 2013). It may be speculated that this finding is due to the fact that persons once victimized feel and express higher perceived risks (Reyns, 2013).

Preventive actions pertaining to identity theft

Identity thieves make use of a variety of means to obtain personal information (e.g., Allison et al., 2005; Reyns, 2013). Some low-tech approaches include the theft of wallets, purses and dumpster diving (Allison et al., 2005). A person's wallet too often contains a driver's license, debit cards, and credit cards. Identity thieves can use credit cards or a driver's license to open a new account. Dumpster diving, according to Allison et al. (2005), is done to "obtain personal information by going through someone's garbage" (p. 19). Many people discard mail that contains their personal information without shredding such letters and enclosures. Some high-tech means include the use of the Internet, pretext calling, and skimming (Allison et al., 2005). Skimming is where identity thieves use electronic equipment to read the information off of a debit/credit card and use that information to create a new debit/credit card to be sold or used later (Allison et al., 2005). Thieves may also use pretext calling to contact victims, set up a false emergency, and in the process obtain their victim's personal information (Allison et al., 2005). The advanced technology of the Internet allows tech-savvy identity thieves to perform skimming and pretext calling online at relatively low cost. The typical scenario is that a victim receives a fake e-mail from their bank asking the victim to take some account action to avoid having their account being frozen. The thieves then skim that account information and gain access to the victim's bank account and stored personal information.

The research done on identity theft suggests that attaining arrest for identity theft is extremely difficult (Allison et al., 2005). In an early empirical study, using data from a large Florida police agency, Allison et al. (2005) found that the clearance rate for identity theft was about 16 per 100 in 2000, 13 per 100 in 2001, and only 4 per 100 in 2002. The low clearance rate for identity theft highlights the great importance of preventive actions. Reyns (2013) recommend that preventive approaches focus on the key areas of Internet-based banking, online shopping and purchases, file downloading, and communicating. Reyns's (2013) recommendation is not to abandon these practices, but rather to carry them out exclusively through a *secure connection*. Performing online activities using a public Wi-Fi portal greatly raises the risk of victimization.

The FTC website on identity theft (https://www.consumer.ftc.gov/topics/identity-theft) provides a valuable resource for persons seeking to reduce the risk of identity theft. For example, people are urged to never remove their social security cards from a secure location, to shred unwanted documents, credit cards, checks, bank statements, and similar documents before discarding them. Stored data should be encrypted, passwords should be private, and personal information should not be overly shared on social media. The FTC also suggests that people consider purchasing identity theft protection services. For instance, credit monitoring services are available from Equifax, Experian, and TransUnion providing notification whenever a client's identity is used in a financial transaction. Identity theft insurance can also be purchased. The NCVS ITS survey includes questions related to such preventive actions. For example, survey respondents were asked about their actions taken to check credit reports, change passwords, purchase identity theft protection services, check bank statements, and shred any documents containing personal information received in the past 12 months.

Data

NCVS data has been used in numerous victimization studies and it develops many supplements with different points of focus such as the School Crime Supplement (e.g., Baek et al., 2019; Hu et al., 2020; Nguyen et al., 2020), the Identity Theft Supplement (e.g., Harrell, 2019; Ylang, 2020), and the Stalking Victimization Supplement (e.g., Ngo, 2019). This study uses data from three iterations of the NCVS ITS survey. The survey process documents incidents of victimization in considerable detail (Randa & Reyns, 2019). In order to maximize the number of available variables and cases for analysis, we aggregate three waves of the ITS conducted by the Bureau of Justice Statistics (BJS) in 2012, 2014, and in 2016. After combining these three datasets, the database used for this study contains 224,551 cases.

Dependent variables

In line with previous research on identity theft (e.g., Copes et al., 2010; Golladay & Holtfreter, 2017; Piquero et al., 2011), we focus our attention on six dependent variables. The first three concern survey respondents' existing accounts. The variable "misuse of checking/saving" documents victimization associated with existing accounts, including associated debit or ATM cards. It asks if the survey respondent had experienced this type of victimization in the past 12 months (1 = yes, 0 = no). The variable "misuse credit card" documents if the respondents' existing credit cards had been misused in the same time period (1 = yes, 0 = no). The third variable is intended to serve as a catch-all for "misuse other types" and asks if the respondents' other existing accounts such as telephone, cable, PayPal and iTunes accounts had been misused by others during the past year (1 = yes, 0 = no).

The fourth dependent variable documents if survey respondents' personal information had been misused to "open new accounts" such as telephone, credit card, bank, loan and online payment accounts in the past 12 months (1 = yes, 0 = no). The fifth dependent variable "personal information fraudulent" asks if their personal information was misused for other fraudulent purposes such as securing a job, receiving medical care, or renting a residence (1 = yes, 0 = no). The sixth dependent variable "any identity theft" is a composite measure created based on the five previous variables, which designates if a respondent had been a victim of any of these types of identity theft in the past 12 months (1 = yes, 0 = no).

Independent variables

We employ the same demographic characteristics used to predict identity theft victimization in prior research. The variables "gender" (1 = male, 0 = female), "age" (a continuous variable ranging from 16 to 90), and "race" (1 = white, 2 = African American, 3 = Asian, and 4 = other races) follow conventional self-identification specification formats. The variable "ethnicity" is used to identify Hispanic persons of any race (1 = yes, 0 = no). Formal education levels are measured by the variable "education" featuring four ordinal groups (1 = less than high school, 2 = high school and associate degree, 3 = BA/BS degree, and 4 = MA degree and higher). The variable "job" documents employment status (1 = yes, 0 = no). The variable "married" documents marital status (1 = yes, 0 = no). The variable "income" documents the respondents' self-reported annual household income (1 = less than 10,000, USD 2 = 10,000 USD-$19,999, 3 = 20,000 USD-$29,999, 4 = 30,000 USD-$39,999, 5 = 40,000 USD-$49,999, 6 = 50,000 USD-$74,999, and 7 = 75,000 USD+).

We also document respondents' frequency of residential relocation in the past five years knowing that the likelihood of letters bearing personal information being misdirected and subject to theft by identity thieves increases with frequency of relocation. The variable "moving" is coded 0 = not moved, 1 = moved once, 2 = moved twice, 3 = moved three times, 4 = moved four times, 5 = moved five times, and 6 = moved six+ times. Additionally, in order to account for respondents' susceptibility to dumpster diving we document the conditions of the communities in which respondents reside. Specifically, the two binary variables "gated" and "access" document if a respondent's residence lies within a gated area and whether they maintain access control to their private residence (1 = yes, 0 = no). Finally, regarding personal background characteristics we document whether a person had **ever** been a victim of identity theft. Persons who have been affected by data breaches where personal identifying information has been sold to nefarious third parties are at heightened risk of revictimization. We use the binary NCVS ITS variable "prior victim" to identify such persons (1 = yes, 0 = no).

Previous studies have shown that *Internet-based behavior* (e.g., shopping, downloading, banking) may affect identity theft victimization (e.g., Reyns, 2013). Here we use three variables to capture respondents' online activities. The variable "online shopping" measures online shopping frequency (0 = never, 1 = 1–50 times, 2 = 51–100 times, 3 = 101–150 times,

4 = 151–200 times, 5 = 201 and more times). The variable "payment credit" measures if respondents use credit cards to complete online purchasing (1 = yes, 0 = no). The variable "payment debit" measures if respondents use debit cards to make purchases online (1 = yes, 0 = no). We differentiate use of credit cards and debit cards because these are two quite different products. Debit cards are usually linked to a person's checking account, representing how much money a person *owns*. Credit cards often involve a credit line, representing how much money a person can *borrow*. Another differentiation we make is that of misuse of checking/saving accounts and misuse of credit cards; these differentiations are factored into our dependent variables.

Finally, with respect to preventive actions seven distinct variables are employed. The first asks respondents if they have checked their credit report in the past 12 months (1 = yes, 0 = no). The second asks if they have changed the passwords on any of their financial accounts in the past year (1 = yes, 0 = no). The third inquires into the purchase of either credit monitoring services or identity theft insurance (1 = yes, 0 = no). The fourth documents if respondents have shredded and/or destroyed any hard copy documents containing personal information (1 = yes, 0 = no). The fifth asks respondents whether they check their banking statements for suspect charges (1 = yes, 0 = no). The sixth variable asks if respondents use security software programs to protect against loss of credit cards/card theft (1 = yes, 0 = no). The seventh variable asks if the survey respondent has purchased identity theft protection from a commercial company (1 = yes, 0 = no). Since we combine three waves of cross-sectional data, a control variable "year" is also used, with the coding being (1 = 2012, 2 = 2014, 3 = 2016).

Analytical strategies

In recent years a number of scholars, primarily statisticians and computational social scientists, have raised questions about conventional approaches to large N research in criminal justice and related public policy areas. For the most part, social science researchers generally interpret results by analyzing the statistical significance, directionality and effect sizes of theory-derived hypothesized predictor variables (Shmueli, 2010). However, some scholars have questioned the use of regression analysis for *forecasting* purposes. It has been argued that regression analyses should be properly viewed as a form of modeling for testing the adequacy of hypothetical relationships derived systematically from theoretical reasoning (Berk, 2012; Breiman, 2001; Shmueli, 2010). Additionally, it is argued by some such critics of regression analyses that *p*-values are more properly associated with explanation of past behavior, not prediction of future behavior (Shmueli, 2010).

The machine learning approach focuses precisely on forecasting. The machine learning approach involves dividing large N datasets into two parts: (1) training data and (2) test data. The researcher uses training data to build a mathematical model of the structuring of the data in the training subset, and then uses the test data subset to assess the model's predictive ability (Russell & Norvig, 2016). A machine learning approach has some additional noteworthy features. While various assumptions as to the distributional qualities and covariance of variables (e.g., normality, collinearity, etc.) must be met in regression analysis (Warner, 2013), the development of machine learning algorithms generally requires fewer distributional and covariance assumptions being met than does conventional statistical analysis (Shmueli, 2010).[1] Importantly, machine learning accommodates very large datasets while regression has problems with "everything being significant" in such analyses (Berk,

2012; Shmueli, 2010). If used properly, machine learning algorithms can be at least as good as traditional statistical approaches such as OLS regression, and it may be better when dealing with complicated and nonlinear relationships (Berk & Bleich, 2014; Duwe & Kim, 2017). Inquisitive researchers using all forms of advanced statistical modeling do get quite involved in "tweaking" variables in different ways (e.g., adjusting cutting points on scales, collapsing categories, etc.) to attain optimal performance in their models; researchers using machine learning algorithms are inclined to do the same thing when possible. The machine learning approach, however, minimizes such researcher speculative manipulations in the forecasting process (Duwe & Kim, 2017). The objectivity of data analysis is thereby enhanced in machine learning.

Additionally, traditional statistical approaches tend to remain stable across the time. For example, the formula for the OLS regression has remained largely unchanged since its original development, although researchers can use some processes such as bootstrapping and other forms of imputation to achieve better results in some cases. In contrast, machine learning algorithms can be developed quickly and improvements in forecasting accuracy can be ongoing. In this regard, Duwe and Kim (2017) have evaluated the performance of 12 supervised machine learning algorithms and conclude that the newer algorithms generally perform considerably better than the older ones as new test data become available.

Machine learning approaches have been used by criminologists for predicting recidivism among offenders (e.g., Duwe & Kim, 2017). We explore here whether a comparable application of machine learning algorithms can be done to forecast identity theft victimization. Three commonly used machine learning algorithms are employed in this study to forecast identity theft victimization – namely, logistic regression, decision tree, and random forest. We picked these three algorithms because of their records of good previous performance, simple parameter selections, ease of tuning, as well as the fact that our dependent variables are dichotomous variables and hence amenable to machine learning analysis.[2]

Logistic regression is a statistical algorithm which uses a probabilistic logistic function to model the behavior of a binary dependent variable (Kleinbaum et al., 2002). While the term logistic regression contains the word "regression," it is not a regression model along the lines of the conventional Ordinary Least Squares (OLS) family of statistical operations. The logistic regression model is able to classify cases based on probabilistic odds ratios (Hosmer et al., 2013). The logistic regression algorithm provides a formula that tells the researcher precisely how independent variables are used to predict dependent variables, a formula which "offers a relatively high degree of transparency" (Duwe & Kim, 2017, p. 576). The logistic regression algorithm can be "trained" with a series of data samples to refine its predictions of reoccurring outcomes. The trained logistic regression algorithm is used in category assignment prediction (e.g., recidivist/non-recidivist, crime victim/non-victim, successful vs. unsuccessful employment hire, etc.). A limitation of logistic regression algorithm is that it cannot solve non-linear problems. Also, the logistic regression algorithm generally requires its dependent variable to be strictly dichotomous.

A decision tree algorithm uses a tree-like conceptual model and flowchart-like structure to document decisions and assess their possible consequences (Safavian & Landgrebe, 1991). Nodes and corresponding branches are key elements in the tree-like model. Every node represents a feature tested, and its branches represent test results. A leaf node, which does not have any branch, represents a specific diagnostic result (Friedl & Brodley, 1997). The outcomes of events can be decided through the tree-like structure according to the attributes of the events. The decision tree algorithm findings are relatively easy to interpret (Duwe & Kim, 2017). Decision tree algorithms are widely used in business decision analysis to help identify potential investment strategies (e.g., Foster et al., 2010; Takieddine & Andoh-Baidoo, 2014; Zurada et al., 2014). Unlike the logistic regression algorithm, a decision tree algorithm can be used when a dependent variable has multiple values.

An "overfitting" limitation sometimes constrains the use of decision tree algorithms Trained decision tree algorithms tend to perform well in situations where well established data parameters and predictable decisional pathways already exist, but it is less well suited for use in prediction tasks where marked uncertainties obtain in either regard (Liaw & Wiener, 2002). In order to correct the overfitting problem, a random forest algorithm is often introduced as an analytical tool. The random forest algorithm expands the scope of the traditional decision tree algorithm. Unlike the decision tree algorithm that runs cases throughout a single tree, the random forest algorithm can construct a set of potential trees and select the best model for obtaining optimal classification results. The random forest algorithm draws sub-samples from the training sample, with replacement, and uses these multiple samples to train multiple potential decision trees (Breiman, 2001, 1996). These features make random forest algorithms more accurate on predictions compared to decision tree-derived algorithms in many circumstances, but not always. Additionally, a random forest algorithm constructs decision trees with controlled variance and selects some case features, instead of all features, to evaluate the results (Amit et al., 1997). In the current study, the number of trees in the random forest algorithm is selected to be the same as the number of features, an analytical choice which achieves the best prediction results. The calculation of feature importance in a random forest algorithm is accomplished by averaging feature importance in all potential viable trees identified. A limitation of the random forest algorithm concerns the interpretation of the results. Compared to the decision tree algorithm, which only has one tree, the random forest algorithm creates a large number of trees making interpretation more difficult.

We compare the efficacy of these three machine learning algorithms vis-a-vis three evaluative criteria: the overall percentage of correct classification, the receiver operating characteristics (ROC), and the area under the ROC curve (AUC). A classification table was produced to capture *type 1* (false positive) and *type 2* errors (false negative) associated with each of the three approaches. A classification table indicates how likely a given survey respondent's classification on the binary dependent variable would be correct based on the independent variables being used. In addition, a commonly used approach to comparing analytical model outcomes is to calculate the area under the ROC curve (i.e., AUC) (Bradley, 1997). The AUC represents "the probability that the classifier will rank a randomly chosen positive instance higher than a randomly chosen negative instance" (Fawcett, 2006). In other words, an AUC indicates if two randomly selected respondents are selected – one is an identity theft victim and one is not – what is the likelihood that the model will distinguish between the two based on these particular independent variables (i.e., predictive discrimination). Customarily, if a model AUC falls between 0.9 and 1.0, the model is considered robust. If the AUC falls in the range of 0.8–0.9, the model is considered good. If the AUC falls in the 0.7–0.8 range, the model is considered to be fair. A model AUC of less than 0.7 is considered poor.

Also, to illustrate how each independent variable impacts the predictive accuracy, we employ the concept of *variable criticality*. The concept measures how predictive accuracy would change if we eliminate one independent variable. For instance, assume a model with ten variables has a predictive accuracy of 0.90. When we eliminate variable A and use the rest of the nine variables, the predictive accuracy becomes 0.89; the variable criticality of A is 0.01. When we eliminate variable B and use the rest of the nine variables, the accuracy becomes 0.88; in this hypothetical case the variable criticality of B is 0.02. Carrying out this process *seriatim* allows us to compare both model performance and the relative importance of independent variables. In general, variables with higher variable criticality are more important (i.e., more significant predictors) in the predictive model than variables with lower variable criticality.

Findings

Table 1 displays descriptive statistics for the dependent and independent variables. About 9% of all respondents in this sample have experienced at least one type of identity theft. Within five types of identity theft, misuse of checking/saving accounts (45%) and misuse of credit/debit cards (51%) were the most common types of victimization. The three other types – misuse of other types (8%), open new accounts (6%) and personal information fraudulent (5%) – were substantially less common.

Regarding independent variables, the sample contained more female respondents (53%) than male respondents (47%). The average age of the respondents was approximately 49. The majority of the respondents were White, followed by African Americans and Asians. Most of the respondents were non-Hispanic Whites. The average education level among the respondents was between high school and BA/BS degree. Over half of the respondents were married and were employed. The average household income was between 40,000 USD and 49,999. USD The majority of the respondents did not move frequently, and only a small proportion of them lived in a gated community with access control. About 10% of the respondents had experienced identity theft sometime in the past.

The majority of the respondents did not shop online frequently. About 40% of them used credit cards to purchase things online, and about 26% of them used debit cards. Regarding the seven preventive actions, the most common actions adopted by the respondents were checking banking statements for suspect charges (78%) and shredding/destroying documents containing personal information (70%), followed by checking credit reports (42%) and frequently changing the passwords for financial accounts (34%). The other three preventive actions (i.e., purchasing credit monitoring services, using security software programs, and purchasing identity theft protection) were only infrequently taken.

Six groups of datasets were created, and each group was examined by three machine learning algorithms. Group 1 used all cases in the sample with the dependent variable as identity theft victim (1 = yes and 0 = no). We randomly assigned all cases into training group (with 80% of cases) and test group (with 20% of cases). The algorithms we selected created a model based on the training group and used the model to make predictions in the test group. The algorithms ran without a problem on the first group; however, when it came to five different types of identity theft the algorithms tended to classify all cases into category 0 because the proportion of category 1 was quite limited. To address this problem, we matched the number of cases with category 1 with randomly selected cases

Table 1. Descriptive statistics of dependent and independent variables.

Variables	N (%)	Min.	Max	Mean	S.D.
Dependent Variables					
Identity Theft (any type)	19,427 (8.7)	0	1	0.09	0.28
Misuse Checking/Saving	8,695 (3.9)	0	1	0.04	0.19
Misuse Credit Card	9,911 (4.4)	0	1	0.04	0.21
Misuse Other Types	1,627 (0.7)	0	1	0.01	0.09
Open New Accounts	1,167 (0.5)	0	1	0.01	0.07
Information Fraudulent	866 (0.4)	0	1	0.00	0.06
Independent Variables					
Gender	104,730 (46.6)	0	1	0.47	0.50
Age	-	16	90	48.63	18.23
Race	-	-	-	1.26	0.65
White	185,455 (82.6)	0	1	-	-
African American	24,103 (10.7)	0	1	-	-
Asian	9,897 (4.4)	0	1	-	-
Others	5,094 (2.3)	0	1	-	-
Ethnicity (Hispanic)	28,229 (12.6)	0	1	0.13	0.33
Education	-	1	4	2.26	0.84
Job (Employment status)	130,772 (58.2)	0	1	0.58	0.49
Married	123,223 (54.9)	0	1	0.55	0.50
Income	-	1	7	5.03	1.97
Moving	-	0	6	0.69	1.14
Gated	17,619 (7.8)	0	1	0.08	0.27
Access (Controlled)	16,872 (7.5)	0	1	0.08	0.26
Prior Victim	23,624 (10.5)	0	1	0.11	0.31
Online Shopping	-	0	5	0.63	0.73
Payment Credit	90,579 (40.3)	0	1	0.40	0.49
Payment Debit	58,186 (25.9)	0	1	0.26	0.44
Preventive Action 1	94,799 (42.2)	0	1	0.42	0.49
Preventive Action 2	76,295 (34.0)	0	1	0.34	0.47
Preventive Action 3	19,120 (8.5)	0	1	0.09	0.28
Preventive Action 4	157,453 (70.1)	0	1	0.70	0.46
Preventive Action 5	174,945 (77.9)	0	1	0.78	0.41
Preventive Action 6	36,360 (16.2)	0	1	0.16	0.37
Preventive Action 7	9,580 (4.3)	0	1	0.04	0.20
Year	-	-	-	2.14	0.83
2012	64,132 (28.6)	0	1	-	-
2014	64,287 (28.6)	0	1	-	-
2016	96,130 (42.8)	0	1	-	-

within the 0 category to create a new group wherein cases with both 1 and 0 values were in equal presence. Next, we randomly assigned cases of the newly created group into a training group (with 80% of cases) and a test group (with 20% of cases). In this manner, we created analytical groups 2–6 based on the five types of identity theft. To examine whether training and test groups are comparable, Table 2 was constructed as an assessment. Based on Table 2, the descriptive statistics for the training group and the test group with respect to within-group comparisons indicated that the two groups were virtually identical. When it came to between-group comparisons, however, some noteworthy differences are in evidence. For instance, group 3 had a higher average age than other groups, suggesting that victims of credit card misuse tend to be older than victims of other types of identity theft. A similar pattern could also be found in regard to household income. Victims of misuse of credit cards have a higher household income than victims of other types of identity theft.

Figures 1-3 display the results of using the group 1 dataset – any type of identity theft victimization. The *confusion matrixes*[3] indicate that the logistic regression algorithm had

Table 2. Descriptive statistics of the training and test datasets.

	Group 1		**Group 2**		**Group 3**		**Group 4**		**Group 5**		**Group 6**	
	ID Theft Victimization		Misuse Checking/Saving		Misuse Credit Card		Misuse Other Types		Open New Accounts		Information Fraudulent	
	Training	Test	Training	Test	Training	Test	Training	Test	Training	Test	Training	Test
	N =179,640	N =44,911	N =13,914	N =3,479	N =15,858	N =3,966	N =2,604	N =652	N =1,868	N =468	N =1,386	N =348
	Mean	Mean	Mean	Mean	Mean	Mean	Mean	Mean	Mean	Mean	Mean	Mean
Gender	0.47	0.46	0.46	0.46	0.48	0.47	0.46	0.48	0.49	0.45	0.45	0.44
Age	48.65	48.52	46.91	47.56	50.03	50.07	46.65	47.20	47.62	48.30	48.59	47.22
Race	1.26	1.26	1.25	1.27	1.23	1.22	1.29	1.29	1.31	1.33	1.28	1.31
Ethnicity	0.13	0.13	0.12	0.11	0.10	0.09	0.11	0.10	0.13	0.13	0.13	0.13
Education	2.27	2.26	2.33	2.35	2.52	2.52	2.39	2.38	2.37	2.35	2.33	2.36
Job	0.58	0.58	0.65	0.64	0.63	0.63	0.62	0.60	0.62	0.60	0.58	0.59
Married	0.55	0.55	0.56	0.56	0.62	0.62	0.55	0.51	0.53	0.55	0.53	0.56
Income	5.03	5.03	5.18	5.18	5.45	5.47	5.17	5.06	5.07	5.00	4.99	4.98
Moving	0.68	0.69	0.83	0.79	0.65	0.64	0.85	0.85	0.79	0.82	0.81	0.82
Gated	0.08	0.08	0.09	0.08	0.08	0.09	0.07	0.09	0.08	0.10	0.09	0.07
Access	0.08	0.08	0.08	0.08	0.08	0.08	0.07	0.10	0.08	0.09	0.08	0.08
Victim (any type)	0.11	0.11	0.14	0.14	0.16	0.17	0.17	0.16	0.16	0.15	0.16	0.14
Online Shopping	0.63	0.64	0.81	0.78	0.87	0.89	0.86	0.93	0.77	0.74	0.73	0.77
Payment Credit	0.40	0.40	0.45	0.44	0.58	0.59	0.49	0.49	0.44	0.43	0.42	0.46
Payment Debit	0.26	0.26	0.40	0.39	0.23	0.24	0.35	0.36	0.29	0.30	0.30	0.31
Preventive Action 1	0.42	0.43	0.50	0.50	0.51	0.52	0.52	0.52	0.57	0.52	0.52	0.48
Preventive Action 2	0.34	0.35	0.49	0.48	0.47	0.48	0.52	0.47	0.49	0.46	0.45	0.46
Preventive Action 3	0.09	0.09	0.12	0.12	0.14	0.14	0.15	0.15	0.19	0.18	0.15	0.16
Preventive Action 4	0.70	0.71	0.75	0.74	0.78	0.77	0.75	0.74	0.75	0.75	0.75	0.75
Preventive Action 5	0.78	0.78	0.86	0.86	0.86	0.86	0.84	0.87	0.83	0.83	0.82	0.83
Preventive Action 6	0.16	0.16	0.20	0.19	0.21	0.21	0.23	0.25	0.23	0.24	0.21	0.21
Preventive Action 7	0.04	0.04	0.06	0.06	0.06	0.06	0.07	0.07	0.11	0.11	0.09	0.09
Year	2.14	2.14	2.22	2.21	2.23	2.23	2.20	2.17	2.21	2.23	2.22	2.25

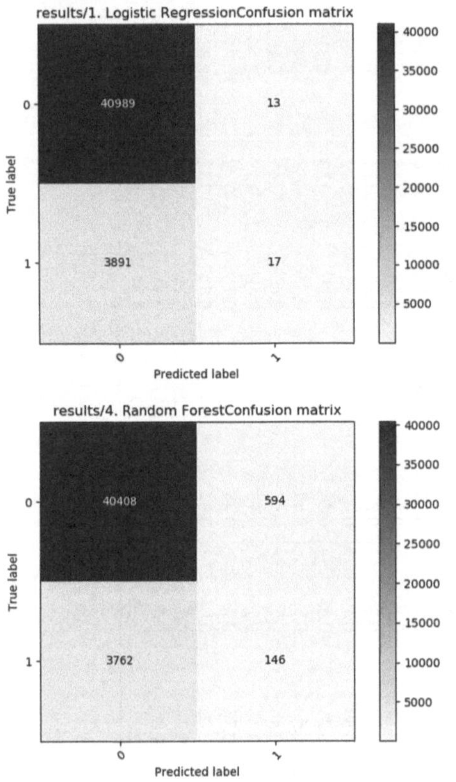

Figure 1. Confusion matrix of logistic regression, decision tree, and random forest of group 1.

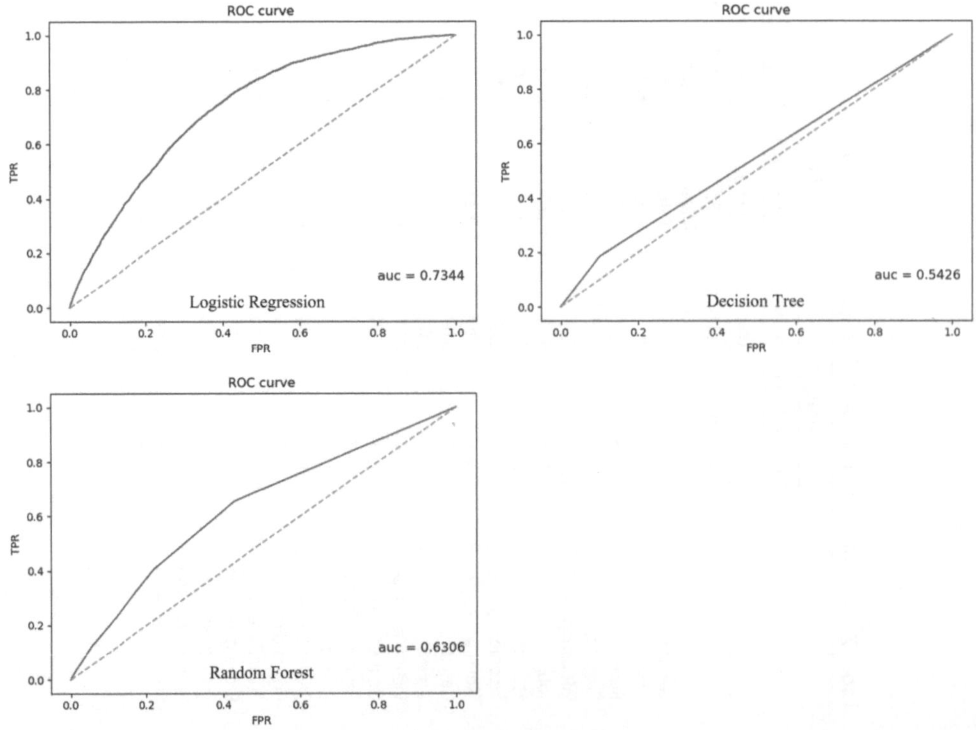

Figure 2. ROC and AUC of logistic regression, decision tree, and random forest of group 1.

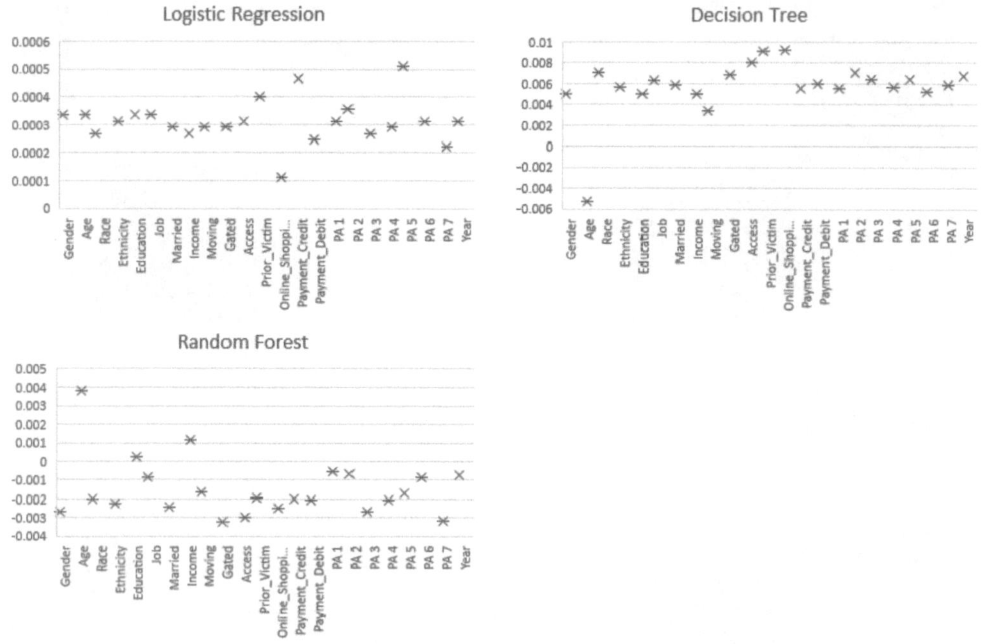

Figure 3. Feature criticality of logistic regression, decision tree, and random forest of group 1.

the highest accuracy, followed by the random forest algorithm and then the decision tree algorithm. The ROC and AUC curves suggested that the logistic regression algorithm achieved fair predictive discrimination, while the decision tree algorithm and the random forest algorithm produced poor predictive discrimination. The feature criticality figure indicates that payment with credit card and preventive action 5 (i.e., checking banking statements for unfamiliar charges) seemed to be most influential in the logistic regression algorithm.

Figures 4-6 show the results of using the group 2 dataset involving misuse of checking/saving accounts. The confusion matrixes indicated that the random forest algorithm had the highest predictive accuracy, followed by the logistic regression and decision tree algorithms. The results for the ROC and AUC curves also indicated that although both the random forest and the logistic regression algorithms had fair predictive discrimination, the random forest algorithm performed a little better than the logistic regression. The feature criticality figure indicated that consistency occurred across all three algorithms: *payment with debit cards* seemed to be the most influential predictor of misuse of checking/saving accounts. The random forest algorithm also suggested that age and preventive actions 2 and 5 (i.e., frequently changing passwords of financial accounts, checking banking statements for suspect charges) were important in predicting such victimization.

Figures 7-9 set forth the results of using the third group of datasets involving the misuse of credit cards. The confusion matrixes suggested that the logistic regression algorithm performed a little better than the random forest algorithm, with the decision tree algorithm producing the worst accuracy. The results for the ROC and AUC curves suggested that the logistic regression algorithm had good predictive discrimination, the random forest algorithm had only fair predictive discrimination, and the decision tree

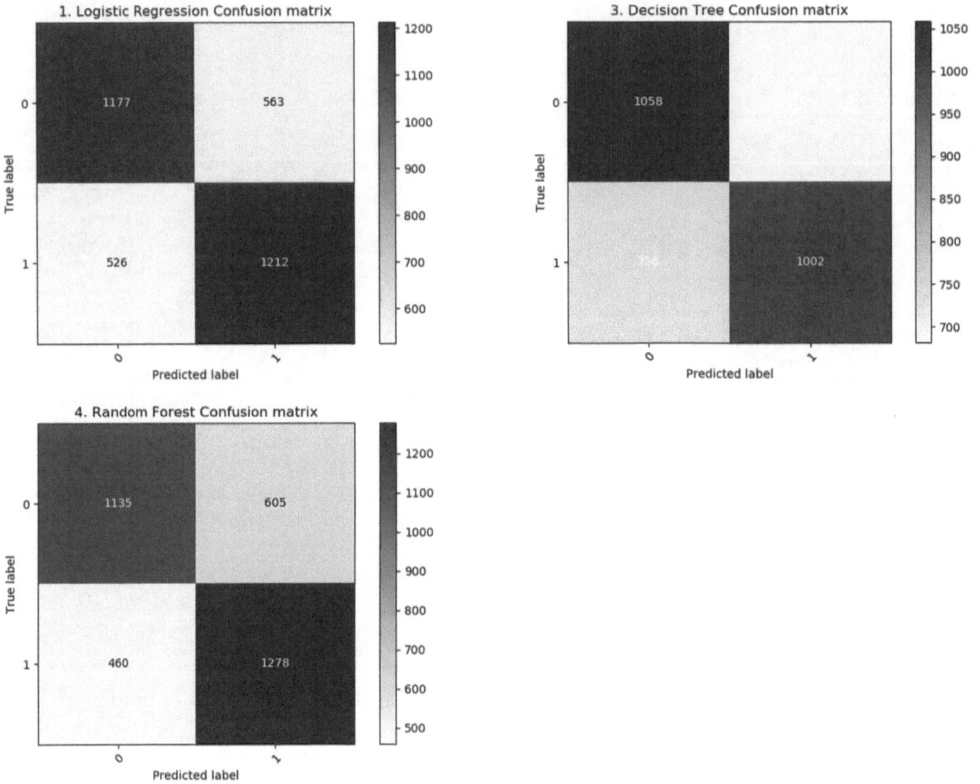

Figure 4. Confusion matrix of logistic regression, decision tree, and random forest of group 2.

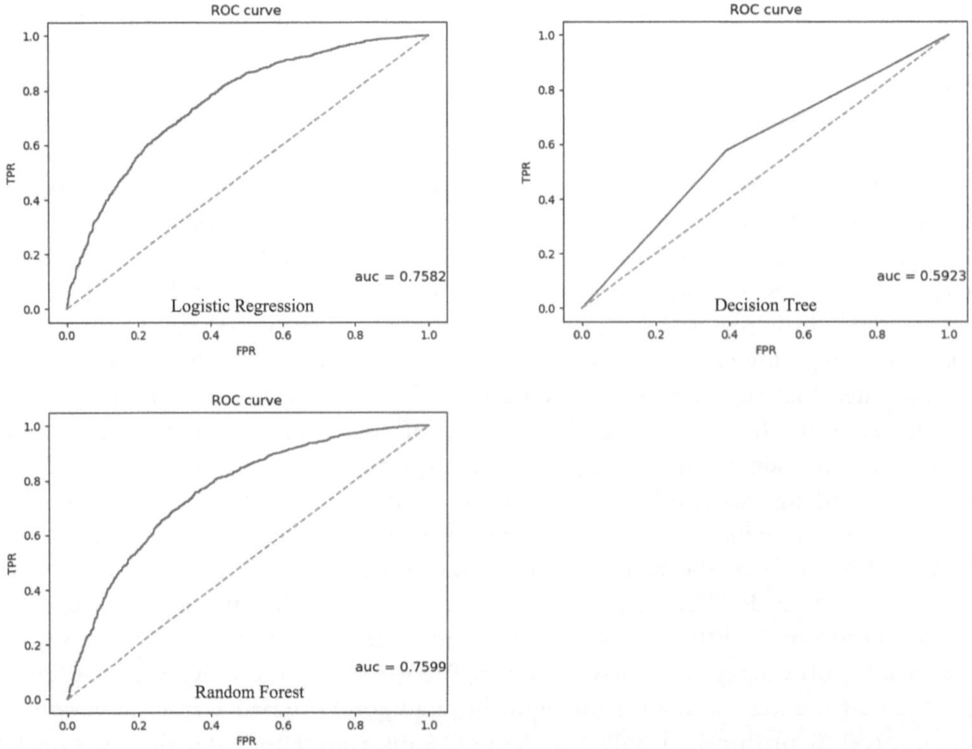

Figure 5. ROC and AUC of logistic regression, decision tree, and random forest of group 2.

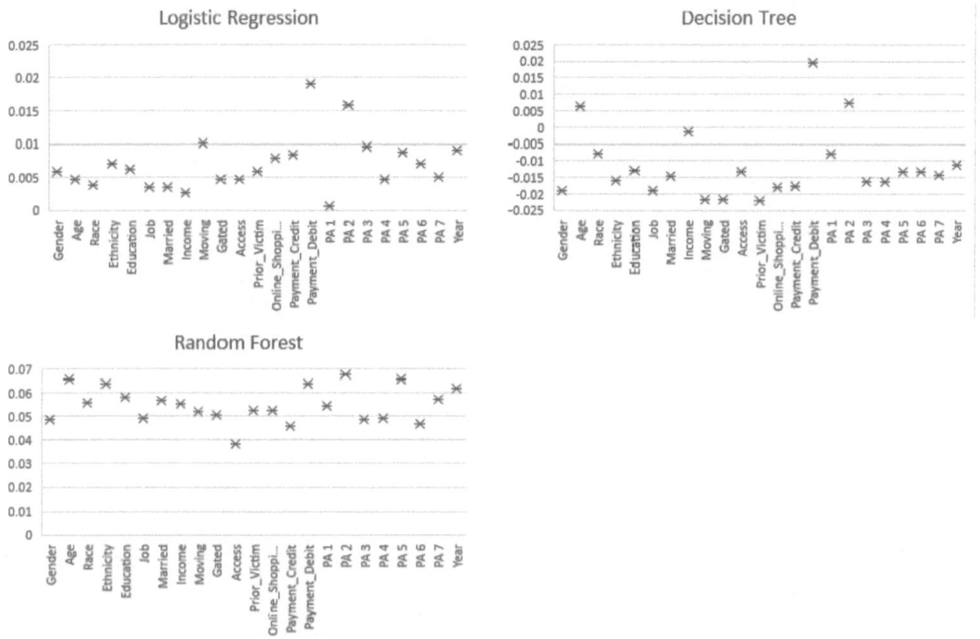

Figure 6. Feature criticality of logistic regression, decision tree, and random forest of group 2.

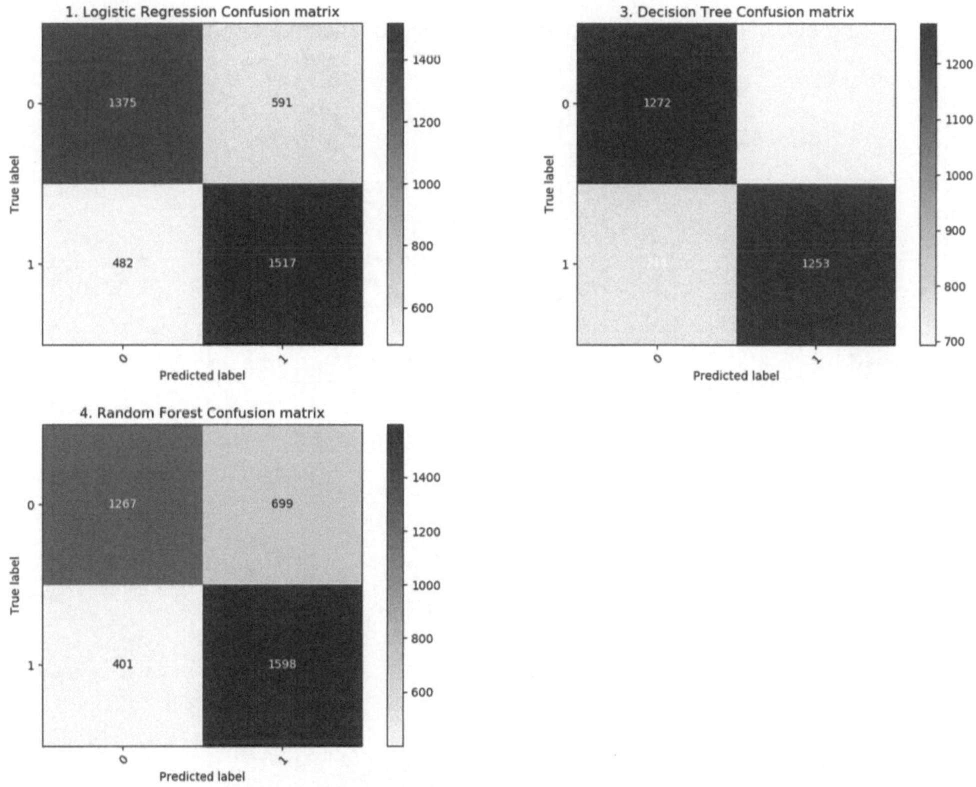

Figure 7. Confusion matrix of logistic regression, decision tree, and random forest of group 3.

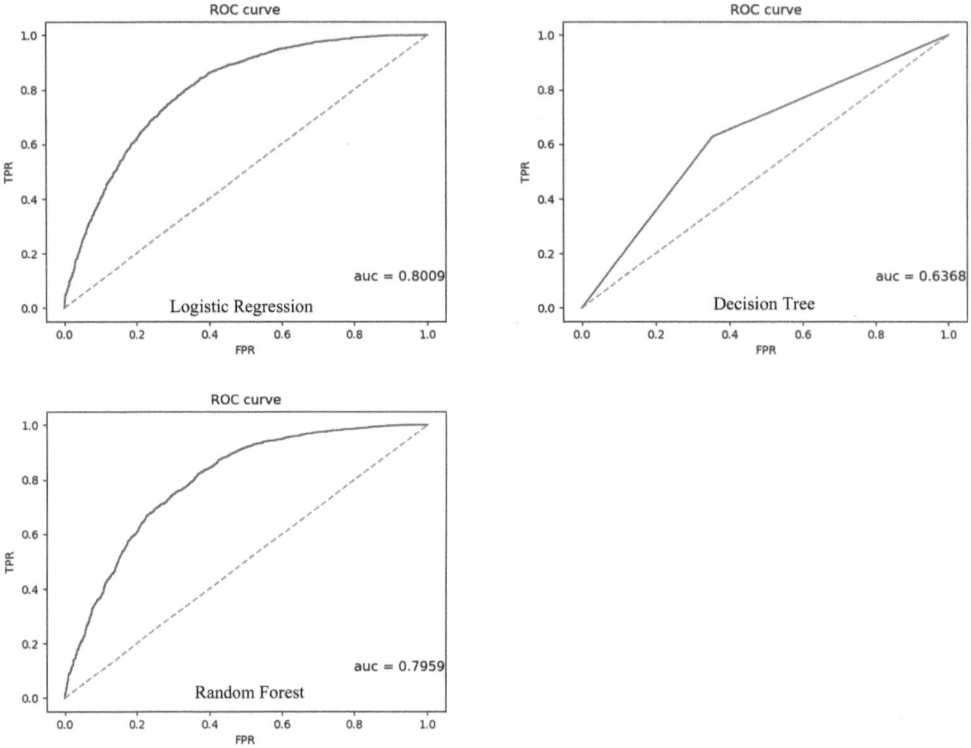

Figure 8. ROC and AUC of logistic regression, decision tree, and random forest of group 3.

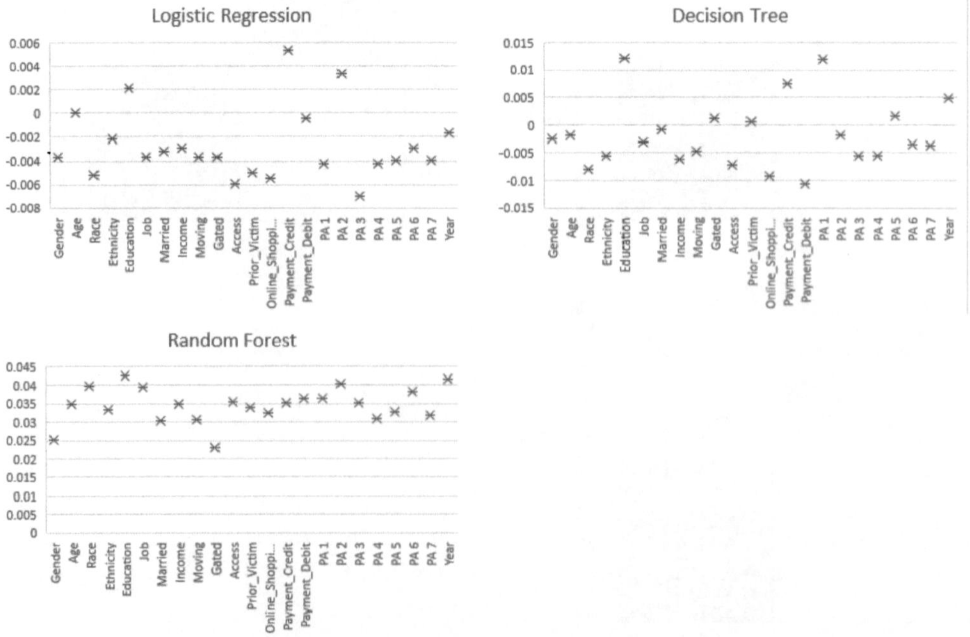

Figure 9. Feature criticality of logistic regression, decision tree, and random forest of group 3.

algorithm had poor predictive discrimination. Based on the feature criticality figure, educational level and preventive action 2 (i.e., frequently changing passwords of financial accounts) seemed to be most influential across all three algorithms. Specifically, payment with credit card was the most influential predictor according to logistic regression algorithm.

Figures 10-12 show the results of using the group 4 dataset involving misuse other types. Based on the confusion matrixes, the logistic regression algorithm performed a little better than the random forest algorithm on overall accuracy. However, the results for the ROC and AUC curves indicated that the random forest algorithm produced slightly better predictive discrimination. Again, the decision tree algorithm did not perform very well in terms of either overall accuracy or predictive discrimination. The feature criticality figure indicated that preventive action 1 (i.e., checking credit report) seemed to be important in prediction with both the logistic regression and the random forest algorithms. The most influential predictor in the logistic regression algorithm was preventive measure 2 (i.e., frequently changing passwords of financial accounts), and the most influential predictor in the random forest algorithm was payment with debit card.

Figures 13-15 show the results of using the group 5 dataset involving the opening of new accounts. The ROC and AUC curves suggested that the logistic regression algorithm produced an overall higher level of accuracy and predictive discrimination than the random forest algorithm, and the decision tree algorithm performed rather poorly. The feature

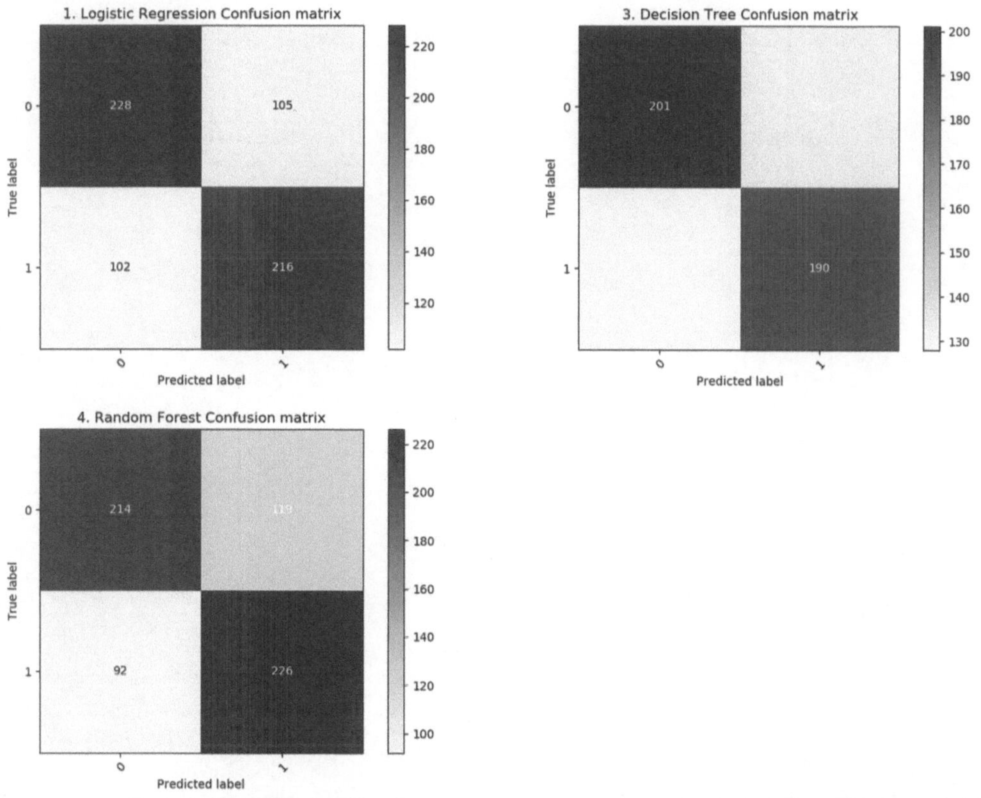

Figure 10. Confusion matrix of logistic regression, decision tree, and random forest of group 4.

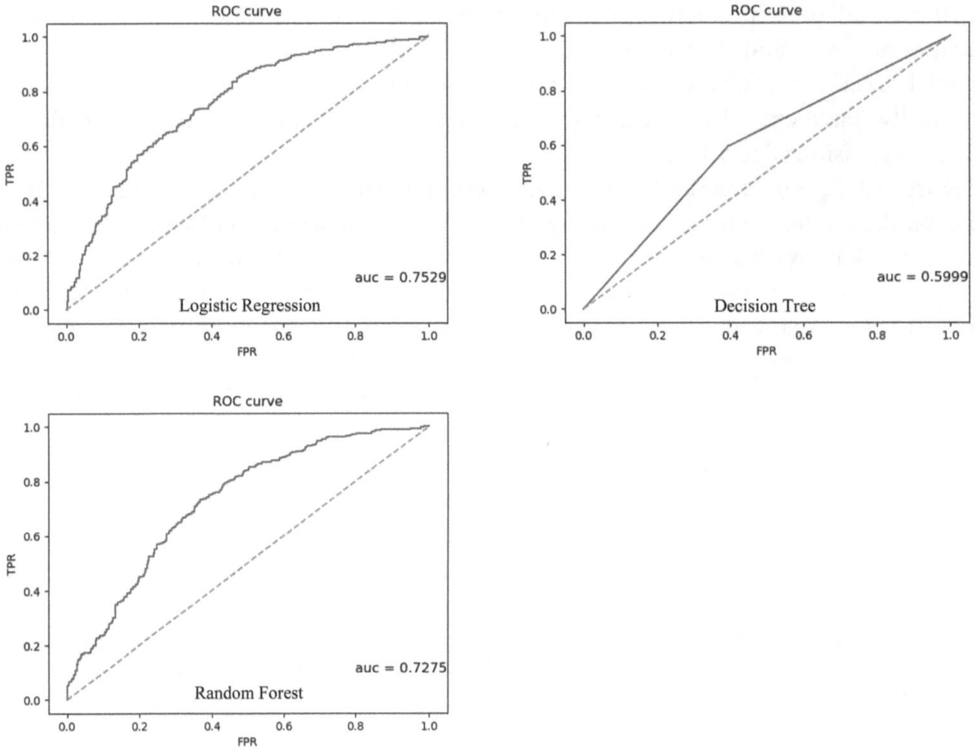

Figure 11. ROC and AUC of logistic regression, decision tree, and random forest of group 4.

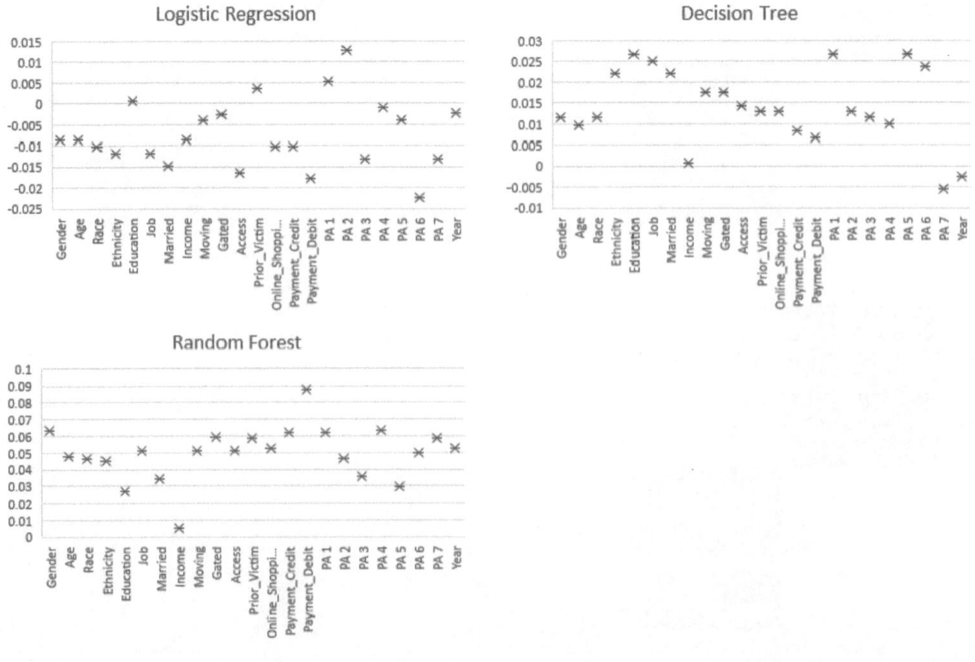

Figure 12. Feature criticality of logistic regression, decision tree, and random forest of group 4.

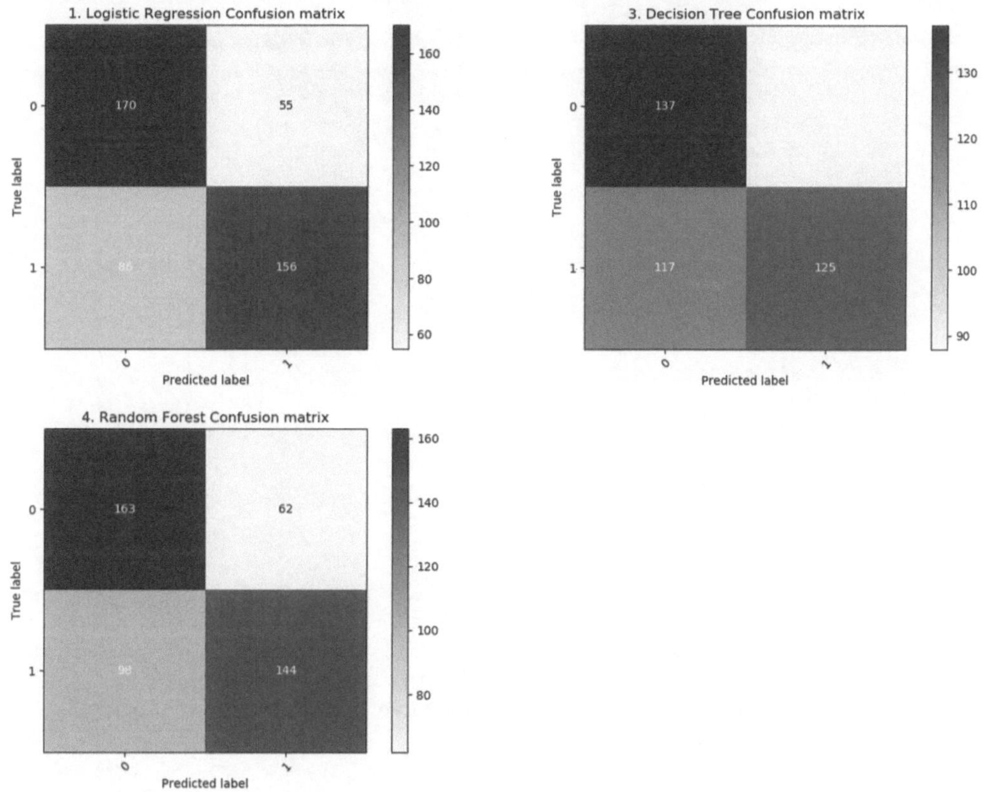

Figure 13. Confusion matrix of logistic regression, decision tree, and random forest of group 5.

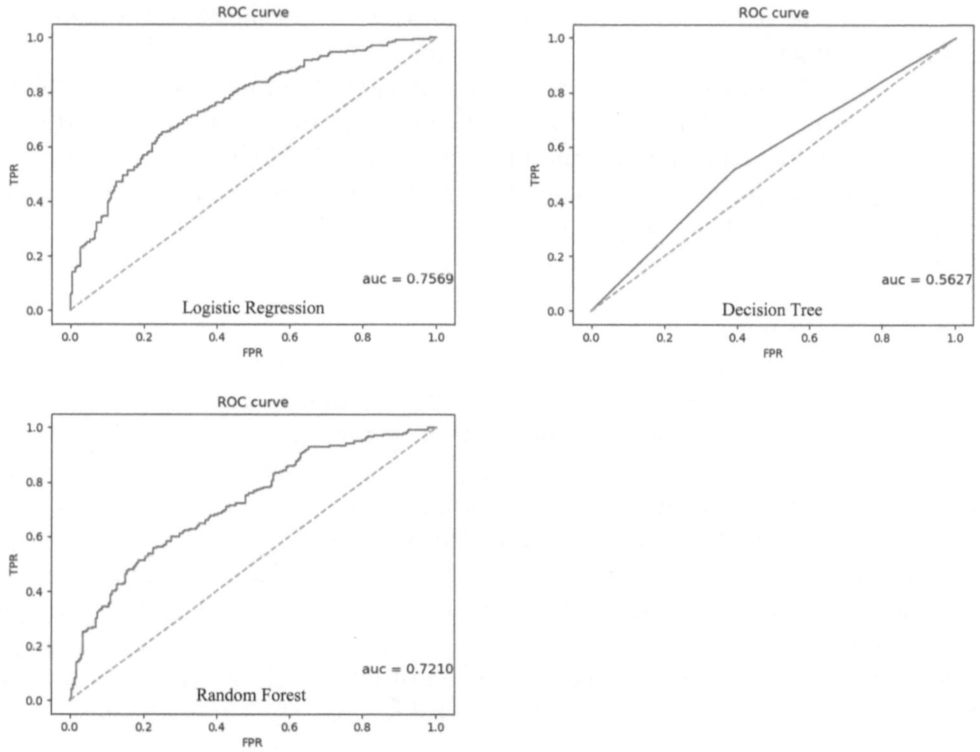

Figure 14. ROC and AUC of logistic regression, decision tree, and random forest of group 5.

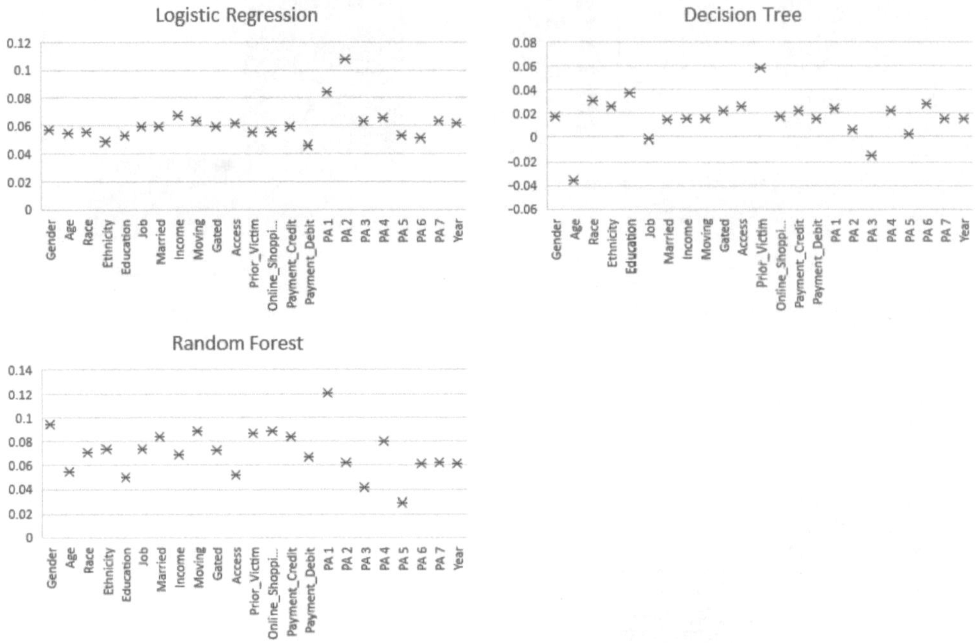

Figure 15. Feature criticality of logistic regression, decision tree, and random forest of group 5.

criticality figure suggested that preventive action 1 (i.e., checking credit report) was important in both logistic regression and random forest algorithms, and preventive action 2 (i.e., frequently changing passwords of financial accounts) was most influential in the logistic regression algorithm.

The last set of Figures 16-18 shows the results of using the group 6 dataset relating to personal information fraudulent. Once again, the logistic regression algorithm performed better overall than the random forest and the decision tree algorithms. However, the ROC and AUC curves results indicated that all these algorithms demonstrated poor predictive discrimination. That is, if two randomly selected respondents are selected – one is a victim of personal information fraudulent and one is not – all three algorithms would barely distinguish between the two based on this set of independent variables. This could very well be due to the fact that the sample size was quite small.

To sum up the findings, among the three machine learning algorithms tested, the logistic regression algorithm had the best predictive accuracy on overall identity theft victimization, misuse of credit cards, misuse of other types, and the opening of new accounts. The random forest algorithm had the best predictive accuracy on the misuse of checking/saving accounts. None of the three algorithms could accurately predict fraudulent use of personal information. Regarding demographic independent variables, respondent age and educational level might be two of the most influential predictors of identity theft. Regrading online activity and preventive actions, online payment with credit and debit cards, preventive action 1, and preventive action 2 (i.e., checking credit report, frequently changing passwords of financial accounts) could have the most influential impact on identity theft victimization.

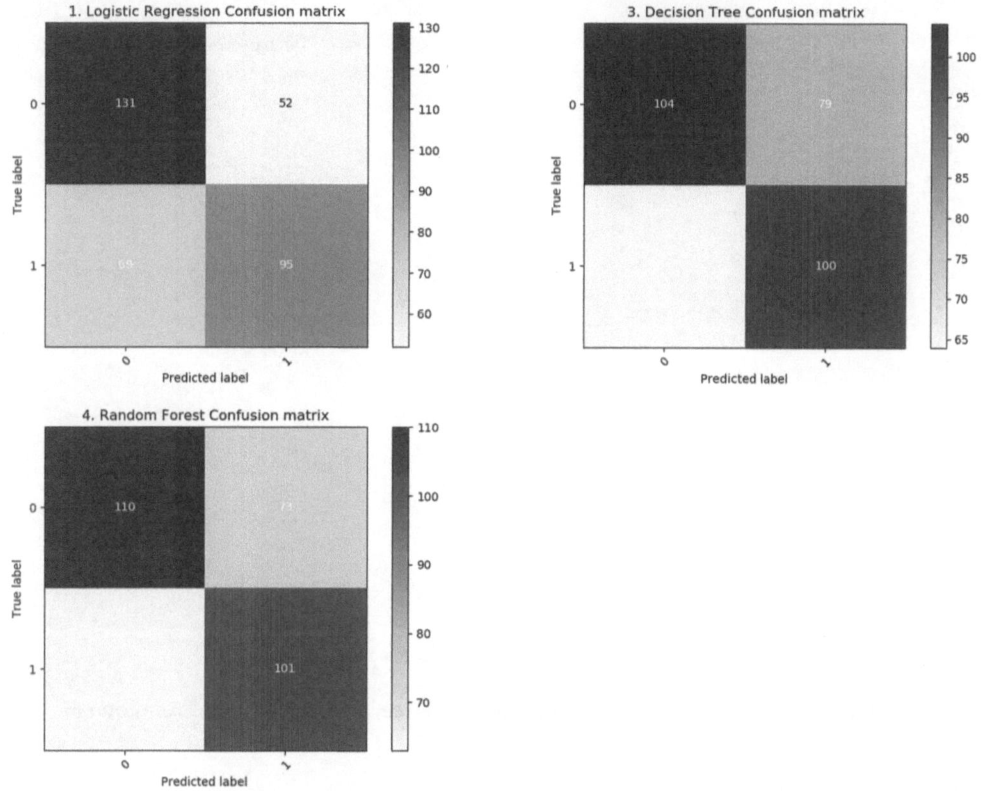

Figure 16. Confusion matrix of logistic regression, decision tree, and random forest of group 6.

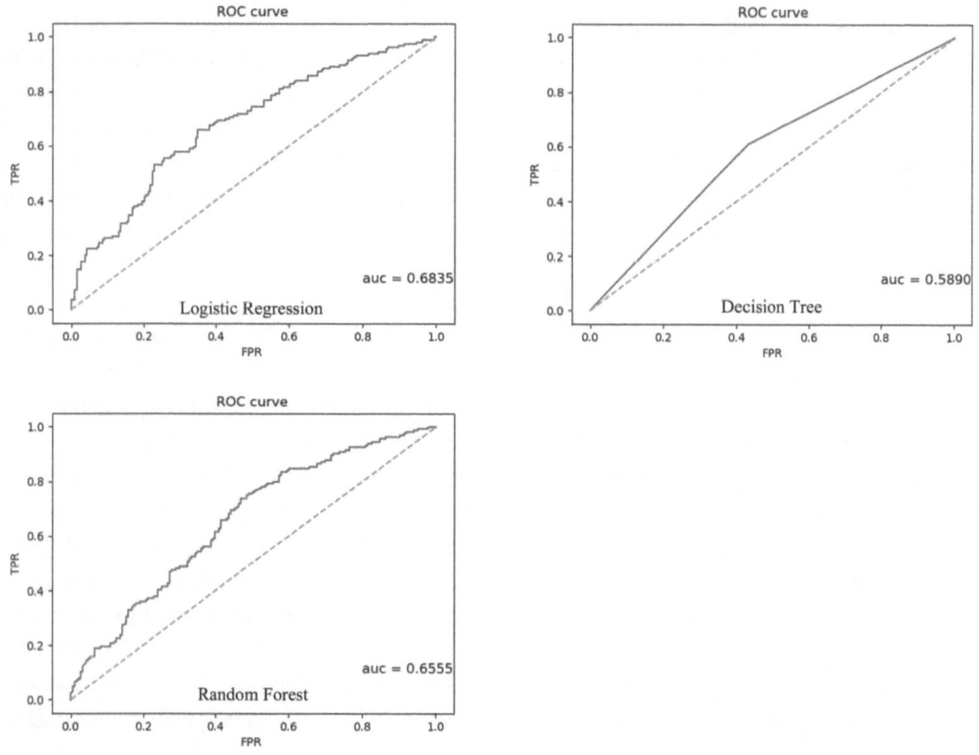

Figure 17. ROC and AUC of logistic regression, decision tree, and random forest of group 6.

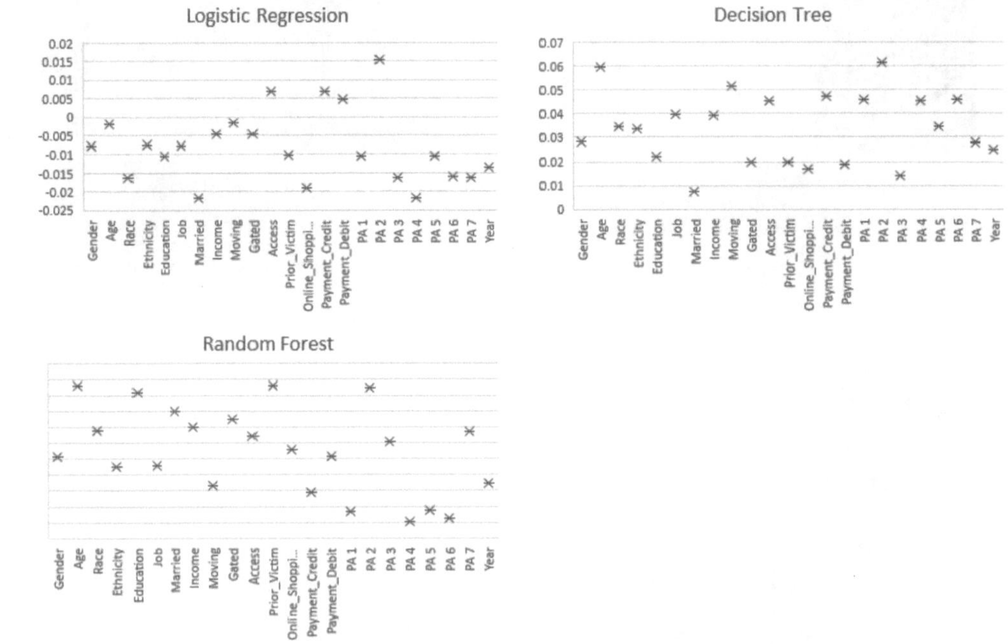

Figure 18. Feature criticality of logistic regression, decision tree, and random forest of group 6.

Discussion and conclusion

The current study has some definite limitations, of course. For example, the cross-sectional nature of the NCVS ITS data do not permit us to establish solid causal connections between preventive actions and identity theft victimization. Future research would benefit greatly from a longitudinal research design. Also, machine learning approaches benefit from large N datasets. Although the first three groups of data used in the current study can be viewed as large N datasets (N_1 = 224,551, N_2 = 17,393, and N_3 = 19,824), the remaining three groups have a relatively small sample size (N_4 = 3,256, N_5 = 2,336, N_6 = 1,734), a fact which may somewhat limit the use of machine learning approaches in the area of survey-based data archives. Future research can be done in which more years of NCVS ITS datasets are combined to enhance the number of observations available for analysis.

Another noteworthy limitation of this study is associated with the machine learning algorithm process itself, one which is justifiably criticized by some scholars for its "black-box" quality. For example, it is difficult to graphically display how alternative decision trees "grow" in the random forest algorithm progress. The black-box mystery aspect associated with machine learning approaches may be a serious problem, but perhaps not a deadly one; one way of addressing this issue may be by improving the transparency of the algorithm development process (e.g., see Zeng et al., 2017). Future research will explore different machine learning approaches. Besides three machine learning algorithms we used in the current study (i.e., logistic regression, decision tree, and random forest), other algorithms have been widely used in the machine learning literature such as the support vector machine (SVM) approach (Bennett & Demiriz, 1999; Cauwenberghs & Poggio, 2001) which has been shown to be an efficient classifier for some types of large N explorations. Further progress may well occur in enhancing the amount of transparency of the process of determining the elements of forecasting algorithms.

The current study apples machine learning approaches to forecasting identity theft victimization. Among many machine learning algorithms, we assessed the performance of three: 1) logistic regression; 2) decision tree; and, 3) random forest. We explore two research questions: 1) Can these three algorithms be used to forecast identity theft victims? and 2) Which algorithm performs best in forecasting? Our findings suggest logistic regression and random forest algorithms generally perform well in forecasting identity theft victimization. Regarding forecasting different types of identity theft victimization, the logistic regression algorithm performs better than the alternatives in predicting overall identity theft victimization, misuse of credit cards, misuse of other types, and open new accounts; the random forest algorithm performs best in predicting misuse of checking/saving accounts. The results reported here confirm some previous findings regarding age and educational level correlates of identity theft victimization (Anderson, 2006; Golladay & Holtfreter, 2017).

Online activity, particularly online shopping frequency and online payment with credit and debit cards, are also shown to be closely associated with identity theft victimization (Holtfreter et al., 2008; Pratt et al., 2010; Reyns, 2013). For example, the current study found that online payment with debit cards is a significant predictor of misuse of checking/saving accounts (Figure 6) and online payment with credit cards is a significant predictor of misuse of credit cards (Figure 8). This study also found that with respect to the seven preventive actions listed in the NCVS ITS survey, the two most influential preventive actions are checking credit reports and frequently changing passwords of financial accounts.

These findings generate both research and policy implications. First, some machine learning algorithms such as logistic regression and random forest algorithms apparently can be used successfully in forecasting identity theft victimization. Both logistic regression and random forest algorithms can achieve a fair level of prediction of identity theft victimization. The ROC and AUC curves results suggest that logistic regression and random forest algorithms generally achieve fair predictive discrimination. In the important area of misuse of credit cards, the logistic regression algorithm achieves good predictive discrimination (Figure 8). The findings reported here add to the current literature showing that machine learning approaches can be used in a criminal justice/criminology in a number of areas such as forecasting victimization, recidivism, informing arraignment decisions, and determining the costs of intervention programs (e.g., Barnes & Hyatt, 2012; Berk et al., 2009; Berk et al., 2016; Manning et al., 2018; Neuilly et al., 2011).

Second, the findings of this study also partially support the argument advanced by Duwe and Kim (2017) that the newer machine learning algorithms generally perform better than algorithms developed earlier. Overall, the random forest algorithm performs much better than its forerunner the decision tree algorithm in predicting identity theft victimization. However, the logistic regression algorithm generally performs a little bit better than the random forest algorithm, with the sole exception of predicting misuse of checking/saving accounts. These findings suggest that social science research can benefit from researchers making greater use of machine learning algorithms as a supplement to traditional statistical approaches.

Third, as identity theft becomes more common (Harrell, 2019) an increasing number of people will likely start taking preventive actions. Our results suggest that some "old-fashion" preventive actions may no longer be effective. For example, shredding/destroying documents with personal information is not associated with remaining safe from identity theft victimization. The findings reported here suggest that in the digital age online shopping with credit and/or debit cards are both activities significantly related to identity theft victimization; these results are consistent with findings previously reported in the research literature (e.g., Holtfreter et al., 2008; Pratt et al., 2010; Reyns, 2013). Therefore, preventive actions related to online activities seem to be crucial in preventing identity theft. The current study, indeed, found that frequently changing passwords of financial accounts is significantly related to identity theft victimization. However, we found that employing commercial services related to identity theft protection (e.g., credit monitoring) appears to have little bearing on remaining safe from experiencing identity theft. Those persons taking these protective steps might be doing so because they were victims in the past and initiated these protective behaviors in reaction. In any case, it would have been reassuring to see evidence that the self-protective actions were associated with being among the non-victim group of survey respondents.

With these findings, we also propose a policy of requiring commercial companies which sell identity theft protection to clarify the content of their advertisements. Many current advertisements imply full protection upon purchase. Based on our findings, this may not be the case. Identity theft protection companies may provide useful surveillance on if a customer's identity has been stolen (i.e., credit monitoring) and help recover loss (i.e., identity theft insurance), but they seem to be able to do little with regard to preventing a customer from being an identity theft victim. Our findings suggest that in the digital age the most effective way of reducing probability of being an identity theft victim is to continually exercise great care in selecting the websites we browse and in making the online payments we do.

Notes

1. Notably, many outcomes of the current study suggest the highest predictive accuracy coming from the logistic regression algorithm, which is still not completely free from the various distributional and covariance assumptions of a regression model.
2. Notably, decision tree modeling and random forest modeling are identified as classifier processes, and they can both be used when a dependent variable is categorical or continuous.
3. In the field of machine learning, the overall percentage of correct classification is presented by a confusion matrix. Also known as an *error matrix*, the confusion matrix is a table that visualizes algorithm performance (Stehman, 1997). Each column shows the counts in a true label and each row shows the counts in a predicted label, and vice versa (Powers, 2011). For example, Figure 1 suggests that in the logistic regression model the number of correct classifications is 41,006 (40,989 + 17) and the number of wrongful classifications is 3,904 (3,891 + 13). Therefore, the overall percentage of correct classification is 91.31%.

Disclosure statement

No potential conflict of interest was reported by the author(s).

ORCID

Xiaochen Hu http://orcid.org/0000-0002-3060-8530
Nicholas P. Lovrich http://orcid.org/0000-0002-9173-547X

References

Allison, S. F., Schuck, A. M., & Lersch, K. M. (2005). Exploring the crime of identity theft: Prevalence, clearance rates, and victim/offender characteristics. *Journal of Criminal Justice, 33*(1), 19–29. https://doi.org/10.1016/j.jcrimjus.2004.10.007

Amit, Y., Geman, D., & Wilder, K. (1997). Joint induction of shape features and tree classifiers. *IEEE Transactions on Pattern Analysis and Machine Intelligence, 19*(11), 1300–1305. https://doi.org/10.1109/34.632990

Anderson, K. B. (2006). Who are the victims of identity theft? The effect of demographics. *Journal of Public Policy & Marketing, 25*(2), 160–171. https://doi.org/10.1509/jppm.25.2.160

Baek, H., Andreescu, V., & Rolfe, S. M. (2019). Bullying and fear of victimization: Do supportive adults in school make a difference in adolescents' perceptions of safety? *Journal of School Violence, 18*(1), 92–106. https://doi.org/10.1080/15388220.2017.1387133

Barnes, G. C., & Hyatt, J. M. (2012). *Classifying adult probationers by forecasting future offending.* National Institute of Justice. Retrieved February 4, 2020, from https://www.ncjrs.gov/pdffiles1/nij/grants/238082.pdf

Baum, K. (2006). *Identity theft, 2004.* Bureau of Justice Statistics. Retrieved January 22, 2020, from https://bjs.gov/content/pub/pdf/it04.pdf

Baum, K. (2007). *Identity theft, 2005.* Bureau of Justice Statistics. Retrieved January 22, 2020, from https://www.bjs.gov/content/pub/pdf/it05.pdf

Bennett, K. P., & Demiriz, A. (1999). Semi-supervised support vector machines. In *Advances in neural information processing systems* (pp. 368–374). http://papers.nips.cc/paper/1582-semi-supervised-support-vector-machines.pdf

Berk, R. (2012). *Criminal justice forecasts of risk: A machine learning approach.* Springer Science & Business Media.

Berk, R., & Bleich, J. (2014). Forecasts of violence to inform sentencing decisions. *Journal of Quantitative Criminology, 30*(1), 79–96. https://doi.org/10.1007/s10940-013-9195-0

Berk, R., Sherman, L., Barnes, G., Kurtz, E., & Ahlman, L. (2009). Forecasting murder within a population of probationers and parolees: A high stakes application of statistical learning. *Journal of the Royal Statistical Society: Series A (Statistics in Society), 172*(1), 191–211. https://doi.org/10.1111/j.1467-985X.2008.00556.x

Berk, R. A., Kriegler, B., & Baek, J. H. (2006). Forecasting dangerous inmate misconduct: An application of ensemble statistical procedures. *Journal of Quantitative Criminology, 22*(2), 131–145. https://doi.org/10.1007/s10940-006-9005-z

Berk, R. A., Sorenson, S. B., & Barnes, G. (2016). Forecasting domestic violence: A machine learning approach to help inform arraignment decisions. *Journal of Empirical Legal Studies, 13*(1), 94–115. https://doi.org/10.1111/jels.12098

Bradley, A. P. (1997). The use of the area under the ROC curve in the evaluation of machine learning algorithms. *Pattern Recognition, 30*(7), 1145–1159. https://doi.org/10.1016/S0031-3203(96)00142-2

Breiman, L. (1996). Bagging predictors. *Machine Learning, 24*(2), 123–140. https://doi.org/10.1007/BF00058655

Breiman, L. (2001). Random forests. *Machine Learning, 45*(1), 5–32. https://doi.org/10.1023/A:1010933404324

Carriquiry, A., Hofmann, H., Tai, X., & VanderPlas, S. (2019). Machine learning in forensic applications. *Significance, 16*(2), 29–35. https://doi.org/10.1111/j.1740-9713.2019.01252.x

Cauwenberghs, G., & Poggio, T. (2001). Incremental and decremental support vector machine learning. In *Advances in neural information processing systems* (pp. 409–415). http://papers.nips.cc/paper/1814-incremental-and-decremental-support-vector-machine-learning.pdf

Chapple, M. (2019). *Taking social security numbers public could fix our data breach crisis.*CNN Business Perspectives. CNN (Cable News Network). Retrieved January 27, 2020, from https://www.cnn.com/2019/06/05/perspectives/labcorp-quest-diagnostics-data-breach-social-security-numbers/index.html

Copes, H., Kerley, K. R., Huff, R., & Kane, J. (2010). Differentiating identity theft: An exploratory study of victims using a national victimization survey. *Journal of Criminal Justice, 38*(5), 1045–1052. https://doi.org/10.1016/j.jcrimjus.2010.07.007

Copes, H., & Vieraitis, L. M. (2009). Bounded rationality of identity thieves: Using offender-based research to inform policy. *Criminology & Public Policy, 8*(2), 237–262. https://doi.org/10.1111/j.1745-9133.2009.00553.x

Cowley, S. (2019). *Equifax to pay at least $650 million in largest-ever data breach settlement.* The New York Times Business. New York Times. Retrieved January 27, 2020, from https://www.nytimes.com/2019/07/22/business/equifax-settlement.html

Duwe, G., & Kim, K. (2017). Out with the old and in with the new? An empirical comparison of supervised learning algorithms to predict recidivism. *Criminal Justice Policy Review, 28*(6), 570–600. https://doi.org/10.1177/0887403415604899

Fawcett, T. (2006). An introduction to ROC analysis. *Pattern Recognition Letters, 27*(8), 861–874. https://doi.org/10.1016/j.patrec.2005.10.010

Federal Trade Commission. (2019). *Consumer sentinel network.* Federal Trade Commission. Retrieved January 22, 2020, from https://www.ftc.gov/system/files/documents/reports/consumer-sentinel-network-data-book-2018/consumer_sentinel_network_data_book_2018_0.pdf

Foster, B. P., Zurada, J., & Barney, D. K. (2010). Could decision trees help improve farm service agency lending decisions? *Academy of Information and Management Sciences Journal, 13*(1), 69–91. https://ir.library.louisville.edu/cgi/viewcontent.cgi?article=1361&context=faculty

Friedl, M. A., & Brodley, C. E. (1997). Decision tree classification of land cover from remotely sensed data. *Remote Sensing of Environment, 61*(3), 399–409. https://doi.org/10.1016/S0034-4257(97)00049-7

Golladay, K., & Holtfreter, K. (2017). The consequences of identity theft victimization: An examination of emotional and physical health outcomes. *Victims & Offenders, 12*(5), 741–760. https://doi.org/10.1080/15564886.2016.1177766

Golladay, K. A. (2017). Reporting behaviors of identity theft victims: An empirical test of Black's theory of law. *Journal of Financial Crime, 24*(1), 101–117. https://doi.org/10.1108/JFC-01-2016-0010

Harrell, E. (2015). *Victims of identity theft, 2014.* US Department of Justice, Office of Justice Programs, Bureau of Justice Statistics. Retrieved January 22, 2020, from https://bjs.gov/content/pub/pdf/vit14.pdf

Harrell, E. (2019). *Victims of identity theft, 2016.* US Department of Justice, Office of Justice Programs, Bureau of Justice Statistics. Retrieved January 20, 2020, from https://www.bjs.gov/content/pub/pdf/vit16.pdf

Harrell, E., & Langton, L. (2013). *Victims of identity theft, 2012.* U.S. Department of Justice, Office of Justice Programs, Bureau of Justice Statistics. Retrieved January 22, 2020, from https://www.bjs.gov/content/pub/pdf/vit12.pdf

Holtfreter, K., Reisig, M. D., & Pratt, T. C. (2008). Low self-control, routine activities, and fraud victimization. *Criminology, 46*(1), 189–220. https://doi.org/10.1111/j.1745-9125.2008.00101.x

Holtfreter, K., Reisig, M. D., Pratt, T. C., & Holtfreter, R. E. (2015). Risky remote purchasing and identity theft victimization among older Internet users. *Psychology, Crime & Law, 21*(7), 681–698. https://doi.org/10.1080/1068316X.2015.1028545

Hosmer, J. D., Lemeshow, W., & Sturdivant, R. X. (2013). *Applied logistic regression* (Vol. 398). John Wiley & Sons.

Hu, X., Wu, J., DeValve, M. J., & Fisher, B. S. (2020). Exploring violent crime reporting among school-age victims: Findings from NCVS SCS 2005-2015. *Victims & Offenders, 15*(2), 141–158. https://doi.org/10.1080/15564886.2019.1705452

Kleinbaum, D. G., Dietz, K., Gail, M., Klein, M., & Klein, M. (2002). *Logistic regression.* Springer-Verlag.

Liaw, A., & Wiener, M. (2002). Classification and regression by randomForest. *R News, 2*(3), 18–22.

Manning, M., Wong, G. T., Graham, T., Ranbaduge, T., Christen, P., Taylor, K., Wortley, R., Makkai, T., & Skorich, P. (2018). Towards a 'smart'cost–benefit tool: Using machine learning to predict the costs of criminal justice policy interventions. *Crime Science, 7*(1), 12. https://doi.org/10.1186/s40163-018-0086-4

Morgan, R. E., & Oudekerk, B. A. (2019). *Criminal victimization, 2018*. Bureau of Justice Statistics. NCJ, 253043. Bureau of Justice Statistics. Retrieved July 2, 2020, from https://www.bjs.gov/content/pub/pdf/cv18.pdf

Neuilly, M. A., Zgoba, K. M., Tita, G. E., & Lee, S. S. (2011). Predicting recidivism in homicide offenders using classification tree analysis. *Homicide Studies, 15*(2), 154–176. https://doi.org/10.1177/1088767911406867

Ngo, F. T. (2019). Stalking: An examination of the correlates of subsequent police responses. *Policing: An International Journal, 42*(3), 362–375. https://doi.org/10.1108/PIJPSM-12-2017-0157

Nguyen, K., Yuan, Y., & McNeeley, S. (2020). School security measures, school environment, and avoidance behaviors. *Victims & Offenders, 15*(1), 43–59. https://doi.org/10.1080/15564886.2019.1679307

Piquero, N. L., Cohen, M. A., & Piquero, A. R. (2011). How much is the public willing to pay to be protected from identity theft? *Justice Quarterly, 28*(3), 437–459. https://doi.org/10.1080/07418825.2010.511245

Pontell, H. (2002). Pleased to meet you . . . won't you guess my name: Identity fraud, cyber-crime, and white-collar delinquency. *Adelaide Law Review, 23*(2), 305–328.

Powers, D. M. (2011). Evaluation: From precision, recall and F-measure to ROC, informedness, markedness and correlation. *Journal of Machine Learning Technologies, 2*(1), 37–63.

Pratt, T. C., Holtfreter, K., & Reisig, M. D. (2010). Routine online activity and internet fraud targeting: Extending the generality of routine activity theory. *Journal of Research in Crime and Delinquency, 47*(3), 267–296. https://doi.org/10.1177/0022427810365903

Randa, R., & Reyns, B. W. (2019). The physical and emotional toll of identity theft victimization: A situational and demographic analysis of the national crime victimization survey. *Deviant Behavior, 41*(10), 1290–1304. https://doi.org/10.1080/01639625.2019.1612980

Rebovich, D. J. (2009). Examining identity theft: Empirical explorations of the offense and the offender. *Victims & Offenders, 4*(4), 357–364. https://doi.org/10.1080/15564880903260603

Reisig, M. D., & Holtfreter, K. (2013). Shopping fraud victimization among the elderly. *Journal of Financial Crime, 20*(3), 324–337. https://doi.org/10.1108/JFC-03-2013-0014

Reisig, M. D., Pratt, T. C., & Holtfreter, K. (2009). Perceived risk of internet theft victimization: Examining the effects of social vulnerability and financial impulsivity. *Criminal Justice and Behavior, 36*(4), 369–384. https://doi.org/10.1177/0093854808329405

Reyns, B. W. (2013). Online routines and identity theft victimization: Further expanding routine activity theory beyond direct-contact offenses. *Journal of Research in Crime and Delinquency, 50*(2), 216–238. https://doi.org/10.1177/0022427811425539

Russell, S. J., & Norvig, P. (2016). *Artificial intelligence: A modern approach*. Pearson Education Limited.

Safavian, S. R., & Landgrebe, D. (1991). A survey of decision tree classifier methodology. *IEEE Transactions on Systems, Man, and Cybernetics, 21*(3), 660–674. https://doi.org/10.1109/21.97458

Shmueli, G. (2010). To explain or to predict? *Statistical Science, 25*(3), 289–310. https://doi.org/10.1214/10-STS330

Slosarik, K. (2002). Identity theft: An overview of the problem. *The Justice Professional, 15*(4), 329–343. https://doi.org/10.1080/0888431022000070458

Stehman, S. V. (1997). Selecting and interpreting measures of thematic classification accuracy. *Remote Sensing of Environment, 62*(1), 77–89. https://doi.org/10.1016/S0034-4257(97)00083-7

Takieddine, S., & Andoh-Baidoo, F. K. (2014). An exploratory analysis of internet banking adoption using decision tree induction. *International Journal of Electronic Finance, 8*(1), 1–20. https://doi.org/10.1504/IJEF.2014.063996

Warner, R. M. (2013). *Applied statistics: From bivariate through multivariate techniques* (2nd ed.). SAGE Publications.

White, M. D., & Fisher, C. (2008). Assessing our knowledge of identity theft: The challenges to effective prevention and control efforts. *Criminal Justice Policy Review, 19*(1), 3–24. https://doi.org/10.1177/0887403407306297

Ylang, N. (2020). Capable guardianship against identity theft: Demographic insights based on a national sample of US adults. *Journal of Financial Crime, 27*(1), 130–142. https://doi.org/10.1108/JFC-12-2018-0140

Zeng, J., Ustun, B., & Rudin, C. (2017). Interpretable classification models for recidivism prediction. *Journal of the Royal Statistical Society: Series A (Statistics in Society), 180*(3), 689–722. https://doi.org/10.1111/rssa.12227

Zurada, J., Kunene, N., & Guan, J. (2014). The classification performance of multiple methods and datasets: Cases from the loan credit scoring domain. *Journal of International Technology and Information Management, 23*(1), 57–82.

The Identification of a Model Victim for Social Engineering: A Qualitative Analysis

Kevin F. Steinmetz

ABSTRACT

End users present a key challenge for the protection of contemporary information security systems. The manipulation of people through deceit to gain access to sensitive information and otherwise secure systems is known to hackers, information security practitioners, and other technologists as "social engineering." To date, little research has investigated the attributes that people who engage in such deception – so-called "social engineers" – associate with vulnerable targets. To address this gap, this study engages in a grounded theory-based analysis of interviews with nonprofessional and professional social engineers. The results describe six attributes of a "model victim" for social engineers, a hypothetical person considered particularly susceptible to social engineering deceptions: (1) *prized*, (2) *uninformed*, (3) *unconcerned*, (4) *outgoing*, (5) *connected*, and (6) *controlled*. Additionally, this study describes heuristic categories described by participants to help make decisions about target vulnerability which include target *socio-demographic characteristics*, *social roles*, and *organizational positions*. Implications for theory, future research, and policy are considered.

Introduction

The key challenges facing information security are not found in faulty hardware or software. Instead, one of the most significant vulnerabilities comes from the end-user. A recent report from Verizon (2019, p. 5) claims that 32% of data breaches in their study involved phishing e-mails.[1] The Internet Crime Complaint Center (Internet Crime Complaint Center (IC3), 2020, p. 19) reports that personal data breaches, phishing/vishing/smishing/pharming scams, and business e-mail/e-mail account compromises were among the most frequently reported online crimes in 2019.[2] The manipulation of people through deceit to gain access to sensitive information and otherwise secure systems is known to hackers, information security practitioners, and other technologists as "social engineering" (Hadnagy, 2018; Mitnick & Simon, 2002).[3] It is usually associated with tele-mediated strategies like phishing (e-mail-based) or vishing (phone-based) scams though social engineers describe in-person deceptions within their purview (Hadnagy, 2018; Mitnick & Simon, 2002).[4]

To date, research has investigated the harms caused by internet-facilitated frauds (e.g., Button & Cross, 2017; Cross et al., 2016, 2018; Whitty & Buchanan, 2016), the strategies used by such fraudsters (e.g., Button & Cross, 2017; Cross et al., 2018; Holt & Graves, 2007; Leukfeldt et al., 2017a, 2017b; Lusthaus, 2018; Leukfeldt, 2014a; Whitty, 2013), and the characteristics associated with victimization (e.g., Button & Cross, 2017; Holtfreter et al., 2008; Lee & Soberon-Gerrer, 1997; Whitty, 2019). Little research, however, has investigated the attributes that people who engage in social engineering deceptions associate with vulnerable targets (Hutchings, 2013). To address this gap, this study engages in a grounded theory-based analysis of interviews with nonprofessional and professional social engineers. The latter population consists of security auditors who use social engineering techniques to test organizational information security systems (Caldwell, 2011). While these participants may not have illicit or illegal motivations underlying a large proportion of their activities, they do often use the techniques of fraudsters to great effect to compromise organizational security. Considering that their livelihoods hinge on their ability to conduct effective deceptions, such participants are a valuable source of insights regarding perceived target vulnerability for information security-oriented deceptions. Additionally, it is not uncommon for criminal hackers to matriculate into legitimate security positions later in life (Taylor, 1999).[5]

The themes described in this analysis, when considered *in toto*, comprise what this study terms a *model victim* for social engineering, a hypothetical person perceived as particularly susceptible to deception or otherwise likely to be exploited by fraud perpetrators should their paths cross. The term is not to be confused with Nils Christie's (1986, p. 18) concept of the "ideal victim," or a victim most likely to be "given the complete and legitimate status of being a victim" by others when targeted by a crime (see also: Cross et al., 2019). This study does not suggest that social engineers share consistent and uniform views of target susceptibility. Instead, this study argues that the model victim emerges when considering the aggregated views of social engineers toward potentially vulnerable victims. Examining the model victim may be useful for criminologists interested in the decision-making processes of social engineers, perceptions of targets among deception perpetrators, and the identification of risk factors associated with victimization.

Participants described six general attributes associated with individuals thought to be susceptible to social engineering deceptions. They are (1) *prized*, (2) *uninformed*, (3) *unconcerned*, (4) *outgoing*, (5) *connected*, and (6) *controlled*. This analysis argues that such traits collectively constitute a model victim for social engineering. In addition to the traits associated with a model victim, this analysis also identified heuristics used by social engineers to help identify the presence of the aforementioned traits in a target. Heuristics are a kind of perceptual short-hand used to quickly solve what Simon and Newell (1958) call "ill-structured problems." In the case of social engineering, these heuristics involve the use of imperfect but practical associations between directly observable attributes and perceived latent vulnerabilities. This study describes three heuristic categories that manifested in participant responses: *socio-demographic characteristics*, *role*, and *position*. Before describing the results in detail, two areas of criminological and victimological research are reviewed which inform the current analysis on attributes associated with model social engineering victims. The first includes criminological research on offender target selection while the second concerns victimological research examining traits associated with fraud victimization. After reviewing the relevant literature, the methodological approach of the study is described.

Literature review

A burgeoning literature has emerged exploring social engineering. For instance, scholars have cataloged the various techniques, psychological tendencies, biases, and emotions said to be exploited by social engineers (e.g., Abraham & Chengalur-Smith, 2010; Atkins & Huang, 2013; Chantler & Broadhurst, 2006; Goel et al., 2017; Huang & Brockman, 2011; King & Thomas, 2009; Kopp et al., 2015; Norris et al., 2019; Twitchell, 2009; Williams et al., 2017). Relatedly, research has probed the content of fraudulent e-mails to uncover possible mechanisms that may drive their relative success (e.g., Atkins & Huang, 2013; Ferreira & Teles, 2019; Holt & Graves, 2007; Huang & Brockman, 2011; King & Thomas, 2009). Another body of scholarship has investigated the ability of persons to discern between legitimate and fraudulent e-mails (Jackobsson et al., 2007; Karakasiliotis et al., 2006; Lawson et al., 2017; Parsons et al., 2019; Sarno et al., 2019). Despite these and other advances, little research to date has considered the target selection or traits associated with victim vulnerability from the perspective of social engineering perpetrators.[6] As such, this review considers two adjacent areas of relevant research. The first explores criminological research on perpetrator target selection. The second area of research reviewed explores traits associated with online fraud victimization including social engineering.

Perpetrator target selection

The criminological literature has examined target selection among a variety of offenders. Most of this literature tends to approach the issue from a rational choice perspective – offenders select their targets for rational reasons that, to one degree or another, minimize costs and maximize benefits (Clark & Cornish, 1985; Cornish & Clarke, 1986). Scholarship on burglars suggest that offenders look for signs that a dwelling is accessible, unoccupied, and likely to contain valuables (Hough, 1987; Wright & Decker, 1994). Burglars make these determinations based on information gained by knowing occupants personally, receiving an informed tip, and through casual surveillance of a pre-identified location (Wright & Decker, 1994, p. 101). Though Hough (1987) argues that burglars are generally bad at selecting appropriate targets, Wright et al. (1995) conclude that experience yields expertise in their experimental study comparing assessments of photographs of dwellings by active burglars to non-burglars, finding that burglars were better at identifying likely candidates for burglary.

Target selection has also been examined among robbers with research finding that robbers prioritize victims who are distracted, easy to approach, likely to be carrying cash, and appear unlikely to resist and report the crime (Deakin et al., 2007; Wright & Decker, 1997). As a result, robbers are said to focus on targeting other people involved in illicit activities like drug dealers and men seeking prostitutes because they are unlikely to report the crime to officials (Wright & Decker, 1997). They may also target people seen as community outsiders and easy targets. Stereotypes about race, gender and age may also be used to assess likelihood of victim resistance (Wright & Decker, 1997). Jacobs (2010) adds that robbery target selection may be a result of serendipity, chance opportunities for which a robber has to be prepared and energized to capitalize on when they emerge.

In her study of street-robbers, Miller (1998) examined the role of gender in target selection. She found that men appeared to target other men involved in illicit street activities or who otherwise appear "flashy" (Miller, 1998, p. 47). Though women were viewed as less likely to resist or retaliate, they were viewed by men as peripheral to street activities and less lucrative. Further, victimizing women is a potential threat to a man's "badass" masculine status (Miller, 1998, p. 50). Additionally, men were said to become more vulnerable to robbery if they were accompanied by a woman. Women, on the other hand, were found to target other women (usually younger women) because they were viewed as less likely to be armed or resist (Miller, 1998, p. 51). They may also target men who appear to have plenty of cash on hand by using sexual advances to compromise their ability or willingness to resist being robbed. In short, gender norms and situational dynamics shape target selection by both men and women.

Related to robbery, Topalli et al. (2015) discuss the role of "perceptual skills" in carjacking. These skills involve "knowing which vehicles are appropriate to take and which drivers and situations will mitigate the potential for resistance or retaliation by a driver" (Topalli et al., 2015, p. 21). In other words, the priority among offenders engaged in violent thefts when identifying likely victims is determining the potential haul and the likelihood of resistance, retribution, and reporting to the police.

Other studies have examined target selection fraudsters. Ethnographic accounts of con-artists finds that the most important trait of a potential mark is a victim's "larceny" or "a kind of inner thought process wherein the victim of a con is thinking of how he or she might steal from the con artist" (Williams & Milton, 2015, p. 2; see also: Maurer, 1940). In other words, the mark has to have some degree of dishonesty and greed which can be cultivated by the con-artist from "simple latent dishonesty to an all-consuming lust which drives the victim to secure funds for speculation by any means at his comment" (Maurer, 1940, p. 117). Though con-artists may prefer victims from certain occupations, socio-economic classes, races, or genders, Maurer (1940, p. 108) claims that "no profession, occupation, race or sex has a corner on the never-failing supply of marks." Jacques et al. (2014) examined "rip-offs" perpetrated by drug dealers against customers. They found that drug dealers were more likely to "rip-off" customers seen as unlikely to be repeat customers, not worth the dealer's time, having committed some slight against the dealer, likely to be unaware they were ripped off, or, if they are aware of being ripped off, unlikely to retaliate or take their business elsewhere (Jacques et al., 2014).

Limited research has examined target selection within the area of "cyberfraud." While not addressing target selection specifically, Button and Cross (2017, p. 65) detail mechanisms through which fraudsters may curate rosters of potential victims. These may be garnered from both licit sources like marketing lists, telephone directories, and shareholders lists as well as illicit sources that track individuals who have previously fallen for frauds. Social networking sites may also be scoured for potential victims. Fraudsters may also target affinity groups – "groups who have some common bond or link" (Button & Cross, 2017, p. 67). Finally, fraudsters may engage in targeted advertising of their illicit schemes on legitimate venues like eBay or Craig's List. The authors do not explore, from an offender's perspective, what makes for an attractive mark specifically.

One of the only studies that specifically examines target selection among fraud perpetrators is Hutchings (2013) study of former fraud and hacking offenders. She concludes that fraudsters were generally motivated by financial gain (in terms of both "need" and "greed") and engaged in cost-benefit decision making regarding perceived risks and rewards of their activities when selecting targets. According to her, hackers and related fraudsters select their targets because they are (1) known or accessible, (2) morally or ideologically offensive to the perpetrator, (3) perceived as having personally aggrieved the offender, (4) viewed as easy targets or have known vulnerabilities, (5) selected based on chance, or (6) particularly lucrative. It is difficult in this study, however, to disentangle which of these elements are specific to fraud target selection or hacking selection.

Fraud victim characteristics

The current study examines traits social engineers ascribe to vulnerable targets. An adjacent area of the literature to consider are studies that examine the characteristics of fraud victims. Scholars have generally examined three types of characteristics associated with fraud victimization: socio-demographics, dispositional traits, and routine activities or lifestyle considerations. Regarding socio-demographic characteristics, age is likely the most controversial. Popular media and law enforcement outlets often claim that aging populations are at greater risk of fraud, a claim which has some support in the research (Lee & Soberon-Gerrer, 1997; Whitty, 2019). Scholars, however, have questioned this relationship, arguing that while aging populations are more likely to be victimized by fraud compared to other types of crime, this does not mean they themselves are more susceptible relative to younger folks (Button & Cross, 2017, p. 54). Some studies indicate that aging populations are *less* likely to fall for frauds compared to younger individuals or that there is no age effect (Button & Cross, 2017, pp. 23–24; Muscat et al., 2002; Sarno et al., 2019; Titus & Gover, 2001; Titus et al., 1995). Regarding education, some hold that less-educated individuals are more vulnerable to fraud (Fischer et al., 2013; Lee & Soberon-Gerrer, 1997). Other studies, however, find that education either has no effect or may actually increase fraud susceptibility (Drew & Cross, 2013; Whitty, 2018; Titus & Gover, 2001; Titus et al., 1995).[78] Evidence also indicates that members of higher socio-economic classes and managerial and professional occupations are more vulnerable to fraud (Button & Cross, 2017, p. 53). Some scholars also claim that previous victimization status is a predictor of future victimization (Maurer, 1940; Titus & Gover, 2001). Though evidence is limited, race and gender appear to have little to no relationship to fraud susceptibility and victimization (Broadhurst et al., 2019; Lee & Soberon-Gerrer, 1997; Titus et al., 1995).

Research has also investigated the dispositional characteristics of fraud victims. For instance, impulsivity, low self-control, or risk-taking proclivities, dispositions toward addiction, willingness to trust, commitment to reciprocity, investment in committed lines of action, desire to please others, and obedience to authority have all been linked to fraud victimization (Fischer et al., 2013; Holtfreter et al., 2008, 2010; Whitty, 2013, 2018, 2019; Titus & Gover, 2001; Van de Weijer, 2020; Van Wyk & Benson, 1997; Workman, 2007, 2008). Specific to romance scams, one study found that people with a tendency to idealize romantic partners were more likely to be defrauded (Buchanan & Whitty, 2014). Relatedly, socially isolated individuals have been found to be more susceptible to fraud (Fischer et al., 2013; Lee & Soberon-Gerrer, 1997; Whitty, 2018).[9] Additionally, research has investigated the role of prior experiences and education with social engineering as well as confidence in one's ability to use computers effectively (Vishwanath et al., 2011). Though such research may be useful, Button and Cross (2017, p. 63) argue that dispositional research should be treated with caution as such studies tend to cast victimization as a result of some personal failing on part of the victim while ignoring the acts and skills of offender.

Finally, scholars have explored the relationship between victim routine activities and online fraud victimization (Bossler, 2020; Hutchings & Hayes, 2009; Leukfeldt, 2014b; Leukfelt & Yar, 2016; Ngo & Raymond, 2011; Pratt et al., 2010; Reyns, 2013, 2015, 2018;

Van de Weijer, 2020). Pratt et al. (2010), for instance, found that time spent online and internet shopping behaviors significantly predicted likelihood of being targeted for online fraud, even when sociodemographic variables were taken into account. For Reyns (2015), routine activities related to online exposure (online banking, making travel arrangements, online shopping, and social networking) were all significant predictors of phishing e-mail receipt. Phishing also increased for persons with personal information made available online or, counter-intuitive to expectations, if they purposefully provided inaccurate personal information to websites. Finally, his analysis found that guardianship behaviors like deleting e-mails and changing passwords were related to phishing but in unexpected directions – both behaviors were associated with increased phishing, though this may be attributed to a problem of temporal ordering. In other words, people may delete more e-mails and change passwords because they receive more phishing e-mails. Despite such studies, it should be noted that not all research supports the connection between routine activities and phishing (Ngo & Raymond, 2011).

Methods

The current study addresses the question "*what are the attributes social engineers ascribe to susceptible marks?*" by examining qualitative semi-structured interviews drawn from a National Science Foundation-funded research project of social engineers and information technology professionals (n = 54). This analysis draws from a subsample of 37 interviews with social engineers including both nonprofessionals (n = 7) and professionals (n = 30). The latter include security auditors who use social engineering techniques to test information security systems. Seventeen interviews with IT security professionals (e.g., CIOs and CISOs) were excluded from the analysis because these individuals do not engage in social engineering but, rather, protect their organizations against information security threats (including social engineering).

Participants were recruited through both purposive and snowball sampling strategies. Researchers traveled to hacking conventions (in-person events for hackers and other technology enthusiasts) and corporate security conferences to network and solicit participation, a strategy used in previous studies of hackers (Bachmann, 2010; Holt, 2009, 2010b; Schell & Holt, 2010; Schell & Melnychuck, 2010; Steinmetz, 2016). The researchers also cold-called information security contractors identified through internet search engines. Finally, we relied on interviewees to provide references to others possible participants. Individuals were considered viable for recruitment if they espoused or demonstrated participation in social engineering activities. The 37 interviews included in this study totaled 73 hours ranging from 43 minutes to 4 hours and 4 minutes in length ($\bar{x}$ = 1 hours and 59 minutes). Table 1 presents descriptive statistics for the participants. The sample is predominantly male, white, and relatively educated. These demographics roughly mirror other studies on hacking and related populations (Bachmann, 2010; Holt, 2009, 2010b; Schell & Holt, 2010; Steinmetz, 2016). For reasons of human subjects ethics, we avoided recruiting minors meaning that adults of various ages ($\bar{x}$ = 36.8) comprise our sample.

The research was approved by our institution's review board.[10] Informed consent was gathered and each participant was assigned a pseudonym to protect their identity. Interviews were conducted through encrypted voice over internet protocol (VoIP)

Table 1. Descriptive statistics of study sample.

Variable		n(percent)
Age		Range: 25–57, = 36.8
Race		
	White	33 (89.19%)
	Asian	1 (2.70%)
	African American	2 (5.41%)
	Bi-Racial	1 (2.70%)
Gender		
	Male	28 (75.68%)
	Female	9 (24.32%)
Education		
	High School Diploma/GED	2 (5.41%)
	Some College	4 (10.81%)
	Associate's Degree	4 (10.81%)
	Bachelor's Degree	17 (45.95%)
	Graduate Education	10 (27.03%)
Self-Described Socio-Economic Status		
	Lower/Working Class	2 (5.41%)
	Lower-Middle Class	2 (5.41%)
	Middle Class	14 (37.84%)
	Upper-Middle or Above	19 (51.35%)
Illegal Social Engineering Participation		15 (40.5%)
Harmful Social Engineering Participation		13 (35.14%)

programs and were audio-recorded and transcribed. Personal information has been scrubbed from transcripts to ensure confidentiality. Electronic data is stored on hardware encrypted external media.

The current analysis focuses on interview descriptions of social engineering frauds. During the interviews, participants were asked to describe their first social engineering experiences, favorite or most successful social engineering engagements, as well as engagements that may have been illegal or harmful to others. They also often provided examples of social engineering scenarios in response to an assortment of other questions presented in the interviews. They were also asked explicitly to describe the characteristics of "good" and "bad" targets at both the individual and organizational levels. This analysis focuses on their descriptions of characteristics associated with individual-level marks. The narratives and advice provided were analyzed for the common themes using a grounded theory-based approach which involves the transformation of data into concepts which are then summarized into broader analytic categories through open, axial, and selective coding strategies (Charmaz, 2002; Corbin & Strauss, 1990; Glaser & Strauss, 1967). Open coding involves comparisons between units of data and the assignment of conceptual labels. Axial coding means that concepts are compared to each other and categories are developed to organize the concepts. The process of comparing each level of analysis (data, concepts, and categories), refining these levels, and developing core categories to organize to totality of the data is *selective* coding (Corbin & Strauss, 1990, p. 14). It is at this stage of analysis that explanations for the patterns in the data are unified through common mechanisms. In the case of the current analysis, the core categories resulted in discrete categories of traits which participants appeared to directly associate with susceptibility to social engineering deceptions. Additionally, the results of the analysis also revealed perceived victim characteristics which serve as indirect indicators that victims may be vulnerable to deception. Both these traits and heuristics are described in the results. The Atlas.ti qualitative data analysis software was used to organize the data and facilitate the grounded theory analysis.

Results

In describing the traits that make for a vulnerable target from their perspective, some participants simply stated that everyone is susceptible to social engineering. When asked "what makes for a good target?" Daniel stated "they're human." Others explained that what makes for a good target is situationally dependent – that there are no set characteristics of the model target. Yet, when examining the responses in greater depth through a grounded theory-based analytic method, most participants described general characteristics that coalesce into what this analysis terms a "model victim." According to this study, a model victim is composed of six traits. The first is that a model victim is *prized* for some resource or experience they offer to the social engineer. The next three traits refer to the disposition of the model victim – that they are *uninformed, unconcerned*, and *outgoing*. The final two traits are social; they pertain to the mark's relationships with others or their situational constraints. These traits are described as *connected* and *controlled* respectively. In addition to these traits, participants also described certain demographic characteristics, social roles, and hierarchical positions that potential victims may occupy which serve as heuristic devices indicating the likelihood that a mark will possess some combination of the aforementioned traits. The frequencies of participants who mention these traits and heuristics are presented in Table 2.

Traits

Prized

To start, a model victim must be of some value to the social engineer (n = 10).[11] All other considerations proceed from this point. A person may have available to them some resource desired by the social engineer such as systems access or money (see also: Hutchings, 2013; Maurer, 1940). For instance, Mark, a security auditor, preferred to target organizational executives because "they have the most authority":

> If I can manipulate an executive at a high level, I can get that person to transfer 50 million dollars, right? Fifty million dollars is a pretty big, you know, incentive. If I call somebody at a very junior level, they don't have the rights and permissions and authority to be able to do any of that.[12]

For him, then, executives are prime targets because of the authority and access they wield in the organization to make large-scale financial transactions. Others may be targeted because

Table 2. Themes.

Theme	*f* (n = 37)
Traits	
Prized	10
Uninformed	18
Unconcerned	19
Outgoing	23
Connected	16
Controlled	14
Heuristics	
Demographics	9
Role	12
Position	13

Note: Frequencies refer to the number of participants who described the theme in their interviews.

of the information available to them. Edward explained that he likes to approach executive assistants because they often have access to privileged information that could be leveraged.

> If you go to, mostly 90 percent probably or more, to a CEO or CFO's assistant and ask 'em if they have the file, they will. The file will be their boss's full name, date of birth, social security number, password number, credit cards, and PIN codes on the credit cards and security codes, and addresses, and everything else because who makes the reservations for these people? Who's the one that has to handle all the travel and the purchases and buying things? It's the assistant.

The social engineer may also value a target because of the potential emotional thrill that may be gained – that deceiving the victim promises to be fun or thrilling, a finding that resonates with other criminological studies (e.g., Tunnell, 1992). It is also worth noting that for many of the security auditors, the organizations they target were not selected by them but, instead, based on a contract with a client. "Our targets are defined based on a customer" explained Zeke. He added, however, that "you have targets inside of that company that you go after." Within these pre-selected organizations, individuals may be chosen because of the resources available to them. Regardless, an individual is selected as a potential victim because of what they offer to the social engineer.

Uninformed

For social engineering, a model victim is uninformed of the risks posed by their actions, either due to ignorance or a lack of proper training (n = 18). For many of the participants, good targets are those who have not been trained or empowered within their roles to identify and stop deceptive encounters. Thus a mark to avoid, as Edna explained is "someone who's been trained." In one example, she cited "interns or new hires" as vulnerable targets "because they don't know internal policies and a lot of times they don't even if they're suspicious of something, they don't know who to go to, or they're embarrassed to report something." Persons more knowledgeable in general about security risks are also to be avoided. For this reason, participants often advised avoiding people in information technology roles as they are assumed to be more alert and aware of information security risks – that "technically savvy people tend to not be good targets" (Harold).

Unconcerned

While some marks may not know the security risks their actions create, a potential mark may also be "someone who doesn't care" (Eugene). These potential marks are considered passive, complacent, apathetic, or otherwise unwilling to inquire, investigate, or halt a deceptive encounter. They are, in other words, *unconcerned* with mitigating information security risks (n = 19). Diminished concern with information security matters may be a result of a target's lack of commitment to their occupation, a point Ida made when describing retail work: "Retail. Retail's always the easiest because the employees tend to not care as much. They're, they're just there for an hourly paycheck, they're not getting paid very well and they, they're not gonna be there for very long." From this perspective, the retail worker is not invested in their organization and its interests and is thus likely not going to be an adequate guardian to prevent fraud. Similarly, people are seen as vulnerable for "just kind of goin' through the motions" (Clarence). Anna explained that she can target "the people who are kind of zoning out":

> It's like you get in your car, you drive to work, and then you get there and realize you don't remember the drive, you know, and that's because your brain's sort of been somewhere else and you're doing all these automatic things.

A mark may also be unconcerned with security risks because their attention is directed elsewhere – "a good target is a distracted or busy target" (John). Conversely, participants indicated that difficult targets exercise what Malcolm called "discernment" whereby a person is "on guard with the types of information that they give up." Similarly, Anna added that "the bad targets are the ones that are paying attention. The ones that are thinking, you know?" Be it from situational disinterest, boredom, a lack of commitment, or otherwise elected to place their attention elsewhere, a good mark is unconcerned with what is happening during a social encounter.

Outgoing

Participant responses indicate that a person who is willing to engage with others may be viewed as vulnerable to deception (n = 23). Friendly and helpful people were repeatedly cited by participants as good targets because they could be asked to surrender coveted resources under the auspices of altruism or social decorum. In this vein, Zeb stated that he prefers "super friendly" marks as he believes they "are more susceptible, especially when I'm super friendly with them, 'cause we're both super friendly and now we're just super friends." Relatedly, a good mark is a talkative mark. "Someone that is talkative tends to be kind of my, my favorite," explained Gus, "because you can ask them like a fairly specific question that could have a short answer but if they like to expand on things, you're likely to glean more information from that response." People who want to help were also considered good targets. Arlo enthusiastically exclaimed his preferred mark was "the type of person who always wants to help" – someone who is willing to accommodate others. From this perspective, the outgoing are more trusting and eager to please.

On the other hand, the unhelpful or rude were said to be harder to exploit. Eustace succinctly explained that a bad target is "Somebody who's grumpy." Similarly, Bernard claimed that a bad target is "jaded" or "angry" and, as a result, "gonna question every damn thing you do and make it really hard to fool them." A bad mark was also one considered to be socially awkward or averse to social interactions. Zeke advised avoiding "socially awkward folks that don't necessarily interact with human beings on a regular basis" because they are more difficult to engage with a pretext.

Connected

Participant responses indicate that a person may be perceived as exploitable if they are socially networked to many people or, conversely, relatively isolated (n = 16). In a curvilinear fashion, a model social engineering victim may be over-connected *or* under-connected to others. Specifically, under-connected refers to an individual's diminished social support network. Such persons may be lonely (Fischer et al., 2013; Lee & Soberon-Gerrer, 1997; Whitty, 2018). Reflecting on "romance scams" – frauds which exploit a mark's desire for romantic companionship to extract money – Harold claimed that the social engineer wants,

> Someone who's isolated, who doesn't have a lot of people in their life, who can say, "Gosh, that's the stupidest thing I've ever heard of." ... You know, so someone who's isolated makes the best mark with regards to those kinds of scams.

Similarly, individuals who are tenuously connected within a community may also be vulnerable as they lack the support and integration necessary to make use of communal resources (like the police). Here, Harold explained a scam used against immigrants where the fraudster claims to be law enforcement and will deport the mark unless paid a sum of money. According to him, these frauds are successful because immigrants maintain weak connections within a community because of their status as non-citizens. Additionally, a social engineer may target someone who has weaker connections to their organization. For instance, during security audits Patrick claimed to sometimes pick "sales people who are remote, who are not gonna be in the headquarters all that often" because it will be easier for him to pretend to be an organizational insider. The person who works remote may not have the requisite familiarity with other organizational members to discern legitimate from illegitimate organizational actors.

Over-connected, in this context, refers to people who have engendered a diverse assortment of connections to others, particularly online. Social media in particular is viewed as a boon for social engineers. As Daniel explained, an "easy target" is "someone who is prolific on social media." He added that,

> I'll hear people say, "Well, I don't put everything on Facebook." And I go, "You're right but between your LinkedIn, your Twitter, and your Facebook, think about what I have. You know, Facebook I have your favorite foods, your favorite restaurants, where you go on vacation, you know, your friends, your family, all your likes, your dislikes, your groups that you're a part of. On LinkedIn, I have your college, your high school, and your work history, and usually a picture of you, and on Twitter, especially if you use Four Square with Twitter, I have where you are right now and what you're doing right now throughout the day. So if those three social medias [*sic*] alone, forget about all the others, but those three alone, allow me to basically stalk you in every way possible."

Because the internet is an archival medium, active participation in online social life means a person is likely creating a reservoir of information. From this view, the more online connections a person fosters, the bigger this reservoir becomes. In other words,

> The more you can find out about a person, especially if they have a very public social media profile, you know, their likes and dislikes – you can, you can, you can create a more realistic phishing email or a phone pretext. (Herbert)

Additionally, a wide-ranging social network also gives a broader assortment of potential pretexts that can be used to garner trust from a mark. A social engineer may appear as any number of friends, family members, or coworkers within a potential mark's social network. Social media provides an accessible way to map out a potential mark's relational network to identify potential pretexts.

Controlled

While not explicitly using the language of social control, many of the participants invoked the role of personal and social controls on a potential target (n = 14). Similar to the *connected* theme, the results indicate a curvilinear relationship between control experienced and vulnerability to social engineering. A person who is relatively unrestrained in their behavior may be more willing to violate rules and act in their self-interest, which may be detrimental to the organization, others, or themselves. Yet a person who is over-controlled may be more willing to genuflect to authority or follow organizational policy to the letter (even if requests appear below-board) which can also be exploited.

Regarding under-controlled targets, some participants commented on arrogance or *hubris* as traits which may allow potential marks to think that they are either too intelligent to be defrauded or that the rules do not apply to them. Claire stated that, "in some cases, it is an arrogance thing," that some people think "Oh, I am way too smart to fall for that." Walter commented that regardless of the training provided or the policies enacted, some people will believe they are above compliance:

> You think you're the authoritative figure and you can decide for yourself what is right and what is wrong and what is an attack and what is not an attack, and you throw the policies out the window and ignore them because you think you're the authority or you think you're able to do that on your own and that's when you fail.

Similarly, a potential mark may be someone who feels that policy can be violated if they believe they are providing assistance to the social engineer. In other words, it is,

> Someone that wants to do the right thing but may not want, you know, may not stick to the rules explicitly . . . they see the rules and things that are there kind of as guidelines but not really as hard and fast rules. (Dorian)

Either because of some belief that the rules do not apply to them or that the situation justifies rule violation, participants argued that a good mark is someone who is not full bound by policy.

A mark may also fail to follow rules or act in an insecure manner because of a lack of investment by an organization. For instance, they may be insufficiently trained. Training is often framed as a method for raising awareness of security risks. Yet it also serves as a mechanism of social control – a way to inform others of the rules and possible consequences of rule violation. Additionally, employees may fail to follow policy because a perceived lack of commitment to them on the part of the organization. Returning to Ida's example concerning the risks posed by retail employees, she remarked that such employees are vulnerable because they are insufficiently paid and their tenure is likely limited. Instead, well compensated employees who have been with an organization for a long period of time are "grateful for the, the job that they've had, and the, the lifestyle that it's allowed them to live. Those people are gonna be a little more locked down."

Participants also indicated that targets may be vulnerable precisely because they respond to mechanisms of social control – that they are perhaps *over-controlled*. For example, participants commented on the role of authority in selecting a target. The idea is to pick a target that will comply with requests from an authoritative pretext – their employer, law enforcement, or some other figure. While the use of authority in fraud has been thoroughly documented by scholars (e.g., Chantler & Broadhurst, 2006; Huang & Brockman, 2011), it is worth noting that the façade of authority used by a social engineer is an attempt to take advantage of social control mechanisms to which the mark responds. For instance, Zeke described dressing in a suit and adopting an agitated disposition during a security audit. He approached a potential mark in a parking lot who appeared to be lower in status in his target company because they drove a "rust bucket" or an old and inexpensive automobile. As he explained, "lower-end employees will not, you know, challenge somebody that may be, you know, senior in rank." Either because of fear of reprisal, respect for authority, or a generally compliant disposition, such marks are made pliable by the rules that govern conduct between status positions. Additionally, targets may be rendered vulnerable by over-control if they are made to feel powerless. For example, Harold claimed that lower-level employees often make good targets if the social engineer can give them a sense of power they may otherwise feel they are lacking. As he explained,

> You know, so asking people for help and putting myself in a position where I seem to be the person who's weak, that they can be generous and help. If you're going after a low level person, that's, they like, it shares with them the sense of power that the social engineer is often after himself.

In this sense, an employee may be deprived of a sense of agency or autonomy within their organization and helping the social engineer (albeit under false pretenses) may be a way to feel that they are of consequence.

Heuristics

In addition to the aforementioned traits, participants described heuristics that can expedite the potential identification of a target victim. These heuristics involve more directly observable characteristics of a target thought to indicate underlying exploitable traits including certain demographic characteristics, roles, and positions within an organizational hierarchy. Importantly, this analysis does not claim that these heuristics are valid indicators of deception vulnerability, only that participants reported using such heuristics as a practical matter.

Demographics

A potential target's demographic characteristics, namely their age, gender, or a combination of both, may be considered indicators of susceptibility to social engineering (n = 9). Regarding age, younger people were sometimes described as more likely to comply with authority. As Zeke explained, people "relatively younger in nature will respect, in most cases, you know, director, VP positions, things like that." They may also be more connected and thus have a greater online footprint: "I can track where they are, what they're doing, who they're talking to, because they're just, you know, millennial, online, loud mouth, they're great for targets because, you know, you know everything about their life" (Donnie). Despite prevailing wisdom that older individuals are susceptible to deception and fraud, some participants also warned that they may be more difficult to social engineer because of their unwillingness to engage in discussions over technology:

> Like old folks and technology, like if you're talkin' about like mainframe admins, like they don't want to talk to any human being whatsoever, they want their mainframes to run and they're cool with that. They don't want to deal with any BS or anything. (Zeke)

Yet they are also viewed as potentially valuable targets because they may be socially-isolated.

Gender was also viewed as a demographic variable where trait vulnerabilities might cluster differentially. For instance, Joan noted that, because she is a woman, she is able to get men to break protocol because they may appreciate the attention from the opposite gender: "So, yeah, I think just giving people the time of day, especially with male to female interactions is generally what works well." In other words, they may act upon baser sexual inclinations and fail to follow proper security practices. Yet the most commented upon demographic characteristic combines both gender and age; older women were viewed as the most difficult targets because they "are not interested in taking any crap from you" (Joan), "want nothing to do with me and some of them have been kind of mean and made me cry" (Marilyn), "always had a guard up" (Eustace), "they care" (Eugene), and "they're also mothers so they have a day-to-day training regime with social engineers, mainly children." They are concerned and willing to be unkind if necessary. One participant, Tara, claimed that she has had success targeting older women because they "just want to help."

Role

The aforementioned traits may be viewed as endemic to particular social or organizational roles (n = 12). This analysis clusters these roles into two categories: "regulators" and "accommodators." Regulators are roles which are thought to, by virtue of their charge, be more vigilant and aware of potential security risks. These are also individuals thought to be imbued with more power to make key security decisions. These roles are thought to be less-than-model victims for social engineering deceptions and include information technology workers (including IT security), military and intelligence personnel, law enforcement, security guards, and medical doctors and psychiatrists. Marilyn, for instance, cautioned against targeting IT workers because "not only are they more trained to look for red flags but they'll be more likely to, like, sound an alarm." Bernard added that,

> There's a big issue with the type of people that go into IT and like engineering and things like that, are generally are not the type of people that are very social. So they, you know, live in their own little, their own little filter bubble, and they sit in an office every day, and they're paranoid all the time because that's what they do, you know?

The inquisitive nature of these roles were also viewed as a problem for the social engineer: "they're gonna counter you with really probing questions, you know, so it could kind of knock you off your pretext" (Herbert).

Accommodators are roles thought to prioritize the facilitation of social interactions over security needs. They may also be positions which are subordinated – not given the power to make key security decisions. Receptionists, assistants, retail workers, sales and marketing representatives, helpdesk operators, healthcare workers, customer service providers, human resources representatives, catering services, cashiers, and corporate communications associates were all mentioned by participants as roles vulnerable to social engineering. One reason these occupations are considered vulnerable is because of their orientation toward helping: "help desks are designed to help you, that's what they do, right? So, you know, if you can take advantage of that help" (Zeke). Marilyn said that "people like that are just kind of naturally in a mode of answering questions and helping people." Additionally, such roles are considered vulnerable because of their lack of knowledge about technology combined with their privileged access:

> Pick sales or marketing people, executing assistants, people that, people, or, I mean, people that are generally not as tech savvy but that still would have access to accounts and key information to the organization that could be utilized for further compromization. (David)

Finally, accommodators were viewed as good targets for social engineering because some may simply not care about security, instead devoting all of their attention to their primary service provision duties. Bernard highlighted this issue with hospitality workers (hotels, restaurants, etc.):

> The people that work there, the actually workers, the waiters, or the people that work at the desk, they do not give a shit. They just don't. I mean, you're not gonna make 'em care. They don't care about locking up the PIN, they don't care about people's credit cards, they might very well be stealing the credit cards themselves. I mean, they just don't care and you're not gonna make them care. But we've forced all these like security policies and procedures on them, well, they just find a way around it and they'll keep doing that until we can make it work.

Position

Similar to the role heuristic, the aforementioned traits were also associated with a potential mark's position within an organizational hierarchy (n = 13). Each position, described here generally as "low," "medium," and "high," were thought to have their own potential advantages or disadvantages pertaining to exploitable traits. Generally, participants described individuals at the top or the bottom of an organizational hierarchy being more desirable marks for various reasons. For instance, some participants claimed that top level administrators or executives are likely to fall for a ruse:

> People think that the higher level, the more intelligent, the more you'll be able to catch on to things. But, really, C-levels are [laughs] the people who click my links in phishing, or who entered in their credentials like a lot more than I would expect.

Similarly, August said "c-level guys, they're you know, they click on everything." Such executives are also valued because of the possible rewards involved. As Zeke explained in a previous example,

> If I can manipulate an executive at a high level, I can get that person to transfer 50 million dollars right? ... If I call somebody at a very junior level, they don't have the rights and permissions and authority to be able to do any of that.

At the same time, some participants argued that high-level executives and administrators were poor targets because they "tend to have less patience for things that require their time" (Marilyn).

On the other hand, lower-level employees may be considered "low-hanging fruit" (Mark). For instance, Muriel claimed to target lower-level employees who are not trained and may not understand their importance in regards to security – that she targeted those "who don't often get trained, or who don't think that what they do is important." In a prior example Edna claimed to prefer interns and new hires because they are less aware of security policy and may be uncertain about how to handle a problematic situation. Zeke also claimed previously that lower-level employees are more susceptible to requests and pressure from perceived employees: "lower-end employees will not, you know, challenge somebody that may be, you know, senior rank." Further, lower-level employees were said to be generally tasked with helping others and in subordinated positions – traits which can be exploited. You can "take a low-level employee and make them feel special" to ply information and access from them (Harold). In total, people at the lower levels of an organizational hierarchy were viewed as less likely to be adequately trained and invested in security. They are also the ones most likely to be in subordinated positions and tasked primarily with providing aid to others within and outside the organization.

Most participants focused on the top or the bottom levels of an organization. Some, however, prioritized those in the middle of the organizational hierarchy. Patrick, for example, claimed that he targets people "who can get me the information I need but are maybe not as regarded as like a VIP of the company" like facility managers. He explains that "they have access to all the buildings" and "a lot of the information that I wanted" but "they're not somebody who gets a lot of attention and is a target for, you know, people don't usually need to talk to them or want to talk to them, right?" In other words, they have the desired access and information but may also be less vigilant and more outgoing because they are not inundated with requests for their time and attention.

Discussion and conclusion

The results of this study identified six general characteristics that participants ascribe to susceptibility to social engineering deceptions. When considered in tandem, these six characteristics can be amalgamated into what this study terms a "model victim" – a hypothetical person considered particularly vulnerable to social engineering. First, the mark should have something to offer the social engineer, be it a resource (money, information, or access) or some experience (thrills). The model victim is also uninformed and unconcerned about information security risks – "don't know" and "don't care" respectively. They also are friendly and helpful. A model victim is also either socially isolated or broadly connected and visible across social networks. Finally, a model victim is one that experiences too much control or too little. Three of these traits – *uninformed, unconcerned*, and *outgoing* – are considered *dispositional* traits associated with perceived target vulnerability. The *connected* and *controlled* traits are *social*. They refer to the relational networks and situational constraints in which the model victim is embedded.

To further explore why the dispositional traits of the model victim may be associated with target vulnerability, this analysis relates these traits to what Erving Goffman (1971, p. 252) calls the "*Umwelt*" or the perceptual region around a person "from within which signs for alarm can come." Applied to deception, the *Umwelt* refers to the ability of a mark to identify the ill-intent or deceit of an actor during a social encounter. To slip through this metaphorical perimeter, the social engineer must accomplish one or both of the following tasks: (1) create a ruse designed to avoid presenting signs of alarm or, important for this analysis, (2) choose a mark less likely to identify signs of alarm. A target with a weaker *Umwelt* may be uninformed of the signs of alarm related to information security risks – they have fewer alarms to trip, so to speak. Additionally, the social engineer may not raise suspicion within the *Umwelt* if the target does not prioritize the identification and mitigation of security risks. In a sense, the alarms may be present but ignored or disabled. Additionally, a mark may not register signs of alarm if they are friendly, helpful, or otherwise outgoing in their disposition. Their guard will be lowered for the sake of facilitating and encouraging social engagement. Thus these traits impact the permeability of perceptual zone of disquiet of the mark. Participant's responses indicate that this zone may be bolstered through efforts to educate the individual on security risks and investments to promote the prioritization of information security among relevant actors.

Participant responses also indicate a perceived curvilinear relationship between "connectedness" within social networks and deception vulnerability. On one end, a person may be viewed as susceptible to social engineering if they are socially isolated. On the other, being over-connected may also introduce points of vulnerability. While these dynamics may apply to other forms of deception more broadly, the perceived relationship between connectedness and social engineering vulnerability may be tied to the changing nature of social networking in the information age. In their study of social networks, Raine and Wellman (2012, pp. 9, 12) argue that contemporary society is characterized by "networked individualism" where people are increasingly embedded in multiple diffuse social networks mediated through communications technologies to "meet their social, emotional, and economic needs." Networked individualism requires a willingness to engage in "'remote relationships – in both the physical and emotional sense of the word" (Raine & Wellman, 2012, p. 13). Raine and Wellman (2012) argue that networked individualism is "both socially liberating and socially taxing" because it provides tremendous freedom to connect to others but also places the onus on the individual to curate and maintain such relationships. Relevant to social engineering, increased reliance on remote relationships means that individuals have to keep track of relationships in sufficient detail todiscern legitimate from illegitimate correspondences. They also have to develop skills in discerning authenticity and trustworthiness across mediated communications.[13] Further, it also places a greater burden on individuals to manicure their online identities to reduce their "data exhaust" – the surplus data which can be mined from internet activities (Zuboff, 2015). In short, the particular character of contemporary social networks may create the conditions of social isolation and saturation in weak social ties that are thought to be exploitable by social engineers (Granovetter, 1985).

The issue of regulation or control also became evident in this analysis. In particular, this study suggests that a model victim is one that experiences too much or too little control. This finding resonates with Tittle's (1995) control balance theory which argues that deviance may stem from an individual experiencing too much control relative to the amount of control they exercise (a "control surplus") or too little (a "control deficit"). In particular, this study supports Piquero and Hickman's (2003) theoretical extension which posits that both control deficits and surpluses increase victimization risks. They argue that "individuals with control deficits do not have the confidence and/or skills to defend themselves against those who may victimize them" (Piquero & Hickman, 2003, p. 286). Similarly, our study finds that a mark may be considered vulnerable, for example, because of a perceived tendency to acquiesce to authority either due to a personal disposition or organizational policy and culture. Additionally, low-level employees or those in organizations with rigid rules and formal structures may "become passive, withdrawn, and submissive" creating a situation in which the mark may respond to attempts by the social engineer to exploit their "desire for autonomy" (Piquero & Hickman, 2003, p. 285). Regarding control surpluses, such individuals "indirectly place themselves at risk for victimization because they come to perceive that there is relatively little to restrain their actions" (Piquero & Hickman, 2003, p. 287). In this sense, the mark may ignore information security risks because they may not feel that the rules apply to them or to the situation due to "feelings of impunity, invulnerability, and 'untouchability'" (Piquero & Hickman, 2003, p. 286).

It is also worth noting that the dispositional traits described in this analysis (*uninformed, unconcerned*, and *outgoing*) may be interrelated with the social traits (*over- or under-connected* and *over- or under-controlled*). For instance, an outgoing individual may well be over-connected. Additionally, a person who is not outgoing but still desires social connections may feel isolated (or *under-connected*) and similarly vulnerable to deception.

Friendly and helpful individuals may also be more willing to violate protocol under the auspices of providing assistance. Potential marks who are undertrained in security risks (*uninformed*) or do not care about said risks (*unconcerned*) may not adhere to proper security practices (*under-controlled*). Similarly, a person who is all too aware of protocol (*informed*) and concerned about respecting policy (*concerned*) may be easier to coerce for fear of consequences (*over-controlled*).

Finally, this study explored heuristics participants described as indicating susceptibility to social engineering including sociodemographic characteristics (age and gender), role, and organizational position. Previous qualitative studies also describe similar factors being used for target selection, though they do not explicitly frame such factors as heuristic devices (e.g., Deakin et al., 2007; Miller, 1998; Wright & Decker, 1997). For instance, Wright and Decker (1997) found that robbers tended to associate being white, a woman, and elderly with a diminished likelihood of resistance. Such assessments rely on generalities about social categories. Evidence indicates that heuristics are useful in making quick decisions but also introduce the potential for bias and misjudgment as heuristics are often imperfect tools used for assessment (Pogarsky et al., 2017), a fact also recognized by at least one participant.[14] This analysis suggests that target selection research should clearly differentiate between observable criteria used by decision-makers and the underlying latent traits associated with vulnerability.

The use of heuristics by social engineers bears implications for rational choice theory. Rational choice theory argues that crime is the result of a decision-making process where offenders weight the perceived benefits of crime against possible costs (Clark & Cornish, 1985; Cornish & Clarke, 1986). Rational choice theorists have recently begun to consider the role of heuristics in criminal decision making (e.g., Collins & Loughran, 2018; Pogarsky et al., 2017; Schneider & Ervin, 1990). From this perspective, individuals may rely on "experience-based shortcuts" when rationality is "bounded" such as in situations of uncertainty (Pogarsky et al., 2017, p. 91). This study lends credence to these claims, demonstrating that participants use heuristics when considering the individuals most susceptible to social engineering, though further research is necessary to determine whether such heuristics are actually used during the target-selection process in real-time.

The use of heuristics also gives a reason to contemplate the role of social structure and culture in decision-making and perceptions of victim susceptibility. Speaking to the heuristics described by participants in our study, the meanings ascribed to gender, age, roles, and status positions are not formed in a vacuum. Rather, they are a product of both experience and socialization. For instance, heuristics may rely on learned stereotypes about social categories like gender. Exploring the connection between individual decision making and social structure through heuristics may necessitate adopting approaches which examine the relationship between agency, situational context, and social structure like Giddens's (1990) structuration theory, Bourdieu's (1980/1990) field theory, and cultural criminology (Ferrell et al., 2015). Examining heuristics in decision making in such a manner may allow researchers to explore how levels of analysis interrelate. Future research should consider these approaches.

The objective of this study was to examine the traits participants ascribe to vulnerable persons which, when examined in the aggregate, constitute a "model victim" – a hypothetical person particularly susceptible to social engineering deceptions. Because the data is retrospective, it is impossible to know if these traits and heuristics are used in real-time to make decisions about target selection. This is not a problem limited to the current study (e.g., Deakin et al., 2007; Jacobs, 2010; Jacques et al., 2014; Miller, 1998; Topalli et al., 2015; Wright & Decker, 1994, 1997). More research is necessary to investigate the decisions making processes of social engineers and deception perpetrators more generally. The results also illuminate the ways that participants think about the individuals they deceive which may be useful for criminologists and victimologists interested in how perpetrators understand vulnerability and victimization.

Assuming that there is validity to the traits described in this analysis – that the attributes of the model victim align with actual vulnerabilities – the results bear implications for policy and practice. First, individuals should be educated on security risks. Organizations should also invest (financially and culturally) in their members so such individuals feel committed to the organization and its security. Relatedly, organizations should empower their members to make key security decisions. This suggestion is perhaps counter to conventional wisdom which emphasizes regulating individual decision making through policy. Yet, if organizational actors have little to no autonomy, they may be less likely to halt frauds that exploit organizational processes or unconcerned with flagrant attempts to commit deception. That said, some regulation of decision making is necessary. These policies should be clear and easy to follow and the reasoning underpinning such policies should be made evident to members. An additional consideration is that collective efficacy should be shored up within organizations and among individuals to reduce vulnerability. Collective efficacy refers to "the willingness" of people "to intervene for the common good" (Sampson et al., 1997, p. 919). As described in this analysis, individuals with strong social ties to others may be insulated from the isolation conducive to social engineering. Such individuals may be able to lean on others to validate that a social engineering attempt is a ruse. They are also less likely to fall for the promises made by social engineers because they gain fulfillment from their current social networks. Finally, collective efficacy may also restrain individuals from acting in their own self-interest at the expense of others. The results also may contribute to the production of effective security awareness training programs. In addition to teaching individuals about various types of social engineering attacks and organizational policies, such programs should clearly detail the importance of vigilance against social engineering – the stakes facing both individuals, organizational stakeholders, and the organization itself. Training should also encourage individuals to work cooperatively to address security issues. This may involve encouraging individuals to communicate with others about possible social threats and ask questions about information security a judgment free environment.

Notes

1. Use of official and business statistics have limitations, particularly when describing internet-facilitated crimes (Yar, 2008). Yet these statistics are still useful for demonstrating that such frauds are a problem, even if they may not be the most accurate in communicating the precise prevalence or harm caused by such frauds.
2. The Internet Crime Complaint Center (IC3) (2020, p. 27) defines "phishing/vishing/smishing/pharming" scams as "unsolicited email, text messages, and telephone calls purportedly from a legitimate company requesting personal, financial, and/or login credentials."
3. The term "social engineering" originates in the late 1800s to describe reformatory attempts to use social science and policy to increase the efficiency and effectiveness of organizations and

institutions (Hatfield, 2018). There is little evidence to suggest that the term was adopted by hackers, phone phreaks, and other technologists with this history in mind.

4. Cross (2019, p. 129) has described illicit activities that drift between on- and off-line vectors as "cyber-enabled offenses."
5. 40.5% our participants report engaging in criminal social engineering in some capacity at some point in their lives, a figure derived from self-report questions. In total, fifteen participants admitted to or described engaging in some form of illegal social engineering (3 nonprofessional social engineers and 12 security auditors). Additionally, this percentage does not count two security auditors who reported finding out in retrospect that their activities were illegal while conducting a security audit.
6. One analytic literature review by Tetri and Vuorinen (2013) describes three procedural dimensions of social engineering including persuasion, fabrication, and data gathering. The authors specifically note that data gathering can be useful for target selection but do not go into the elements that comprise a suitable target.
7. To our knowledge, only one study finds a connection between being less educated and likelihood of fraud victimization (Lee & Soberon-Gerrer, 1997).
8. Whitty's (2018) conclusion regarding the role of education is specific to romance frauds and is restricted to middle-aged women.
9. Whitty (2018) did not directly measure social isolation. Instead, this study examined the role of kindness, finding that less kind individuals were more likely to be subjected to romance scams. The authors then posit that one reason for the association may be that less kind may be indirectly measuring social isolation (pp. 108–109).
10. The IRB protocol number for this study is 8194.
11. While only ten participants openly invoked the need for a target to have some valued resource, this is likely because this requirement was often taken for granted. Further, no one provided counter-evidence that this theme was considered unimportant
12. The author is uncertain if the participant could actually extract 50 million dollars from an executive in this fashion. The claim is likely an exaggeration to help make their argument that social engineers may select a target for the authority they possess within an organization. Hyperbole aside, the point still stands that authority is a potentially desired resource for the social engineer. We did ask multiple participants if they personally knew of organizations who sustained significant losses to this degree and answers were generally negative, those some claim to know some organizations that did sustain such losses. This adds credence to the idea that this claim may tend toward hyperbole.
13. Various authors have explored the development of trust online (e.g., Henderson & Gilding, 2004). Criminologists have also explored the development of trust in online black market networks (e.g., Dupont et al., 2016; Lusthaus, 2018).
14. Bernard recognized that the use of heuristics was more probabilistic. He explicitly noted this while explaining that he might target nurses because they tend to be helpful. He added a caveat, stating that there is "some percentage of 'em, maybe a quarter of 'em that are just mean."

Acknowledgments

The author would like to acknowledge Richard Goe and Alexandra Pimentel, who were both involved in the data gathering process for this study. Additionally, appreciation is given to Ken Tunnell who provided invaluable feedback on a prior draft.

Disclosure statement

No potential conflict of interest was reported by the author(s).

Funding

This work was supported by the National Science Foundation under [grant number SES #1616804].

References

Abraham, S., & Chengalur-Smith, I. (2010). An overview of social engineering malware: Trends, tactics, and implications. *Technology in Society*, *32*(3), 183–196. https://doi.org/10.1016/j.techsoc.2010.07.001

Atkins, B., & Huang, W. (2013). A study of social engineering in online frauds. *Open Journal of Social Sciences*, *1*(3), 23–32. https://doi.org/10.4236/jss.2013.13004

Bachmann, M. (2010). Deciphering the hacker underground. In T. J. Holt & B. Schell (Eds.), *Corporate hacking and technology-driven crime* (pp. 105–126). IGI Global.

Bossler, A. (2020). Contributions of criminological theory to the understanding of cybercrime offending and victimization. In R. Leukfeldt & T. J. Holt (Eds.), *The human factor of cybercrime* (pp. 29–59). Routledge.

Bourdieu, P. (1980/1990). *The logic of practice*. Stanford University Press.

Broadhurst, R., Skinner, K., Sifniotis, N., Matamoros-Macias, B., & Ipsen, Y. (2019). Phishing and cybercrime risks in a university student community. *International Journal of Cybersecurity Intelligence and Cybercrime*, *2*(1), 4–23. https://vc.bridgew.edu/ijcic/vol2/iss1/2/

Buchanan, T., & Whitty, M. T. (2014). The online dating romance scam: Causes and consequences of victimhood. *Psychology, Crime & Law*, *20*(3), 261–283. https://doi.org/10.1080/1068316X.2013.772180

Button, M., & Cross, C. (2017). *Cyberfrauds, scams and their victims*. Routledge.

Caldwell, T. (2011). Ethical hackers: Putting on the white hat. *Network Security*, *(2011*(7), 10–13. https://doi.org/10.1016/S1353-4858(11)70075-7

Chantler, A., & Broadhurst, R. (2006). *Social engineering and crime prevention in cyberspace*. Queensland University of Technology. Technical report Retrieved from http://eprints.qut.edu.au/7526/1/7526.pdf.

Charmaz, K. (2002). Qualitative interviewing and grounded theory analysis. In J. F. Gubrium & J. A. Holstein (Eds.), *The handbook of interview research* (pp. 675–694). Sage.

Christie, N. (1986). The ideal victim. In E. A. Fattah (Ed.), *From crime policy to victim policy: Reorienting the justice system* (pp. 17–30). The Macmillan Press.

Clark, R. B., & Cornish, D. B. (1985). Modeling offenders' decisions: A framework for research and policy. *Crime & Justice*, *2*(1985), 147–185. https://doi.org/10.1086/449106

Collins, M. E., & Loughran, T. A. (2018). Rational choice theory, heuristics, and biases. In W. Bernasco, J. van Gelder, & H. Elffers (Eds..), *The Oxford handbook of offender decision making*. Oxford University Press. [online version] https://doi.org/10.1093/oxfordhb/9780199338801.013.1

Corbin, J., & Strauss, A. (1990). Grounded theory research: Procedures, canons, and evaluative Criteria. *Qualitative Sociology*, *13*(1), 3–21. https://doi.org/10.1007/BF00988593

Cornish, D. B., & Clarke, R. V. (1986). *The reasoning criminal: Rational choice perspectives on offending*. Springer-Verlag.

Cross, C. (2019). Is online fraud just fraud? Examining the efficacy of the digital divide. *Journal of Criminological Research, Policy and Practice*, *5*(2), 120–131. https://doi.org/10.1108/JCRPP-01-2019-0008

Cross, C., Dragiewicz, M., & Richards, K. (2018). Understanding romance fraud: Insights from domestic violence research. *British Journal of Criminology*, *58*(6), 1303–1322. https://doi.org/10.1093/bjc/azy005

Cross, C., Parker, M., & Sansom, D. (2019). Media discourses surrounding 'non-ideal' victims: The case of the Ashley Madison data breach. *International Review of Victimology*, *25*(1), 53–69. https://doi.org/10.1177/0269758017752410

Cross, C., Richards, K., & Smith, R. G. (2016). The reporting experiences and support needs of victims of online fraud. *Trends & Issues in Crime and Criminal Justice, 518*, 1–14. https://www.aic.gov.au/sites/default/files/2020-05/tandi518.pdf

Deakin, J., Smithson, H., Spencer, J., & Medina-Ariza, J. (2007). Taxing on the streets: Understanding the methods and process of street robbery. *Crime Prevention and Community Safety, 9*(1), 52–67. https://doi.org/10.1057/palgrave.cpcs.8150033

Drew, J. M., & Cross, C. (2013). Fraud and its PREY: Conceptualising social engineering tactics and its impact on financial literacy outcomes. *Journal of Financial Services Marketing, 18*(3), 188–198. https://doi.org/10.1057/fsm.2013.14

Dupont, B., Côté, A., Savine, C., & Décary-Hétu, D. (2016). The ecology of trust among hackers. *Global Crime, 17*(2), 129–151. https://doi.org/10.1080/17440572.2016.1157480

Ferreira, A., & Teles, S. (2019). Persuasion: How phishing emails can influence users and bypass security measures. *International Journal of Human-Computer Studies, 125*(May 2019), 19–31. https://doi.org/10.1016/j.ijhcs.2018.12.004

Ferrell, J., Hayward, K., & Young, J. (2015). *Cultural criminology: An invitation* (2nd ed.). Sage.

Fischer, P., Lea, S. E. G., & Evans, K. M. (2013). Why do individuals respond to fraudulent scam communications and lose money? The psychological determinants of scam compliance. *Journal of Applied Social Psychology, 43*(10), 2060–2072. https://doi.org/10.1111/jasp.12158

Giddens, A. (1990). *The consequences of modernity*. Stanford University Press.

Glaser, B. G., & Strauss, A. L. (1967). *The discovery of grounded theory*. Aldine Publishing Company.

Goel, S., Williams, K., & Dincelli, E. (2017). Got phished? Internet security and human vulnerability. *Journal of the Association for Information Systems, 18*(1), 22–44. https://doi.org/10.17705/1jais.00447

Goffman, E. (1971). *Relations in public: Microstudies of the public order*. Basic Books.

Granovetter, M. (1985). Economic action and social structure: The problem of embeddedness. *American Journal of Sociology, 91*(3), 481–510. https://doi.org/10.1086/228311

Hadnagy, C. (2018). *Social engineering: The science of human hacking*. Wiley.

Hatfield, J. M. (2018). Social engineering in cybersecurity: The evolution of a concept. *Computers & Security, 73*(March 2018), 102–113. https://doi.org/10.1016/j.cose.2017.10.008

Henderson, S., & Gilding, M. (2004). "I've never clicked this much with anyone in my life": Trust and hyperpersonal communication in online friendships. *New Media & Society, 6*(4), 487–506. https://doi.org/10.1177/146144804044331

Holt, T. J. (2009). Lone hacks or group cracks. In F. Schmalleger & M. Pittaro (Eds.), *Crimes of the internet* (pp. 336–355). Pearson Education.

Holt, T. J. (2010). Examining the role of technology in the formation of deviant subcultures. *Social Science Computer Review, 28*(4), 466–481. https://doi.org/10.1177/0894439309351344

Holt, T. J., & Graves, D. C. (2007). A qualitative analysis of advance fee fraud e-mail schemes. *International Journal of Cyber Criminology, 1*(1), 137–154. http://www.cybercrimejournal.com/thomasdanielleijcc.pdf

Holtfreter, K., Reisig, M. D., Piquero, N. L., & Piquero, A. R. (2010). Low self-control and fraud: Offending, victimization, and their overlap. *Criminal Justice and Behavior, 37*(2), 188–203. https://doi.org/10.1177/0093854809354977

Holtfreter, K., Reisig, M. D., & Pratt, T. C. (2008). Low self-control, routine activities, and fraud victimization. *Criminology, 46*(1), 189–220. https://doi.org/10.1111/j.1745-9125.2008.00101.x

Hough, M. (1987). Offenders' choice of target: Findings from victim surveys. *Journal of Quantitative Criminology, 3*(4), 355–369. https://doi.org/10.1007/BF01066836

Huang, W., & Brockman, A. (2011). Social engineering exploitations in online communications: Examining persuasions used in fraudulent emails. In T. Holt (Ed.), *Crime online: Correlates, causes, and context* (pp. 87–111). Carolina Academic Press.

Hutchings, A. (2013). Hacking and fraud: Qualitative analysis of online offending and victimization. In K. Jaishankar & N. Ronel (Eds.), *Global criminology: Crime and victimization in a globalized era* (pp. 93–114). CRC Press.

Hutchings, A., & Hayes, H. (2009). Routine activity theory and phishing victimisation: Who gets caught in the 'net'? *Current Issues in Criminal Justice, 20*(3), 433–452. https://doi.org/10.1080/10345329.2009.12035821

Internet Crime Complaint Center (IC3). (2020). *2019 internet crime report*. Federal Bureau of Investigation. Retrieved February 19, 2020, from https://pdf.ic3.gov/2019_IC3Report.pdf

Jackobsson, M., Tsow, A., Shah, A., Blevis, E., & Lim, Y. (2007). What instills trust? A qualitative study of phishing. In S. Dietrich & R. Dhamija Eds., *Financial cryptographic and data security: 11th international conference, FC 2007, and 1st international workshop on useable security, USEC 2007, Scarborough, Trinidad and Tobago, February 12-16, 2007*. Revised Selected Papers (356–361). Springer-Verlag.

Jacobs, B. A. (2010). Serendipity in robbery target selection. *British Journal of Criminology, 50*(3), 514–529. https://doi.org/10.1093/bjc/azq002

Jacques, S., Allen, A. & Wright, R. (2014). Drug dealers' rational choices on which customers to rip-off. *International Journal of Drug Policy, 25*, 251–256.

Karakasiliotis, A., Furnell, S. M., & Papadaki, M. (2006, December 4-5). Assessing end-user awareness of social engineering and phishing. *Proceedings of the 7th Australian information warfare and security conference*, Edith Cowan University, Perth, Western Australia. http://ro.ecu.edu.au/isw/12

King, A., & Thomas, J. (2009). You can't cheat an honest man: Making ($$$s and) sense of the Nigerian e-mail scams. In F. Schmalleger & M. Pittaro (Eds.), *Crimes of the Internet* (pp. 206–224). Prentice Hall.

Kopp, C., Layton, R., Sillitoe, J., & Gondal, I. (2015). The role of love stories in romance scams: A qualitative analysis of fraudulent profiles. *International Journal of Cyber Criminology, 9*(2), 205–217. https://www.cybercrimejournal.com/Koppetal2015vol9issue2.pdf

Lawson, P., Zielinska, O., Pearson, C., & Mayhorn, C. B. (2017). Interaction of personality and persuasion tactics in email phishing attacks. *Proceedings of the Human Factors and Ergonomics Society Annual Meeting, 61*(1), 1331–1333. https://doi.org/10.1177/1541931213601815

Lee, J., & Soberon-Gerrer, H. (1997). Consumer vulnerability to fraud: Influencing factors. *The Journal of Consumer Affairs, 31*(1), 70–89. https://doi.org/10.1111/j.1745-6606.1997.tb00827.x

Leukfeldt, E. R. (2014a). Cybercrime and social ties: Phishing in Amsterdam. *Trends in Organized Crime, 17*(4), 231–249. https://doi.org/10.1007/s12117-014-9229-5

Leukfeldt, E. R. (2014b). Phishing for suitable targets in the Netherlands: Routine activity theory and phishing victimization. *Cyberpsychology, Behavior, and Social Networking, 17*(8), 551–555. https://doi.org/10.1089/cyber.2014.0008

Leukfeldt, E. R., Kleemans, E. R., & Stol, W. P. (2017a). Cybercriminal networks, social ties and online forums: Social ties versus digital ties within phishing and malware networks. *British Journal of Criminology, 57*(3), 704–722. https://doi.org/10.1093/bjc/azw009

Leukfeldt, E. R., Kleemans, E. R., & Stol, W. P. (2017b). Origin, growth and criminal capabilities of cybercriminal networks: An international empirical analysis. *Crime, Law, & Social Change, 67*(1), 39–53. https://doi.org/10.1007/s10611-016-9663-1

Leukfelt, E. R., & Yar, M. (2016). Applying routine activity theory to cybercrime: A theoretical and empirical analysis. *Deviant Behavior, 37*(3), 263–280. https://doi.org/10.1080/01639625.2015.1012409

Lusthaus, J. (2018). *Industry of anonymity: Inside the business of cybercrime*. Harvard University Press.

Maurer, D. W. (1940). *The big con: The story of the confidence man*. Anchor Books.

Miller, J. (1998). Up it up: Gender and the accomplishment of street robbery. *Criminology, 36*(1), 37–65. https://doi.org/10.1111/j.1745-9125.1998.tb01239.x

Mitnick, K., & Simon, W. L. (2002). *The art of deception: Controlling the human element of security*. Wiley.

Muscat, G., James, M., & Graycar, A. (2002). *Older people and consumer fraud* (Report No. 220). Australian Institute of Criminology.

Ngo, F. T., & Raymond, R. (2011). Cybercrime victimization: An examination of individual and situational level factors. *International Journal of Cyber Criminology, 5*(1), 773–793. https://www.cybercrimejournal.com/ngo2011ijcc.pdf

Norris, G., Brookes, A., & Dowell, D. (2019). The psychology of internet fraud victimization: A systematic review. *Journal of Police and Criminal Psychology, 34*(3), 231–245. Online First. https://doi.org/10.1007/s11896-019-09334-5

Parsons, K., Butavicius, M., Delfabbro, P., & Lillie, M. (2019). Predicting susceptibility to social influence in phishing emails. *International Journal of Human-Computer Studies, 128*(August 2019), 17–26. https://doi.org/10.1016/j.ijhcs.2019.02.007

Piquero, A. R., & Hickman, M. (2003). Extending Tittle's control balance theory to account for victimization. *Criminal Justice and Behavior, 30*(3), 282–301. https://doi.org/10.1177/0093854803030003002

Pogarsky, G., Roche, S. P., & Pickett, J. T. (2017). Heuristics and biases, rational choice, and sanction perceptions. *Criminology, 55*(1), 85–111. https://doi.org/10.1111/1745-9125.12129

Pratt, T. C., Holtfreter, K., & Reisig, M. (2010). Routine online activity and internet fraud targeting: Extending the generality of routine activity theory. *Journal of Research in Crime and Delinquency, 47*(3), 267–296. https://doi.org/10.1177/0022427810365903

Raine, L., & Wellman, B. (2012). *Networked: The new social operating system.* The MIT Press.

Reyns, B. W. (2013). Online routines and identity theft victimization: Further expanding routine activity theory beyond direct-contact offenses. *Journal of Research in Crime and Delinquency, 50* (2), 216–238. https://doi.org/10.1177/0022427811425539

Reyns, B. W. (2015). A routine activity perspective on online victimisation: Results from the Canadian General Social Survey. *Journal of Financial Crime, 22*(4), 396–411. https://doi.org/10.1108/JFC-06-2014-0030

Reyns, B. W. (2018). Routine activity theory and cybercrime: A theoretical appraisal and literature review. In K. F. Steinmetz & M. R. Nobles (Eds.), *Technocrime and criminological theory* (pp. 35–54). Routledge.

Sampson, R. J., Raudenbush, S. W., & Earls, F. (1997). Neighborhoods and violent crime: A multilevel study of collective efficacy. *Science, 277*(5328), 918–924. https://doi.org/10.1126/science.277.5328.918

Sarno, D. M., Lewis, J. E., Bohil, C. J., & Neider, M. B. (2019). Which phish is on the hook? Phishing vulnerability for older versus younger adults. *Human Factors: The Journal of the Human Factors and Ergonomics Society, 62*(5), 704–717. https://doi.org/10.1177/0018720819855570

Schell, B. H., & Holt, T. J. (2010). A profile of the demographics, psychological predispositions, and social/behavioral patterns of computer hacker insiders and outsiders. In T. J. Holt & B. H. Schell (Eds.), *Corporate hacking and technology-driven crime: Social dynamics and implications* (pp. 190–213). IGI Global.

Schell, B. H., & Melnychuck, J. (2010). Female and male hacker conference attendees: The autism-spectrum quotient (AQ) scores and self-reported adulthood experiences. In T. J. Holt & B. H. Schell (Eds.) *Corporate hacking and technology-driven crime: Social dynamics and implications* (pp. 144–168). IGI Global.

Schneider, A. L., & Ervin, L. (1990). Specific deterrence, rational choice, and decision heuristics: Applications in juvenile justice. *Social Science Quarterly, 71*(3), 585–601.

Simon, H. A., & Newell, A. (1958). Heuristic problem solving: The next advance in operations research. *Operations Research, 6*(1), 1–10. https://doi.org/10.1287/opre.6.1.1

Steinmetz, K. F. (2016). *Hacked: A radical approach to hacker culture and crime.* NYU Press.

Taylor, P. A. (1999). *Hackers: Crime and the digital sublime.* Routledge.

Tetri, P., & Vuorinen, J. (2013). Dissecting social engineering. *Behaviour & Information Technology, 32*(10), 1014–1023. https://doi.org/10.1080/0144929X.2013.763860

Tittle, C. R. (1995). *Control balance: Toward a general theory of deviance.* Westview Press.

Titus, R. M., & Gover, A. R. (2001). Personal fraud: The victims and the scams. In G. Farrell & K. Pease (Eds.), *Repeat victimization: Crime prevention studies* (Vol. 12, pp. 133–151). Lynne Rienner.

Titus, R. M., Heinzelmann, F., & Boyle, J. M. (1995). Victimization of persons by fraud. *Crime & Delinquency, 41*(1), 54–72. https://doi.org/10.1177/0011128795041001004

Topalli, V., Jacques, S., & Wright, R. (2015). "It takes skills to take a car": Perceptual and procedural expertise in carjacking. *Aggression in Violent Behavior, 20*(January-February 2015), 19–25. https://doi.org/10.1016/j.avb.2014.12.001

Tunnell, K. D. (1992). *Choosing crime: The criminal calculus of property offenders*. Nelson-Hall.

Twitchell, D. P. (2009). Social engineering and its countermeasures. In M. Gupta & R. Sharman (Eds.), *Handbook of research on social and organizational liabilities in information security* (pp. 228–242). IGI Global.

Van de Weijer, S. (2020). Predictors of cybercrime victimization. In R. Leukfeldt & T. J. Holt (Eds.), *The human factor of cybercrime* (pp. 83–110). Routledge.

Van Wyk, J., & Benson, M. L. (1997). Fraud victimization: Risky business or just bad luck. *American Journal of Criminal Justice, 21*(1), 163–179. https://doi.org/10.1007/BF02887448

Verizon. (2019). *2019 data breach investigations report*. Retrieved August 20, 2019, from https://enterprise.verizon.com/resources/reports/2019-data-breach-investigations-report.pdf.

Vishwanath, A., Herath, T., Chen, R., Wang, J., & Rao, H. R. (2011). Why do people get phished? Testing individual differences in phishing vulnerability within an integrated, information processing model. *Decision Support Systems, 51*(3), 576–586. https://doi.org/10.1016/j.dss.2011.03.002

Whitty, M. T. (2013). The scammers persuasive techniques model. *British Journal of Criminology, 53* (4), 665–684. https://doi.org/10.1093/bjc/azt009

Whitty, M. T. (2018). Do you love me? Psychological characteristics of romance scam victims. *Cyberpsychology, Behavior, and Social Networking, 21*(2), 105–109. https://doi.org/10.1089/cyber.2016.0729

Whitty, M. T. (2019). Predicting susceptibility to cyber-fraud victimhood. *Journal of Financial Crime, 26*(1), 277–292. https://doi.org/10.1108/JFC-10-2017-0095

Whitty, M. T., & Buchanan, T. (2016). The online dating romance scam: The psychological impact on victims – Both financial and non-financial. *Criminology & Criminal Justice, 16*(2), 176–194. https://doi.org/10.1177/1748895815603773

Williams, E. J., Beardmore, A., & Joinson, A. N. (2017). Individual differences in susceptibility to online influence: A theoretical review. *Computers in Human Behavior, 72*(July 2017), 412–421. https://doi.org/10.1016/j.chb.2017.03.002

Williams, J. & Milton, T. B. (2015). *The con men*. Columbia University Press.

Workman, M. (2007). Gaining access with social engineering: An empirical study of the threat. *Information Systems Security, 16*(6), 315–331. https://doi.org/10.1080/10658980701788165

Workman, M. (2008). Wisecrackers: A theory-grounded investigation of phishing and pretext social engineering threats to information security. *Journal of the American Society for Information Science and Technology, 59*(4), 662–674. https://doi.org/10.1002/asi.20779

Wright, R., & Decker, S. H. (1994). *Burglars on the job: Streetlife and residential break-ins*. Northeastern University Press.

Wright, R., & Decker, S. H. (1997). *Armed robbers in action: Stickups and street culture*. Northeastern University Press.

Wright, R., Logie, R. H., & Decker, S. H. (1995). Criminal expertise and offender decision making: An experimental study of the target selection process in residential burglary. *Journal of Research in Crime and Delinquency, 32*(1), 39–53. https://doi.org/10.1177/0022427895032001002

Yar, M. (2008). Computer crime control as industry: Virtual insecurity and the market for private policing. In K. F. Aas, H. O. Gundhus, & H. M. Lomell (Eds.), *Technologies of insecurity: The surveillance of everyday life* (pp. 189–204). Routledge-Cavendish.

Zuboff, S. (2015). Big other: Surveillance capitalism and the prospects of an information civilization. *Journal of Information Technology, 30*(1), 75–89. https://doi.org/10.1057/jit.2015.5

Index